News Writing

ed Press

MOSCOW — Ambassadors of the United States, Britain and France made formal protests yesterday to the Soviet Union over recent interference with Western access to Berlin.

Communist East Germany has been delaying traffic on highways linking West Germany and Berlin following ment of a West environment West Berlin two The Soviet bloc hat West Germany of the agency's counter agree-

men y.

The three Moscow embassies declined to give details, but in Washington a State Dept. spokesman said the embassies had delivered oral protests that the traffic delays violated the 1971 four-power agreement on Berlin.

The latest Berlin difficulties prompted the United States last week to break off talks with East Germany on establishing relations between the two countries. Until then the diplomatic negotiations had appeared to cessful and were that em soon be open

In holdi
the Berlin t
East German
guards have qu
travelers in an eff
identify and turn
employees of the envir
ment agency.

West German For
Minister Hans-Die
Genscher has warned
East Germany could
trying to raise itself to
statu of Berlin a
ena power through
interference with tr
traffic. The signatorie
agreement
tates, Brit

News Writing

GEORGE A. HOUGH 3rd

Michigan State University

HOUGHTON MIFFLIN COMPANY / BOSTON

Atlanta
Dallas
Geneva, Illinois
Hopewell, New Jersey
Palo Alto
London

Selections on pp. 45, 136, 144, reprinted courtesy of the *Boston Globe*.

Selections on pp. 20, 38, 39–40, 45–46, 48, 63, 64, 131–32, 135, 147, and 180, reprinted courtesy of the *Buffalo Evening News*.

Selections on pp. 44, 72, 110, and 149–51, reprinted with permission from the *Chicago Daily News*.

Selections on pp. 27, 42, 58, 97, and 126, reprinted with permission from the *Chicago Sun-Times*. Selection on p. 42 is by Dennis Fisher; selection on p. 97 is by David S. Robinson.

Selections on the following pp. reprinted courtesy of the *Detroit Free Press*: p. 35 (February 24, 1973); p. 56 (May 25, 1973); p. 61 (December 18, 1972); p. 126 (November 18, 1962); p. 128 (August 18, 1966); pp. 132–33 (December 13, 1968); p. 161 (January 13, 1966); p. 180 (February 3, 1973); p. 199 (May 28, 1973).

Selections on pp. 29, 50, 126, 154–56 copyright © 1973 by the *Los Angeles Times*. Reprinted by permission.

Selections on pp. 60, 89, 94, 126, 127, 128, 142, 152, 162, 169, 178, © 1965, 1966, 1968–71, 1973 by the New York Times Company. Reprinted by permission.

Selection on p. 27 reprinted by permission of the *New York Post*. Copyright © 1973, New York Post Corporation.

Selections on pp. 19, 21, 24, 27, 29, 34, 35, 43, 50, 60, 65, 91, 107, 116–17, 121, 123, 124, 127, 128, 129, 135, 158, 162, 178, 179, 190, reprinted by permission of *United Press International*.

Photograph on p. 1 by Cary Wolinsky from Stock Boston; photograph on p. 87 by Ken Regan from Camera 5; photograph on p. 169 by Dan McCoy from Black Star.

Printed in the U.S.A.

Library of Congress Catalog Card Number: 74–17877

ISBN: 0–395–18593–9

for Mary Lu

CONTENTS

News Writing is organized as a teaching text, intended for use in beginning news writing and reporting courses. It is also a self-learning text, written with the expectation that it could be used away from the classroom as well as in it.

The level of instruction is aimed primarily at the beginner who is endeavoring to learn news writing. The more experienced teacher may find some things in the text that seem too simple or obvious. But what is simple or obvious to the experienced teacher may not be so familiar to the beginning teacher or to a person with limited professional experience or training. A number of points in *News Writing* were included with that in mind.

The text is the outgrowth of a lifetime in journalism, divided between newspaper work as a reporter and an editor, and the teaching of journalism. It was shaped by my own experience and by the needs of the courses in news writing and reporting offered at Michigan State. It is also a response to the needs of students who want to learn about news writing, written out of more than 15 years of experience in teaching the hows and whys of news writing and newsroom practices.

News Writing is a different kind of a text. It is different in that it deals only with news writing, a craft important in itself and one that requires the full attention of both teacher and student. *News Writing* is also a new text, treating news writing broadly and deeply at a time when great changes have been taking place in the newsroom. The influence of broadcast journalism, of advocacy journalism, of the "new journalism," and of the new technology in newspaper production have been widely felt in the newspaper world, and this study of the writing craft reflects changes due to those influences.

As a text, *News Writing* is as far as possible descriptive rather than prescriptive. That is, it attempts to describe news writing techniques and practices currently in use on well-edited newspapers. It attempts to show beginners how it is done, *not* how the author thinks it ought to be done.

Examples have been selected from a wide range of newspapers in order to make them as representative as possible of good newsroom practices.

No attempt has been made to make style consistent in these examples. News style varies among newspapers on some points and some of these differences are quite apparent among examples included in this text. It should be remembered that the examples are intended to show writing technique, organization and structure, not style.

As additional features the text includes a glossary, a bibliography and a style guide. They provide the beginning news writer with useful reference material that is readily available: definitions of some of the most common words in newspaper parlance, a list of books and periodicals that have proved indispensible to news writers, and a basic style guide, based on current newspaper usage.

ACKNOWLEDGEMENTS

I am indebted to a great many people for assistance at one time or another with this text. I am indebted to the many students, past and present, who tested my ideas, my insights and my writing assignments; to my colleagues in the School of Journalism at Michigan State University; to my co-workers and friends at the Lansing *State Journal;* to Gordon A. Sabine, teacher and friend, who brought me to Michigan State and introduced me to college teaching; to Mrs. Virginia Brenner and Mrs. Nina Burton, the School of Journalism secretaries who helped at so many times and in so many ways; to Betty, Beverly and Barbara for their help with typing chapters in this text and its workbook; to my wife, Mary Lu, herself a working journalist, to whom this book is dedicated, for the help and encouragement she has given me through the years.

Finally, but really first of all, I am indebted to George A. Hough Jr. and Clara Sharpe Hough, editors and publishers of the *Falmouth Enterprise,* for having taught me about news writing when I was a green beginner.

George A. Hough 3rd
East Lansing, Michigan

News Writing

PART ONE

Basic Skills

CHAPTER ONE

News, the Newspaper and the News Writer

BEFORE WE TURN to the main purpose of this text, the business of learning to be a news writer, perhaps we should define a few terms. Just what is news? Where does the news writer practice his craft? What kind of work do news writers do?

THE NATURE OF NEWS

News is both a commodity and a state of mind. As a commodity, news is gathered, processed, packaged and sold by newspapers and news services. As a state of mind, it excites, interests and holds the attention of millions of people every day of the year. This, of course, is not a definition of news; a good definition is hard to find, although many attempts have been made.

One of the great city editors of all time, Stanley Walker of the *New York Herald-Tribune*, didn't think there was a definition of news. News, he said,

is more unpredictable than the winds. Sometimes it is the repetition with new characters of tales as old as the pyramids, and again it may be almost outside the common experience.

You will find that Walker was right. Much news is routine and repetitious, although even then it may be interesting, even exciting, to many people. Births, deaths and marriages are hardly new, but they are news, and stories about them are printed and avidly read.

Some news is so strange that we can hardly accept it. Many people did not believe that men had actually landed and walked on the moon, though the event was seen on television and reported on the front page of every daily newspaper. Such an event was just too far outside common experience for some people.

Joseph Pulitzer, nineteenth-century publisher of the *St. Louis Post-Dispatch* and the *New York World*, had his own view of news. He instructed his staff to look for stories which were,

original, distinctive, dramatic, romantic, thrilling, unique, curious, quaint, humorous, odd and apt-to-be-talked-about.

Since Pulitzer's newspapers were highly successful—the *World* at one time had a circulation of more than a million—Pulitzer must have had a fairly good insight into the nature of news.

Charles A. Dana, editor of the old *New York Sun*, had his eye on his readers when he defined news as "anything that will make people talk." Arthur McEwan, editor of the *San Francisco Examiner* under William Randolph Hearst, is quoted as saying that news is "anything that makes a reader say, 'Gee, whiz!'" And Turner Catledge, a former managing editor of the *New York Times*, called news "anything you can find out today that you didn't know before."

None of these definitions are satisfactory, though they touch on aspects or qualities of news which are real and understandable. Nearly all, for example, imply that news is timely, recent, new. They imply also that news is of interest to people; that is, they will react to it and talk about it. Pulitzer's directive implies further that news ought to be out of the ordinary, not routine.

Some other frequently mentioned qualities of news include proximity: the geographical proximity of local news, and the psychological proximity of news which has direct, personal effect on the reader. Other very real elements of news are emotional appeal, human interest, conflict, sex and significance.

Another definition, one we shall hear again, says that news is not anything that happens, but just those things reported and made known to the public through publication or broadcast.

What Newspapers Print

If news is not the event, but the *report* of the event, then we ought to turn to the pages of the newspaper to find our definition. For all practical purposes, at least to the newsman, news is what newspapers print. News is the story the reporter is assigned to, the story the news writer pounds out on the typewriter, the story with picture and headline which the reader sees in the newspaper.

To observe news in its natural habitat, then, all we have to do is turn to the newspaper itself. Here we quickly see that news is a tremendously varied commodity. Some news stories are routine, others highly unusual. Some are a paragraph or two in length, others fill column after column. And the subject matter comprises many, many topics and touches the interests of many different people.

We cannot here attempt an exhaustive survey of what newspapers print. But we can quickly review the main outline as we look from the front page through the various other pages and sections of the newspaper.

Newspapers print stories which have so much reader interest that they appear on the front page under bold headlines: stories about significant events such as wars, peace treaties, the deaths of kings and presidents, elections, floods, strikes, great storms and acts of Congress. Other stories are so routine that they can often be reported in a few lines or by simple entries in lists of births, deaths, marriages, divorces, hospital admissions or traffic court dispositions.

The departmentalization of the newspaper is a further clue to the nature of news. Newspapers have pages for sports, for stories about the business world, for news of special interest to women. Some newspapers publish columns or pages to interest teen-agers or the elderly. Newspapers print news about food, clothing, fashions, home furnishings and home repairs, gardening, social problems and personal relationships—all of interest to both men and women and to readers of all ages.

You will find much about politics and government in newspapers, and much about people in politics and government—the globe-trotting of presidents, foreign ministers and secretaries of state, for example. Newspapers also print stories about books, music, art, architecture, records, stamps, coins, bridge and chess. They print stories about events of interest only in the newspaper's hometown, as well as news from around the state, the region, the nation and the world. And they print many technical stories of limited interest to the average reader: about law, education, science and religion.

Newspapers tend to specialize, too, in their approach to news. Some smaller city newspapers concentrate largely on local news. Newspapers like the *Chicago Tribune* and the *Minneapolis Star* and *Tribune*, are regional papers, concentrating on news from their own city and several surrounding states. The *New York Times* is almost a national newspaper, specializing in news

On The Inside

Akron Beacon Journal

Fig. 1.1 *A newspaper's index gives clues to what editors think is news and suggests their knowledge of what readers will look for inside the paper.*

of national and international importance, especially news of politics and government, economics and social issues originating in Washington. The *Wall Street Journal* is concerned with the business world. *Women's Wear Daily* devotes its attention to the women's clothing industry.

Newspapers are not all alike, despite some obvious similarities in the way they treat major stories. The circulation and the number of pages a newspaper publishes make a great difference. Small newspapers have limited space and print fewer and less varied news stories. Larger newspapers have more space, print more news and more varied news stories, and respond to the needs of a more diverse audience.

What Readers Read

Newspaper readers read everything in the newspaper. Few read every story in the paper, but some do. So diverse are the interests of newspaper readers that it has been said that every reader reads a different newspaper.

Daily newspaper circulation in the United States exceeds 62 million copies a day* and the people who read them read them thoroughly. A study of newspaper readership has shown that 71 per cent read their newspaper page by page, another 27 per cent scan their paper; while only 2 per cent open their paper to read a specific item.

Another study tried to determine what pages get the heaviest traffic and came up with the following figures:

All pages	84%
General news pages	88
Women's pages	85
Business, finance pages	75
Sports	75
Obituaries	87
Amusements	80
Editorial	87
Columnists	86

These figures reveal some of the special interests of newspaper readers: sports, women's news, obituaries, business and finance. But, what is especially interesting is the fact that 84 per cent of all newspaper readers read something on every page of the newspaper and that 88 per cent are interested in everything.

Newspaper readers read what interests them, skip what does not, and this influences what editors put into their newspaper. This accounts for the limited amount of international news in most newspapers and for the concentration on local news in many newspapers.

After the full impact of the energy crisis struck the American public, critics asked why newspapers hadn't warned their readers about it. The

*The figures in this chapter were obtained from *Facts About Newspapers—1973*, published by the Newspaper Information Service of the American Newspaper Publishers Association; from bulletins of the ANPA Research Insitute; from *Newsprint Facts*, published by the Newsprint Information Committee; from the 1973 *Editor and Publisher International Yearbook*; and the 1972–73 edition of the *Occupational Outlook Handbook* of the U.S. Department of Labor.

answer was simple: newspapers respond to reader interests and readers had shown little or no interest in what they thought were abstract discussions of future shortages. Who is interested in speculation about shortages in a land of plenty?

Newspaper editors are also painfully aware that the reading public tends to like good news and dislike bad news. Much of the criticism of newspapers stems from this fact. When the newspaper reports crime, corruption in public office, unemployment and increased taxes, readers send letters of complaint to the editor. "Why don't you print only good news?" they ask.

On the other hand, newspaper readers apparently enjoy conflict and violence. Stories about violent crimes, murders, battles and wars, conflicts between nations and political parties, staged conflicts in sports arenas and even competition between the sexes—remember Bobby Riggs?—attract readers.

While many newspapers try to give their readers a balanced ration of news, making a real effort to report important stories whether readers will like them or not, some newspapers are guided by the apparent interests of their average reader. If news can be loosely defined as what you find printed in the newspaper, so can reader interest. Newspapers generally respond to what their readers will pay to read. What you find in the pages of a newspaper, is what the readers of that paper want to know about.

THE NEWSPAPER

The Industry

Millions of men, women and children in the United States receive news stories via the newspaper and its related agencies: the two press associations and the supplementary news services.

There are in the United States more than 1,700 daily newspapers, ranging in size from giants like the *Los Angeles Times* to small city dailies like the Mount Pleasant (Texas) *Tribune* which has a circulation on four nights a week of less than 4,000. There are, in addition, some 9,500 weeklies, semiweeklies, and triweeklies. Most dailies are evening newspapers. Of the 1,761 dailies listed in the 1973 *Editor and Publisher International Yearbook*, 337 are morning papers and 1,441 are evening papers. Sunday editions are published by 605 dailies.

Few dailies have large circulations. In this country only 12 daily papers have circulations of more than half a million; more than 1,000 dailies have circulations of less than 25,000; and 275 have circulations under 5,000.

A handful of newspapers stand head and shoulders above the rest in terms of size and quality. The list of the 10-best newspapers by any standards usually includes the *New York Times*, the *Wall Street Journal* and the *Washington Post*. Others on the 10-best list vary from year to year depending on who makes up the list. In 1973 *Time* magazine named the following as this country's leading newspapers: the *Boston Globe, Chicago Tribune, Los Angeles Times Louisville Courier-Journal, Miami Herald, Milwaukee Journal, Newsday, New York Times, Wall Street Journal* and the *Washington Post*. Other highly regarded newspapers often included among the 10-best are the *Christian Science Monitor, St. Louis Post-Dispatch, Minneapolis Star and Tribune, Detroit Free Press, Providence Journal and Bulletin* and the *Baltimore Sun*.

Some of the criteria used to rate newspapers are: quality of news content, editorial pages, crusades for better government or community service; size of daily readership; advertising volume; sometimes even the attractiveness of makeup and typography.

The largest newspapers in the United States, by circulation standards, are the *New York News, Wall Street Journal, Los Angeles Times, New York Times, Chicago Tribune, New York Post, Philadelphia Bulletin, Detroit News, Detroit Free Press, Chicago Sun-Times, Los Angeles Herald-Examiner* and the *Washington Post*.

It is interesting to note that while most daily newspapers are published in one-newspaper communities, these 12 giants are published in six cities; and only five of them appeared on *Time* magazine's list of leaders. Nearly all, however, are among the top-10 in terms of advertising volume. The *Detroit News* carries more advertising than any other evening newspaper in the United States, the *Los Angeles Times* leads among morning newspapers.

An important part of the newspaper industry are the two large press associations: the co-operative Associated Press and the privately owned United Press International. These wire services employ thousands of reporters, writers and editors in this country and throughout the world, and produce millions of words of news copy every day for transmission to their newspaper members or clients. There are, in addition, a number of supplemental news services, including the *New York Times* news service, the *Los Angeles Times* and *Washington Post* news service, and the *Chicago Tribune–Knight Newspapers–New York Daily News* news services. These services distribute news and features written for their own newspapers to subscribing papers throughout the country. Some newspaper groups, like the Gannett newspapers, also have news services; but they serve primarily members of their own group.

An important, but less widely recognized, aspect of the industry is the newspaper that is published especially for a special interest group. These include daily and weekly papers published for religious groups, blacks, American Indians, Chicanos, college student bodies, members of labor unions and members of particular professions, businesses and trades. The black-owned *Chicago Daily Defender, Women's Wear Daily*, the *American Metal Market, Variety*, the *Racing Form* and *Rolling Stone* are a few examples. We might also include here the "alternative press," offbeat newspapers like the *Fifth Estate, Great Speckled Bird, Los Angeles Free Press* and the *Village Voice*.

Newsmen

The original purpose of the newspaper was to bring news and information to a concerned and interested public. Today, despite the fact that newspapers are a big business and medium for more than a billion dollars worth of advertising annually, news is still the main reason for the newspaper's existence. And because of this, the men and women who report, write and edit the news are the most important workers in the industry. It is their work that attracts the 62 million readers every day who, in turn, attract the advertising revenues that make the newspapers such a profitable business.

Newsmen* are highly skilled professionals. They are, to a large extent, college educated; many are graduates of schools and departments of journalism. Masters degrees are not uncommon in the newsroom and reporters, editors and special writers with Ph.D.s are not unknown.

The work these people do is interesting, exciting, sometimes glamorous, sometimes dangerous. Newsmen cover politics, government, public schools, trials and public hearings. They also cover floods, hurricanes, earthquakes, riots and wars. Newsmen question presidents at the White House, have access to national and world leaders. They sometimes find themselves in the thick of tear gas used by riot police or near enough to hear the whine of an assassin's bullets. Newsmen, like soldiers, are killed in wars, taken prisoner, carried forever on lists of those missing.

The work newsmen do is often routine, sometimes even dull. Newsmen cover weddings and funerals, write paragraphs about PTA meetings, and collect lists of births, court appearances and traffic offenses at the county courthouse. They cover dull public meetings at night, trail futureless office seekers through the snow in New Hampshire, start work at 6 a.m. so they can take stories over the telephone from correspondents.

Newspapers and the men and women who write for them have influence. Their reports affect the

---

Newsmen, in this discussion and wherever it occurs later in this text, is used in its broadest sense: the men and women who write for newspapers, wire services, and other news services. The *-man* in this word should be taken, and any good dictionary should bear this out, to mean *person* in a context where sexual distinctions are not relevant.

outcome of elections, influence votes in state legislatures and in the Congress of the United States, and cause industrial leaders to ponder plans for marketing a new product or building a new plant. This is why presidents and vice presidents get upset at what newspapers print: the public does respond to what it reads in the newspaper.

The daily and weekly newspapers of this country, the wire services and the supplemental news services and syndicates employ many news writers, reporters and editors. In 1970, according to the U.S. Department of Labor, some 39,000 reporters were at work in the industry. About 35 per cent of these were women.

The news staff of a paper will vary from four or five persons at the smallest dailies or weeklies to hundreds at the largest newspapers. The *Bergen Record*, in Hackensack, N. J., has a circulation of 151,000 and a staff of 145 in its newsroom. In San Jose, Calif., the morning *Mercury*, with a circulation of 131,000, and the evening *News*, with a circulation of 75,000, have a combined staff of 147.

The staff of the *New Orleans States-Item*, circulation 125,000, consists of 1 editor, 1 news editor, 1 city editor, 2 assistant city editors, 23 reporters, 8 copy editors, 1 makeup editor, 1 sports editor, 7 sports writers, 1 society editor, 2 women's news editors, 1 fashion editor, 3 columnists, 1 editorial cartoonist, 3 editorial writers, 1 secretary-researcher, 2 reporters in an outside news bureau in the state capital at Baton Rouge and another in Washington.

The newspaper industry offers many opportunities for interesting and rewarding careers. The Department of Labor estimates that there are more than 1,000 openings each year on newspapers, with wire services, supplemental news services and newspaper syndicates. The *Milwaukee Journal* estimates that it has about 12 openings a year on its news staff. *Editor and Publisher* lists from a dozen or so to 25 or 30 openings on newspapers every week.

Many newspapers offer summer internships for beginners. The *St. Petersburg Times* has offered an extremely effective summer internship program for many years, and the Lansing, Mich., *State Journal* has an intern program that hires college students for three months.

Newspapers regularly interview graduating seniors on college campuses and many editors keep in close touch with schools and departments of journalism in a continuing search for talent.

News Writing

In this text news writing means writing about events and activities for publication in a newspaper or distribution by a wire service or other news service. These are the stories you will find in any newspaper: routine stories, unusual stories, unimportant stories, significant stories—all kinds.

Excluded from our discussion of news writing are such specialized forms as editorials, columns, larger interpretive or investigative stories, series, reviews and critical writing, handouts, press releases and broadcast news copy. However, if you master the basic techniques discussed in this text, you will not find it difficult to learn to handle more specialized forms.

This text makes no distinction between news and features. Its aim is to help you master the skills of organization, structure and exposition that will enable you to write about any subject in a variety of ways.

Some news writers are generalists, while others prefer to specialize in sports, the outdoors, theater, politics, social issues or some other area. Some writers have a special touch for feature leads or are especially good at explaining complicated matters such as school finances or foreign policy. Still other writers are especially good at explaining people: Alden Whitman of the *New York Times* is a master craftsman of the extended biographical sketch and writes many of the *Times's* obituaries.

As you practice the craft of news writing, you will learn much more about the work of newsmen, about news and news values, and about newspapers, wire services and related news agencies. This brief introduction should give you your bearings as you prepare to enter the rewarding world of journalism.

CHAPTER TWO

Preparing News Copy

JOURNALISM is a highly creative profession, or trade, if you wish. But it also involves a considerable amount of routine and systematization. One of the areas in which this routine and systematization is very important is in the preparation and handling of copy intended for publication. All copy prepared for a printer is, by tradition and necessity, handled in much the same way. There are, of course, minor differences in detail from one newspaper to another, but in the main all news copy goes through the same procedures.

Standards and uniformity are necessary because of the vast amount of copy handled each day in the newsroom. A small newspaper will handle hundreds of pages of copy and a large metropolitan newspaper will handle thousands every day. On the smallest newspaper all copy may be seen by a single editor and a single copy desk, perhaps even a one-man copy desk. On a large newspaper half a dozen editors may handle copy for a dozen or more news departments, and special pages and special copy may be handled by two, three or more copy desks. In so huge an undertaking there is so much copy, all of it in small bits and pieces, constantly on the way through production channels, that a system is necessary if errors are to be avoided.

All news writers must begin by learning the basic, inviolable rules of copy preparation. Newsmen and newswomen are highly trained professionals. If you want to be accepted as a journeyman among journeymen, you will have to prepare and handle copy in a professional way. You wouldn't want it said of you, as it was said about one newcomer to a newspaper, that "you don't even know how to put the paper in your typewriter."

TYPING SKILLS

All copy intended for publication is typed. The news writer should be able to type using the touch system, not the two-finger hunt-and-peck approach. Newsmen of past generations were not always good typists and many of them typed with two fingers all their professional lives. Today, however, that frequently isn't enough.

There is a technological revolution under way in newspaper production and more and more newspapers are going to highly automated and computerized systems for setting type and printing the newspaper. Offset and cold-type processes are replacing the familiar linecasting machines and printing presses of the past. Many of the changes will have little effect on the newsroom. Some will. In many newsrooms the manual typewriter is being replaced by the electric typewriter so that copy can be fed into computer systems by means of an optical character reader. When the Richmond, Va., newspapers changed to photocomposition and installed the optical character reader, management sent some staff members back to school to learn to type on the electric typewriters the new system required (see Fig. 2.1).

EDI. OR DATE	DEPT.	STORY NO.	SLUG NEW	REW.	WRITER	PAGE	HEAD	WIDTH

Δ HD 18　　*Board to Discuss*

0 → Δnl nl eh cit 1243 RANDOLPH rop 1-2-18 (hask)

Randolph Renewal

Δhd18 Δsp Board to Discuss

Randolph Renewal

1 —
→

Δtx　　　　The Randolph Planning Study Board will hold its (regular)

　　　　　　　　　/Planning/

monthle meeting Tuesday, July 10, at 8 p.m. in the Randolph Planning

　　/y/

2 — Office, 1610 Winder St.

　　　　　(The current status of urban renw renewal efforts in Randoph ↓AREA

　　　　　　　　　　//　　　/ the Randolph area /

will be discussed as the renewal program has been approved by HUD.

　　　　/./

3 — 　　　　Also, the sistrict district of the Randolph planning board

　　　　/ΔP Randolph/Also　　　　　23　　24 will be held for

will hold district meetings July 9, 13 and 14 to discuss ion of the new

//　　　　/also will be held for discussion of/

urban renewal program.

　　　　　　　　　　next Monday at

　　　　　(The meetings will be held july 9, 7:30 p.m. at the West End

　　　　　　　　/next Monday at/　　　/ at the /

Richmond Community Action Program Center, 1401 Idlewood Ave.; July 23 at

　　　　　　　　　　　　　　　　　　　　　/ at/

8 p.m. at the Randolph office; and July 24 at 8 p.m. at Second Baptist

Church, 1400 Idlewood Ave. Δ #　　⌗

Fig. 2.1 *News copy at the Richmond, Va., newspapers is written on specially ruled copy paper with electric typewriters. Note how changes and corrections made by copy editors have been typed in so they can be read by the optical character reader.*

Fig. 2.2 *Reporters at the* Cadillac (Mich.) *Evening News write their news copy on the keyboard of a video display terminal. They see what they write on the terminal screen. Copy goes from the VDT directly into the newspaper's photocomposition system. Photo by* Cadillac Evening News.

In some newsrooms writers are already writing their copy on video display terminals (see Fig. 2.2). These machines operate almost like a typewriter, although they have many more keys, a built-in electronic eraser and a television screen instead of paper.

Technology is not going to make the reporter and news writer obsolete, but it is going to require that he be brighter, better educated and a more careful workman. It is important that the aspiring news writer be able to type more skillfully and turn out cleaner copy than was necessary in the past.

Copy Paper

In the newsroom copy is typed on copy paper, the same paper that the newspaper is printed on. This is a wood pulp paper with a soft finish; it is cheap and perishable, but ideally suited to newsroom use. In most newsrooms copy paper is salvage cut from the unused paper left on the cores of newsprint rolls when they are taken off the press, usable paper which would otherwise be wasted.

In making the change to photocomposition some newspapers have begun to use a better grade of paper with preprinted lines indicating margins and location of identifying notations. A piece of this type of copy paper appears in Fig. 2.1.

Wire services and some newspapers give their news writers books, sets of copy paper with carbon paper interleaved. These books are slipped into the typewriter and the news writer can produce an original and one or more carbon copies. In some newsrooms the books are also imprinted with lines indicating the location and width of margins.

All copy paper is a standard 8½ by 11 inches. Some Canadian newspapers use half sheets, 5½ by 8½ inches, but this is not often done in this country. Standardization of the size of the copy paper makes it easier to handle the thousands of pieces of copy that come out of the newsroom in a single day.

Copy is always double or triple spaced. No news copy is ever single spaced because it would be hard to read and impossible to edit. And, of course, copy is typed on one side of the paper only.

Carbon Copies

Many newspapers require their news writers to make a carbon, sometimes two carbons, of everything they write. In some newsrooms, the writer is provided with books, in others just carbon paper. Carbon copies are called *dupes,* short for duplicates, and sometimes *flimsies,* because the second sheets in books are very light and flimsy paper.

Margins

Margins on news copy should be generous, at least an inch at left and right. Copy with good wide margins not only looks a lot neater, but it is easier to read and edit than copy crowded out to the margins. Where copy is handled as separate pages, it is best to leave a one-inch margin at the bottom of the page. Where it is the practice to paste all the pages of a news story together into a long strip, the top and bottom margins must be adequate for the overlapping required in the pasteup.

At the top of the first page it is necessary to leave an extra deep margin, from four to five inches. If a standard sheet of copy paper is folded the short way, no more than two or three lines should show above the fold. On the second and succeeding pages, a margin of an inch and one-half or so usually suffices. For utmost clarity, indent generously for each paragraph. Six or eight spaces should be enough.

All this is good practice on newspapers where typesetting is manual, where copy is punched onto tape or set directly on a linecasting machine by a human operator, or where it is typed manually on paper for photo-offset reproduction.

Where copy is to be read by an optical character reader, margins may be different, as you can see by referring again to Fig. 2.1.

Typewriter Tricks

The Dash Typewriters do not have a symbol for the dash and all too frequently news writers garble their copy by using the hyphen in its place. There is a great deal of difference between the hyphen and the dash. The dash separates. The hyphen joins. When you want a dash, hit the hyphen key twice and leave an extra space on either side. Some examples:

```
      He ordered the youth to serve a 10-day

sentence -- to be served on weekends to avoid

missing school.

      He was rescued -- he later learned -- by

a man passing by on his way to work.

      He said his off-the-record remarks had

been misinterpreted -- at least by some people.
```

Number One Many typewriters do not have an arabic numeral *one* on the top line of the keyboard. If your typewriter does not, you can use the lower case letter l as a substitute.

Clean Copy

News writers are expected to turn in copy that is clean and accurate. Clean copy means copy that is reasonably free from typing errors, typewritten revisions and penciled changes. Clean copy is the result of practice and experience, but also the result of following a few basic rules.

Strikeovers Don't strike over letters. If you make a mistake, and you catch it while the page is still in your typewriter, use the letter *X* to obliterate the error. Then type in the word correctly. When you back up and strike over a letter, it is not always possible to determine just what letter you mean. Ambiguity of this kind, especially in names, is dangerous.

Deletions Use the letter *X* to obliterate and delete. Don't use the virgule, or slant, it doesn't do a good enough job.

Word Division Never divide a word at the end of a line. It is easier to read whole words than parts of words and you don't want editors or typesetters to have to guess your meaning. Compound and other hyphenated words can be confusing if divided.

Spacing Never single space; always double or triple space. Don't add extra space between paragraphs, but keep the same spacing throughout your copy.

All Caps Type all your copy in upper and lower case. Do not type words in all caps for emphasis or special effect.

Indenting Indent only for paragraphs. If the copy desk wants your story or any part of it indented, a copy editor will mark it and it will be set in that way. News writers are not concerned with typography.

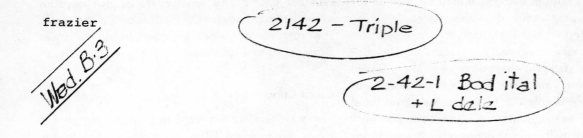

frazier

Wed. B.3

2142 – Triple

2-42-1 Bod ital
+ L dele

~A triple-header lottery drawing is in store for Muskegon
thursday   eleven-
~~tomorrow~~ with an ~~11~~ person Super Drawing and the regular weekly drawing in the morning and the third Millionaire Drawing in
the evening.

~By day's end, more than $2 million will ~~have been~~ be
                  BC
given away ~~since the~~ (Super Drawing) contestants at the 9:45 a.m.
event will share $580,000, millionaire   ing   has
                  ~the ~~big~~ drawing starts at 6:45 p.m.,
~~In the evening, there will be~~ prizes of $1,000,000, million,
                      awards and
$50,000, and seven at $5,000 ~~each in addition to~~ 100 consolation
purses
~~prizes~~ of $1,000 each.

~All three events are scheduled for the L. C. Walker
Arena.

~None of the ~~170~~ Super Drawing contestants is from
                                       from
the Lansing area, but there are ~~run~~ seven Mid-Michigan~~ians~~ in
the semi-finalist lineup for the Millionaire Drawing, including
William Jacovac and Kannikar Parchai for Lansing.
        BC
    ~(Others are ~~participating will be~~ George Black and Sylvia
Nabb of Pinckney, Joseph Young of Gregory, Mrs. Allene Foland, of
Pompeii, and Maynard Helmer of Ionia.

\#

###

Fig. 2.3 *A page of local news copy from the Lansing, Mich.
State Journal. You can compare the editing done on this copy with
the story as it appeared in the paper in Fig. 2.4.*

PROFESSIONAL PRACTICES

Paragraphing

If you look again at Figs. 2.1 and 2.4, you will see that in the news writer's original copy the paragraphs are quite short. No paragraph is more than four lines long, several are only three lines and one paragraph consists of only two lines, a single sentence. There are a number of reasons for seeing that paragraphs in news copy are kept quite short, one of the chief reasons being mechanical: short, typewritten copy looks a lot longer when it is set in type in narrow newspaper columns.

If you look at the pages of any newspaper you will see that the columns are quite narrow, usually less than two inches wide. Compare the news story written for the Lansing, Mich., *State Journal* (Fig. 2.3) with the story as it appeared in print (Fig. 2.4). The last paragraph of the copy is two and one-half typewritten lines. In print the same lines grow to five and one-half lines.

You can estimate roughly that every line of typewritten copy will be two lines of type. Keep the paragraphs in your copy short. Long paragraphs look uninviting on the newspaper page. They do not attract readers.

Copy Control

Identification Since a newspaper may process anywhere from several hundred to several thousand news stories on any given day, there has to be a system for keeping track of all this copy. The very simplest system calls for news writers to put their name and an identifying key word on each page of their copy. For example:

```
sinclair/armed robbery
```

On the second page, the identification would be:

```
sinclair/armed robbery/2-2-2-
```

This tells the editor that the story was written by a reporter named Sinclair and that it is about

Triple Treat

Muskegon Hosts Lottery

A triple-header lottery drawing is in store for Muskegon Thursday with an eleven-person Super Drawing and the regular weekly drawing in the morning and the third Millionaire drawing in the evening.

By days's end, more than $2 million will be given away.

SUPER DRAWING contestants at the 9:45 a.m. event will share $580,000. The millionaire drawing, starting at 6:45 p.m. has prizes of $1 million, $50,-000, seven $5,000 awards and 100 consolation purses of $1,-000 each.

All three events are scheduled for the L. C. Walker Arena.

None of the Super Drawing contestants is from the Lansing area, but there are seven from mid-Michigan in the semifinalist lineup for the Millionaire Drawing, including William Jacovac and Kannikar Parchai for Lansing.

O T H E R S A R E George Black and Sylvia Nabb of Pinckney, Joseph Young of Gregory, Mrs. Allene Foland of Pompeii and Maynard Helmer of Ionia.

Fig. 2.4 *The news story in Fig. 2.3 looked like this in the newspaper. Note what happened when the writer's paragraphing was changed and how on the copy the printer was instructed to set the bold-face read-ins.*

an armed robbery. And, of course, all pages after the first are numbered. Here is another example:

```
kennedy center -- WITH ART

sun local -- marcia
```

This indicates that the story is about the John F. Kennedy Center, a school for trainable mentally handicapped children, and that there are photographs to go with it. The story is intended for the Sunday paper and for a local news page or section. And the writer's name is Marcia.

Some newspapers use a slightly more complex system of identification. Note the identifying information required on copy written for the Richmond newspapers (Fig. 2.1).

Slug Lines The identification of the story—in the examples just cited the words *armed robbery* and *kennedy center*—are called *slugs* or *slug lines*. They are also sometimes called *guides* or *guide lines*. When an editor tells you to "slug that story *fatal"* he means that you should use the word *fatal* as the identifying slug line.

Slug lines are important because they make it possible to keep track of the story as it moves through production channels from the typewriter to the printed page.

Slug lines are usually brief, somewhere between one and four words. One or two words are preferable. The slug line should be very specific because there may be two stories of a similar nature and the editors must be able to tell them apart. Slugs like *speech*, or *police* or *accident* are inadequate. It would be better to use slug lines such as *commencement, robber shot* or *grand ledge fatal*.

Slug lines must appear on every page of news copy.

More When copy runs to more than a single page, every page except the last must be marked with a special symbol to indicate incomplete copy. Traditionally, the word *more* serves this purpose.

The word *more* should either be centered just below the last line of copy or appear near the end of the last typewritten line—in other words, located where the editors, copy editors and typesetters will spot it easily.

```
East Lansing police officer jotted down the

license number of their car the night of the

robbery.

        Ingham County Prosecuting Attorney

Edgar T. Beach tried the case for the state.

        Judge Hooper also sentenced two area

men to prison Monday.  Both had pleaded guilty to

charges of attempted burglary.

        They are:

                        more
```

Thirty At the end of a news story, after the last paragraph, an *end mark* is typed or written in to indicate that the copy is now complete.

```
smith -- burglars 2-2-2


        They were sentenced to three to five

years at Southern Michigan State Prison at

Jackson.

        They were arrested with two other

ex-convicts after an Owosso police officer jotted

down the license number of the car in which they

were riding the night of the burglary.

                        ##
```

The symbol shown is not the only end mark news writers use. You may also use the traditional *30* or *thirty,* either written as an arabic numeral or spelled out, or the word *end.* Press association writers usually use their initials as an end mark.

One Page at a Time Each page of news copy should be complete in itself. This simply means that the last paragraph on each page is complete and that you start a new paragraph at the top of the next page. The need for this is purely mechanical: in both hot-type and cold-type production the different pages of a news story may get separated. It would be impossible to match up the segments of the story if paragraphs or sentences were continued from one page to the next.

Don't break paragraphs at the bottom of the page.

Editing Your Copy

The last step in writing a news story comes after the story is complete and the last sheet of copy paper is out of the typewriter. Experienced news writers at this point take the time to read their copy over carefully, word by word and line by line. They look for typing errors, mistakes in spelling or usage, points of style or writing faults that they can correct themselves before turning their copy over to the editor.

The usual newsroom practice is to make such corrections with a copy pencil. This is a rather fat pencil with a broad, soft lead ideal for writing on the soft surfaces of copy paper. Newspapers supply their staffs with copy pencils. Ball point pens and pencils with very hard lead are not suitable for editing copy.

Newspapers that use cold-type composition and optical character readers edit copy with a special pen or pencil that cannot be read by the optical character reader. Corrections indicated this way are typed in after the copy leaves the copy desk. You can see how this is done in Fig. 2.1.

Editing Marks

In the newsroom a set of traditional symbols are used to indicate changes that should be made in the copy. These are called *copy editing marks* and are somewhat different from the proofreading marks used to indicate needed corrections on proofs.

Copy editing marks are always made within the copy at the place where the error occurs or where the change is wanted. They are never made in the margins.

Here's the system:

Paragraph When you wish to indicate that a paragraph should start where there is no paragraph break in the copy, make a neat right angle, like this:

```
    Mason police said Emery failed to stop at

the intersection and drove in front of the truck.

Emery told police he saw neither the stop sign

nor the approaching truck.

    He was issued a ticket for failure to yield

the right of way.
```

The copy desk usually marks paragraphs that were indented properly on the typewritten copy, as you can see was done on the copy in Fig. 2.4. Another mark often used to indicate a new paragraph break is this:

```
approaching truck. He was issued a ticket for
```

Capitalization When you want a lower case letter changed to a capital, draw three short horizontal lines under the letter:

```
in the south today, there is a tendency to
```

Lower Case When you want a capital letter changed to a lower case letter, draw a slant line through the letter like this:

```
the Democratic system is best, the mayor said
```

Abbreviations To abbreviate a word spelled out in the copy, circle the word:

```
the election will be held November 1
```

To spell out a word abbreviated in the copy, circle the word:

```
in Aug. the committee held a public hearing
```

The circle means "do the opposite" and is usually an adequate instruction. If there is any reason to think that the copy desk or anyone else might not know the form you are requesting, cross the word out and write it in above the line

```
                        Auditorium
at the meeting in the Aud last night they
```

Numbers Arabic figures can be changed to words or vice versa by circling them:

```
was at least 5 or more, the mayor said
```

```
called for at least eleven new members
```

Transposition Where words or letters have been typed in the wrong order, indicate the proper order with the transposition symbol which encloses the letters or words to be changed around:

residetn/ of Baton Rouge will speak at the

that is all for now," (said/he).

If the copy desk or anyone else might not be able to follow a transposition corrected in this way, cross out the entire word or words and print them in above the line:

was a ~~residetn~~ \resident/ of Baton Rouge who would

never before, "~~said he~~, \he said/ "would I think

Insertion To insert a word or a letter within a word, print it neatly above the line and indicate its intended position with a bracket. Add a small caret below the line to indicate again where the insertion is to be made:

refused (any) help from the senate committee to

asked for any support he could get from

Space When figures or words are improperly divided by unwanted space, indicate that the space is to be closed up by inserting a short curved or flat line above and below the place where the change is wanted:

he gave his book to an other man who

the judge ordered him to pay a $1 00 fine.

This mark means close up and leave no space, so it can only be used to close up space within a word or a set of figures.

When words or figures are improperly run together and there is no space where there should be, separate the words or figures thus:

he gave another man his only book

the horses finished in 1, 2, 3 order

Another acceptable mark to indicate where space is needed:

he gave another man his only book

Punctuation When it is necessary to add or insert punctuation it can be done this way:

asked for what cant be done easily /No, she said

without looking up. can't do it that way Not

on your "Why not " she asked him quickly.

apparently not " the speaker said. that will be

all, he said

No Paragraph When the copy has been indented for a paragraph and it is later decided not to paragraph at this point, run a guide line connecting last word of one paragraph to the first word of the next:

to help the Administration. But, he said, that

is not enough.

When that was done, he ordered the

arrest of the other members of the team.

Deletion When it is necessary to delete, to take out a letter or word, do it this way:

used his best judgement to give her

was ~~totally~~ destroyed by fire last night

Note carefully that when a letter is deleted the close-up symbol appears above and below the line and means *close up and leave no space.* When a word is deleted the close-up symbol is a flat or slightly curved line above the typewritten line and means *close up to normal spacing.* These marks are not interchangeable. The second close-up symbol not only indicates normal spacing, but also carries the eye over the deleted matter:

The No. 9 spot ~~andxthen~~ went to ~~thexgreatxnexx~~

Smith who was named chairman of the new

committee.

Extensive Deletion Where there are extensive deletions, it is a good idea to draw a connecting line to indicate the correct reading:

A Washington county sheriff's officer ~~whexexwnexx~~

~~xomxxffanxthexxhtt~~ jotted down the license of the

~~whtexxthexhexxxwentxtexxthexx~~ car ~~the~~ in which the

men were riding.

Since the purpose of the guide line is to carry the eye to the next word in the same line, it is not used at the beginning or end of a line where deletions are not extensive:

they were especially interested in the way

~~inxwhighx~~ in which the Court's decision was

reached last year. Congressional ~~nowxixxtt~~

districts were not affected.

Verification Names and figures in your copy which might be questioned by the copy desk should be marked to indicate that you have verified them and know them to be correct. A small *OK*, circled, will usually do. Some newspapers prefer that you draw a box around the item, and others use *CQ* as an indication that the item is correct:

Dr. Eugene Guthrie; business, Henry Ford II;

Dr. Eugene Guthrie; business, Henry Ford II;

Dr. Eugene Guthrie; business, Henry Ford II;

CHAPTER THREE

Basic News Story Organization

EVERY WRITER has to work within the conventions of some literary form, whether it is the novel, essay, biography, play, poem or news story. Whatever information, ideas or emotions the writer wants to communicate, they have to be communicated in that form. News writing is often regarded as highly stylized and conventional. "You have to write everything the same way," the critics charge. Not so. News writing is no more restrictive a form than the short story, the sonnet, or the haiku. News writing does make use of a number of conventional organizing devices, since experience has shown them to be useful for conveying information to newspaper readers. But once you have mastered these basic conventions, you will have ample opportunity to exercise your creativity and imagination.

News writing demands discipline, but it also demands imagination, perception, humor, sympathy and taste. News writing is more flexible and open to innovation today than it has ever been—try reading a newspaper story written in 1890 or 1900. Today's news writer relies on tried and true news writing techniques, but he also makes use of unconventional and creative ones.

BASIC ORGANIZATION

The news story can be organized and told in a variety of ways, but basically it consists of a beginning (*lead*), a middle (*body or development*) and an end (*conclusion*). See Fig. 3.1.

There are many ways of writing a lead. One basic type of lead is the *summary lead* which is constructed around the five Ws: *who, what, when, where, why* and *how.*

The body, or development, of a story elaborates on the facts predicted in the lead. The body may be brief or it may be very long. In the one-paragraph news story, the lead and the body are one and the same.

News stories may or may not require a conclusion. Some stories tell what they have to tell and then stop; others have carefully contrived conclusions. Some conclusions carry the point of

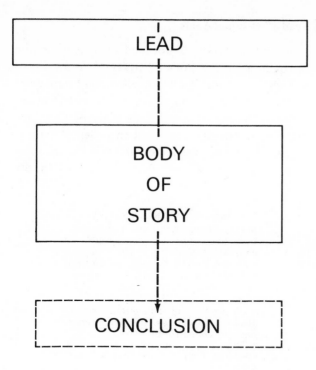

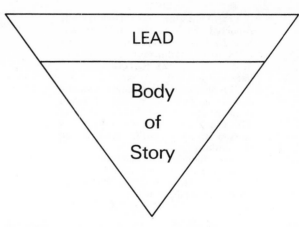

Fig. 3.2 *The traditional and useful inverted pyramid form calls for a summary lead and supporting facts arranged in a descending order. The facts most easily dispensed with are placed at the peak of the inverted pyramid.*

Fig. 3.1 *The basic structure of the news story. All news stories have a* lead—*a starting place; and all have a* body—*the development of facts introduced in the lead. The* conclusion *is optional and found most often in feature stories.*

the story; others serve to emphasize the significance of the facts presented in the lead and body.

VARIATIONS

The Inverted Pyramid

Many single-incident news stories are presented in the *inverted-pyramid* format (Fig. 3.2). This consists of a summary lead and a development made up of details arranged in descending order of importance: the most important facts coming right after the lead, and the least important facts coming at the end.

The inverted-pyramid story has no conclusion. This format has one advantage—the story can be cut, paragraph by paragraph, from the bottom up. Let's look at a good example of a single-incident story that uses the inverted-pyramid format:

> PHILADELPHIA—UPI—The YMCA announced Saturday the purchase of a 620-acre camp site in the Pocono Mountains about 15 miles northeast of Jim Thorpe, Pa.
>
> The site, covered by thick woods and bisected by a stream, will be used to expand the YMCA's present camping program for young adults.
>
> The local YMCA now operates three camps near Downington, Pa.

The first paragraph of this story is a summary lead containing all the essential facts; the second paragraph contains the explanatory detail; and the third paragraph contains some additional details not predicted in the lead. If space limitations had demanded that this story be cut, the last paragraph could have been trimmed off and the story would have remained intact. If necessary, the second paragraph could also have been trimmed and the story—now consisting of nothing but the original lead—would still stand. The summary lead in an inverted-pyramid story contains all the essential facts. Here is another example:

> A $45,000 blaze destroyed a truck and its contents of lumber at a south Arlington warehouse early today.

The Arlington Fire Department reported that one fireman, Pvt. Albert R. Stutz, suffered a foot injury in fighting the blaze at the Morgan Millwork Co., 521 S. 15th St., just before 6 a.m.

The fire caused considerable smoke and soot damage to the finished lumber stored in the warehouse. The truck that was destroyed was backed up to a loading dock inside the building.

Fire officials said they still were investigating the cause of the blaze which erupted before the firm's employes arrived for work.

Washington Evening Star

This story, consisting of a summary lead and three paragraphs of additional information, is a little longer than the first example. The additional information is carefully arranged in descending order of importance: injury to the fireman in the second paragraph, damage to the warehouse in the third paragraph and the investigation—a routine matter—in the final paragraph.

LEAD

Fact 1

Fact 2

Fact 3

Fact 4

Fig. 3.3 *A summary lead can be followed by paragraphs containing facts of relatively equal importance. Fact 4 is as necessary to the story as Fact 1.*

Lead-Plus-Equal-Facts

Many news stories do not lend themselves to the restrictions of the inverted-pyramid form. These are stories whose details are all equally important so that they cannot be eliminated to meet the demands of space. Details in the body of the story are not necessarily presented in order of importance, but they always appear in some logical order (Fig. 3.3). You can see how this works in the following story:

WASHINGTON—The Urban Mass Transportation Administration has approved five key subcontracts vital to expediting the engineering planning of the Buffalo-to Amherst rapid rail transit system, Rep. Jack F. Kemp (R., Hamburg) said today.

Approved as subcontractors to Bechtel Associates, the prime engineering consultants, were:

The Anderson Drilling Co., of Orchard Park for drilling and soil sampling.

The J. H. Robinson Co. of Erie, Pa., for lab testing and rock samples.

Transit & Tunnel Inc. of Buffalo for studies on underground construction and costs.

Urban Engineers of Buffalo for engineering support services.

Calspan Corp. of Buffalo for safety engineering studies.

Buffalo Evening News

Since the summary lead mentions the approval of *five* subcontracts, the body of the story must identify all five subcontractors. Otherwise the reader—who can count, after all—will ask, "Where's the rest of the story?"

A number of situations call for the lead-plus-equal-facts format. An accident story that starts out like this, for example:

Four persons were treated Saturday at City General Hospital for minor injuries suffered in four separate accidents.

This story has to explain each accident, identify the people involved and explain the nature of their injuries. Similarly, if a lead reports that a speaker made three major points, the story has to tell what the three points were. The following lead also calls for explanation of five items:

> City Council will be asked to approve purchases of $165,000 when it meets Tuesday night.
> The five bids Council will consider:

The Chronological Account

When news stories report action or a series of related events, chronology is the answer to the problem of organization (Fig. 3.4). In these cases the lead may be a summary or a partial summary. The partial summary is not complete, but merely gives some idea of the nature of the story without disclosing its outcome. Or the lead may be a convenient starting place, such as the first episode of the story. The body of the story is then told in strict chronological order. It may be told briefly or at some length, but it is always chronological.

The conclusion in a chronological account may be either the final episode in the sequence of events or it may be a statement of some fact outside the chronology. In either case, this format does have an identifiable conclusion; it cannot be cut by throwing paragraphs away.

Let's look at an example:

> GRANTHAM, ENGLAND—AP—Dr. F. J. Hopkins-Musson had an emergency call Tuesday night and his car wouldn't start.
> Another driver stopped to help, lifted the hood of the doctor's car and lit his cigarette lighter to get a better view of the engine.
> There was an explosion and the doctor's automobile was wrapped in flames.
> Somebody called the fire department. By the time firemen arrived, the doctor had fainted. His car was in ruins—and the good Samaritan had gone without leaving his name.

The lead in this story is just a starting place—the first event in the chronology—with no hint as to how the story will end. The facts are related in choronological order, and the story is told briefly.

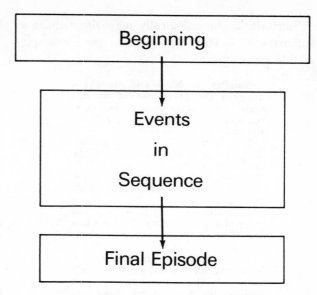

Fig. 3.4 *The chronological story has a lead, the beginning; a development, the events of the story told in sequence; and a conclusion, often just the final event in the chronology, but sometimes a formal close or punch line.*

It ends with the final episode in the sequence of events. There are also some elements of a formal conclusion. The story could have ended with the doctor in a faint and the car in ruins, but the writer has added a punch line: the helpful passerby disappeared without a trace.

The lead of a chronological story may also be a *partial summary*, telling only enough to give an idea of the story and to catch the reader's interest. The partial summary is careful to avoid revealing the outcome:

> SUGAR LAND, TEX.—UPI— The burglars were professionals, the sheriff's deputies agreed. They just had a bad day.
> The burglars:
> —Pried open the back door of the Sugar Land State Bank and broke into the cashiers' drawers. They were empty.
> ——They used a compressor drill to get into the main vault, but it led only to a storage vault.
> ——Finally, they bored into what they thought was the main vault. Bursting through a wall, the burglars ended up outdoors on U.S. 50.

Stories told chronologically may also require a summary lead. The following is a good example of this approach:

> Bandits, one black and one white, dragged the proprietor of an all-night party store back to her cash register early today and forced her to hand over $96 in cash.
>
> The robbers also took $58 from the purse of Ella Hill who runs the Quik Pix Party Store at 5127 S. Waverly, and then shut her in the store's bathroom while they made their getaway.
>
> Mrs. Hill told city police she was stooped down stocking shelves when the two men entered the store about 1:30 a.m.
>
> The black man walked up behind her, grabbed her by the hair, held an object she believes was a gun against the back of her head and pulled her to the cash register, she told police.
>
> After he forced her to open the till, the white man grabbed $20 in quarters and $76 in small bills.

> The first man then shoved her inside the bathroom and closed the door. When she came out, $58 from her purse was also missing, she told officers.
>
> The victim said that once she heard the gun click as if the hammer had fallen against an empty chamber.
>
> Mrs. Hill said the white man was wearing a blue and white striped shirt and blue jeans. She didn't get a good look at his partner.
>
> Lansing, Mich., *State Journal*

The first two paragraphs of this story are a summary lead. The chronological account begins in the third paragraph with the entry of the two men and ends in the sixth paragraph as the woman emerges from the bathroom. The final two paragraphs are outside the chronology, but are included to add interesting and useful information. Description of the two bandits provides a conclusion and brings the story up to date: These are the men the police are seeking.

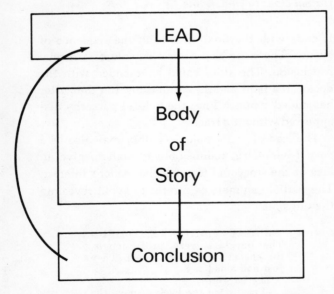

Fig. 3.5 *The more rigidly structured news story with a formal conclusion looks like this. The lead carries the reader into the story; the body of the story reveals the details in some logical order; and there is a formal conclusion which often ties back to the lead in the same way that the lead ties in to the body.*

Stories with a Conclusion

The chronological stories we have just looked at have conclusions of a kind. Now let's look at stories that require a more formal conclusion, one designed to leave the reader with a specific set of facts or point of view. The *formal conclusion* is more than just a stopping place, a final event in a chronology or an additional detail. The function of the formal conclusion is much like that of the summary lead: it brings the body of the story to a head just as the summary lead brings the story to a head. The formal conclusion ties together the loose ends of the story. In many instances it refers the readers back to the lead (Fig. 3.5) by repeating a theme or a word introduced in the lead. For example:

> Two men who were Boy Scouts so long ago they had forgotten what troop they belonged to remembered enough of their first-aid training Sunday to save a drowning boy.

Jerry Huntley and William Ishom Jr., both 21 and of the 700 block of Sedgewick Street, heard screams, ran out of the house, swam 75 feet into nearby Ohio Creek and pulled unconscious Grover Wade from beneath the water. Wade, 11, of the 200 block of East Brombleton Avenue, came to after 20 minutes of artificial respiration applied by the men.

"The boy would have drowned," said Detective P. G. Shaner, "if it weren't for the immediate and intelligent response of these men. When I got there, they had him in perfect artificial respiration position —feet slightly raised, head to the side and tongue out."

The boy told police he had waded into the creek with two friends and slipped into a hole. He was in fair condition in Norfolk General Hospital Sunday night.

Huntley said they spotted the boy floating face down and by the time they reached him, he had slipped beneath the water.

"First aid is something that sticks with you," Ishom said. "You never forget it."

But when he was asked what troop he and Huntley had belonged to, he answered: "It's been so long ago, I couldn't tell you."

Norfolk (Va.) *Virginian-Pilot*

The lead in this story sets the stage and tells in summary form what the story is about and how it came out. The body of the story is developed chronologically, then shifts to summary statements of the boy's and his rescuers' versions to fill in the details. In the formal conclusion—the last two paragraphs—the writer reiterates the feature angle introduced in the lead: the rescue of a drowning youngster by two former Boy Scouts who remembered their first-aid training. A secondary feature angle, is also introduced in the lead and reiterated in the conclusion: the fact that the former Scouts could not remember what troop they had belonged to. Words from the lead, *first aid* and *troop*, are brought back in the conclusion. The effect here is to swing from the end of the story back to the beginning and remind the reader of the feature angle which makes the story interesting. Lead and conclusion serve to contain the story and to em-

phasize the unusual circumstances that make it interesting.

Here is another story with a formal conclusion:

PALO ALTO, CALIF.—AP—All told it was a pretty cool operation.

Jose Garza, 26, told police he was going about his clerking duties in a 7–11 store when an armed man walked in and forced him into the beverage cooler so he could rifle the till.

Garza was cooling his heels, and everything else, when the refrigerator door was opened by a customer. The customer was surprised to find the shelf tenanted by other than bottles and things.

"I'm being robbed," Garza gasped. The customer tackled the robber as he was going out the door.

The man was identified as Robert McQueen, 18. Police charged him with robbery.

When Garza defrosted himself, he gave the customer, Spencer Perkins, 22, a six-pack of beer for his help.

The lead on this story merely characterizes the story that follows as a "pretty cool operation." The body is told chronologically and the story ends with the arrest of the robber and the reward for the customer who apprehended him. The final paragraph is more than a stopping place. The words "defrosted himself" are perfectly calculated to reiterate the "cool operation" theme.

The Suspended-Interest Story

Finally, there is a specialized story form, the *suspended-interest or pyramid* form. This is most frequently used to tell short, humorous stories, the kind editors call "page brighteners." The suspended-interest story is tricky to write because the writer must be careful to save the best for last (Fig. 3.6). Just as in telling a joke, if the writer gives too much away before the end, the effect is lost. Deftly told, a good joke makes the audience laugh at the right moment—after the punch line is delivered. So it is with the suspended-interest

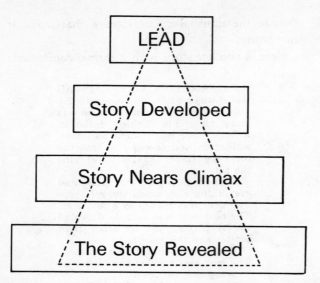

Fig. 3.6 *The suspended interest story is carefully structured so that the lead does not give away the outcome of the story. The details are arranged so as to carry the reader on to the final paragraph where the punch line is revealed.*

story: properly crafted, it will make the reader smile, even laugh, at the end.

The following story is deftly told and the punch line is withheld until the very end:

> BALTIMORE—UPI—Ronald Sapia wishes his dog would bite.
>
> Mr. Sapia, manager of a local shopping center, was taking his sheepdog for a ride in his automobile when he was approached by a blond youth.
>
> "Does your dog bite?" the youth asked.

"No," Mr. Sapia said.

The youth pulled a revolver, ordered Mr. Sapia and the dog out, and stole the car.

Here is another example of a story that would not have the same effect if the outcome were revealed in the summary lead:

> SALT LAKE CITY—AP—The message from Multnomah County, Ore., police asked Salt Lake City officers to arrest and serve a felony warrant on a man wanted in Oregon.
>
> "He is reported to be residing at 244 E. Fourth South, Salt Lake City," the letter said.
>
> Local police weren't able to locate the man immediately. The address is that of the police department.

Beginning news writers won't need all these story forms right away. They are presented here to give you a few worthwhile ideas. First of all, there are some story forms that you can use while you learn the rudiments of news writing. Second, even given these forms, you will still have plenty of room for flexibility and creativity. News writing is not rigid and inflexible. Although there are customary ways of organizing facts and ideas, you will have ample opportunity to tell a story in a way that fits the circumstances of your story and suits your personal taste.

You will find the inverted-pyramid and the lead-plus-equal-facts formats especially useful in the beginning. Later chapters will discuss chronology, the feature format, and other ways of organizing and writing news stories in greater detail.

CHAPTER FOUR

Writing the Lead

THE SUMMARY LEAD

CHAPTER 3 discusses the *summary lead* as a means of beginning a news story. This type of lead tells the gist of the story so completely that in some instances it can stand by itself as a story.

The summary lead answers these questions:

- What happened?
- Who was involved?
- Where did it happen?
- When did it happen?
- Why did it happen?
- How did it happen?

These are the five Ws of journalism—actually five Ws and an H—which provide the news writer with a means of organizing a story. If the five Ws are answered in the first paragraph or two, the framework of the entire story is there (Fig. 4.1). All that remains is to flesh it out with supporting detail.

The five Ws perform two important tasks: they provide the first paragraph, or the first couple of paragraphs of the story; and they serve as a framework for the body of the story. Take a look at this news story:

> CINCINNATI, OHIO—AP—An airman was killed today in a one-car accident on U.S. 52 just east of Cincinnati.

> Killed was Carl F. Wolfe, 21, Battle Creek, Mich. The Ohio Highway Patrol said he was stationed at Shaw Air Force Base in South Carolina.

This news story is really nothing but a lead. It tells *what* happened (an airman was killed), *when* it happened (today), *where* it happened (just east of Cincinnati), *how* it happened (in a one-car accident). The *who* of the lead is reported in general terms in the first paragraph, where the victim is described as an airman, and in detail in the second paragraph, where he is identified fully by name, age and address. The only question not answered

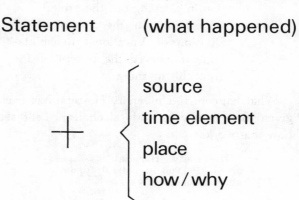

Statement　　(what happened)

+ { source
time element
place
how / why }

Fig. 4.1 *The* summary lead *stresses* what *happened. Other elements are secondary and are included to* explain and support *the statement of* what *happened.*

is *why?* Perhaps the cause of the crash was not known at the time the story was written and transmitted.

This is a *single-incident* story: it has only one thing to tell us. Single-incident stories can be effectively organized around the five Ws. Leads based on the five Ws give us most of the information we want to know, especially if we are in a hurry. This is why summary leads are a good way to start a news story. Let's see how a news story can be written using a summary lead built around the five Ws. We will begin with the *what.*

The What of the Story

If you were to analyze the stories in any issue of a newspaper, you would probably find that the *what* is the most common starting place. So, starting with what happened, let's see how the following facts can be arranged into a news story:

Fact 1: a grant of $100,000

Fact 2: by the federal government

Fact 3: made to University Hospital

Fact 4: to be used for research into early detection of alcoholism among industrial workers

Fact 5: the hospital will work with the state Division of Vocational Rehabilitation in carrying out the project

Fact 6: Robert Jackson, the director of the Division of Vocational Rehabilitation, announced the receipt of the grant this morning

What happened? University Hospital has been given some money to study alcoholism. Let's see how that works:

> University Hospital has been given $100,000 in federal funds to study alcoholism.

That's an accurate statement, but a little too general. The hospital is not going to study alcoholism, but, one aspect of it. Let's try again:

> University Hospital has been given $100,000 in federal funds for

research into the early detection of alcoholism among industrial workers.

The project will be undertaken jointly by the hospital and the state Division of Vocational Rehabilitation, Robert Jackson, director of the division, said today.

We now have a concise summary, one that could either stand by itself or serve as the summary lead for a considerably longer story.

Now, looking at the two news stories—the one about the airman and the one about the federal grant—we can broaden our definition of a summary lead. We can now say that a summary lead consists of

1 A statement of what happened;

2 A time element;

3 Identification of the place where the story happened;

4 Something of the circumstances, how or why the event happened;

5 Some identification of the people involved in the story.

One further element is almost always necessary if the lead is to be complete: *attribution*, citation of the source of the story. In most news stories all information included in the story is attributed to some clearly identified source, the police, the governor's office, a spokesman for the hospital. See, for example, the following story:

> PULLMAN—AP—The dining hall at a YMCA Boy Scout camp near this southwestern Michigan community burned early Tuesday in what Allegan County sheriff's deputies called a $40,000 blaze.
>
> Deputies said the blaze was traced to temporary space heaters being used to keep the dining hall warm while a new heating system was installed at the camp.
>
> Camp Channing is 20 miles southwest of Allegan near Lake Michigan.

The first paragraph of this story is a good summary: it tells what happened, where it happened, when it happened, and it identifies the source of the story. The second and third paragraphs just add details.

We now have a clear picture of what a summary lead looks like: it is a simple sentence built around the five Ws with the emphasis on *what* happened. This may be called a *what lead* and is frequently used and easy to write. Here are two more examples:

> Ronald W. Braun, 22, of Manchester, has been bound over for arraignment in Circuit Court April 24 on a charge of murder in connection with the fatal shooting of his brother-in-law.
> *Jackson* (Mich.) *Citizen Patriot*

> A six-year-old girl who was critically injured in a five-story fall from the balcony of her mother's Key Biscayne apartment died Tuesday in Mercy Hospital.
> *Miami Herald*

The Who of the Story

The *who* of the story is a little more complicated than the *what*. Sometimes the *who* is included as part of the statement of what happened, as it was in the story about the airman; sometimes it appears in the identification of the source; and sometimes there is no *who* in the story at all.

In the following example, the *who* is part of the attribution:

> LONDON—International Harvester Co. will focus European investments in continental plants rather than in Great Britain, Brooks McCormick, president and chief executive officer, said here today.
> *Chicago Sun-Times*

In the following lead, the *who* is part of the explanation of what happened:

> CLOVIS, N.M.—UPI—Police say Ralph Madrid drove his car through the wall of a house, rammed two other cars, struck the side of a railroad overpass and then apparently jumped off a bridge.

In the next lead, the *who* gets more emphasis, but is still part of the explanation of what happened:

> Claire Boothe Luce's "The Women" will start rehearsals March 5 for an April 25 bow at the 46th Street Theater.
> *New York Post*

In the next lead, the *who* is not a person, but a couple of organizations:

> The League of Women Voters Monday joined the Chicago Crime Commission in a watchdog effort aimed at ending long-term continuances in Cook County court cases.
> *Chicago Sun-Times*

These summary leads were written primarily to tell what happened or what is happening and the names appearing in them are incidental to the events. They were not designed to say anything about anyone. A *who lead*, on the other hand, emphasizes a person or persons and is quite another thing, as we shall see later in this chapter.

The Other Ws

What leads are most common, and *who leads* come next. The other Ws are seldom emphasized. Diligent search through newspaper pages will, sooner or later, uncover a lead which starts with a time element, a reference to where the story occurred or to the circumstances surrounding the story —why and how. But these are occasional solutions to occasional problems.

Where The location of a story is usually of some interest and it often rates a mention in the lead. Sometimes the dateline serves this purpose; and sometimes a reference to a local street or landmark or the word *here*, tells us that we are reading a local story. News writers seldom emphasize the location of the story, although once in a while they do:

> At a private brunch this morning at the Scottsdale Hilton Hotel, guests are being served a new meatlike product that contains no meat.
> *The Arizona Republic*

It is more usual to place the where element as well as the when element after the verb:

> CINCINNATI, OHIO—AP—An airman was killed today in a one-car accident *on U.S. 52 just east of Cincinnati.*

How or Why The circumstances surrounding an event, the *how* and *why* of the story, are usually left for the second or third paragraph of the lead, or even for the body of the story. However, there are times when the circumstances are so much a factor that they must be explained with the *what* or the *who* of the incident:

> Just as he's done each morning for the past several years, Calvin S. Bryant, 50, of Miami Shores, awoke Monday, dressed and started his keep-trim jog around the block.
> He had hardly been gone a minute when a hit-and-run car glanced off two palm trees, jumped the curb and onto the sidewalk and struck Bryant from behind, killing him, police said.
> *Miami Herald*

It is more usual to subordinate the *why* and *how* to the *what* and *who,* as in the following leads:

> A six-year-old girl was critically injured Monday when she fell from a second-story window at her home on the west side.

> A 73-year-old man, struck by a hit-run car as he crossed the street near his home, died Monday in Madison General Hospital.

When The time element is important in news stories and is almost always included in the lead. But it is seldom advisable to start with a phrase like "'At *10 a.m. today*," or, "*At 5 p.m. Monday.*" Time elements belong farther along in the first sentence and appear most comfortably after the verb. For example:

> The dining hall at a YMCA Boy Scout camp near this southwestern Michigan community burned *early Tuesday* in what Allegan County sheriff's deputies call a $40,000 blaze.

> Donald L. Kaminski, who had been the world's second-longest living heart transplant patient, died *today.*

More about the When

Our discussion so far has lumped the time element, the *when* of the lead, with the minor Ws, the *where, why* and *how.* We will have to take a closer look at the time element in news leads, however, because it is more important and prominent than we have suggested. Journalism lives by the clock; there is an urgency about speeding the news to readers that prompts news services and newspapers to value the timeliness of the news highly. "Now, now, now," the front page news story says. "Today, today, today." Your daily newspaper cannot bring the news to your doorstep as quickly as radio and television can bring it into your living room; but it does get it there pretty fast. And leads on stories that are breaking when the paper goes to press, inevitably remind us of that currency by jamming a *today* into the first sentence of the lead. For example:

> WOUNDED KNEE, S.D.—AP— Women and children were being evacuated *today* from Wounded Knee and militant Indians were reported beefing up their forces as a government deadline to leave the hamlet approached.

Since news writers usually do have to include a time element in their lead, the only question is, Where is it best to put it? As we have already suggested, the time element most commonly appears after the verb:

> Two eight-year old boys were kidnaped *Saturday* from the neighborhood playground where they had been playing.

The time element may also fit comfortably at the end of the sentence after the other elements that follow the verb:

> More than 15,000 protestors paraded through downtown streets *Saturday.*

Newspapers and wire services have a tendency to push the time element as far forward in the first sentence as possible, often putting it just before the verb:

> Members of Local 43 *Saturday* ratified a new three-year contract with Central States Power Co.

There is some flexibility, as you can see, in placing the time element in a sentence. Much will depend on how the sentence sounds. If you read it aloud and the time element sounds awkwardly placed—move it. There are several places to put it, as the above examples show.

Present Tense Using the word *today* in a lead is not the only way to make it timely. Another useful tactic is to write in the present tense rather than in the past tense:

> DETROIT—UPI—The Detroit Police Department which rarely uses women in any unit other than its women's division, is planning to use female police officers in its controversial STRESS units to help catch rapists.

No mention of today or the day of the week here: just the implied currency of the phrase *is planning*. Emphasis on timeliness can also be found in leads that look ahead:

> Masonic services *will be* held today for Lee A. Jennings, 76, of Brooklyn, who died Saturday. Funeral services *will be* Wednesday.
> *Jackson* (Mich.) *Citizen Patriot*

Present Perfect Sometimes there is a good reason for not emphasizing the time element in the lead. If a story is several days old it might still be news, but the paper might not want to call attention to the fact that it had either missed the story at first or had been slow getting it into the paper. Or, if the story is a news feature, possibly an interview, the time element is not important. In such cases, the writer can use the present perfect: *has seen, has given, has heard, has asked.* The present perfect conveys immediacy even when it is used to describe past events; it allows the writer to avoid pinpointing the time of the action. For example:

> A physician *has complained* to state and federal agencies that the move to install X-ray machines at airports to speed inspection of carry-on baggage is a hazard to the health of airline employes operating the equipment.
> *Los Angeles Times*

VARIATIONS OF THE SUMMARY LEAD

The Blind Lead

The lead not only summarizes the story it introduces, but it also gets the reader interested enough to read on. This is a difficult job in an age when we have many distractions and when there is so much competition for our time. We spend very little time with our newspapers and we tend to read only those items that look interesting. We skim and we skip. If a summary lead packed full of details looks too formidable we will skip past it. If a lead is too long we will hurry on to something that looks more appealing.

The *blind lead* is a useful device for dealing with this problem. It omits names and specifics and relies on a general summary, short and pithy, to catch the reader's interest. It is the idea, not the specific details, that snags us:

> DETROIT—AP—A maintenance worker plunged 20 floors down an elevator shaft Friday and suffered only a fractured ankle and hand cuts.
> Glen Roberts, 39, of suburban Warren, was helping install an elevator at an apartment building under construction when he apparently slipped.

> AUGUSTA, GA.—AP—A Negro minister has become the second member of his race in a little more than a year to win a seat on the Augusta City Council.

The Rev. C. S. Hamilton, president of the Augusta Chapter of the National Association for the Advancement of Colored People, defeated the incumbent Councilman Eugene Tudor and two other white opponents in a city election....

These leads suggest a good reason for using the blind lead: although the circumstances or events reported in the stories are interesting enough to attract the reader's attention, the names mean very little. The blind lead can avoid losing readers who might not pay attention to a story about unfamiliar people by emphasizing the interesting facts and playing down the names. The Augusta, Ga., story suggests another use of the blind lead: to get around the problem of the long and unwieldy identification. A general description is often more appropriate than name, age, address, title and so on.

The blind lead has the further advantage of brevity: it presents an idea quickly and clearly because it is not concerned with details. But this also means that it is effective only if what happened is sufficiently intriguing to catch the reader's attention; it is a good lead only when *what* happened is more important than *who* it happened to. Where the name in the story is an important one or one the reader will recognize immediately, the blind lead is not necessary: in fact it may be weaker than a lead built around the name.

Delayed Identification

Somewhere between the blind lead, which shuns detail, and the summary lead, which may have too much detail, there is the *delayed identification lead*. Here the name is given in the first sentence of the lead, but full identification is held off until the second paragraph or even much later. For example:

John L. Rainey, 73, remained in critical condition in the intensive care unit at Mound Park Hospital last night. He was struck by a car Saturday night.

Rainey, 315 24th St. S., suffered a broken pelvis, right ankle and col-

lar bone when he was struck while crossing Central Avenue at 21st Street. He was knocked 37 feet from the point of impact.

St. Petersburg Times

In this example the delayed identification device is used, much like the blind lead, to keep the first paragraph brief. Delayed identification is more likely to be used when the *who* has some recognition factor. For example, if the name John Lindsay appeared in the first paragraph, he would be identified as "the former mayor of New York City," in the second paragraph.

The following lead suggests another possible use for the delayed identification device: to fool, rather than inform, the reader.

Milwaukeean Gay Reineck wrote the draft board Thursday that its notice to report for a physical won't be obeyed.

For one thing, Gay once was assigned to a barracks at an air force base and decided not to stay. For another, Gay is busy teaching the third grade at Maple Tree school, 644 N. 107th st.

But mainly, Gay Reineck, 25, of 3914 W. Sheridan St., won't report for the draft physical because she's a girl.

Milwaukee Journal

OTHER ASPECTS OF THE LEAD

Datelines

Some of the leads used as examples in this chapter have had *datelines* and some have not. When do we use a dateline? The general practice is to use a dateline when a story originates outside the city in which the newspaper is published, or outside the city and its immediate environs. Stories that originate outside the newspaper's own city and suburbs are not local and a dateline is used to tell the reader where the event took place. In newspaper terminology such stories are trade area, state, regional, national or foreign stories.

The term *dateline* may be confusing because the dateline often does not include a date. In fact, a better name for it might be identification line. In any case, it is the line preceding the first sentence of the lead which tells the copy's point of origin and sometimes, but not always, the date the story was written and mailed, telephoned or otherwise transmitted to the newsroom. The *New York Times* always includes the date in its datelines.

Datelines appear on all stories originating with the Associated Press or United Press International. Stories originating from other sources—correspondents, supplementary news services, the newspaper's state capital or Washington bureau—are also identified by datelines. When staff members are sent on assignment out of town, the stories they bring or send back to the newspaper carry datelines.

Credit Lines

In addition to datelines, news stories may also carry a credit line. Stories originating with the Associated Press and United Press International, carry the initials AP or UPI immediately after the point of origin of the story:

> NEW ORLEANS—AP—Fire Monday night destroyed a warehouse . . .

> SEATTLE—UPI—FBI agents said Monday that they had identified . . .

In the above examples the dateline identifies both the place of origin and the originator of the story. Most credit lines are carried as separate lines that precede the first paragraph of the lead and give information not included in the dateline:

From Our Capital Bureau

From Our Washington Bureau

Special to the State Journal

From Journal Wire Services

The fourth credit line in the examples above is taken to mean that stories from both the Associated Press and United Press International were rewritten and combined into one.

The use of datelines and credit lines varies from paper to paper and the newspaper's preferences are usually set forth in a stylebook similar to the *Beginner's Basic Guide to News Style* at the back of this book. For the moment, it is enough to note that local news stories carry no datelines.

Short Paragraphs

The tendency in news writing today is toward brevity: news stories are shorter; leads are shorter; sentences are, on the average, shorter than they were 20 or 30 years ago; and paragraphs are shorter. Newspaper readers spend less time with their newspapers than they once did and brevity in news writing is one way to meet the readers' needs. In addition, there are good mechanical reasons for writing shorter copy. Over the past 30 years newspaper columns have been narrowed to save expensive newsprint. One result of setting type into long, narrow columns is that in type copy becomes twice as long as the typewritten original. Long columns of uninterrupted lines of type appear dull; and dullness repels readers. Shorter copy results in shorter stories in type. The extra white space gained at the beginning and end of shorter paragraphs brightens the page, and both the page and the stories on it look more inviting.

Short Sentences

A widespread interest in readability over the past 30 or so years has made the news writer acutely aware of the length of sentences. Readability formulas suggest that shorter sentences are easier to read than long ones. This does not mean that long sentences are necessarily hard to read. But you should bear in mind that when sentences begin to get long, they may also be getting awkward and hard to follow.

No one can or should be expected to write every sentence in exactly 18 words, or whatever the magic number may be at the moment. News writing has to be flexible: some sentences will be short, some long, and some will fall in between. A close examination of a few hundred sentences taken at random from a well-edited newspaper's local stories will show that extreme sentence length is usually avoided, but that sentence length varies depending on what the writer has to say.

A good rule of thumb for writing leads is to keep sentences fairly short. If the first sentence of your lead gets up to 25 or 30 words, it would be a good idea to go over it carefully to see if it is clear and readable. A word count alone will not help, because long sentences can be just as clear as short sentences. But if you read the sentence aloud to yourself, your ear will often detect problems in word order, arrangement of ideas or length. If you stumble, so will your reader. So, if the sentence is wordy, take out a word here and there; if it includes too much information, delete some facts and use them in the next sentence or in the next paragraph. For example:

> WILLIAMSBURG, MICH.—AP —Continuing mysterious natural gas eruptions near this northern Michigan community have forced at least 25 families from their homes, authorities report.

Although this lead contains only a single sentence and that sentence has only 21 words, a more direct and readable sentence is possible:

> Continuing natural gas eruptions have forced at least 25 families from their homes near this northern Michigan community.

Only three words have been deleted from the original lead: *mysterious* and *authorities reported*. The phrase *near this northern Michigan community* has been moved to the end of the sentence. The result is more readable, not because it is shorter, but because it is simpler, and because it deals with only one aspect of the story. The secondary element, the mysterious nature of the eruptions, can be dealt with in a later paragraph. The source of the story, attribution, can surely come later on, too.

One other point: good writing calls for rhythm and pace. Sentence length must vary or the pace will be difficult for the reader. Too many long sentences will be hard on the reader; too many short sentences and one-sentence paragraphs will have a singsong feel. Vary the length of your sentences. Vary the number of sentences in your paragraphs.

There are no absolute rules in this matter: only general guidelines. You will have to develop your own style, your own rhythm and pace.

The Lead as a Unit

The lead is not always a single sentence in a single paragraph, except in very brief news stories. The longer the story, the longer the lead. Leads may consist of as many paragraphs as the complexity or length of the story demands. If the story is very long or complex, it may require a lengthy introduction. The lead in the following story consists of three substantial paragraphs:

> BATAVIA—A state trooper was injured while writing a summons last night when another auto hit his car.
>
> Trooper Walter C. Flinkmann, 29, of Troop T was treated and released at St. Jerome Hospital here. He suffered left leg and hand injuries.
>
> The accident happened at 8 p.m. five miles west of the Batavia interchange on the New York Thruway.
>
> Lt. A. Gallion of Troop T said Trooper Flinkmann was parked in the center mall writing a summons for a motorist charged with a moving violation when his car was struck by one driven by Jack Sullivan, 67, of Buffalo. Sullivan was charged with speeding.
>
> The lieutenant said the injured officer and Troopers J. M. Law and N. J. Birner had been on radar duty and that one of the officers was flagging traffic when an unidentified motorist just ahead of Sullivan jammed on his brakes. He said Sullivan steered onto the mall to avoid

hitting the other auto, but struck the troop car instead.

The other troopers were not injured.

Rochester Times Union

The lead of this story is completely routine: it starts with a statement of what happened and how, it identifies the person involved and gives some details about the nature of his injuries, and it tells you where and when the accident occurred. The development of the story clearly begins in the fourth paragraph, with the chronological account of the accident. So the lead and the body of the story, and the dividing point between them, are clearly identifiable.

The point is that the lead is a clearly identifiable unit, separate from the body of the story: the lead is a summary; the body is a detailed account of the incident. Don't think of the lead as a paragraph or a sentence, but as the opening of your story. Make your lead complete whether it takes one, two or more paragraphs.

Using Paragraphs

As we have just seen, the lead may consist of more than one paragraph. There is a good reason for this: if all the facts that belong in the lead were jammed into a single, long sentence or a single, long paragraph, the result would be hard to read and understand. It is for this reason that the various ideas or facts that belong in the lead are presented one at a time in as many paragraphs as necessary. For example:

> An explosion and fire early Sunday injured three persons, one of them seriously, and destroyed seven inner city apartment units.
>
> All the apartments were in a building that had recently been condemned.
>
> Four fire companies responded to the fire which broke out at 8:17 p.m. at 1144 South Cedar. The fire was controlled within minutes.
>
> Sean Graham, 25, who lived in one of the apartments, was badly burned. He suffered first and second degree burns over 60 per cent of his body.

This is, perhaps, an overly simplified lead, but the point it makes should be taken seriously. In writing a lead, present each bit of information concisely and directly, one at a time. Keep your sentences fairly short. Present your points in several, short paragraphs. And vary the number of sentences in your paragraphs.

Attribution

Most leads give some indication of the source of the story. When an attribution appears in the lead, it usually comes at the end of the first sentence, or in the second paragraph. In other words, it is seldom the most prominent element. In the following lead, the attribution comes at the end of the first sentence:

> ST. IGNACE—AP—April traffic on the Mackinac Bridge set a new high for the month, the Bridge Commission reports.

In the next example, attribution comes at the beginning of the first sentence of the lead and somewhat overshadows the statement of what happened. It is usually best to avoid this arrangement unless the source is of major importance:

> DETROIT—AP—The Federal Bureau of Investigation says three men have been arrested in connection with armed robberies of several Detroit area banks.

Some leads need no attribution. In the story about trooper Flinkmann, for example, the source wasn't mentioned until the fourth paragraph, in the body of the story. When the source is relatively unimportant, it can often be included in the body of the story; or, when the facts can stand by themselves, the source can sometimes be omitted. Attribution allows the reader to judge the story's credibility. However, no reader would seriously question the validity of an unattributed lead like the following:

> Today is Thanksgiving, the oldest and most traditional American holiday.
>
> *San Francisco Examiner*

Generally, in unattributed stories, the facts stand or fall on their own merits, as in the Thanksgiving Day lead. In some cases, the reader is expected to accept the newspaper and its news staff as a reliable source of information. The reporter's or news writer's by-line or the Associated Press and United Press International logotypes also indicate a source, even when there is no attribution in the story itself.

As a general rule, however, you should get your facts from reliable and identifiable sources and you should credit these sources in your story. Some indication of the source of a story is almost always necessary. And it generally goes in the lead.

Emphasis on People

Most leads are constructed around the *what* of a news story, but since people are almost always involved, the *what* and the *who* often overlap. A lead which reports that 21 people were killed in weekend traffic accidents across your state reports not only what happened, but who it happened to. But since names do not usually appear in the first few paragraphs of such a story, this is not really a *who lead*. Even stories about speeches may emphasize what the speaker said and play down the identity of the speaker, at least in the first paragraph of the lead. In stories like these what happened or what was said is emphasized, while who it happened to or who said it, is played down. This kind of lead should perhaps be called a *who–what lead* since it does include both elements.

The true who lead is constructed around the name, personality or record of a well-known person: the President of the United States is the most obvious example. Here, without question, the story is interesting because of the person involved, even when it is not interesting because of what was said or done. Most people can go to church on Sunday morning, for example, without getting their names in the newspaper. When the President goes to church, even if he goes every Sunday, it is

news. Of course, stories about the President are usually a little more significant than that, but the principle is the same: the who lead is built around a name that is news in itself. Here are a few examples:

> WASHINGTON—President Nixon asked Congress yesterday to provide America's poor with free legal assistance "independent of political pressures."
> *Arizona Republic*

> Mayor Daley offered the ultimate rebuttal yesterday to criticisms of the Loop as a crimeridden area.
> *Chicago Tribune*

So many of the news stories coming out of Washington involve important people whose names are news in themselves, that a large percentage of stories carrying Washington datelines are written with who leads. If you think of who leads as "Washington leads" it will help put the who lead in proper perspective. Save the who lead for the big names.

News stories are sometimes about people who are not particularly well known, but who are interesting or newsworthy nevertheless. When a who lead is used in stories about less well-known people, the lead will have to include more than the name to carry it off:

> CHICAGO—UPI—Michael Norman Stavy Jr. is a student at the Chicago Circle branch of the University of Illinois. He has high hopes.
> He's running for the board of trustees. Not just of Chicago Circle, the newest extension of Illinois' traditional Champaign-Urbana campus, but election to the state's highest educational governing body.

This is obviously a who lead, but it is based, not on the person's importance, nor on the fact that he is well known to the reading public—he's not—but because he is doing something interesting. The following lead is about a man who became newsworthy because something highly unusual happened to him.

ALPENA, MICH.—AP—Donald L. Kaminski, who had been the world's second-longest living heart transplant patient, died today.

Obituaries, of course, are stories in which the person's name or identity is given as much prominence as possible. Obituaries require who leads, as this example shows:

GLOVERSVILLE, N.Y.—AP— George J. Burns, a standout outfielder for the New York Giants from 1911 to 1921, died here today after a long illness. He was 75 years old.

CREATIVE LEADS

All the leads we have discussed so far have been written in normal word order as conventional declarative sentences. Once in a while, however, the nature of the story you are writing demands something different. There are many ways to inject variety in your news writing and we will discuss some of them later in this text. At this point we will suggest one way of making a lead different: variation in grammatical structure.

Questions Leads can sometimes be pepped up by switching from the declarative sentence to the interrogative:

Anyone want a nice cat to give the premises a homey touch?
Norfolk (Va.) *Virginian-Pilot*

Do your children turn instinctively from Bach to "rock?"
Detroit Free Press

Once in a while a *question lead* will provide a bit of variety, but don't write too many of them. Master the more usual ways of writing leads first.

The Imperative Another way to change pace is to shift from the indicative to the imperative:

Go to the trout canals of Hudson. Or nearer home, you may want to take a whack at bass fishing in Lake Seminole.
St. Petersburg Times

WASHINGTON—AP—If a wolf is at your door, be kind to it.

Direct Address Still another variation is direct address, the writer talking directly to the reader:

WASHINGTON—UPI—You are an exporter in Chicago, Paris or Tokyo. You want an agent or outlet in Aden, Moscow or Zambia.

Merry Christmas, Charlie Bishop, wherever you are.
Philadelphia Bulletin

These last suggestions for attaining variety are just that: suggestions. They are not common in news writing, but do show how occasional departures from the usual approach can help spark up a story. The competent professional will use tricks when they are needed, but for the most part will rely on commonly used sentence patterns and normal word order. This is not for lack of imagination or because of an inability to manipulate the language, but because talking to readers in direct, everyday language provides the surest means of being understood.

Originality and creativity are possible in even the simplest sentences and the most routine kinds of leads. Compare the obituary lead we cited earlier with a similar lead—but one with an important difference:

George J. Burns, a standout outfielder for the New York Giants from 1911 to 1921, died here today after a long illness. He was 75 years old.

Bertha Hamblin Boyce died at the Fraser Nursing Home Saturday morning. It was the 56th day of the 102nd year of her life.
Falmouth (Mass.) *Enterprise*

Structure and organization are important, but what is going to count in the long run is the imagination and creativity the writer brings to the conventional forms of organization and structure.

CHAPTER FIVE

Developing The Story

IN PREVIOUS CHAPTERS we saw that a news story consists of a *lead*, the *body* or *development* and sometimes a formal *conclusion*. In this chapter we will look closely at how the body of the story is developed and how it flows naturally out of the lead. To do this, we will examine a few different types of news stories in some detail. As you know by now, while there are some general principles about news writing, there are no absolute rules. Leads can be written in many ways; so can the rest of the news story. What follows here are some workable, easy-to-follow solutions to a few, fairly simple, writing problems.

ORGANIZING DIFFERENT STORIES

Experienced writers know that a story's subject matter will dictate the way it is organized and written. For example, we saw in Chapter 4 that most routine, single-incident stories open with a summary lead. If the event the story reports is the most interesting or important element, the lead emphasizes what happened. If the person in the story is well known, the lead may emphasize who was involved.

When we get past the lead and think about ways to organize the rest of the story, the facts of the story will generally provide a clue as to how the story should be written. For example, stories that report a sequence of events are best organized in chronological order. This allows the reader to follow each event in the sequence as easily as an eyewitness. Once the summary lead sets the stage, the reader has no problem keeping the action straight.

Routine, single-incident stories can be quickly and easily put together using the inverted-pyramid format: a summary lead presents the outline of the story and the details follow in descending order of importance.

Humorous or light stories are often written in the suspended-interest format. Here, again, the nature of the story dictates the form. If you have a funny story to tell, you proceed through it step by step and end with a punch line.

This chapter will analyze the organization and structure of several types of routine news stories: single-incident stories; stories about coming events; stories that involve several related incidents; stories that carry lists of names; complicated stories; action stories; and obituaries. These are routine stories, the type published every day in the newspapers you read. You will write a lot of them yourself as you become a professional news writer.

Single-Incident Stories

Routine stories involving a few, closely related facts about a single incident or event are most easily written in the inverted-pyramid format. Such stories begin with a summary lead and are developed by explaining in some detail the bare facts given in the lead. For example:

> Three men, arrested last August in a disturbance at Kercheval and Pennsylvania, have been bound over for trial on charges of rioting and inciting to riot.
>
> Russel Marcilis, 26, of 5390 Holcomb; Jerome Evans, 19, of 2512 Garland; and J. B. Whitfield, 22, of 2594 Pennsylvania, were examined yesterday in Recorder's Court before visiting East Detroit Municipal Judge Calvin C. Rock.
>
> Jefferson Station patrolmen testified at the examination they saw the men tossing rocks and other objects at firemen who were fighting a blaze in a drugstore on Aug. 10 near the intersection.
>
> They said the defendants were later discovered hiding under a rear porch at 2129 Pennsylvania.
>
> Whitfield was released on $1,000 bond, and Marcilis and Evans on $500 bonds, pending trial.
>
> *Detroit News*

This story begins with a summary lead explaining what happened: three men have been bound over for trial. The rest of the story is elaboration and explanation. Let's look at the four paragraphs that make up the body of this story and see what the writer did.

The first paragraph of the development (the second of the story) identifies the three men mentioned in the lead by name, age and address. In addition, the circumstances under which they were bound over for trial are explained: they were in court the previous day at an examination presided over by a visiting judge.

The next paragraph explains the lead's reference to a disturbance. Without this explanation, the reference in the lead would make one wonder about the relationship between the reported disturbance and the charges of rioting and inciting to riot. This paragraph makes that relationship clear.

The following paragraph explains the arrest mentioned in the lead. And the fourth and final paragraph of the development elaborates on the fact that the three men have been bound over for trial: they have been released on bond and the amount of the bond is given.

In the following story, the development builds out of a solid summary lead and the information is arranged carefully in order of importance:

> Eleven trapped persons were rescued by Oakland firemen in a five-alarm blaze that broke out yesterday in a 24-unit, three-story stucco apartment building at 450 40th St.
>
> Firemen carried six persons from the roof and five from third-floor windows down ladders that were run up against the smoke-filled building where the fire was mainly confined between interior walls.
>
> The fire apparently started in the basement near the furnace and sent flames shooting up through the walls, according to L. A. Toellner, chief of the department's fire prevention bureau. He estimated approximately $50,000 damage to the structure.
>
> A force of 110 firemen and 22 pieces of equipment responded to the alarm at 5:40 p.m. and had the fire under control in an hour and 20 minutes, preventing it from spreading to adjoining apartment houses.
>
> The building was declared uninhabitable by Acting Chief John P. Gai after the fire and the Red Cross helped the building's 25 tenants, several of them elderly, find temporary shelters.
>
> An investigation was under way last night to determine the cause of the fire.
>
> *San Francisco Examiner*

The first paragraph of the development explains how the 11 trapped people were rescued: six from the roof and five from windows.

The second paragraph explains how the fire started and builds on a phrase from the lead: *blaze that broke out.* The extent of the damage is also included here.

The third paragraph amplifies the lead's indication that this was a serious fire—*a five alarm blaze*—by telling how many firemen and pieces of equipment were needed to put the fire out and how long it took them.

The fourth paragraph rounds the story out: the building is so damaged as to be uninhabitable and temporary housing is being found for the tenants.

The fifth and final paragraph of the development is a minor detail and a routine fact: fire departments always try to find out what or who started the fire. Such an obvious and commonplace fact only pads the story. Learn to save space by omitting details that don't add to the story, or that don't need to be said.

Here is another single-incident story that reports not only what happened, but who it happened to in the summary lead:

> Miss Jennifer Dawson, a Carroll College senior, has begun work in a youth ministry at Roundy Memorial Baptist Church, 4819 N. Ardmore Ave., Whitefish Bay.
>
> A reception was held Sunday at the church for Miss Dawson, a native of Wisconsin and a National Presbyterian Scholarship student.
>
> For the past year Family Service has had an outpost counseling service at the church, with a trained counselor available to parents or youths in the north shore area. The addition of Miss Dawson will make possible the expansion of the service, the Rev. Martin Linwood Whitmer, pastor, said.
>
> *Milwaukee Sentinel*

The development here consists of only two paragraphs which follow and build on a summary lead. The first paragraph of the development adds details about the start of the new job; and the second explains the nature of the work the new staff member will undertake. Note the additional link between the lead and the body of the story: Miss Dawson is mentioned by name in each paragraph of the story.

Coming Events

News stories about coming events are comparatively easy to develop from a summary lead. For example:

> The Behavior Therapy Institute will hold a series of meetings dealing with "practical ways of working with learning disabled children."
>
> The series of eight meetings will take place at the West Branch YMCA, 5515 Medical Circle, on Wednesday evenings from 7:15 to 9:15, beginning today.
>
> The course is being taught by Dr. Roger A. Severson, clinical psychologist and specialist in learning disabilities, and three other members of the Behavior Therapy Institute.
>
> The series is intended for parents who wish to work with their own learning disabled child in the home, and persons who are interested in becoming paraprofessionals in the schools.
>
> Training fee is $50. Persons desiring further information should write the Behavior Therapy Institute, 154 Nautilus Drive, or call 837-3693.
>
> Madison, Wis., *Capital Times*

There is nothing unusual about the summary lead here, except that it deals with something that is about to happen rather than with something that has already happened. What is different about this story is the greater emphasis in the development on *where* and *when*. Details that would be unimportant in a story about an event that has already taken place, are essential to a story about a coming event. Before an event, it is important to inform readers of the day and the hour and to be specific about where the event or program will take place. The story must define the audience: Who is invited? Who ought to be interested? And there will often be details about admission: What will it cost? Where can one get tickets? Explanation of the program, of course, is cast in the future: what *will* happen rather than what has happened. Let's look at another story about a coming event:

> William M. E. Clarkson, a Presbyterian lay leader and president of the Graphic Controls Corp., will speak at 7 PM tomorrow in University Presbyterian Church. His topic, in the church's series of bi-monthly Open Door meetings, will be "Living Your Christianity."
>
> *Buffalo Evening News*

This is typical of stories about scheduled speeches or programs. Stories of this type name and identify the speaker, mention the subject of the speech, identify the sponsor of the talk or the circumstances under which the speaker will appear. Again, the story must be specific about *where* and *when*:

> The Wayne County Women's Republican Club will meet at 1:30 p.m. tomorrow in the Italian Room of the Tuller Hotel. Guest speaker will be Mrs. Philip Barth, president of the Republican Women's Federation of Michigan. Her topic will be "Women in Politics—1973".
>
> *Detroit News*

Although these last two stories are organized differently, they both deal with the same items of information: a speaker, the topic, the organization being addressed or sponsoring the talk, the place, the day, the hour of the program. There is a handy mnemonic formula to help you organize this set of facts quickly and efficiently: "STOP digging here." This memory jogger says: Write the story in this order—speaker, topic, organization, place, day and hour. For example:

> Charles Mills, district supervisor for Parents Without Partners, will speak on leadership at a general meeting of the local chapter of the organization at the Statler Plaza Thursday at 7:30 p.m.

Not all stories about coming events concentrate on the speaker and the title of the speech. The following story, for example, emphasizes a sponsoring organization:

> The Women's Cancer Association at the University of Miami will sponsor its annual Holiday and World-Wide Bazaar Dec. 2 and 3 at Bayfront Auditorium.
>
> Admission is free and the public is invited to enjoy the foods and music of more than a dozen ethnic groups. Gifts will be sold at booths.
>
> All proceeds will go toward cancer research at the university. Hours are 10 a.m. to 5 p.m. Dec. 2 and from noon to 5 p.m. on Dec. 3.
>
> *Miami Herald*

This story has a summary lead which names the organization, tells what it will do and where and when it will do it. Additional details are supplied in two supporting paragraphs: the nature of the event, free admission, the beneficiary and the exact dates and times.

Related-Incident Stories

Many single-incident news stories break down naturally into several parts which are outlined in the summary lead. For example:

> Three men were fined for drunken driving in Traffic Court Monday. Two other drunken driving charges were filed and another was reduced to a lesser charge.

In this lead the general idea is "several people in court on drinking and driving charges." The body of the story will have to deal with the fact that, although the charges were similar, the defendants were not all treated alike.

A similar complication arises in the following news story:

> The National Endowment for the Arts has made grants to the Albright-Knox Art Gallery and the Buffalo Museum of Science to employ visiting specialists for two projects.
>
> The Albright-Knox will receive $8,500 to hire a specialist, as yet unchosen, to do research for a catalog of the collections, concentrating on art works prior to 1945.
>
> The gallery is working with a commercial publisher on its catalog of contemporary works of art, to be published sometime early next winter.
>
> The Museum of Science has engaged Mrs. Joan Hartman, a scholar and writer in Oriental art, associated with the China Institute, New York, to prepare a catalog of its collection of Chinese jades. The project is expected to be undertaken next spring. The museum's grant is for $3,125.
>
> The Museum of Science has an enormous collection of Chinese jades gathered by its late patron, Chauncey J. Hamlin. Because of insufficient funds, none of these jades is on display.
>
> Dr. Virginia L. Cummings, director, said because of the size of the

collection a decision has been made to concentrate only on the archaic jades, which number about 150.
Buffalo Evening News

The lead makes it clear that we are dealing with a single story, not two stories, by identifying the single source of the grants and explaining that the grants are for the same purpose: to provide funds for visiting specialists. The body of the story is organized into two parts, the first dealing with the larger grant to the art gallery, the second dealing with the smaller grant to the science museum. Each grant is discussed separately. There is no mixing, no jumping back and forth. The story could be outlined thus:

1) Summary lead reporting two grants, one to an art gallery, one to a science museum;
2) Two paragraphs explaining what the gallery will do with its grant;
3) Three paragraphs explaining what the museum will do with its grant.

Stories with Many Names

Names make news, according to newspaper tradition, and newspapers do carry many stories that contain anywhere from two or three names to long lists of them. These are not difficult stories to write, once you know how. The following is a good example of a routine story full of names:

New officers of the Senior Methodist Youth fellowship will be installed at 7 P.M. Sunday at John Wesley Methodist Church. Parents are invited to attend.

Officers are Richard Williams, president; Jill Propes, vice-president; Margaret Morton, secretary; Jacquelyn Reynolds, treasurer; Martha Waight, chair of faith; Robert Williams, chair of fellowship and refreshments; Richard Morton, chair of witness; and Helen Nickerson, chair of outreach.
Falmouth (Mass.) *Enterprise*

The summary lead explains that the story is about an installation of officers and tells where and when it took place. The body of the story is

simply a list of the new officers arranged logically: name first, then the office to which the person was elected. A simple system of punctuation helps maintain the structure: the name is followed by a comma and the office by a semi-colon.

The next example presents the same kind of problem, but this time the list includes names, ages and addresses:

Eight persons were treated at hospitals Sunday after eating food left over from a wedding reception Saturday night.

They had gathered at the home of Mr. and Mrs. Alois V. Andrews, 5674 N. 27th st., Glendale. The Andrews' daughter, Janet, 19, married Phillip Dahlen, 20 of 3273 N. 11th st.

The eight persons, all relatives of the newlyweds became ill after eating ham, turkey and potato salad, Glendale police said.

Six were in satisfactory condition Monday at St. Michael hospital. They are Mrs. Duane Hoppe and Miss Carol Andrews, both of 5674 N. 27th st., Glendale; Mrs. William Buchmann, 51, Mrs. Hattie Stamm, 81, and Walter Daehn, 62, all of 2528 N. 18th st.; and Mrs. Fred Mueller, 60, of 4670 N. 19th pl.

The bridegroom's parents, Mr. and Mrs. Olfer Dahlen, 3273 N. 11th st., went to the county general hospital where they were treated and released.
Milwaukee Journal

This is a tightly organized and simply told story. Everything in the development explains some point made in the 18-word summary lead. The first paragraph of the development explains the reference to a wedding reception; the next paragraph explains the reference to left over food; and the third and fourth paragraphs list the eight persons mentioned in the lead. Note, too, the way the names are organized: first, according to the hospital that treated them, and second, according to their home addresses. Punctuation follows the same pattern as the previous story: name, comma, age, comma, address, semi-colon.

The story in Fig. 5.1 contains a long list of colleges and sums granted to them under the National Defense Education Act. The body of the

Twenty-two Michigan colleges and universities will get a $4,377,922 slice of the National Defense Education Act student loan money for 1965–66.

University of Michigan will get the second largest allocation, $874,176, Rep. Weston E. Vivian, D-Ann Arbor, announced. U of M was topped by the Michigan State University allocation of $913,275.

Eastern Michigan University, Ypsilanti, got a big chunk—$344,194. Central Michigan University, Mount Pleasant, will receive $313,795.

Rep. Paul H. Todd Jr., D-Kalamazoo, announced allocations for colleges in his district.

The Third District grants:

Western Michigan University, Kalamazoo, $355,323; Kalamazoo College, $50,258; Albion College, $70,645; Kellogg Community College, Battle Creek, $2,581; Nazareth College, $7,268; Olivet College, $38,905.

Other Michigan allocations include:

Calvin College, Grand Rapids, $88,379; Calvin Theological Seminary, Grand Rapids, $5,233; Grand Rapids Junior College, $14,718; Hope College, Holland, $65,412; Flint Community Junior College, $23,367; Saginaw Valley College, $67,292; Alma College, $72,680; Ferris State College, Big Rapids, $11,927; Concordia Lutheran College, Ann Arbor, $6,342; Davenport College of Business, $39,974; Delta College, $17,298.

Grand Rapids Press

Fig. 5.1 *A logically-organized story with many names.*

story is organized logically around the lump sum introduced in the lead. The list is in this order: name, comma, sum of money, semi-colon.

The one-paragraph summary lead in Fig. 5.1 explains what the story is about and suggests the way it will be developed: by breaking down the lump sum and telling what each college and university received.

The development begins in the second paragraph, where the universities with the largest allocations are identified. This paragraph seems a little odd, since it gives the second largest allocation before the largest. There is a reason for this, however: the University of Michigan is the oldest and most prestigious university in the state, and it is usually mentioned first.

Other sizable allocations are listed next, followed by two lists of smaller allocations: one list of allocations granted to colleges in the Third Congressional District, and a second list covering the rest of the state. It would have been easy to organize the list in other ways—in alphabetical order, for example.

The names of the two congressmen don't really have to be included; they are there for political reasons. The administration generally accords congressmen and senators the privilege of announcing large grants, building contracts and other major expenditures in their districts and, in making the announcement, to take some of the credit. The names do serve as an attribution, although the fact that the allocations were made from NDEA funds would probably have sufficed.

Complicated Stories

Some stories can get complicated even though they revolve around a single idea. See Fig. 5.2 for a good example.

Although Fig. 5.2 is not an action story there is a chronology around which the facts can be organized. As we follow the chronological development of the story we are also told how the check passers' scheme worked.

Complicated stories require a special effort from the writer; they need a crystal clear lead and a logical and coherent development. The story in Fig. 5.3 is a good example of a newspaper writer making an involved legal decision understandable.

The story in Fig. 5.3 has a two-paragraph lead. The first paragraph is a precise statement of the outcome of the law suit. The second identifies the parties to the dispute.

The development begins in the third paragraph of the story with an explanation of the judge's order. The substance of the judge's order is then clearly spelled out point by point in an itemized list. The precincts affected by the injunction are then identified and the role of the bilingual special judges—which probably should have been point four in the itemized list—is explained.

Next, the story quotes verbatim from the judge's order and quotes a statement by the head of the group that has asked for the injunction. Two paragraphs about another election issue also before the courts conclude the story.

Although this story is somewhat involved, it is

A check-passing ring has been printing and cashing bogus payroll checks totalling more than $3,000 drawn on Kalman W. Abrams Metals, Inc., 58 9th Ave. NE, according to Minneapolis police.

Capt. Joseph Rusinko, head of the Forgery and Larceny Division, said the checks which began appearing Dec. 8, were made out to James Flint and Robert Larson, two men who lost their driver's licenses in street robberies.

He said Flint and Larson are not employes of Kalman W. Abrams Metals, Inc., and that two men had been using the stolen licenses to cash

Summary lead.

First appearance of the checks and explanation of technique used to cash them.

the checks.

The bogus checks were discovered when the owner of a bar where one check was cashed called the company. The number of the bogus check did not correspond to the company's number series, Rusinko said.

The last check appeared last Thursday, but Rusinko believes the men are still in the Twin Cities area.

He warned merchants to be "especially alert this time of year for bogus payroll checks," particularly during rush hours and on weekends.

Discovery that checks were bogus

Last checks appear.

Warning to merchants.

Minneapolis Tribune

Fig. 5.2 *A complicated story developed chronologically.*

A U.S. District Court Judge on Tuesday ordered the Chicago Board of Election Commissioners to print election materials in Spanish for next Tuesday's general election in 326 precincts and 11 wards.

Judge Philip W. Tone made the ruling in response to a suit filed by the Puerto Rican Organization for Political Action against election board chairman Stanley T. Kusper Jr. and the other two board members.

Tone also ordered the board to make "all reasonable efforts" to appoint qualified bilingual election judges in the precincts. The judge issued a preliminary injunction to ensure that the board would:

1) Affix directions for voting machines in Spanish to specimen general election ballots.

2) Print posters in Spanish advising voters of who is entitled to assistance.

3) Print instruction cards in

Spanish to be affixed to model voting machines.

The order applied to certain precincts in the 1st, 7th, 25th, 26th, 30th, 31st, 32nd, 33rd, 43rd, 44th and 46th wards. Most Spanish-speaking voters reside in those wards.

The board was also ordered to station bilingual special judges, appointed to tally the judicial retention ballots, as interpreters outside the voting booths in Spanish-speaking precincts, wherever possible.

In a memorandum issued by the judge in support of his order, he noted that the board's announcement last week that certain election materials would be printed in Spanish "is not ground for denial of the injunction."

"It is significant that the board took no steps to provide election assistance in Spanish prior to the commencement of this action," Tone

said.

"The enforcement of the important rights should not depend . . . on the voluntary acts of the defendants or upon my prediction that defendants will do what they say they intend, but will not agree, to do," he said.

Hector Franco, president of the Puerto Rican Organization, said in a press conference at the Federal Building, 219 S. Dearborn:

"We're satisfied with the judge's order."

He said as many as 125,000 Spanish-speaking persons could benefit from the bilingual instructions and assistance.

Meanwhile, Operation PUSH filed a motion before U.S. District Judge Julius J. Hoffman challenging the removal of seven voters from election rolls by a Board of Election Commissioners canvass.

Hoffman said he would rule on the matter Monday.

Chicago Sun-Times

Fig. 5.3 *A complicated story helped by a clear lead.*

not hard to understand. The lead introduces the general problem and the specific details are explained carefully in the body. The opposing parties in the case, the Puerto Ricans and the election board, are introduced in the first part of the story. The writer has taken things one at a time and has spelled out each fact carefully before going on to the next. There are quite a few points in the judge's order, but they are presented seriatim in a careful build up, not thrown at the reader all at once.

The story could be summarized thus:

- A court order issued
- In response to a suit filed by Puerto Ricans against the election board
- A preliminary injunction requires the board to do certain things
- The order applies only to certain things
- The judge issued a memorandum in support of the injunction
- The complainants have a comment on the order

GREENSBORO, N.C.—UPI— Two robbers fled a surrounded bank with six hostages yesterday and tried to find a plane in which to escape.

They were captured later in an exchange of shots at a roadblock.

FBI agent Victor Holdren was wounded in the left arm and three of the hostages and one of the bandits were injured slightly when their car crashed at the roadblock.

The suspects, Bobby Charles McManus, 30, of Atlanta, and Stanley Eugene Crawford, 24, of Greensboro, were taken before a U.S. commissioner early today and jailed under $100,000 bond each on a bank robbery charge.

"We're thanking God that we got those people out of the car," said police Maj. Ed Weant.

The bandits, wearing ski masks and carrying pistols, tripped a silent burglar alarm after entering the Lawnsdale branch of Wachovia Bank and Trust Co. about 5 P.M.

Seeing the bank quickly surrounded by police, the bandits used bank manager Peter Davenport Jr. and a customer, Roger Alden, president of Alden Steel Co., and four woman tellers as shields to make their getaway.

Police promised them safe conduct to the local airport and said a jetliner would be waiting to take them wherever they wanted to go.

Davenport was forced to bring a money sack containing an unknown quantity of the bank's money which was later recovered.

At the airport, the runways were empty. Officer W.O. Yokeley said, "They stayed for 35 minutes, driving around the runways and taxiways."

They left and eventually got onto Interstate 85. The highway patrol massed patrol cars across all four lanes and the median of I-85 near Hillsborough.

As the gunmen approached the roadblock, they swerved across the median, met more patrol cars, and spun back across the median. Two highway patrol vehicles deliberately sideswiped the station wagon before it plowed into an FBI vehicle.

Witnesses said about eight shots were fired before the two gunmen gave up.

Fig. 5.4 *An example of effective use of summary and chronology.*

The story is complicated and somewhat technical because it includes legal terminology. But it is organized logically and developed one point at a time; the language is clear and specific.

Action Stories

Stories reporting action require a combination of techniques to keep things straight for the reader. The basic techniques are summary and chronology. The story in Fig. 5.4 shows how both are used effectively.

The two-paragraph summary lead sets up the action and explains its outcome. The story is developed in two parts. The first part is a summary of the results of the attempted robbery, the chase and the capture at the roadblock:

> FBI agent Victor Holdren was wounded in the left arm and the three hostages and one of the bandits were injured slightly when the fleeing car crashed at the roadblock.
>
> The suspects, Bobby Charles McManus, 30, of Atlanta, and Stanley Eugene Crawford, 24, of Greensboro, were taken before U.S. commissioner early today and jailed under $100,000 bond each on bank robbery charges.
>
> "We're thanking God we got those people out of the car," said police Maj. Ed Weant.

The second part of the development is a carefully sequenced explanation of the attempted robbery, the taking of the hostages, the flight and the capture at the roadblock. The chronology flows smoothly along and the only attribution is the direct quotation from the police officer describing the robbers' actions at the airport. The final paragraph, after the action is over, quotes eyewitnesses as to the amount of gunfire at the roadblock.

In Fig. 5.5, the action is not quite as thrilling, but chronology makes it possible to explain a fairly complicated confidence game.

Here is a lead from another action story that uses the techniques of summary and chronology:

> Two gunmen methodically robbed a cleaner's shop of more than $200 yesterday, ripping a phone from the wall to prevent an alarm being given during the holdup, and binding and gagging two clerks with adhesive tape to provide time for a getaway.

This lead summarizes the holdup and then gives some details about the robbery and the escape of the robbers. The next paragraph introduces another angle:

> Another cleaner's establishment was robbed later in the day by a single gunman who escaped with about $10.

Greed apparently was the undoing of a female confidence artist arrested by Oak Park police after she tried to bilk a 72-year-old housewife of her $6,000 savings.

The 26-year-old suspect originally promised to sell her elderly victim several thousand dollars in negotiable stock certificates for $1,000, according to Oak Park Police Sgt. George Lavery.

The two women went Friday to Oak Park Federal Savings & Loan Assn., where the victim was to withdraw the $1,000 and turn it over to the con artist.

In this version of the "pigeon drop," Lavery said, the younger woman would then have disappeared leaving the victim without either money or stock.

When the elderly housewife came out of the bank with the money the con artist noticed that the savings passbook listed another $4,900 on deposit, Lavery said.

"So she sold the lady on paying the $4,900 for more stock and sent her back inside the bank to make a second withdrawal," the police sergeant said.

At this point, the teller became suspicious, and police were called. The suspect, identified as Judy Gilmore, 26, of 6409 S. Eberhardt, was arrested in a cab outside the financial institution, 1001 Lake, in the suburb.

Chicago Daily News

Fig. 5.5 *Chronology in a news story.*

An account of the first holdup is then given in chronological sequence:

> The Holland Cleaners in the 2100 block of Madison Avenue was held up yesterday morning as two clerks, Miss Deborah Washington, 16, and Mrs. Christine Matthews, 32, were confronted by two gunmen.
>
> Miss Washington was talking on the phone when the bandits entered. One grabbed the handset away and ripped the phone from the wall. The second put a pistol against Mrs. Matthews and told her to open the cash register.
>
> Before running off with more than $200, the bandits took the two clerks to the back room, one gunman saying, "Don't be nervous; we're not going to hurt you."
>
> Miss Washington said she worked herself loose from the tape bonds and got help from an adjoining laundry.

The second holdup is then described in two paragraphs of summary:

> In the second holdup, Mrs. Lucile Francis, 40, told police she was alone in the Brilliant Cleaners, in the 2300 block of Harford road when a young gunman demanded "all the money."
>
> He was unsatisfied with the amount in the cash register, she said, and she gave him a cash envelope from beneath the counter. Total loss of about $10 was described as "nominal."

Baltimore Sun

Obituaries

The obituary, a routine type of news story, presents its own special problems of organization. The obituary, or *obit* as it is generally called in the news room, is tricky to write for a number of reasons. First of all, it involves a great deal of information which must be organized coherently. Second, it requires absolute accuracy. No one enjoys writing obits because they are boring after a while, but they are an important part of the day's news and you can learn something useful about news writing by mastering the various ways of putting together the day's obits.

Obituaries are built around four sets of facts:
1) Who died and under what circumstances.
2) The surviving relatives.
3) The funeral and burial arrangements.
4) The deceased's occupation or profession.

These four aspects of the obituary can be presented in different order, but they are all essential. Note the arrangement in this obit:

> Sidney Edward Pavek, 67, of 1300 Oakland road NE, a salesman for Armstrong's and a Cedar Rapids resident for 10 years, died Wednesday following a long illness.
>
> Born Oct. 24, 1896, at LaCrosse, Wis., he was married to Viola Coburn Nov. 2, 1921, at Des Moines. He was a veteran of World War I.
>
> Surviving are his wife; a daughter, Mrs. Charles Welsh of Cedar Rapids; two grandchildren; a

brother, George, of Winona, Minn.; and a sister, Helen Schneyer of LaCrosse.

Mr. Pavek was a member of Immaculate Conception church.

Memorial services: Immaculate Conception church at 10:30 a.m. Friday by the Rt. Rev. Msgr. William A. Roach. Burial: Mt. Calvary cemetery.

The Rosary will be recited in the Turner chapel at 8:15 p.m. Thursday by Msgr. Roach. Friends may call at the chapel.

Cedar Rapids Gazette

This obituary consists of

1) A summary lead naming and identifying the man who died and giving some information about the circumstances of his death;

2) A paragraph of biographical information;

3) A list of surviving relatives;

4) Plans for religious services and burial.

The routine nature of the obit is emphasized in the next-to-last paragraph of the obit where the services are given in a list rather than in complete sentences.

Another obit, in the same order, but in more detail:

Louis M. Kirstein, 65, of 395 Revere Beach pkwy., Revere, a former mayor of Revere, died yesterday at the New England Rehabilitation Center in Woburn.

He was born in Boston and lived most of his life in Revere. He was graduated from Northeastern University Law School and for many years conducted a real estate and insurance business on the North Shore.

He was elected mayor in February 1953 by the Revere City Council and served for a year. He later served two terms on the city council.

Mr. Kirstein was an Army veteran of World War II. He served in the European Theater.

He was a member of the B'nai B'rith and the Jewish War Veterans post of Revere.

He leaves two daughters, Ann and Marjorie Kirstein, both of Chestnut Hill; a brother, Samuel Kirstein of Brooklyn; and two sisters, Mrs. Edith Schusterman of Indiana and Mrs. Anne Selya of Revere.

Funeral services will be tomorrow at 11 a.m. at the Torf Funeral Chapel, 151 Washington ave., Chelsea.

Boston Globe

Other arrangements are possible. The following obit begins with the plans for services:

Services for Mrs. Maggie C. Bell, 84, of 202 Post Ave., will be held at 1:30 p.m. Friday at the Hebble Funeral Home. She died at her home Tuesday.

Mrs. Bell, widow of John Bell, was a native of Scotland. She came to Battle Creek in 1913 from Montreal.

Mrs. Bell is survived by two daughters, Mrs. Isabelle C. Blankenship of the Post avenue address and Mrs. Janet S. Dines of Kalamazoo; three grandchildren and four great-grandchildren.

She was a member of the Trinity Lutheran Church and the church's Mary Martha Circle. Mrs. Bell was a life member of the White Shrine of Jerusalem and the Bryant Chapter of the OES. She was a past president and member of the Lodge 87 auxiliary of the Locomotive Firemen and Engineers.

Battle Creek, Mich., *Enquirer and News*

The following obituary uses still a different arrangement: services and identification in the first paragraph; circumstances of death; biography; and survivors.

Paul E. Gardner, 88, retired president of the Buffalo Welding Supply Co., was buried today in Acacia Park Cemetery, Pendleton, following funeral services in the Leo Vandercher & Son Funeral Home, 2549 Main St.

Mr. Gardner of Wallace Ave. died Wednesday (Nov. 28, 1973) in the Presbyterian Home, 900 Delaware Ave. after a long illness.

He joined Buffalo Welding Supply in 1943 as a salesman when the company was on East Ferry. He became president and a co-owner in 1954. He retired in 1961.

Born in Coraopolis, Pa., Mr. Gardner came to Buffalo in 1917 and formed the old Meldrum Motor

Corp. at 1081 Main St. He served as the company's vice president and treasurer for 16 years until he began working for Buffalo Welding.

He was a member of the Buffalo Consistory, the Ismalia Shrine Temple and was an elder of Central United Presbyterian Church.

Surviving are his wife, the former Anne MacArthur, and a brother, Frank J. of Beaver Falls, Pa.
Buffalo Evening News

Notice that the date and year have been added in parentheses after the day of death is given. Obits have a high readership. They are often clipped, pasted in scrapbooks or mailed to faraway friends or relatives. They are a matter of family record. The exact date inserted this way in the obit makes it a more accurate record.

Identification in the obit is usually simple: by job, trade, profession, public offices held, books written. Sometimes the identification is geographical: "So-and-so was a resident of this community for 25 years." Women are frequently identified by giving the husband's name: "Mrs. So-and-so was the wife of Mr. So-and-so."

Some people are best identified by recalling their part in some past news event. In the following obit, the single event that made this man newsworthy many years ago takes up most of the obit. The obit begins with a summary lead recalling the tie to the newsworthy event, and continues with a lengthy description of the incident, notice of the services and mention of the survivor.

John F. Hammond, 78, who was once asked by Robert Ripley of Believe It or Not fame to tour the United States as the man who survived a 12-story fall, died Tuesday in an Atlanta hospital. He lived at 937 Center St. NW.

In 1929 Mr. Hammond, who was painting the outside of the Healey Building, plunged 12 stories from his scaffold through a skylight and lived to tell about it.

His co-worker, who had only started on the job that morning, fell first from the scaffold, grasping at the ropes and plunging to his death. Mr. Hammond was able to hold on for a little less than a minute before he lost his grip.

After the fall, which permanently injured his left leg, the subsequent publicity, the offer from Ripley, and 18 months in the hospital, Mr. Hammond told friends all he wanted to do was to "go back to work."

Born in Rome, Mr. Hammond was a member of the North Atlanta Baptist Church.

Funeral services will be held at 11 a.m. Thursday in Lowndes Chapel. The Rev. A. L. Kendrick will officiate and burial will be in Crest Lawn Memorial Park.

Survivors include a brother, Will Hammond, Newman.
Atlanta Constitution

THE LEAD AS A CLUE

We have so far been working under the assumption that the nature of the story dictates the way the body of the story will be developed. We have seen, for example, that action stories are usually best told in chronological order. And we have seen the way that stories about coming events and obituaries are organized to answer specific questions that grow out of the circumstances of the story. In the same way, the nature of the lead may determine how the story is organized and developed.

A question lead provides a good illustration. If you ask a question in a lead, the body of the story has to be organized and developed in such a way that the question is answered. Take this Associated Press lead:

Has a pair of off-duty, allegedly drunken Saginaw police officers been given preferential treatment by State Police officers who arrested them?

The development follows the clue provided in the lead, answers the question in the affirmative and goes on to give the supporting detail. The first paragraph of the body of the story:

George Thick, Saginaw County prosecutor thinks so.

"Quite frankly, the agencies didn't handle this as they normally would," Thick said Friday. "I'm afraid it's because other police officers were involved."

In the same way, words, phrases or numbers used in a lead will determine the way the body of the story is developed. For example, this lead:

Four persons were treated Saturday at Marion General Hospital for minor injuries suffered in separate accidents. They later were dismissed.

Marion, Ind., *Chronicle Tribune*

The story that follows, will have to identify the four people, tell what happened to them and, treat *all four* accidents. The lead that starts, "Eight people were injured," or "Five local residents were appointed," or, "Twenty-two colleges and universities," has to account for all 8, 5 or 22 in the body of the story.

CHAPTER SIX
Elements of Cohesiveness

IN THE LAST chapter we saw how the story itself tends to shape the way it is written. We also saw how the structure of the lead can shape the development of the story.

Another influence on the structure and organization of the news story is the need to make it hang together so that it is readily understandable. The reader must be able to grasp immediately the relationships between the various parts of the story and the relationships between facts, names, ideas and numbers. There must be an internal organization that is consistent with the nature of the story.

Logical Order

A good example of internal organization can be found in stories about the election or installation of officers in a club or other organization:

> Mrs. George E. Punter as president heads a single slate of officers to be presented to Junior Board of Meyer Memorial Hospital at a

> luncheon Dec. 6 at the hospital. Also on the slate are:
> First vice president, Mrs. Alfred A. Adler; second vice president, Mrs. J. Walter Frey; corresponding secretary, Mrs. H. Jack Mengle; recording secretary, Mrs. Charles D. Molnar; treasurer, Mrs. Seymour E. Weissman.
> *Buffalo Evening News*

Here we have several different levels of organization: a summary lead is followed by an orderly development of the story; a slate of officers is listed in descending order of importance; and the name of each office is consistently followed by the name of the person nominated for that office.

Other stories may present more possibilities, but some organizational principles are always selected and consistently maintained throughout the story or within the different sections of the story. In disaster stories, the logical way to organize the victims names is the dead first, injured second: from the most serious to the least serious. This ranking might also be used in a list of injured persons' names, where the most seriously injured would be listed first and the least seriously injured last. Where no other logical order is possible, names can be listed alphabetically or chronologically, in birth announcements, for example. Sometimes names are arranged geographically, local names first, names of those living in the paper's circulation area second, all others last. In stories reporting several events, the most recent is often discussed first and the less recent last.

The Bridge

Nowhere is coherence more important in a news story than at the point where the lead ends and the development begins. The lead and the development are two separate structures, each with its own form and organization. Since the lead comes first and the body second, it seems that any reader should be able to move from one to the other without getting lost. But this will happen only if the news writer provides an easy transition—a kind of *bridge* over which the reader can proceed to the body of the story.

The bridge can be such a natural progression of thought or sequence of facts that the reader is not conscious of it. Or, it may be more obvious. The following paragraphs from the *Washington Post* show how the gap between the lead and body of a story can be bridged subtly and unobtrusively:

> A Cardozo High School student was kidnaped at gunpoint from the school yesterday in what Washington police robbery squad officials said was a case of mistaken identity.
> Ronald K. Sewell, 18, a Cardozo junior, was kidnaped by two men about 11:40 a.m. while walking in a first-floor hallway in the school.
> Police said that Sewell was approached by two men. One asked: "Are you Ronnie Sewell?" When Sewell said yes, they told him . . .

The first paragraph of this story is a summary lead. It is also a blind lead that describes but does not name the high school student. The second paragraph is part of the lead and also the first part of the body of the story: it completes the lead by

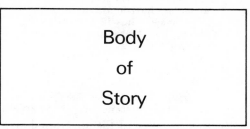

Fig. 6.1 *The writer must lead the reader from lead to body with a bridging device.*

naming the student and also begins the chronological account of the kidnaping.

There is a clear-cut division here between the lead and the body of the story: the lead is a summary; the body is a chronology and narrative. The two merge in the second paragraph. The key to this subtle bridging is that the subject is the same in both parts of the story—kidnaping. The reader is kept on the track by a careful repetition of key ideas:

First paragraph	A Cardozo High School student kidnaped
Second paragraph	Ronald K. Sewell, 18, a Cardozo junior kidnaped two men
Third paragraph	Sewell two men

Notice that the student's identification or name appears in each of the first three paragraphs, that the word *kidnaped* is used in the first two paragraphs, and that the words *two men* appear in the second and third paragraphs.

In the following story, the bridge is accomplished by an obvious device: a question and a projected answer.

When a poll last spring showed Democrat Daniel Walker running 2 to 1 ahead of Gov. Ogilvie, there were many who wrote off the Republican incumbent on Nov. 7.

But early last month the polls showed Ogilvie nosing ahead of Walker, and political pros now rate the contest a toss-up.

How did the governor with the dour demeanor manage to close the gap on his charismatic challenger?

The answer lies in a complex of factors, but there are some that stand out:

Chicago Tribune

The story goes on at some length to explain four major factors: prestige of the governorship, a substantial campaign fund, a willingness to engage in debates, a campaign designed to neutralize Walker's major advantages.

Bridging is most important in stories where there is a clear-cut difference between the lead and the body of the story. It is best accomplished by maintaining a clear, obvious story line, that is, by staying on the same subject until the gap between bridge and body is closed. Linking paragraphs by repeating names and key words facilitates the bridge.

Linking by Repetition

Repeating names and key words and phrases is also helpful in tying the story together. In the following story note how the words *counterfeit* and *counterfeiting* run throughout:

PHILADELPHIA—UPI—Secret Service agents raided a house yesterday and seized a quarter-million dollars in "high quality" counterfeit bills.

Special agent Myron Weinstein and his men also seized a complete counterfeiting plant and plates for $5 notes.

Raymond Blunt Jr. and John E. Polidoro, both of Philadelphia, and Robert W. Ribel, of Lower Southampton, Pa., were arrested.

They were charged with counterfeiting and were released on $25,000 bail each following a preliminary hearing.

Weinstein said the counterfeit bills first appeared in Maryland last month, then were found circulating in Delaware and eastern Pennsylvania.

He said they were the first counterfeit bills found in some time which used multicolored threads similar to those in real money.

Now read the *Los Angeles Times* story in Fig. 6.2 and note the many different forms the linking words take.

The key words and phrases in the *Los Angeles Times* story are repeated frequently, though they do not always appear in the same form. *Sheriff's investigators* in the first paragraph appears as *deputies* in later paragraphs. The phrase *smuggling ring* in the first paragraph becomes *the operation* in the second paragraph. The word *arrested*

A *kidnaping* investigation led to the breakup of a *smuggling* ring that charged *$225* each to bring Mexican nationals from Tiajuana to Los Angeles, *sheriff's investigators* said Sunday.

The operation came to light after a 19-year-old South Gabriel housewife told *deputies* her *husband* was *kidnaped* when he failed to pay the *$225* fee.

Deputies said they arranged for Mrs. Guadalupe Placentia to pay the suspected *smugglers* with marked currency, then arrested two men when they returned her *husband*, Carols, 23, to their home.

Taken into *custody* were Jose Torango, 21, of Santa Monica, and Espiridion Gomez, 19, a Los Angeles man.

Placentia led *deputies* to a house at 842 S. California Ave., Venice, where four other persons were *arrested* and nine *aliens*, eight men and a woman, were *taken into custody*, officers *reported*.

The *aliens* were turned over to U.S. Immigration authorities for return to Mexico and the six persons *arrested* were booked on suspicion of *kidnaping* and *smuggling*.

Deputies said they learned the *aliens* were being transported across the border in cars or walked across at deserted locations and collected at a home in San Diego where they stayed from several days to a month.

Later, *they* were driven to the Venice location in the trunks of cars, *deputies* said, and turned loose in Los Angeles after *they* paid the *$225* fee.

Los Angeles Times

Fig. 6.2 *An example of the effective use of linking words.*

in the third paragraph becomes *taken into custody* in the next paragraph. *Aliens* in the next to the last paragraph becomes the pronoun *they* in two references in the last paragraph. The relationships between these sets of words and phrases is close enough that readers cannot fail to make the connections.

Attribution

Attribution is another device that helps support the framework of the news story as it unfolds. You have already been introduced to attribution: it is the identification of the source of the story. Sometimes many references are necessary. In the following brief news story a single attribution is enough. Once it is established that the source of the story is the sheriff's office, there is no need to repeat the fact:

> A two-car accident at the corner of US-131 and Cannonsville Road Friday resulted in minor injuries to one person.
> Sheriff's officers said a car driven by Ernie Ritchie, 73, Rl Cedar Springs, was attempting a left turn off US-131 just as another car was attempting to pass him. The other car was driven by 21-year-old John Princer, Rl Pierson.
> Ritchie was treated for minor scalp lacerations.
> *Greenville Daily News*

The next story is interesting because it shows two types of attribution. The first two paragraphs clearly state who is making the charges about marijuana use and how the charges were made. The final paragraph carefully attributes every statement about the narcotics raid to the police: "they (detectives) said," "police said," "the detectives said." The Associated Press is being very certain readers understand who said what:

> WASHINGTON—AP—John Steinbeck IV, 21-year-old son of the novelist, reports widespread use of marijuana among soldiers in South Vietnam.
> His charges appear in drafts of articles submitted for publication in Washingtonian magazine in December and early next year. In them Steinbeck, who was arrested here Tuesday on narcotics charges, alleges that three-fourths or more of the troops are using marijuana.
> Young Steinbeck is in the Army and recently returned from duty in Southeast Asia. He is stationed in the Army's Office of Information at a military plant here.
> He was arrested a day after detectives raided an off-base apartment they said he rents. In the apartment police said they found 20 pounds of marijuana stuffed in shopping bags and packed in a suitcase the detectives said belonged to Steinbeck.

How much attribution is necessary? Just enough so that the reader always knows the source of any information in the story. In simple stories, like the accident report from the *Greenville Daily News*, one attribution is enough. Where information comes from more than one source, all should be identified. Where it might not be clear where certain information comes from, then attribute again. Another way of looking at it is to say that where facts are obvious and unexceptionable, minimum attribution will do. Where the facts are open to question or are controversial, or where the source is questionable, pin the source down.

In general, attribute enough to make your story clear. If you attribute too much, the city editor or someone on the copy desk will delete the excess attribution. If you don't attribute enough, an irate editor will embarrass you by asking: "Who said that?" or "Where did you get that information?"

Formal Transitions

Transitions are words, phrases, sentences or paragraphs that lift the reader over gaps in the story. Gaps appear, for example, between the lead and body of the story, or between the body of the story and a formal conclusion; where the topic changes; where there is a shift from summary to chronology; or a shift in viewpoint or in time. These gaps have to be bridged or the reader will lose track of what is going on and may lose interest in the story and not finish it. It is the writer's job to hold the reader's attention. Transitions help do this.

Ordinarily, the shorter the story the less it needs formal transitions. We have already seen how linking words, phrases, names and ideas maintain continuity. Linking devices are unobtrusive, but effective. We have also seen how a rhetorical question—a formal transition—can bridge the lead and body.

A shift in subject or place is easily signified by certain transitional words such as *but, however, nevertheless, still.* These words plainly warn the reader to prepare for a shift in attitude or direction. The following transitional paragraph from a *Los Angeles Times* story, for example, indicates that the discussion is about to shift from the Nixon campaign to the McGovern campaign. The warning device is the single word *but*:

> *But* in the McGovern camp the precision and fervor of the spring campaign has not returned.

A transitional paragraph from a news feature that appeared in the *Minneapolis Tribune* clearly indicates a shift in point of view from that of the ex-convicts to that of the townspeople:

> *Meanwhile,* many of the citizens of Clinton were alarmed at the thought of ex-convicts in their community.

Similar transitional paragraphs from a *Detroit News* story show, first, a shift from one person's views to another's, second, a shift in place, third, a shift in time:

> Lafnear, *like Fell*, was encouraged by the cool behavior of the students after the shootings.
>
> *Meanwhile, at the high school*, students milled about, unaware of the fleeing gunman or the wounded classmates.
>
> *After* the word had spread, there was some excitement, but no atmosphere of deep concern.

The following transitional paragraphs, from a story in the *Philadelphia Bulletin*, reports the effect of a school strike on three families. The transitional paragraphs clearly signal the story's progress from one family to the next:

> In Marlene Gordon's home, the effects of the strike on her children, Howard, 11, and Mindy, 9, are just as pronounced.
>
> Cathy Green, *however,* a center city mother, who has two school-age children, tends to take a more balanced view of the school crisis.
>
> A concern over a possible increase in the "drop-out" rate was *also* raised by Veronica Singleton, a Vista Volunteer, who is the mother of a teen-age son.

Transitional paragraphs contain both a transitional word or phrase and some statement about the subject matter of the paragraphs to follow. The only exception in the examples just cited is the paragraph from the *Detroit News* in which two names are juxtaposed in order to show a shift from one point of view to another. In the other examples, the words *but, meanwhile, after, just as, also* signal a shift within the story and warn the reader to be alert for some difference in time, place or point of view.

Pronoun References

Pronouns—principally *he, she, it, they, them, him, her, his*—are commonly used as substitutes for names. This allows for some variation, avoids annoying repetition of a name and is economical of space since pronouns are shorter than most names. Pronouns should only be used if the reader will know who the *he, she,* or *it* refers to. In the story from the *Philadelphia Bulletin* (Fig. 6.3.), notice how the pronouns follow very closely the name they replace.

Do use a pronoun to refer back to a name in a preceding paragraph, but be sure that name and pronoun are close enough together that the reader cannot doubt who the pronoun refers to. If the name is several paragraphs back, it is usually best to repeat it rather than substitute the pronoun. If

Five prisoners used wooden planks from a remodeling job to walk from a second-floor window to the top of a 30-foot wall at the Montgomery County Prison in Norristown yesterday and jump to freedom.

The prisoners, four of whom were awaiting trial, had been helping to prepare a temporary altar for Sunday Mass when the break occurred at about 9 A.M. from the old stone structure in the heart of town.

Guards had taken them to the dining room, officials said. From there they went to a second-floor storeroom for the altar equipment while the guards waited downstairs.

Windows of the storeroom are level with the top of the wall six feet away. The men laid the planks across the space and walked over them. They dropped into a cemetery on the other side.

A 13-state alarm was issued for the arrest of all five, all of whom were wearing the normal prison shirts and dungarees. They might also have been wearing civilian jackets, officials said.

Only one of the escapees was serving time. He was named as Thomas Adam, 22, of the 7300 block of Ryers ave. He had been convicted of robbery charges.

Those awaiting trial were identified as:

Charles Krajci, 23, of the 200 block Roosevelt blvd., charged with burglary; Arthur Andrews, 21, of Warminster, Bucks County, awaiting trial for burglary; Lawrence Fanelli, 23, of Levittown, burglary; and Paul Ruby, 22, of the 7700 block Hasbrook ave., weapons and drug charges.

Philadelphia Bulletin

Fig. 6.3 *Using pronouns.*

there are several names of the same gender in the preceding paragraph, the pronoun may be ambiguous and, again, the name may be more appropriate than a pronoun substitute.

Occasionally a writer senses that a pronoun reference is a bit unclear and attempts to salvage the situation by pairing the pronoun with a noun or name. For example:

> Jon Anderson, who is reviewing plans for Bakalis' office, described the plans as "unusual" and "very imaginative." He said, "I don't know how to describe it (the proposed school)."

This is a badly written paragraph. The pronoun *it*, of course, does not refer to the school, but to the word *plans*. The writer realized something was wrong, but didn't solve the problem by adding *the proposed school* in parentheses. The only cure here is to rewrite the two sentences so that their meaning is clear. This revision would do the trick:

> Jon Anderson, who is reviewing the plans for Bakalis' office, said the new school is hard to describe. He called the plans "unusual" and "very imaginative."

Another example of the same problem:

> Blame for the curb problem has been placed on Ralph Precious, former city manager, by Mayor Leonard Chabala and the village board.
> "I think he (Precious) knew he was leaving and wanted to leave something behind for us to remember him by," Trustee Thomas Streiter (5th) said in November.

Use of the pronoun and name together is clumsy, but necessary unless the writer revises the paragraph that precedes the quotation. Here is one way to solve the problem:

> Mayor Leonard Chabala and the village board blame the curb problem on the former city manager, Ralph Precious.
> "He knew he was leaving and wanted to leave something behind for us to remember him by," Trustee Thomas Streiter (5th) said in November.

In this revision the pronoun *he* follows the name *Ralph Precious* so closely that the reader is not likely to mistake the reference. Another possibility would have been to substitute the name *Precious* for the pronoun in the direct quotation—a perfectly acceptable way of making the direct quotation mean what the speaker intended:

> "I think Precious knew he was leaving..."

Parenthetical Inserts

Parentheses are not much used in news writing, because they tend to interrupt the flow of ideas.

They are used sometimes, however, to further identify a name, title or technical term, as in the following examples from the *Chicago Tribune:*

> Bennett said the youth would be returned to Lake County (Indiana) authorities.
>
> Dr. Raymond Shamberger linked the presence of silenium (a natural preservative) and BHT (man-made) in cereals to the decline of stomach cancer fatalities in these countries during the past 40 years, a recent issue of Supermarket News reports.

Parentheses or brackets are often used to set off background or explanation material inserted in a story, as in this excerpt from the obituary of Charles Correll—the Andy of Amos and Andy:

> Restaurants frequently boosted the volume of their radio sets when the show came on to satisfy customers.
> [In Philadelphia, the program came on Monday through Friday at 7 P.M. for 15 minutes and many movie houses delayed the start of their pictures because of it.]
> In 1960, with television taking more and more of their audience, Amos and Andy left the air.
> *Philadelphia Bulletin*

Parentheses or brackets are used to insert explanations into news copy. Using them for other purposes, however, can be awkward. The parenthetical insert frequently doesn't fit and should be omitted or put somewhere else in the story. The following is an example of an awkward and unnecessary intrusion in a lengthy and involved sentence:

> The evidence is at the H. George Wilde Sports Center at Bordentown/Lenox School, the home away from home for 200-plus hockey players (and there's a waiting list) and a host of volunteer parent/coaches involved in the Tri-town Hockey program.

The following example is both awkward and repetitious:

> Warnke describes himself as "a fat little preacher," and certainly his rhetoric is modest enough. He "got into Satanism" as a high school dope addict ("I was a speed freak," he says) and rose to become a Satanic priest for three California towns.

The parentheses in the following example are completely unnecessary:

> Over 1,600 families in Pittsfield pay more than 35 per cent of their income for housing, which Bogdan said points to the need for decent housing at rents low- and moderate-income families can afford. (Twenty or 25 per cent of income going to housing is usually cited as a realistic budget figure.)

The sentence in parentheses contains such routine information that it hardly needs to be set off by parentheses. If the writer was concerned that the information might be taken as coming from Bogdan, it could have been put in a separate paragraph.

Parenthetical material may be necessary, but the parentheses or brackets themselves are awkward and should be used as little as possible. One way to avoid them is to use dashes instead. Or, it may be better to restructure a couple of sentences. For example, the following excerpt from a story about a new school doesn't really need the parentheses although it does need the information:

> The District 108 school will be built in two-story pods (sections constructed so as to provide for easy expansion) with an absolute minimum of interior walls.

This could be revised in several ways:

> The District 108 school will be built in two-story pods—sections constructed so as to provide for easy expansion—with an absolute minimum of interior walls.

The District 108 school will be built in two-story pods, sections constructed so as to provide for easy expansion, with an absolute minimum of interior walls.

The District 108 school will be built in two-story pods with as few interior walls as possible. Pod is a technical term for sections or units in a building.

Too Much Variation

Inexperienced writers can be very conscious of repetition in their copy, much more so than their readers. The reader is learning something new from the story and is interested in its content. Most readers are unaware of the structure and techniques the writer used. When the writer introduces repetition that makes his story clearer or more cohesive, the reader is helped, not hurt, by repetition. But when the writer goes out of his way to avoid words or phrases important to meaning, the reader may lose his way. In the story in Fig. 6.4, the writer went too far out of his way to avoid repetition.

Note how many different terms the writer has used to avoid repeating a basic term like *spacecraft*:

interplanetary spaceship
Mariner 4
gold and gleaming robot
the 574-pound craft
the streaking craft
the streaking vehicle
the mechanical explorer
the craft
the mechanical marvel
the vehicle

CAPE KENNEDY, FLA.—AP—An interplanetary spaceship named Mariner 4 hurtled toward Mars on a photographic and scientific expedition Saturday and the flight control center reported it was on a course that would enable it to pass close to the red planet next July 14, as planned.

Although the gold and gleaming robot successfully executed early maneuvers, it still must clear several challenging hurdles and survive for a record 7½ months in the hostile environment of space before achieving its goal of Martian exploration.

Mariner 4, packing a camera and a sparkling array of scientific instruments, rocketed away from Cape Kennedy atop a towering Atlas-Agena booster which surged skyward at 9:22 a.m. EST after a perfect countdown.

More than seven hours later, after carefully calculating tracking information on rocket and spacecraft performance, project officials reported the 574-pound craft had been injected into an interplanetary trajectory which, if continued, would miss Mars by about 200,000 miles. They said this miss-distance was well within the million-mile correction capability of a small steering motor aboard the streaking vehicle.

Mariner's project director, Jack James, said that between two and 10 days after launching, when computers have figured the course precisely, a station at Goldstone, Calif., is to send a radio signal to ignite the steering for the proper amount of time to swing Mariner 4 onto a path which would take it within 8,600 miles of Mars. The motor is capable of being fired again later for additional course refinement.

James said satisfactory data could be obtained if the mechanical explorer came within 54,000 miles of the target planet.

At the time of the miss-distance announcement, Mariner 4 was nearly 60,000 miles from earth on its outward journey. It had been injected into space at a speed of 25,598 miles an hour, but had slowed as intended to 9,547 miles as it darted farther from its home planet.

The space agency was hopeful that Mariner 4 would succeed where a twin spacecraft, Mariner 3, failed earlier this month because of structural failure of a protective shroud. The craft represents the last U.S. opportunity to probe Mars for two years.

The spacecraft was to zip across 325 million miles of space before its brief encounter with the planet, which many astronomers believe is inhabited by a basic form of life such as moss-like vegetation.

Mariner 4 was not designed to detect life. Its job is to gather information to help engineers build future life-seeking capsules which the United States plans to land on Mars in 1969.

During a 30-minute fly-by of the planet before sailing past into eternal orbit about the sun, the mechanical marvel is to snap 22 television pictures and its electronic eyes are to scan for scientific secrets such as magnetic field strength, radiation intensity and micrometeoroid frequency.

Project official Glen A. Reiff of the National Aeronautics and Space Administration called the assignment the most difficult ever handed an unmanned U.S. spacecraft.

"It's an incomprehensibly long trip in terms of time and distance," he said. "It's something like 1,400 trips to the moon."

James said the spacecraft's 138,000 parts would have to function in the hostile space environment throughout the long lonely trip.

The vehicle would have to receive and carry out radio commands sent from earth stations and would have to transmit information and pictures from a record 134 million miles in space.

Fig. 6.4 *An example of pointless variation.*

The writer couldn't even refrain from varying the name of Mars with *the red planet.*

This kind of variation is not only pointless, it is confusing. The experienced writer will use precise terminology and correct names, explaining them if necessary, and will save the use of substitute terms for references to technical terms, proper names, or longer, less manageable names. Do you think you would have noticed or been bothered by a more frequent use of the name *Mariner 4,* or the repeated use of a single substitute term such as *spacecraft,* in Fig. 6.4? Probably not.

Sufficient Identification

In news stories it is important to identify people clearly and accurately. No one wants to see his or her name spelled incorrectly, or given the wrong middle initial, street address, profession or job. So there are a number of problems in identifying the people who appear in the news stories you write.

First of all, get the correct identification. This is a matter of careful reporting. Ask people to spell their names for you, verify addresses, titles, ages. If the person is not available, check the information in the best possible source: a city directory, court records, an official printed program, a telephone book.

Second, identify people fully enough so that they cannot be confused with anyone else. It is general newspaper practice to use full names: first name, middle initial and last name.

There are times when it is appropriate to identify people by name and local address only:

> Blake A. Bryant of Providence street is a patient in St. Luke's hospital, New Bedford. Mr. Bryant will be there for a week, undergoing tests.
> *Falmouth* (Mass.) *Enterprise*

In stories about crimes, accidents, disasters and similar occurrences, it has always been customary to identify people by name, age and address:

> Mrs. Ethel Rasner, 58, of the 8200 block of Forrest ave., Stenton, was knocked down and robbed

of about $100 near her home and about a half block from Mayor Rizzo's home yesterday.
> *Philadelphia Bulletin*

Young people are usually identified by naming their parents:

> Sam Mallette, 14, son of Mr. and Mrs. Dolor M. Mallette of 36 Richards road, received rank of Eagle Scout recently in a ceremony at John Wesley Methodist church.
> *Falmouth* (Mass.) *Enterprise*

In many news stories, however, identification must include more information than a person's home address. Public officials are identified by the title of the office they hold: mayor, governor, prosecuting attorney. Legislators are identified by the district they represent and the party to which they belong.

In other cases, the subject of the story will suggest the relevant information to include:

> Larry Nevels, 36, announced Thursday he will be a candidate for the Detroit Common Council in the Sept. 11 primary.
> Nevels is the director of the United Communities Inc., a Detroit service group.
> *Detroit Free Press*

> Euell Gibbons, naturalist and author of "Stalking the Wild Asparagus" and "Stalking the Blue-Eyed Scallop," will speak at the Annual Benefit Lecture for the Woods Hole Library at 9 P.M. Tuesday, July 10, at the Lillie auditorium of the Marine Biological Laboratory.
> *Falmouth* (Mass.) *Enterprise*

Whatever the story, use the identification that is most relevant to the story in which the person appears, and most liable to avoid confusion with another person.

The *Beginners Basic Guide to News Style* at the back of this text discusses this subject in some detail.

CHAPTER SEVEN
Using the Elements of News

IN CHAPTER 4 we saw that the news elements in a story are pretty well summed up by five Ws: *what, who, where, when, why,* and *how.* The five Ws provide a workable approach to writing a lead. They also provide a clue about the nature of news and about the basic interests of newspaper readers. This chapter will treat some basic considerations of news values as they affect the organization and structure of news stories.

THE VALUE OF *WHAT*

In treating events—like fires, accidents, battles and elections—the story always focuses on what happened. The lead summarizes the event and the body presents the details. In writing about a speech, a public hearing or a debate, we emphasize what was said. Again, the lead summarizes and the body concentrates on the specifics, even the exact words, of the speaker or speakers. People read newspapers to find out what happened. They quiz their friends to find out what happened: at court today, at home, at the meeting last night, at the office. A news story that fails to take into account the reader's interest in what happened will not be read.

Among the five Ws, the *what* is really the most important; the *who* follows closely; *where* and *when* come next. In breaking news stories, these are the important elements. The *how* and the *why* of a story are important, but they are generally subordinated to the other Ws. Interpretation and explanation come to a large extent in sidebars, background stories and follow-up stories.

RELATION OF *WHAT* AND *WHO*

Sometimes it is hard to separate the *what* and *who* elements of a story, for not only do things happen, they happen to people and are frequently caused by people. The story in Fig. 7.1, for example, has both *what* and *who* elements. Both elements are important, but *what* is given greater emphasis than *who.*

The story tells what happened: two people were killed in two separate fires. The victims were not prominent people and were probably unknown to most of the *Sun-Times'* hundreds of thousands of readers. Therefore, their identity (the *who*) is of secondary importance to the story. So impersonal is the large urban area today that what happens clearly takes precedence over who is involved. The names of the two victims are almost

Two persons were killed Sunday in separate fires in a Near North Side hotel and a South Side house.

At the Lakeside Hotel, 839 N. Dearborn, a fire that began on the fourth floor and spread to the sixth killed Sidney Green, 74, who lived on the sixth floor.

Second Deputy Fire Marshal James Neville said firemen helped evacuate 30 to 40 persons, most of them elderly, from the building. About 14 persons who lived on the top floors of the hotel were left homeless.

Fireman Daniel Toth, 31, of Snorkel Squad 1, was treated for smoke inhalation at Northwestern Memorial Hospital and released. Two hotel residents, Nick Yakavich, 83, and John Vanderwall, 78, were treated at Henrotin Hospital and released.

Neville said the fire began near the stairway and elevator on the fourth floor. He estimated damage at $20,000. About 100 firemen fought the two-alarm fire.

On the South Side, Paulette Boyde, 22, of 9107 S. Laflin, was killed when fire broke out at the home where she was visiting at 8809 S. Parnell.

Seventh Division Fire Marshal Allen Spearber said the fire began in the living room where Miss Boyde was sleeping. He said seven other persons were evacuated from the home, and he estimated damage at $5,000.

Chicago Sun-Times

Fig. 7.1 *This story emphasizes both* what *and* who.

a minor detail. In smaller cities where people know each other better, this is less true and people are given more prominence in news stories.

The following story, though not exactly comparable to the fire story, is about an event. But it emphasizes the people involved as much or more than the event itself:

Elden W. Middlebrook of Rives Junction won $50,000 today in the largest weekly drawing held so far by the Michigan State Lottery.

Middlebrook, 21, who lives at 3522 Henry Rd., was drawn sixth of 14 persons participating in the $780,000 drawing. The first three numbers drawn won $10,000 each, and the last won the jackpot of $200,000.

That was Larry R. Hypes, 23, of Flint, an employe of the Fisher Body Co.

Middlebrook, who said he may build a home with his winnings, was accompanied at the drawing in Wyandotte by his wife, Renee; his father-in-law, Richard Bunnell, of 4317 Lansing; and a friend, Ralph Stull of 1350 Losey Rd., Rives Junction.

Jackson (Mich.) *Citizen Patriot*

Writing news stories and balancing the news values of *what* and *who* call for judgment and organization. The policies of your newspaper, your editor's views and the circumstances of the story itself usually make it pretty clear at the outset where the emphasis should lie. Striking the right balance between what happened and who was involved is one aspect of judgment about news values.

WHO: PEOPLE AND PERSONALITIES

Human interest, our interest in other people is a basic news concept. Newspaper readers are curious about the everyday activities of their friends and neighbors. They are also curious about people whose names are in the news: statesmen, politicians, theatrical personalities, the husbands and wives of important public figures, athletic stars and many more. And newspapers cater to this interest in a number of ways. The obituary columns get a great deal of attention in the newsroom and are among the most widely read features in a newspaper. The *New York Times* runs extensive biographical sketches in its obituary columns. The *Detroit Free Press* gathers interesting items about people and runs them on the back page of the paper every day under the heading *Names and Faces*. Other newspapers do much the same thing. The *New York Times* makes a point of publishing brief biographical sketches of people in the news in an effort to make the news and the people in it more understandable. The obituary from the *St. Louis Globe-Democrat* (Fig. 7.2) is a good example of a human-interest story that goes way beyond the mere recitation of facts about a person's life. It is a careful marshaling of small facts and colorful details. The direct quotations are a nice touch that brings other people into the story. The story in Fig. 7.3 is a good example of finding human interest in an otherwise routine story. Commencement exercises come every June and they are always much the same. A story about an

'Red' Perryman, a blues legend, dies penniless

By CHARLES J. OSWALD
Globe-Democrat Staff Writer

Rufus (Speckled Red) Perryman, the legendary Barrelhouse blues pianist and songwriter who played before noblemen, died pennyless at Homer G. Phillips Hospital Tuesday, Jan. 2, 1973, at the age of 80.

Best remembered for his thundering piano style and good natured blues shouting, Red's music and fame spanned four generations bringing happiness, laughter and sometimes sentimental tears to millions of Americans.

"IF THERE is or ever was a Barrelhouse style, Speckled Red would certainly have been the embodiment of that style," said Paul E. Affeldt, music critic and president of Euphonic records in Ventura, Calif.

"His erratic, unpredictable, original and often seemingly bumbling style fits the description of experts to a fare-thee-well.

"Red was the most original and inventive blues pinao player.

Red's trademark was the Stetson hat he always wore while playing, the glass of gin that sat on the piano and the crazy left hand that was always "walkin' the base."

MUSIC historians say Red was born in Monroe, La., on Oct. 23, 1892. Shortly afterwards his family moved to Hampton, Ga., near Atlanta, where he grew up.

Red was an albino Negro. His skin was white with a few scattered specks of dark pigmentation which gave rise to his nickname.

During World War I, his family moved to Detroit where Red came under the influence of blues pianists Charlie Spand, Will Ezell, Fishtail and James Heminway.

In 1917, Red took a job working in Miss Fat's Good-Time House in Detroit where he played an old upright when he wasn't mopping up tables.

RED COULDN'T read music but, as he said once, "I got a good ear" and it wasn't long until he was composing his own music.

Red left Detroit in 1929 after making a name "and a whole lot of money." A short time later he was in Memphis and cut his first record "The Dirty Dozens" and "Wilkins Street Stomp" on the old Brunswick label.

For the next 10 years Red continued recording. Some of the most famous recordings during that period were "The Right String but the Wrong Yo Yo," "Goin Down Slow," "Red's Boogie-Woogie," "Cow Cow Blues," "Highway 61 Blues," and "Crying in my sleep."

THOUGH seen occasionally playing in Negro taverns in St. Louis, Red dropped into obscurity around 1938 and worked through World War II as a laborer in produce row. When the war ended, so did his job and he went back to playing the piano in neighborhood taverns.

In 1954 jazz buff and St. Louis detective, Charlie O'Brien found Red and famous blues pianist Henry Brownin St. Louis.

Red played at nightclubs during the heyday of Gaslight Square and in 1959 toured Europe and the British Isles through a U.S. cultural exchange program.

Red's last big public appearance came in October, 1971, when he was the St. Louis Jazz Club's guest of nonor on the steamer Admiral, Jeff Leopold, president of the club said.

"He was just an absolute doll. The most pleasant person I ever talked to," said Olive Brown, "empress of the blues."

In poor health, virtually pennyless and suffering from diabetes Red spent his last years living with the family of Mrs. Minerva Muse at 4515 Newberry Terrace. He underwent surgery three times in 1972 for cancer, the disease he died of Tuesday.

Miss Brown is collecting money to pay for Red's funeral expenses. Friends are asked to send donations to the Speckled Red Burial Fund care of Miss Olive Brown, 6253 Cabanne ave., St. Louis, Mo. 63130.

St. Louis Globe Democrat

Fig. 7.2 *A good example of a human interest story.*

CHICAGO TODAY Photo

Mrs. Antoinette James, M. A., Gemini, musicologist, caseworker, and mother of 10.

Mother of 10 sees doctorate in her future

BY LEONARD ARONSON

"NOW'S THE TIME to start ventures," reads the horoscope of Mrs. Antoinette James, mother of 10, who will receive a master's degree today from the University of Chicago.

In Mrs. James' case, the new venture will be to start on "my doctorate at the U. of C., perhaps in the area of social thought," she said.

A firm believer in the astrological "star system," Mrs. James, a Gemini, went back to school on scholarships after having her eighth child, largely to make sure all her children had the chance to continue their education.

"But most of my children are Geminis, anyway," she noted, citing the Gemini qualities of determination, willpower, wittiness, and restlessness.

"I feel that if I lived or died, they'd all have had the incentive to do it anyway. They all play the piano, love music, and have a lot of irons in the fire."

MRS. JAMES FOR the last 18 months has been working as a caseworker at the englewood office of the Cook County Department of Public Aid. In her master's thesis she compares black and white music and literature.

Her husband, Joseph, an employe of the post office, said, "When she went back to work I had to start doing a lot more around the house." The home is at 8934 S. Wallace St.

"It's a little sacrifice on the husband's part, too," he said, adding that there is a positive side: "I began to see the kids more, and understand them, and appreciate them."

Chicago Today

Fig. 7.3 *Adding interest to a routine story.*

WASHINGTON, Aug. 22 (AP)—The Law Enforcement Assistance Administration awarded more than $2.2-million to 25 states and the Virgin Islands today for planning law enforcement improvements in the current fiscal year.

The money was the first allocated by the agency since July 1.

Charles H. Rogovin, the agency's director, said the grants represented advances on planning allocations that all the states would get after the agency's 1970 appropriation was approved by Congress.

Mr. Rogovin said each advance was about 25 per cent of what the state received for law enforcement planning in the fiscal year 1969.

The grants included:

Alaska, $25,000; Arizona, $52,000; California, $347,000; Colorado, $58,000; Connecticut, $74,000; Delaware, $23,000; Idaho, $37,000; Illinois, $208,-000. Iowa, $71,000; Kansas, $63,000; Louisiana, $86,000; Massachusetts, $116,000, and Michigan, $169,000.

Also, Minnesota, $85,000; Mississippi, $64,000; Montana, $37,000; New Jersey, $143,000; New Mexico, $42,000; Oregon, $59,000; Texas, $208,000; Utah, $42,000; Vermont, $32,000; Virginia, $101,000; Virgin Islands, $26,000; West Virginia, $55,-000, and Wyoming, $30,000.

New York Times

Michigan Awarded Law Fund

WASHINGTON (AP)— Michigan was awarded a $169,000 law enforcement improvement planning grant Friday by the federal Law Enforcement Assistance Administration (LEAA).

Twenty-five other states shared in the $2.2 million allocated. Only California, with $347,000, and Illinois and Texas, with $208,000 each, received more than Michigan.

LEAA director Charles H. Rogovin said the money represents about 25 per cent of what the state received for planning in the previous fiscal year, ended June 30. The money awarded Friday is only an advance on grants to all states which they will receive after the agency's fiscal 1970 budget is approved by Congress.

Lansing, Mich., *State Journal*

Fig. 7.4 *Two AP stories on law enforcement grants.*

unusual person who has earned a degree adds human interest to a usually dull story.

WHERE: THE LOCAL ANGLE

According to a journalistic axiom, things that happen nearby are more interesting to newspaper readers than things that happen in the next state, in another country or on the other side of the world. It is important, then, in writing a news story of special interest to local readers, to organize it so that the local angle is emphasized. The two versions of the Associated Press story in Fig. 7.4 provide a good example of the localizing technique. The *New York Times* version is written from a national point of view: it is datelined Washington, D.C., it emphasizes policy issues and

PATRICK M'GINNIS, A RAIL EXECUTIVE

Head of Four Lines, 68, Dies —Led Investment Firm

CINCINNATI, Feb. 23 (UPI) —Patrick McGinnis, a retired New York businessman and railroad executive, died Tuesday at his home in suburban Glendale. He was 68 years old.

Expert in Securities

Patrick McGinnis started as a clerk in the New York Central System before going to Wall Street, where he became an expert on railroad securities. He became president of McGinnis & Co., an investment concern, and headed four railroads at various times.

He was chairman of the Norfolk & Southern from 1947 to 1952, chairman of the Central of Georgia from 1952 to 1953 and president of the New York, New Haven & Hartford from 1954 to 1956.

In 1965, as president of the Boston & Maine, he and three other members were accused by the Government of selling 10 of the B & M.'s passenger cars to the International Railway Corporation for $250,000, with the cars to be sold the next day to the Wabash Railroad for $425,000. Mr. McGinnis was to have received $35,000 in the deal.

He was sentenced to 18 months in prison and fined $2,500 for his part in the transaction.

Mr. McGinnis was born in Palmyra, N. Y., in 1904, and received his B. S. from St. Lawrence University in 1926. He studied for three years at New York University and then spent two years at Columbia and a year at Brooklyn Law School.

He was manager of the railroad bond department for Lehman Brothers in 1930-31, and then joined Pflugfelder, Bampton & Rust, member of the New York Stock Exchange. He became a partner in 1943. In 1946 he became a senior partner of McGinnis, Bampton & Sellger, and three years later senior partne rof his own company, McGinnis & Co.

He leaves his wife, the former Lucile Whitney; a son, Patrick B.; a daughter, Carol Iveagh, and a brother.

New York Times

Patrick B. McGinnis

Patrick B. McGinnis, retired New York businessman and one-time president of the New Haven railroad, died a week ago today at his home in Glendale, a suburb of Cincinnati. He was 68 years old.

He was only president of the New Haven for three years, 1954 to 1956, and they were years of railroad decline. But he made an impression that has lingered here. He enjoyed making a splash.

In the summer of 1955, Mr. McGinnis rented the Dr. Louis Hutchins house at Nobska for his son-in-law and daughter, Mr. and Mrs. Edward McGrath, their young child and a nurse. Patrick B. McGinnis 3d, the railroad president's son, was at Highfield for several years with the Cross Right Players from Williams college.

The Depot avenue crossing leading to Highfield was elaborately repaired and smoothed in the summer of 1954, when "Packy" McGinnis was among the troupe on Highfield hill. The young actor's father blithely admitted the connection. He said it was too bad Highfield theatre didn't lie beyond every grade crossing in town, in which case they would all be in first rate condition.

Wires were installed on a siding near Depot avenue, so that the railroad president's private car could be placed there while he attended performances at Highfield. Mr. and Mrs. McGinnis attended a memorable party at Highfield, with entertainers imported from the Casino at Falmouth Heights.

In August, 1954, Mr. McGinnis spoke to the Falmouth Rotary club. He said he was going to bring 2,000 passengers a day to the Falmouth station. He did not do this, and before long the trains had stopped altogether. But it was at this meeting that Mr. McGinnis, almost as an afterthought, threw out the suggestion that the overhead signs be taken off Main street. There were none of these protruding and dangling signs on Fifth avenue in New York, Mr. McGinnis pointed out, and Fifth avenue was the wealthiest street of commerce in the world.

Falmouth (Mass.) *Enterprise*

Fig. 7.5 *A news story with a national viewpoint, left, and a local viewpoint, right.*

Crash Kills Two Swimmers

Two members of the Central Michigan University swimming team were killed and two were seriously injured in a car crash early Sunday morning in south-central Indiana.

Twelve swimmers, the team coach and his wife were driving to a holiday training session in Florida when the second car of their three-car caravan swept across the I—65 median and crashed into another auto and then was hit broadside by an oncoming semi-trailer truck.

Dead are James H. Wilson, 19, of Battle Creek, a CMU sophomore, the driver of the car, and Robert C. Currie, 18, of Dearborn, a freshman.

Gregory S. Haliczer, 18, of Lansing was in serious condition late Sunday with a collapsed lung and severe brain concussion at Methodist Hospital in Indianapolis. Michael J. Benda, 21, of Madison Heights was in Robert Long Hospital, Indianapolis, with a fractured pelvic bone. Benda was listed in satisfactory condition.

A fifth youth in the car, Michael Keevan of Lansing, was not seriously injured. Keevan, Benda and Currie were asleep in the back seat of the car, a university official said.

Currie was the son of Mr. and Mrs. Robert C. Currie, 18714

Carlysle, Dearborn. Wilson was the son of Mr. and Mrs. Donald R. Wilson of Battle Creek.

Police said the accident occurred at 12:10 a.m. north of Seymour, Ind. They said Wilson had apparently fallen asleep at the wheel and the car swerved to the left.

THE INJURED IN the other care were all Michigan residents, too. None was seriously hurt.

They are Son Luckett, 62, of Hamtramck, the driver of the car; his wife, 59; Jake Norman, 61, of Detroit, and Irma Griece, 38, of Detroit. All suffered lacerations.

The driver of the truck was not injured.

Indiana State Police said the truck carried Wilson's car 500 feet before coming to a stop on top of it, pinning Wilson, Currie and Haliczer inside.

Al Thomas, director of CMU's physical education department, said swim coach Douglas Morris and his wife, Sue, were taking the youths to a voluntary swimming session.

He said the team had held a swimming meet earlier Saturday at the CMU campus in Mt. Pleasant about 60 miles north of Lansing.

Detroit Free Press

Fig. 7.6 *Contrasting versions of accident story from* Detroit Free Press *and* Lansing State Journal.

Two Local Swimmers Injured

SEYMOUR, Ind.,—Gregory Haliczer, 18, a Sexton High School graduate and a member of the Central Michigan University swimming team, was injured seriously Sunday in a three vehicle accident on Interstate 65 which claimed the lives of two other members of the CMU squad.

Haliczer, son of Mr. and Mrs. S.L. Haliczer, 2515 Concord, was listed in serious condition this morning at Indianapolis Methodist Hospital with head and internal injuries.

ANOTHER SEXTON graduate and member of the CMU team, Mike Keevan, son of Mr. and Mrs. John Keevan, 1618 Stirling, suffered a broken nose and facial cuts in the accident. He was treated and released from a hospital in nearby Columbus, Ind.

Killed in the accident were James H. Wilson, 19, of Battle Creek, and Robert C. Currie, also 19, of Dearborn. Indiana State Police said Wilson apparently fell asleep at the wheel and the car swerved across the center line.

The car was struck broadside by a second car and then struck by a truck.

THE CAR was one of three containing CMU swim team members traveling to Ft. Lauderdale, Fl. for a swimming forum which was scheduled to begin today.

The team had a swim meet at Mt. Pleasant Saturday against Northern Illinois.

Lansing (Mich.) *State Journal*

---

reports the amount of every allocation. The same story was published in the Lansing *State Journal*, but this version is localized to make it more interesting to Michigan newspaper readers: Michigan's share of the $2.2 million is put in the lead, and it was not considered necessary to list all the other states sharing in the grant.

An even more strongly localized story is the obituary of Patrick McGinnis from the *Falmouth Enterprise* (Fig. 7.5). The *New York Times* obituary was written for a national readership. But the *Enterprise* version emphasizes McGinnis' connection with Falmouth, includes local anecdotes and leaves details of his career for the last few paragraphs. To the *Enterprise*, this was a local story, nationally known figure or not.

The Lansing *State Journal* and the *Detroit Free Press* versions of the story in Fig. 7.6 provide another example of localizing. The *Detroit Free Press* circulates throughout Michigan and this story appeared in the state edition which has a substantial readership in the Lansing area. The *Free Press* version is a completely balanced story emphasizing the seriousness of the accident and the deaths of the two college students. The *State Journal*, on the other hand, emphasized the injuries to the two Lansing area students over the deaths of the two students from other cities.

It might be said that local stories such as these are narrow in their point of view, even unbalanced. But, such a charge would be unfair. Most

newspapers in the United States are local newspapers and they serve their readers best by offering them what they want—complete coverage of the local community.

Another approach to localizing can be seen in an excerpt from an Associated Press story as it was published in the Minneapolis *Tribune* (Fig. 7.7). The story has a local angle: the crime was committed in Minneapolis and the accused was arrested and questioned there. But the thrust of the Associated Press story was the U.S. Senate investigation of the treatment of suspects in criminal cases. The story could have been revised and a new lead written to emphasize the local angle, but the *Tribune* editors chose instead to keep the wire story as it was written and to add a parenthetical

WASHINGTON, D.C. — (AP) — When John F. Biron at last confessed to murder, his voice was a h o a r s e whisper.

"Do some thinking," his police interrogators had told him the night before. Their voices had been firm but soft —their questions persistent.

Now it was morning, and Biron was telling a story of a woman beaten and left to die of exposure on a snowy Minneapolis street, a purse snatching turned to murder.

FOR MORE t h a n an hour, a tape-recording of the questioning that led to that confession was played before a Senate subcommittee considering the impact of the Supreme Court decision on the treatment of criminal suspects.

(Biron's confession to taking part in the fatal beating of Mrs. Ann Danielski in North Minneapolis in 1962 actually occurred late in the afternoon — some 24 hours after he was arrested, according to police.

(Mrs. Danielski, 54, had been walking home about 4 a.m. when she was attacked. She died at General Hospital after being found in the snow a b o u t three hours later.)

Only a momentary excerpt of the confession by the 18-year-old youth, was played. Even in the hushed hearing room, his voice could barely be heard.

"HE'S NOW confessing," said Yale Kamisar, former University of Minnesota professor now at the University of Michigan Law School, who played the record. "He's barely audible. To some extent the officers are dictating his confession.

"He's in such a state that he'll say anything."

Minneapolis Tribune

Fig. 7.7 *Parenthetical insert localizing a story in* Minneapolis Tribune.

insert of background information to clarify the local angle—the reference to Minneapolis—in the third paragraph of the lead.

WHEN: TIME AND TIMELINESS

Journalism deals with current events and newspapers have long made a great point of the speed with which the news is brought to the reading public. First radio, then television, took some of the freshness out of the front page. No longer do newspapers issue extras and there are fewer late stories marked *flash* or *bulletin* even in the few metropolitan dailies still pushing street sales. Radio and television news programs bring the public the first word of news events. Newspapers now recognize this and concentrate on depth and completeness in their coverage of the news. There is more feature writing, more interpretive reporting and much less emphasis on haste in getting the news into print.

The news writer, however, cannot ignore the time element in a story. In the first place, a story has to be placed in time; the reader must know when the event took place. In the second place, it is important to establish a clear relationship between the time the events took place and the time the story is being read by the newspaper reader.

The Point in Time

With few exceptions, it is necessary to be specific about the time element in a news story. Depending on the newspaper's style, the word *today* or the day of the week is made an integral part of the lead:

> City Council voted $4.5 million for a new disposal plant Monday night at its regular monthly meeting.

> Four incumbent council members and one challenger were nominated in a light vote in the city primary Tuesday.

> A four-car crash took the lives of four area teenagers early today.

Whether you use *today* or the day of the week is almost entirely a matter of local preference. Your newspaper will have a policy on the matter. And the wire services have their own preferences.

Past Tense News stories about events that have already taken place are written in the past tense and call for active verbs like *said, announced, elected, proposed* or passive verbs like *was elected, was killed, was reported, was seen:*

> The National Labor Relations Board today *was asked* to order a halt to a strike that has shut down construction at the Louisiana Superdome.
> *New Orleans States-Item*

When you write a story in the past tense, be very careful to couple the verb with a time element: *announced Monday, said Tuesday, was killed Wednesday.*

Present Perfect Some leads contain no specific reference to time. This is especially true of features, which emphasize the story and are less concerned with when it happened. The same is true of stories about past events where no specific time is concerned, as in the following item:

> NEW YORK—AP—The gasoline shortage *has produced* a small, shadowy market where some fuel-starved independent gas station chains are paying premium prices to distributors for supplies.

The use of the present perfect implies currency, but avoids specifying an exact time. Verb forms such as these are usual: *has given, has ordered, has told, has been elected, has been honored.* Whereas the past tense requires a specific time element, the present perfect requires its omission:

past tense + time element	was killed Monday said Tuesday Thursday named
present perfect	has been elected has announced

News stories are not always as fresh as they ought to be and the writer or editor may want to disguise this fact. The trick is to avoid mentioning the time at all, as in the following news story:

> A scientist and a businessman have been honored as two "positive personalities" by the city of Philadelphia.
> Mayor Frank Rizzo awarded citations and honorary city badges to Buckminster Fuller and Edward Bizek.
> Fuller is a scientist, poet and inventor of the geodesic dome. Bizek owns Mrs. Paul's Frozen Foods and heads a national campaign against Polish jokes.
> Fuller told a gathering of 100 businessmen that he didn't think of himself as belonging to any particular place or city but that he was part of the "World Man."
> "I feel very strongly about the World Man developing on our continent," he said.
> "What we really call nations are human beings who've been isolated for very long periods from the rest of humanity, have been bred very clearly to such an extent that you can recognize them as being different physically from other people."
> *Miami Herald*

The past tense *awarded* in the second paragraph would ordinarily have been followed by a time element: Monday, Tuesday, today. Its omission is an obvious attempt to avoid being specific. If you can't show that your story is fresh, at least don't admit that it is a little stale by using a giveaway like *last Monday* or the *Time*-style cover-up *one day last week,* or *recently.*

Present Tense Timeliness can sometimes be emphasized by writing in the present tense, as in this lead:

> Professional boxing moves into a new site this evening as Promoter Roy Gill presents a six-bout program in the Holiday Twin Rinks hockey facility at 3465 Broadway, Cheektowaga.
> *Buffalo Evening News*

The Future Stories about events that will take place in the future obviously require careful explanation of the time element and make general use of the auxiliary verb *will*. For example:

> Archbishop Carroll High School *will* hold graduation ceremonies at 8 PM June 22 in Bishop Turner High School, 185 Lang Ave.
> ***Buffalo Evening News***

Day or Date?

The news writer must be sure to make all time references clear and unambiguous. This is usually done by using the full date if the reference is to an event more than seven days before or after the newspaper's date of publication; the day of the week is given if the reference is to an event within seven days of the date of publication. For example, the following story was published on June 18. The events reported were to be held nearly two weeks in the future:

> MACHIAS—A three-day carnival will be featured at the William Weller Hose Company's Field Days, June 29 to July 1, at Gary Herman Memorial Playground, Union St.
> Events include: Parade, 7:30 PM, June 29; fire demonstration, 2 PM, and a firemen's parade, 7:30 PM, June 30; water fight, 1 PM, and a noon chicken barbecue, July 1.
> ***Buffalo Evening News***

There are exceptions to this rule: obituaries often give the day of the week, the month, date and year in order to provide an accurate and permanent record. There are also times when both day and date are needed to avoid ambiguity. Ordinarily, however, one or the other will do.

Time and the Reader

One important thing the news writer must keep in mind about time is the reader's point of view. What does the reader think you mean when you write *today,* or *yesterday* or *tomorrow?* The newspaper helps by establishing a starting place: every page carries a folio that includes the day and date of publication. If he is reading the Monday paper, the reader knows without any doubt that a reference to Sunday means the previous day, *yesterday,* and that a reference to Tuesday means the next day, *tomorrow.* There is little ambiguity.

Some newspapers include the date in their datelines, and this also helps the reader establish points in time. Let's look at the following story from the *Chicago Tribune:*

> WASHINGTON, June 21—The Supreme Court today opened the way for school desegregation suits in northern cities and the possibility of massive pupil busing.

This story appeared on June 22. The dateline on the story is June 21 and the word *today* refers to June 21. This is internally consistent, but externally confusing. *Tribune* readers, especially the hasty ones, who saw the story on June 22 may very well have found the word *today* ambiguous. For this reason few newspapers use dates in datelines and many newspapers prefer to use the day of the week instead of the words *today, yesterday* or *tomorrow.* Very few newspapers use the word *yesterday,* no doubt to avoid the charge that today's newspaper contains yesterday's news. This is the system suggested in the style guide at the back of this text.

In references to months and years it is generally a good idea to avoid using *next* and *last.* If the reference is to the current calendar year, just use the month: June, August, November. If the reference is not to the current calendar year, use both month and year: June 1973, April 1972, March 1976.

Freshening a Story

Leads should always be as up to date as possible. When an event is clearly in the past, your lead will have to reflect this. You can't twist the news to put a *today* lead on a story that broke yesterday. But when a story is a continuing event, like a trial or public hearing, the news writer can choose the

Marje taking Kerner trial stand

BY JOHN McHUGH
and SY ADELMAN

MRS. MARJORIE Lindheimer Everett, who dominated Illinois horse racing for a decade, takes the stand today as the government's first witness in the race track stock bribery trial of former Gov. Otto Kerner.

The apperance of the 51-year-old wealthy sportswoman was to follow more than three hours of opening statements by defense and government attorneys before a newly sworn jury of six men and six women.

Mrs. Everett, acclaimed in the 1960s as the "queen of Illinois racing," is expected to testify as to how she was forced to tender race track stock at below-market value to politicians to safeguard and expand her lucrative racing interests.

United States Atty. James R. Thompson has indicated that he will spell out the charges against Kerner and his former state director of revenue Theodore J. Isaacs, in his opening remarks.

THOMPSON YESTERDAY told presiding Judge Robert L. Taylor that his statement would take at least 1½ hours. The U. S.

District Court judge from Knoxville, Tenn., appeared slightly taken aback.

"I just never heard of opening statements that long," he declared.

"There never has been a case like this," replied Thompson.

"We are talking about eight years of transactions and thousands of pages of documents," Thompson added.

Thompson was referring to Kerner's two terms as governor. A 19-count, 64-page indictment returned by a federal grand jury on Dec. 15, 1971, charged that Kerner and Isaacs engaged in a conspiracy involving bribery, mail fraud, tax evasion, and filing false income tax returns.

KERNER FURTHER WAS charged in the indictment with perjury and giving false statements to the Internal Revenue Service.

Chief defense counsel Paul R. Connolly, a Washington lawyer, joined Thompson in requesting adequate time for opening statements. Connolly told the court his address to the jury would take "every bit of an hour."

THE JUDGE GRANTED 1½ hours to both Thompson and Connolly for their opening statements.

Yesterday also marked the first time that Kerner faced the selected six men and six women who will pass judgment on him after a trial expected to last from six to eight weeks.

The urbane 64-year-old former governor who is now a judge of the U. S. Court of Appeals, sat erect and squarely facing the 12 jurors and six alternates.

Kerner's 12 chosen peers are a fairly representative lot. Some of them have problems of their own, not the least of which has turned out to be the six-to-eight-week sequestration ordered for the jury by Judge Taylor.

MRS. LUCILLE A. Knifke, Chicago, a secretary to the vice president of advertising for Santa Fe Railway, has high blood pressure and requires medication.

Mrs. Betty Jane Hudson, of Chicago, a file clerk with the Cook County Department of Public Aid, has a five-year-old son and no husband. Relatives would have to take care of the boy, she said before being chosen as a juror.

Mrs. Bernice D. Geister, of Palos Heights, has a 16-year-old son. As her husband, a quality control supervisor with Swift & Co., often is required to travel on business trips, she expressed reluctance at leaving the boy on his own.

The other jurors are:
● Mrs. Elizabeth A. Knepper, of Chicago, secretary at a steel treatment company.
● William C. Michael, of Riverdale, a brick mason.
● Mrs. Mary D. Kehart, of Norridge, wife of a retired butcher.
● Louis B. Kinney, of Chicago, an operations agent for American Airlines.
● Mrs. Mattie L. Parker, of Chicago, who has two sons who are Chicago policemen.
● Donald Rogan, of Aurora, a machinist.
● James Robinson, of Chicago, a lift truck operator.
● Delbert D. McKinney, Aurora sheet metal worker. A Navy veteran from 1954 until 1957, he has a wife and two young children. He was reluctant to be away from them for a long time.
● Richard J. O'Brien, of Chicago, a printer. O'Brien, a father of four, is from Dublin, Ireland. He is the only acknowledged horseplayer on the jury.

Chicago Today

Fig. 7.8 *This trial story was made as up-to-date as possible by emphasizing what lay ahead rather than what happened yesterday.*

today angle or the *tomorrow angle* and subordinate the previous day's events. The story in Fig. 7.8 from *Chicago Today* is a good example of this. The story appeared in the Tuesday edition and reported what happened at the opening of the trial on Monday. However, the writers gave their story the most up-to-date look possible by playing up what would happen next instead of what happened last, yesterday. The previous day's events don't enter the story until the fifth paragraph. The story as written is current, it deals with *now* rather than with *then*.

Overdoing It

Many bad leads are written in an obvious attempt to make the story look fresher than it is. The worst offender is the lead which has a *today* where it does not belong:

> PRAGUE—UPI—Western Airline officials said *today* the death toll in the crash *yesterday* of the Soviet-built Tupolev 154 tri-engine jet could have gone much higher if the plane had come down on a highway near the Prague Airport.

This is a second-day story and the first paragraph could easily have been written without referring to the time of the crash. This fact could then have gone in the next paragraph with details of the crash:

> The death toll in the crash of the Soviet-built Tupolev 154 tri-engine jet could have been higher, Western Airline officials say, if the plane had come down on a highway near the Prague Airport.
> The crash Monday killed 77 of the 99 persons on board . . .

Don't force a *today* reference into your lead if it doesn't fit, and don't use more than one time reference in your lead. Keep it simple.

Backgrounding

Part of the news value of many stories lies in the relationship between something that has just happened and something the reader already knows. An obituary will remind readers that "Smith is the man who . . ." and the reader is then able to say to himself, "Why, yes, of course, I remember him." This recognition factor is important and the careful news writer will always try to find a place for the little facts that will jog

LOVELL, WYO.—AP—Little Danny Blackburn, who drew national attention two weeks ago when he was temporarily refused passage on an airplane flight home, has died of cancer.

"Danny was a fighter, all the way through," his father said after the 10-year-old boy died Monday.

Two weeks ago Western Airlines stuck to its interpretation of a Federal Aviation Administration regulation and refused to fly the ailing boy and his oxygen bottle home from Denver, where Danny had undergone a series of brain operations.

The boy flew home via Frontier Airlines which agreed to bend the rule about oxygen because Danny was accompanied by a nurse.

It was known then that Danny, who had been battling brain cancer for 18 months, didn't have long to live. He told his parents he wanted to come home to Lovell, where his grandparents live.

Although home, Danny didn't get to do the things he wanted to do, his father said, "like go to the dime store, or see his grandparents' house."

He drifted off to sleep Sunday "and didn't wake up."

During the last days of his illness, Danny received well wishes from President Nixon, movie star John Wayne, singer Johnny Cash and former astronaut Wally Schirra.

Funeral services are scheduled for Thursday in the Stake Chapel of the Church of Jesus Christ of Latter-day Saints (Mormon).

Fig. 7.9 *Bringing in the background.*

the reader's memory. The story in Fig. 7.9 is built entirely around the recall factor.

The backgrounding and reminding in this story is lengthy and detailed. It may not be necessary to tell your readers quite that much. A few words may do it. But the background, the main outline of an earlier news event or an incident involving someone in the news today, is a very important element of news.

This chapter has dealt with news values in a very limited way. We have touched on four of the six basic news values embodied in the five Ws and added a few words about the technique of building a news story around the reader's interest in past news events. There is, of course, a great deal more to news than has been suggested here. It would be well worth your while to read critically in a good newspaper: the way newspapers handle various stories can tell you a lot that you ought to know about news values. For the moment, though, you have enough background to handle many different kinds of stories. You'll learn more as you practice the craft.

CHAPTER EIGHT

Improving by Revision

COPY FLOWS to the editor's desk from many different sources. Some of it arrives in publishable shape; some of it needs a touch here and there with the copy pencil; and some of it needs thoroughgoing revision. To cope with this daily task of revising and improving copy, the newspaper has a staff of editors and writers.

The editors responsible for pages and departments—city editors, news editors, state editors, sports editors, women's page editors, Sunday editors—all have assistant editors, people on rewrite and copy editors working under them. Editors make decisions about how copy is to be handled and do some editing themselves, although they rarely have time to do more than edit with a copy pencil and perhaps rewrite an occasional lead. Assistant editors do some of this, too, and they may also do some rewriting on the typewriter. Rewrite men, highly skilled writers and reporters, do the bulk of the rewriting—the actual revising and reshaping of news copy. Copy editors or copy readers work mostly with a copy pencil, but they have typewriters, too, and sometimes do a little rewriting on their own.

Much of the effort spent on revising and improving news copy would not be necessary if the news writer had done a better job in the first place. News writers should be aware of the standards for publishable copy and should do their best to deliver it to their editors. This chapter will try to put the problems of rewriting and revising into perspective, to help you see copy from the editor's side of the desk.

THE NEED FOR REVISION

All copy submitted to an editor of a newspaper is subject to some revision. No one writes a perfect story and editors have a knack for spotting weaknesses and for improving raw copy.

Several categories of copy account for most of the materials that must be revised before they are published:

- Stories published in an earlier edition of your newspaper.
- Stories originating with press associations, supplementary news services, the newspaper's bureaus, regional correspondents and readers;
- Stories originating with public relations firms and public relations men (sometimes called public information officers) who work for businesses, industries, state and local government, the federal government, universities, the armed forces and service agencies like the Red Cross and Community Chest.

COMMON WEAKNESSES

No two news stories are alike and it is impossible to draw up a hard and fast list of improvements needed to improve news copy. But there are a few common weaknesses we can discuss.

Badly Written Much news copy, submitted by staff writers and by other sources, is so badly written that it must be revised or rewritten to tighten it up, improve the lead, eliminate clutter and make the story clearer and more readable.

Wordy Some copy is too long, either because it is padded with unnecessary details, or because the desk is short of space.

Wrong Lead Many news stories have the wrong lead. Sometimes the writer uses the wrong angle and the story has to be turned around to bring a more interesting or important fact into the lead. Wire service copy and handouts frequently have to be revised to bring local angles into the lead.

Unprofessional Much news copy, especially that written by stringers or public relations sources, needs to be revised to conform to news style, to eliminate padding and overly commercial details and to improve the writing.

Out of Date News copy is often rewritten to update it. A continuing story, such as a major accident or disaster, may require a new lead for every edition. Yesterday's stories are frequently revised and updated to bring new information to the newspaper's readers.

Missing Facts News stories often have to be revised to fill gaps in information: people are inadequately identified, technical terms are not explained, background that would make the story more understandable is not included.

Many of these problems could be avoided if news writers took the time to read their own copy carefully; to correct small errors in usage and style; to take out unnecessary words and details; to simplify involved sentences; to eliminate clutter in

their leads; and to clarify and simplify their language. If they did these things, fewer news stories would be thrown back at them with a brusk "Here, fix this up."

FORMS OF REVISION

Revision may involve editing, rewriting, or updating. And all of these processes may involve the editor, a rewrite man, a copy editor and the news writer who first wrote the story.

Editing Editing involves minor changes and revisions: a word changed here and there, a sentence shortened, a long word replaced by a simpler one. All of this can be done without the typewriter, with just a touch of the copy pencil. Editing should improve the story, but leave the copy clean enough that it can be punched into tape or set into type by a human operator or scanned by the optical character reader.

Rewriting Rewriting involves major surgery to the entire story or to some part of it. Sometimes, in the case of a breaking story, it may mean completely rewriting the story from one edition of the paper to the next.

Updating Updating is minor surgery and may mean changes to a story still in the editor's hands, revision of a story already set in type or updating of a story published in an earlier edition. Updating might involve writing a *new lead* to incorporate newly reported facts; preparing an *insert* to add something to a story or to replace outdated or erroneous information; or it might require an *add*, new copy at the end of the story.

REVISING YOUR OWN COPY

Bad Writing

Experienced news writers never turn in copy without editing, revising and improving it first. When they take their copy out of the typewriter, they go over it carefully, checking typing, reviewing words and sentences, verifying names, dates, and details from their notes. Only when they are satisfied that they have done the best possible job, do they turn their story over to their editor.

When there is no time for this careful second look news writers may turn their copy in with little or no review. When time is short, editors may also hustle copy to the copy desk. There is a term for this—*railroading*—and news writers and editors know they are flirting with danger when they don't find the time to carefully edit, revise and improve their copy.

News writers who read their own copy and editors and copy readers who review it after them, can make many improvements with just a little thought and a sharp copy pencil. They can eliminate redundancies, substitute specific words for vague ones, find short words to replace long ones, substitute single words for whole phrases, straighten up awkward sentences, clear up ambiguities and explain jargon and gobbledygook.

Wallace Allen, managing editor of the *Minneapolis Tribune*, discussed the need for improved use of the language in an article written for the Associated Press Managing Editors' publication *News*.* His title was, "The Target: Imprecision, Wordiness and Repetition." Below is a brief survey of the kind of misuse of language that Mr. Allen and all editors want news writers to eliminate before they drop their copy on the editors' desks.

Careful editing should catch the use of the wrong word:

- *Congressman* when the writer means *state legislator*.
- *Ceremony* when the writer means *fanfare*.
- *Excessive* when the writer means *extensive*.
- *Conclave* when the writer means *conference*.

Careful editing should catch misspellings that arise through haste, carelessness, poor typing or ignorance:

- *Knit-picking* for *nit-picking*.

*I am indebted to Mr. Allen's article in the APME News for this and several other examples cited here.

- *Site* for *cite*.
- *Irregardless* for *regardless*.
- *Baited* for *bated*.
- *Alright* for *all right*.

Careful editing should eliminate redundancies:

- *Is currently* for *is*.
- *Small in size* for *small*.
- *Past history* for *history*.
- *New discovery* for *discovery*.
- *Served as treasurer* for *was treasurer*.
- *A total of 12* for *12*.

Careful editing should replace vague or neutral words with precise words. Word fads often contribute to the use of vague words. Today's fad word is *received*:

He pleaded guilty and *received* a $10 fine.
He pleaded guilty and *received* a sentence of 10 years.

In both instances a more precise word exists:

- He pleaded guilty and *was fined* $10.
- He pleaded guilty and *was sentenced* to 10 years.

Situation is another fad word, especially among sports announcers who are fond of saying "We seem to be in a first down situation" instead of "It's the first down." Television meteorologists are fond of the word *activity*. They almost inevitably say, "There's going to be some thunder shower activity," when it would be more direct to say, "There will be thunder showers in our area."

Circumlocution, the use of several words when one will do, can be eliminated easily with a copy pencil:

- *For the purpose of* means *for*.
- *In most cases* means *usually*.
- *A sufficient number* means *enough*.
- *Despite the fact that* means *although*.

Ambiguity can be cleared up by careful editing, usually by changing the word order or eliminating a word or two. Ambiguity is often hard for writers to detect in their own writing. They know what they mean and may not realize that someone else could misinterpret their words. For example, can you find two ways to interpret this description: "A Viet Cong prisoner was listed as killed by the Pentagon." The writer who said that a woman had been injured "in a rear end collision" may have meant a collision between automobiles, but the reader could wonder. A lead quoted by Wallace Allen provides a good example of ambiguity resulting from awkward sentence structure:

> The Indonesian native chief American free lance writer and photographer Wyn Sargent married last year is demanding compensation for the 25 pigs killed for the wedding.

Careful editing can save space by substituting short words for long ones:

— *Meet* is better than *encounter*.
— *Buy* is better than *purchase*.
— *Job* is better than *employment*.
— *Begin* is better than *commence*.
— *Person* is better than *individual*.

Careful editing can also eliminate jargon and gobbledygook, the use of technical or "in" language. News writers who use sports terminology in stories about politics or religion are likely to confuse their readers. The writer who said that a candidate "racked up two-thirds of the Republican total" was using jargon. Why "racked up"? It would be clearer to say that the candidate got two-thirds of the Republican vote. And this:

> McCarthy delegates were leading as well as some still running under Johnson's colors.

We can assume the writer meant that delegates pledged to McCarthy and Johnson were leading in early returns. All trades and professions have their own jargon, but it shouldn't creep into news stories. Sports terminology doesn't belong in political copy and academic jargon doesn't belong in

stories on the economy. Why talk about a "downward revision of prices" when you can say simply that "prices will go down." Military jargon should be explained. Do you know what a *riff* is?

> In the second riff since large numbers of U.S. troops began coming home from Vietnam . . . each riffed officer will get 10 days notification before his release.

This discussion is meant to be suggestive, not exhaustive. We introduced it here only to make the point that you should learn to monitor your own news copy, check style, language, spelling and facts before turning it in. News writers are part of the editing process. Editors and copy readers are there to back up the news writer, not to do his work for him. Post mortems on bad copy are embarrassing. After all, would you want to see your errors posted on the office bulletin board with funny remarks attached? Not likely!

Weak Leads

Badly written leads can be found in almost any newspaper. Many of them could have been improved by a little judicious editing. For example:

> Southville's Village Manager's Association (VMA) chose a 45-year-old insurance salesman and a native of Southville Monday as its candidate for Southville village president in the April 3 election.
> The powerful group, whose selections normally win easily, chose Walter P. Mulligan, 15 Droste Circle, to head the board.

This lead contains too much information and is repetitive. Judicious editing could have produced a much more direct lead:

> The Southville Village Manager's Association has named a 45-year-old insurance salesman as its candidate for village president.
> He is Walter P. Mulligan, 15 Droste Circle, a Southville native.
> The election is April 3.

Not all leads are as cluttered as this one was, but writers frequently try to do too much in their leads: making two points instead of one or including qualifications or minor points:

> An agreement for broadly expanded cable television in East Wilmington, with all its potential for public service and entertainment, is set for approval at Tuesday's city council meeting.

This lead would be much more to the point if the aside about the potential of cable television had been used somewhere else in the story. Then the lead could have been rewritten:

> City Council is expected to give its approval to a broadly expanded cable television service at its meeting Tuesday night.

Another lead that needs trimming:

> Four foreign correspondents criticized the American press Wednesday for what they see as its failure to come to grips with important issues in America and a failure to use one of its best weapons, writing, effectively.

This lead should have stopped after the word *issues.* The second point it makes distracts us and lessens the impact of the first point. Again, it would have been better to save the second point for later:

> Four foreign correspondents criticized the American press Wednesday for what they consider its failure to come to grips with important issues.

Leads like these are weak because they are poorly organized, cluttered with unnecessary detail or try to say too many things at once. Previous chapters have shown how leads ought to be written. These examples are a warning: revise, improve, rewrite before you turn your story in, not after the editor returns it and asks you to.

UPDATING THE STORY

News stories frequently have to be revised to add information that was not available at the time the original story was printed. This may mean revising a story that appeared in yesterday's paper or a story that appeared in earlier editions of today's paper. Updating may be limited to such minor details as changing the word *today* to *yesterday* or it might mean completely rewriting the story. When a major story breaks, newspapers may update the story hour by hour throughout a whole day's editions.

On the morning of October 30, 1972, there was a serious train accident in Chicago. The early editions of the afternoon newspapers went to press with scanty details. As the list of dead and injured grew throughout the day and as more details about the crash became available, the story had to be updated. Stories from three *Chicago Daily News* editions for that day are reprinted in Fig. 8.1. The first story contains few details. Much of the information in it was probably obtained hurriedly over the telephone. Later stories became more specific as reporters sent to cover the disaster scene, the hospitals and the morgue began to call in their contributions.

In the Red Flash and Red Streak editions you can see how paragraphs from one edition were picked up and re-used, while the lead and early part of the development were revised, rearranged and updated.

Updating is not always as dramatic as this, but the principle is always the same: it brings new information and additional facts into the story.

Whenever the story to be revised has already been set in type, it is common practice to salvage as much as possible of the original story and of the type already set. To do this the rewrite man works from a proof of the original story or from a copy of the story torn from the most recent edition. The torn copy is pasted vertically on to a sheet of copy paper and marked to indicate deletions or additions.

Revision may take three forms: a *new lead,* an *insert* or an *add* (addition). Fig. 8.2 shows how a

Several persons were reported killed and more than 100 injured Monday when two Illinois Central commuter trains collided at the 27th St. station near McCormick Place.

An old-style commuter train reportedly plowed into the rear of a new double-deck High-Liner commuter train en route to the Loop.

The accident occurred near Michael Reese Hospital, and doctors and nurses rushed to the crash.

All available ambulances and special fire equipment were called in to assist in the removal of the casualties and injured from the wreckage. A temporary morgue was set up nearby for the casualties.

MOST OF the injured were believed to have been in the older train, which has coaches that carry more than 100 passengers. At the height of the rush hour, these trains usually are packed with standees.

Police said about 75 of the injured were taken to Michael Reese Hospital, but others were removed to Mercy and Mount Sinai Hospitals.

At least 29 persons were killed and hundreds injured Monday morning when two Loop-bound Illinois Central commuter trains collided at the 27th St. station near McCormick Place.

Authorities said many more persons were trapped in the tangled wreckage of one of the trains.

Witnesses and surviving passengers said there was screaming throughout the trains when the collision occurred.

"People were flying all over the place," said Mrs. Laureice Browning, 33, of 7614 S. Essex, a passenger on one of the trains. "I just screamed and screamed, and somehow I was able to find my way off of that thing."

THE WRECKAGE of one train leaned nearly all the way off the tracks, sheared completely through by the collision.

Chief Francis Murphy of the Fire Prevention Bureau said, "There's an awful lot of pieces in there. We're trying to work on the live ones."

Sweating, grunting and cursing firemen were using winches, tackle-blocks and other equipment to rip loose large hunks of twisted sheet metal to get at the trapped people.

At least 44 persons were believed killed and more than 300 injured Monday morning when a Loop-bound Illinois Central commuter train rammed the rear of another commuter train at the 27th St. station near McCormick Place.

The death toll made the disaster the second worst train accident in Illinois history.

Many passengers, including some who were seriously injured and maimed, were trapped for hours in the tangled wreckage of the two crowded rush-hour electric trains.

The scene resembled a battlefield, with wreckage strewn over the tracks and bodies hanging out of the shattered railroad cars.

SCREAMING erupted in the trains seconds before impact as some passengers apparently realized they were about to crash.

"People were flying all over the place," said Mrs. Laureice Browning, 33, of 7614 S. Essex, a passenger on one train. "I just screamed and screamed, and somehow I was able to find my way off of that thing."

Sweating, grunting and cursing firemen from all over the city used winches, tackle-blocks and other equipment to rip loose large hunks of twisted sheet metal and free persons trapped inside.

The death and injury toll was expected to rise as more bodies were pulled from the wreckage.

Fig. 8.1 *The process of updating is graphically shown in three news stories from the* Chicago Daily News *for Monday, October 30, 1972. From left to right, stories from the Blue Streak, Red Flash and Red Streak editions which show how the lead of the accident story changed through the day.*

Chicago Daily News

proof or a tearup would be marked to indicate the substitution of a new lead, the insertion of new copy or the addition of new copy at the end of the original story.

The word *rule, turn rule* or just *TR*, written on a proof or a pasted-up clipping tells the printer that a change is to be made. In the hot-metal composing room, the printer inserts a piece of rule (a thin strip of metal) upside down in the story at the point indicated to serve as a physical marker and reminder of the change to be made. The rewrite man writes the new lead, insert or add and slugs it accordingly. Of course, new leads, inserts and adds are written separately and slugged and handled as

Class project doomed by building rules

Design students who spent the last five weeks putting together a garden on the roof of the Human Ecology Building will see this week that their efforts were in vain.

The class project, for Design for Living 143, will be disassembled after Wednesday before either the roof collapses or the first floor ceiling begins to leak.

Maintenance men pointed out to the students midway through the project that the aged building would not support the added weight. *turn rule for insert A*

"We were told all University buildings have to pass regulations and that the University maintenance people must authorize the use of any area for a purpose beyond its intended use," Lois Lund, dean of the College of Human Ecology, said last week.

"The project is most creative and the kind of emphasis we want in our programs but unfortunately does not coincide with regulations and must be taken down," she added.

Thomas Young, instructor of the course, was unavailable for further comment Sunday.

Class project doomed by building rules

turn rule for new lead

~~Design students who spent the last five weeks putting together a garden on the roof of the Human Ecology Building will see this week that their efforts were in vain.

The class project, for Design for Living 143, will be disassembled after Wednesday before either the roof collapses or the first floor ceiling begins to leak.~~

Maintenance men pointed out to the students midway through the project that the aged building would not support the added weight. *pick up as add one*

"We were told all University buildings have to pass regulations and that the University maintenance people must authorize the use of any area for a purpose beyond its intended use," Lois Lund, dean of the College of Human Ecology, said last week.

"The project is most creative and the kind of emphasis we want in our programs but unfortunately does not coincide with regulations and must be taken down," she added.

Thomas Young, instructor of the course, was unavailable for further comment Sunday.

Class project doomed by building rules

Design students who spent the last five weeks putting together a garden on the roof of the Human Ecology Building will see this week that their efforts were in vain.

The class project, for Design for Living 143, will be disassembled after Wednesday before either the roof collapses or the first floor ceiling begins to leak.

Maintenance men pointed out to the students midway through the project that the aged building would not support the added weight.

"We were told all University buildings have to pass regulations and that the University maintenance people must authorize the use of any area for a purpose beyond its intended use," Lois Lund, dean of the College of Human Ecology, said last week.

"The project is most creative and the kind of emphasis we want in our programs but unfortunately does not coincide with regulations and must be taken down," she added.

Thomas Young, instructor of the course, was unavailable for further comment Sunday. *turn rule for add one*

Fig. 8.2 *Instructions for, from left to right, an* insert, new lead *and an* add *written on a proof of the original story.*

separate copy until it comes time to put the type for the new matter with the type of the original story.

New leads are slugged simply *new lead* or *new lede.* Inserts are slugged *Insert A, Insert B, Insert C,* and so on. Even if you write only one insert, it is slugged *Insert A* just in case another insert becomes necessary later on. Adds are slugged *Add 1, Add 2, Add 3* and so on. Again, even if there is only one add it is slugged *Add 1.*

The rewrite man is careful to indicate that a new lead is complete by ending it with the instruction *pick up, pick up earlier, pick up Add 1* or some similar instruction. This tells editors, copy readers and printers down the line that the new lead is complete. A marked-up proof or tearup indicates how much of the original is to be killed and where the new lead and the original story are to be joined. Similarly, inserts are shown to be complete by ending with the notation *end insert A, end insert B* and so on (Fig. 8.3 and 8.4). An add would be marked complete by the notation *end Add 1.* This process may vary somewhat from newspaper to newspaper, but the general principles are the same even if terminology or copy desk procedures differ somewhat.

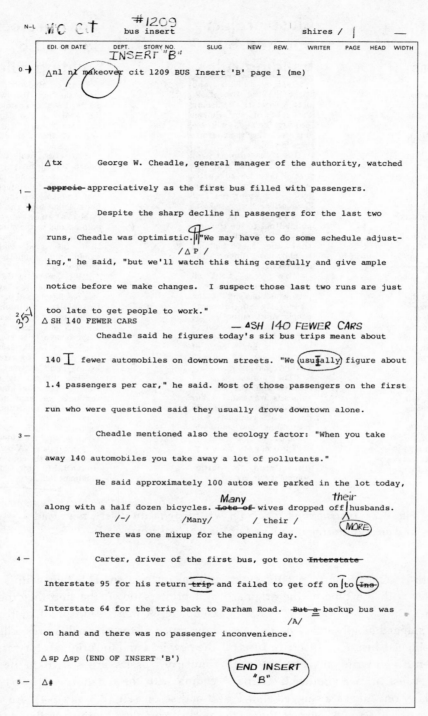

EDI. OR DATE	DEPT.	STORY NO.	SLUG	NEW	REW.	WRITER	PAGE	HEAD	WIDTH

INSERT "B"

△nl nl makeover cit 1209 BUS Insert 'B' page 1 (me)

△tx   George W. Cheadle, general manager of the authority, watched

appreic appreciatively as the first bus filled with passengers.

Despite the sharp decline in passengers for the last two

runs, Cheadle was optimistic. ¶"We may have to do some schedule adjust-
/△P/

ing," he said, "but we'll watch this thing carefully and give ample

notice before we make changes. I suspect those last two runs are just

too late to get people to work."
△ SH 140 FEWER CARS   — △SH 140 FEWER CARS
    Cheadle said he figures today's six bus trips meant about

140 ⊥ fewer automobiles on downtown streets. "We (usually) figure about

1.4 passengers per car," he said. Most of those passengers on the first

run who were questioned said they usually drove downtown alone.

    Cheadle mentioned also the ecology factor: "When you take

away 140 automobiles you take away a lot of pollutants."

    He said approximately 100 autos were parked in the lot today,
                                Many   their
along with a half dozen bicycles. Lots of wives dropped off husbands.
        /-/   /Many/   / their /   MORE
    There was one mixup for the opening day.

    Carter, driver of the first bus, got onto Interstate

Interstate 95 for his return trip and failed to get off on to Ins

Interstate 64 for the trip back to Parham Road. But a backup bus was
                                              /A/

on hand and there was no passenger inconvenience.

△ sp △ sp (END OF INSERT 'B')
                            END INSERT
                              "B"
△ #

Fig. 8.3 *An insert written for a story running in the city edition of the* Richmond (Va.) News Leader. *Writer slugged the story* bus insert, *changed by the copy desk to* 1209 Bus Insert 'B' page 1 (me). *Note the closing reminder* (END OF INSERT 'B').

George W. Cheadle, general manager of the authority, watched appreciatively as the first bus filled with passengers.

Despite the sharp decline in passengers for the last two runs, Cheadle was optimistic.

"We may have to do some schedule adjusting," he said, "but we'll watch this thing carefully and give ample notice before we make changes. I suspect those last two runs are just too late to get people to work."

140 FEWER CARS

Cheadle said he figured today's six bus trips meant about 140 fewer automobiles on downtown streets. "We usually figure about 1.4 passengers per car," he said. Most of those passengers on the first run who were questioned said they usually drove downtown alone.

Cheadle mentioned also the ecology factor: "When you take away 140 automobiles you take away a lot of pollutants."

He said approximately 100 autos were parked in the lot today, along with a half-dozen bicycles. Many wives dropped off their husbands.

There was one mixup for the opening day.

Carter, driver of the first bus, got onto Interstate 95 for his return and failed to get off onto Interstate 64 for the trip back to Parham Road. A backup bus was on hand and there was no passenger inconvenience.

Richmond News Leader

Fig. 8.4 *The revised bus story as it appeared with 'B' in place.*

IMPROVING HANDOUTS

Handout is a catchall term for news stories originating with public relations and public information people. Handouts can be a valuable source of news but they must be screened carefully to determine what, if any, news value each has. Many handouts are too self-seeking, too trivial or too specialized for newspaper use. Other are newsy and can be published with a little editing.

Some handouts contain the germ of an idea or an element of news that can be converted into a readable news story with a certain amount of revision. Sometimes a new lead will do the trick, sometimes a complete rewrite is necessary. Some handouts are much too long and detailed, but are well enough organized that they can be edited. The following news story, for example, originated in the handout shown in Fig. 8.5.

UAW international representative James Ramey, of 200 W. Cavanaugh Road, has been elected to the Board of Directors of the United Way of Michigan.

Lansing (Mich.) *State Journal*

Although the handout is a little too long and detailed, with a little editing it makes a perfectly good news story.

Handouts often fail to get the most important part of the story into the lead. They are written from the point of view of their issuing agency and the agency's idea of news often differs from the newspaper editor's. For example, handouts tend to start with the attribution—identification of the source of the handouts—and to back into the story:

General So-and-So announced today that Private Smith has been awarded the Silver Star.

Handouts often start with the name of the general, the base commander, the attorney general, the governor or the president of the company. Farther down in the story there is news and the news writer or rewrite man has to dig it out and restructure the story.

LOCALIZING

Wire service copy frequently has to be revised to lift buried features into the lead. This is not because the wire services produce badly written copy, but because they generalize their copy for national,

UNITED WAY OF MICHIGAN
Box 1378, Lansing 48904
371-4360
John W. Fisher
July 12, 1973

UAW REP ELECTED TO STATE UNITED WAY POST

(UAW international representative)

James Ramey, of 200 W. Cavanaugh Rd, has been elected to the

the Board of Directors of the United Way of Michigan (UWM)

~~The announcement was made by Aaron M. Shaver, of Battle Creek,~~

~~UWM president.~~

UWM has 25 health and social service agencies as members. It helps

plan programs and provides budgeting services and financial support for

its members.

Funds for UWM come from 150 local united way campaigns conducted

throughout Michigan. Capitol Area United Way is providing $203,841 for

UWM's member services during 1973.

~~Ramey, UAW international representative~~ is a member of the

Michigan Public Transportation Council.

He is vice president and on the board of directors of the

Tri-County Council on Alcoholism and Drug Abuse, and

Ramey is also on the board of directors of the Ingham County

Easter Seals Society and a member of the Victimless Crime Task Force

Committee.

-0-

Fig. 8.5 *A typical handout edited by a Lansing (Mich.)* **State
Journal** *rewrite man to use the main facts of the story. The lead
was strengthened by pulling additional information out of the
fifth paragraph. Later the story was cut back to a single paragraph.*

regional or state use in order to serve as many newspapers as possible with a single story. Few can be tailored to the needs of the individual newspapers. When a wire service story has local appeal, the newspaper usually has to bring the local angle up into the lead. Let's see how this works. Here is an unrevised Associated Press story:

ANN ARBOR—AP—Mary Lou
Keppen, 16, of Dearborn was elec-

ted governor of Wolverine Girls State Saturday by 462 teen-agers attending the annual girls' exercise in government.

Three other 16-year-old high school students won election to other mythical state government administrative posts. They were Betty Massingill of Livonia, lieutenant governor; Thea Schwartz of Farmington, secretary of state; and Lynda Martin of Battle Creek, attorney general.

> The convention named Kellen Largent, 16, of Lansing as chief justice of Girls State Supreme Court, and Ruth Travis, 17, of Caro and Carol Thyer, 17, of Marshall as justices.

This story, from the state wire, was written from as neutral a point of view as possible. The list of elected officers starts with the most important, governor, and works down. But to a newspaper in Lansing, Battle Creek or Marshall, the story is backwards. Each of those newspapers would want to reach down into the story, pull out the name of the local girl and start the story with that in the lead. The Marshall *Evening Chronicle* would, no doubt, want the story to start like this:

> A 17-year-old Marshall girl was elected to the Wolverine Girls State Supreme Court in elections held Saturday.
> She is Carol Thyer, daughter of Mr. and Mrs. . . .

Rewriting wire service copy to make it more interesting to readers in one part of the state is common. Quite often, too, the rewrite man will make a couple of phone calls or check clips in the newspaper library to provide additional background on the local angle. In the Wolverine Girls State story the newspaper might want to add information about the local girl and her activities in high school and the community.

Hometown news releases are a special kind of handout which flood into newspaper offices from camps, schools, colleges, universities and the armed forces. These are standard forms with a blank somewhere in the middle where the name and some brief identification of the local person is inserted. In this way standardized news stories can be localized with a minimum of effort on the part of the originating agency. In the newsroom, however, handouts like these are a nuisance because they can't be edited. The very limited amount of local news is usually buried in a mass of background and detail which is of limited interest to the newspaper. If such stories are to be used, the kernel of local news has to be taken from the middle or end of the handout and made the basis for a new lead.

CHAPTER NINE
Quotations

THE NEWS STORIES we discussed in earlier chapters dealt primarily with factual material: what happened, who it happened to, where and when it happened. Stories of this type are second hand, since they are usually based on facts told to but not observed by the reporter. They are third hand when the reader sees them in his newspaper.

In this chapter we will discuss news stories in which people speak for themselves. Using the exact words spoken by people appearing in news stories is known as *direct quotation* and the words the speakers use are referred to as *direct quotes*. Direct quotation is a useful device, one that breathes life into a story because it enables the participants in an event to speak directly to the newspaper reader rather than indirectly through an intermediary—the reporter or writer.

When the people in our stories start talking for themselves, new writing and organizing problems arise. Just how do we reproduce their words?

REPRODUCED SPEECH

When we quote, that is, give a written or oral report of what someone says, we are reproducing the words, or an approximation of the words, that person used. We are reproducing speech, not creating it. The speaker's words are the original; what we quote in a news story is a reproduction. Let's see how this works.

Every direct quotation originates with someone, somewhere, talking. Visualize, if you will, an episode which might have occurred a few minutes ago on a nearby street corner. You were a witness. A traffic policeman is standing at the curb keeping an eye on the traffic and on pedestrians using the crosswalk. A disheveled man comes up to him. The man's clothes are dirty, his face is cut, his hair is untidy. The police officer turns to him and you hear the following exchange:

Policeman: What happened?
Man: Officer, a guy just held me up. He took my wallet 'n knocked me down.
Policeman: Ya hurt?
Man: Nope, but I'm plenty mad. Kinda dirty, too.
Policeman: Just a minute. Lemme write this down. What'd this guy look like?

That's original speech. You hear it yourself. You may watch the speakers as you listen. You know who said what. Physical movement, relative position of the speakers, differences in voice and tone identify the speakers and their words. But this exchange reproduced by you later on for a friend needs some explaining. You might say something like this:

Hey, did you hear about the mugging? I was right there when this guy told the cop about it. He said he'd been held up. He wasn't hurt. He told the cop he was just mad. Somebody took his wallet and knocked him down.

Later you might see the story in your evening newspaper. This time the man's words look still different:

> An East Monroe man was assaulted and robbed today near Jefferson and McKinley avenues. He told police a short, thickset youth knocked him down and took his wallet.
>
> The mugging victim, John L. Johnson, 23, of 234 Monona St., was not seriously hurt.
>
> "But I'm plenty mad," he told police.
>
> He lost $36, he reported.

As you can see, reproduced speech, secondhand speech, just does not come out like the original. An oral report of what was originally said, like the version you gave your freind, is slightly different from what was said originally: there is a difference in the point of view since you are telling what you heard; and there is a difference in tense since you are speaking in the past tense while the mugging victim and the police officer were speaking in the present tense. The newspaper version is even more unlike the original exchange: the name of the victim, the fact that his wallet contained $36, the location of the mugging, facts you left out of your report, all were added to put the original speech in context.

In the newspaper version, one statement is much like the original and appears as a direct quote. The rest is *summary* or *paraphrase* in the writer's own words. If we had tape-recorded the original exchange we could play it back and check what was originally said against the direct quote:

> "But I'm plenty mad," he told police.

That is what the mugging victim said, as indicated by the quotation marks placed around the statement. The rest of the sentence is background: it tells who was speaking and to whom. This background is important in news stories because it puts the direct quote in context. This is *attribution*; it identifies the source of the quoted words. Attribution is sometimes called a *speech tag*.

The second sentence of the news story about the mugging reports other things the mugging victim said to the police officer. There is an attribution to identify the source of the information, but this time there are no quotation marks around the statement because this is an *indirect quote*. If we replayed our tape recording of the incident, we could verify that the mugging victim did give the officer this information, although in different words and in response to questions the officer asked. We could see, too, that the indirect quote is summarized, reduced to essential facts, and that it is presented more in the news writer's words than in the words of the original speaker.

Indirect quotation, then, tells what the speaker said, without using his exact words. The speaker's words are *paraphrased*, that is, given in the news writer's words, and they are often *summarized*, cut down to bare essentials.

Why Direct Quotation?

News writers gather information, organize it according to the needs of the moment and set down the story in their own words. They identify the source of the story once or twice. And that is about it. Any of the stories in the earlier chapters of this book can serve as examples of this approach. Most stories make use of two basic and important devices of storytelling: summary and paraphrase.

Occasionally, however, someone says something interesting or significant or perhaps just says it so well that the news writer finds it difficult to improve upon. This is where direct quotation comes in. The following story is typical in its use of a single, brief, direct quote:

> Camp Highfields in Onondaga is recovering from a Sunday full of excitement. At the annual Highfields Happening, sponsored by the Lansing Jaycees, more than 2,500 people came out to see the camp and eat chicken barbecue.
>
> "We raised about $1,500, which will help a lot," said Craig Sparks, director of the camp.

The camp offers educational and counseling programs for troubled boys 13 to 17.

The Michigan State University Sky Diving Club provided free entertainment to the guests at the camp.

Lansing Mich., *State Journal*

As you can see, the direct quote adds something to the story. It brings the speaker into direct contact with the newspaper reader and, because the speaker is the source of the news story, the direct quote also functions as an attribution. Direct quotation lends authenticity and credibility to news stories.

Note that the direct quote in this news story is set apart in a separate paragraph. This gives it added prominence and helps call attention to it.

Indirect Quotation

For the moment we are going to talk about indirect quotation in the quite limited sense of any information in news stories—other than direct quotes—that is attributed to the source. Our hypothetical news story about the mugging used indirect quotation:

He told police a short, thickset youth knocked him down and took his wallet.

In the following news story, the second paragraph can be considered an indirect quote. It is attributed, but we can assume that it does not reproduce exactly what the speaker said since it is not enclosed in quotation marks:

Oriole Homes Corp. announced Monday that it has signed a contract to purchase 1,900 acres of real property in Palm Beach County for an undisclosed purchase price.

Jacob L. Friedman, chairman of the board, said the acquired property is in proximity to the corporation's present single family and multi-family construction activities conducted in Broward County.

Oriole is primarily engaged in the construction of residential homes and homesites in Florida and Maryland.

Miami Herald

An indirect quote like the one in this story adds some information, enables the writer to bring the source of information into the story and give it some authenticity and credibility. To this extent, the indirect quote and the direct quote are alike. They differ, however, in that the direct quote is exactly, or almost exactly, what the speaker said, while the indirect quote is more likely to be a summary or a paraphrase.

Indirect quotation is ordinarily just a device for presenting information, not for adding color or interest to the story.

Attribution

In news stories, almost without exception, it is necessary to identify the source of the story, to tell where we got our information. This is usually done by adding a brief phrase like:

police said
the coroner reported
according to the mayor's office
a spokesman for the commission said
she said

Newsmen call this *attribution,* and there are numerous examples of attribution in the stories reprinted in previous chapters. In most brief news stories containing a limited amount of information, attribution need only identify the source of the story. Attribution used with direct or indirect quotation is a speech tag that identifies the person who spoke the original words.

THE GRAMMAR OF QUOTATIONS

Don't be thrown by the suggestion that we are going to talk about grammar. All we are going to do is organize our thinking about the use of direct and indirect quotation, to see how they are handled. Let's look at the following sentences:

He added: "Can't Mr. Dalton see the need to report honestly and openly what is going on in the city?"

"Affluent people are fleeing the city and going to the suburbs," he said.

Bragg said almost everyone who works at Atlantic Sails gets the fever.

"Lyons talks big," said Hart, "but he might make me mad enough to step into the ring with him."

Peck said, "This is the regular disciplinary action we've been using."

If we analyze these sentences, we will notice several patterns. Some of the sentences are in normal word order with the subject first, the verb second and the direct object—in this case a direct quote—third:

Peck said, "This is the regular disciplinary action we've been using."

He added: "Can't Mr. Dalton see the need to report honestly and openly what is going on in the city?"

One of the sentences seems to be in just the opposite order, with the direct quote first, the subject second and the verb third:

"Affluent people are fleeing the city and going to the suburbs," he said.

Another sentence is turned completely inside out with the subject and verb inserted in the middle of the quote:

"Lyons talks big," said Hart, "but he might make me mad enough to step into the ring with him."

And finally, we see that sentences using direct quotation and those using indirect quotation may follow the same word order:

Peck said, "This is the regular disciplinary action we've been using."

Bragg said almost everyone who works at Atlantic Sails gets the fever.

There appear to be different ways to write sentences using direct and indirect quotation, but there are also some conventions, some patterns, to their use.

Type One Quotes

Type One quotes are sentences which follow normal word order: subject + verb + direct object. In newsroom terminology, we can say that Type One quotes put the speech tag first and the direct quote second:

But he added: "Our city's too big to be a one-man show."

A Navy spokesman said, "We can confirm that there are no deaths."

John King, a State Department spokesman, said "there is no credible information available to us which would tend to support these charges."

Type One direct quotes are used more by the wire services than by newspapers. They are perfectly grammatical and understandable, but they do present some problems. One is punctuation. In the first sentence, the speech tag is separated from the direct quote by a colon. In the second, the writer uses a comma. Either is acceptable. In the third example there is no punctuation mark between the speech tag and the direct quote.

Direct quotation is the only instance in written English where a punctuation mark customarily separates a subject and a predicate and, if you are going to use Type One quotes, it would be a good idea to use a colon or a comma.

Indirect quotes commonly use Type One word order and the following are typical examples:

Hadfield said Los Angeles has stopped growing because of poor planning years ago.

Reston said he does not believe the United States is on the verge of a new period of isolationism.

He said his firm could ship component parts into Little Rock or Memphis, which he also praised for their river transportation systems.

Type Two Quotes

Type Two quotes are those in which the direct or indirect quote precedes the speech tag. This is the opposite of Type One word order, but it is perfectly usual. In fact, Type Two word order is much preferred in news writing for direct quotes. Some examples:

> "I would hope that legalized gambling doesn't become a reality," Kuhn said.

> "We need a business man in city hall," he said.

We also find Type Two indirect quotes like the following:

> The scarcity of rain in September isn't unusual, Wassall reported.

> A consumer council would be most significant for business in its product complaint services, Hart suggested.

Type Three Quotes

Speech tags precede the direct or indirect quote in Type One word order and follow the quote in Type Two word order. In Type Three quotes, the speech tag is placed somewhere within the quote. This is a perfectly grammatical and usual arrangement made possible by the fact that the quote is a complete sentence and can stand by itself.

There is really nothing complicated about Type Three quotes. The speech tag is placed at some natural break in the direct quote: for example, between the subject and the verb:

> "My first love," she said softly, "is the city."

> "The problem before me today," said Judge McGee from neighboring Amador County, "is whether the editor of the paper who wrote this article is protected under the Constitution."

The speech tag can also come immediately after the verb in the direct or indirect quote. For example:

> He did not shoot, he said, because he had a can of tear gas in his hand.

> "The crux of the matter is," said Riley, "we've changed the concept of the cultural center."

The speech tag can also come between two sentences joined by linking words such as *and, or, for, but* or *so*:

> "Well, he told me to go there," she said, "but he wasn't there."

> "Audiences are used to it now," she says, "so we'll have to invent something else to startle them."

Speech tags may also be placed between the main part of the direct or indirect quote and a modifying element. For example:

> Typically, he said, elderly mental patients sit next to each other without talking or are apathetic, irritable and forgetful.

> "If we give them up," he said, "we may be defeated, but we won't be destroyed."

These examples of Type Three quotes are illustrative, not exhaustive. Anyone who speaks or writes English easily will be able to sense a natural breaking point in a quote and will be able to put a speech tag in the right place. The real test, of course, is whether the sentence sounds right, whether it is readable.

EXTENDED QUOTATION

The direct and indirect quotes we have examined so far have been single sentences. However, news stories often need to use more than a single sentence of quotation. For example:

> "There is mounting distrust, then an outburst, followed by careful rebuilding," she said. "We are at the final stage now."

The first sentence here is a Type Two quote. The second sentence has no speech tag since the tag at the end of the first sentence serves to identify the source of both. A single speech tag, then, if it comes no later than the end of the first sentence will identify the source of the entire paragraph:

> "One night we made some real good beef stew out of Skippy and baked potatoes and carrots," Arnall said. "For lunch the other day we took cheddar cheese soup and put some Purina in it. Chuckwagon is my favorite dry food."

A Type Three quote may also be used to introduce a whole paragraph of quotation:

> "Lyons talks big," said Hart, "but he might make me mad enough to step into the ring with him. All that talk about me eating that crutch is hogwash. He'll need it to walk on when Mauler gets through with him."

A Type One quote may also be used to introduce a paragraph of direct quotation. In such cases the speech tag and the quote are separated by a colon. Usually, too, the direct quote follows in a separate paragraph.

> Lt. Gov. John Wilder, D-Sommerville, made the same observation about budget growth, and added: "I wonder when the people are going to react adversely."

Another example, this time without putting the quote in a separate paragraph:

> But Arlen C. Christenson, deputy attorney general, said: "We think we have a couple of angles that might get us into court. These may bear fruit very shortly."

Verbatim texts or long excerpts from texts that run over many paragraphs are generally introduced by a speech tag such as this:

> The text of the President's statement:

The full text or the excerpts follow, but without quotation marks. This is a special kind of speech tag and one beginners won't have much occasion to use.

Extended quotation may run over two or three paragraphs but still need only minimum attribution. Note how the single speech tag in the Type Two quote below manages to support two full paragraphs of direct quotation:

> "Hunger is much more of a problem with old people than with children," he said. "A hungry child will climb on a cabinet and get some food if he is hungry, but many older people just don't have the energy to even prepare a meal for themselves.
> "Even a borderline competent parent will feed a child as the best way to get him to shut up. Nobody will do that for an elderly person."

Note that there is no quotation mark at the end of the first paragraph. The closing quotation mark comes only at the end of the entire quotation.

MORE ABOUT ATTRIBUTION

How Many Speech Tags?

If you use only one direct or indirect quote in a story it has to have a speech tag, of course. If you use several sentences of quotation in sequence, quite often one speech tag is enough to identify the speaker. The examples already given in this chapter should guide you in writing short news stories.

The purpose of the speech tag is to identify the speaker. If you have several quotes in a story and each is from a different source, you must tag each one carefully so that your reader won't get lost. But although you must use enough speech tags to avoid confusion, it is a good idea not to use too many. Don't burden your story with more speech tags than it needs. You will develop a feel for the use of attribution and speech tags as you write more news stories. In the meantime, take a careful look at some news stories that depend on one or

Family Charges Cruise Ship Shanghaied Them for Trip

FT. LAUDERDALE, Fla. — (AP) — Theodore Kornowski Jr., his wife and two small children spent four days and $600 on a plush Caribbean cruise they didn't want but couldn't get out of.

"I just can't find enough words to say how lousy it was," said Kornowski after the family flew home from Curacao in the Dutch West Indies.

Kornowski and his family became unwilling passengers on the liner Nieuw Amsterdam Monday when they boarded the ship to wish bon voyage to his wife's mother, Margeurite Mouchard of Ft. Lauderdale. The vessel sailed with them still aboard.

"There were no bells, no one coming around to tell us it was time to get off," said the 29-year-old Kornowski. "We got up to the front deck at five minutes to five and I asked how to get off. They said we were sailing and I looked out a porthole and we were 75 feet from the dock."

Kornowski said he asked the ship's captain to return to the dock, but Kornowski said the skipper replied that that would take too much time.

After a pilot boat and the Coast Guard both refused to fetch his family off the liner, Kornowski, his wife and children settled down to what he described as four days of misery on the Caribbean.

"How can you enjoy yourself with a 6-month-old baby who's going to come down

"How can you enjoy yourself with a 6-month-old baby who's going to come down with the measles?"

with the measles," he said. "We didn't have any toothbrushes or deodorant or anything."

HE SAID THE BABY, Douglas, had been exposed to the measles and started to break out with them Thursday. He said he, his wife, Marilyn, 29, Douglas and a daughter, Cheryl, 4, spent all their time in one small cabin.

"You can't just go up to a dining room without the proper clothes and two kids and enjoy it," he said.

He said his wife cut up towels to use for diapers and washed their only clothes in the cabin's bathroom.

Kornowski said the adventure cost him about $600. He said this included $200 he was charged by the cruise line, which maintained he was at fault, hotel costs in Curacao and $327 for air fare for his family from Curacao back to Ft. Lauderdale.

"We're going to take some action against the cruise line," he said. "It was negligence on the part of the management that we were there."

Fig. 9.1 *Effective use of attribution.*

more sources; for example, the stories in Figures 9.1 and 9.2.

Said and its Variants

When you use direct quotation you enclose a statement between quotation marks. These little punctuation marks are unobtrusive, but meaningful. They inform the reader that whatever is contained between the opening and closing quotation marks is an exact reproduction of what someone said.

The quotation marks are helpful, but they do not intrude. Readers grasp their meaning quickly and go on to read for sense and meaning.

The verb *to say*, generally in the past tense, *said*, is most commonly used in speech tags, and it is a signal much like the quotation marks. The verb *to say* tells the reader that the name it links to the quoted statement is the source of that statement. It is unobtrusive, and should be. Its meaning is so limited that it is almost as mechanical as quotation marks.

Many beginning news writers worry about overusing the verb *to say*. They are concerned about its repeated use in a news story, and frequently try to find synonyms that they can substitute in speech tags. However, there are a number of good reasons for sticking with the verb *to say* and avoiding variations. The verb is short and its meaning is unequivocal. If all you want to do is tag a quote and identify the speaker, it is the ideal verb to use. Its meaning is so limited that the reader catches its signal and goes right on to the quote. It doesn't overload the reader with surplus information. Stick to the verb *to say*. As a writer you may be conscious of its repeated use, but your readers won't be (Fig. 9.1).

If, on the other hand, you do want to tell the reader more than just the identity of the speaker, you will have to find a more meaningful verb. For example, in stories about trials, public hearings or other official proceedings witnesses who appear, give formal testimony under oath. You can, in writing a news story about such proceedings, say that the witness *said*, but it would be more accurate to say that the witness *testified*. In this instance, the verb *to say* is inadequate because it does not convey the special significance of the kind of statement the speaker was making. The verb *to testify* is the only verb that will convey this special significance.

Other special situations call for the use of verbs with particular meanings. Accused persons may *admit* or *confess* or even *affirm*. Injured men may *cry out*; conspirators may *whisper*; and candidates for public office may *thunder forth* their disapproval of their opponents. You have at your disposal a broad range of useful and descriptive words for special situations. But you must be careful to chose one that conveys the exact meaning you want. And you must also be careful not to use verbs that carry too much meaning or a meaning you do not intend. For example, *pointed out* in a speech tag suggests that the statement is a fact; it should not be used if the statement may be only opinion—and only one person's opinion at that. Some words may put a speaker's delivery in an unflattering light. Verbs like *grumbled, insinuated, ranted, stammered, whined* might not be appreciated by the speaker.

Some verbs, like *admitted, confessed, conceded,*

12 women work as Customs inspector

By KAY KIRBY
News Special Writer

There is a sporano note these days at Detroit's ports of entry — the tunnel, the Ambassador Bridge, Metro Airport and even at the riverfront on occasion.

Fifteen attractive young ladies, three U.S. Immigration and 12 U.S. Customs Inspectors; are working the auto lines and Metro Airport, asking questions, looking through cars and luggage and once in a while doing "strip searches."

IF YOU ARE GOING through the tunnel or over the bridge and the U.S. inspector has a soft ladylike voice, don't think she doesn't mean business — she does. Not only is she thoroughly versed in regulations, she is well trained in self-defense and has her own personal radar working for suspicious characters.

How do they know who to pull over for intensive questioning?

It must be a kind of sensory radar, for in a random interview with several inspectors each said in effect, "It's a sense you get — a feeling."

Customs inspector Mary Latiker, of Detroit, put it this way: "You develop sort of a second sense, an instinct. When talking to people on the line, if they look guilty, act nervous or you just 'sense' something is wrong, they you pull them out of line."

A NATIVE OF MISSISSIPPI, Mary graduated from Jackson State College there and did substitute teaching in Detroit for a year before deciding that being a Customs officer was her thing.

"We do all duties, cars, cargo and people — in that order," she said in her soft southern accent. "Many people just don't understand about the $10 limit (for bringing back items purchased in Canada under 24 hours) and we try to explain. Penalties for not declaring are pretty stiff you know."

The biggest problems Mary sees are narcotics and then people who come in without visas. "We see quite a few who have become Canadians and then try to come back without a visa."

ALL THREE LOCATIONS are interesting, often exciting, according to Mary. If she had a choice of spots to work it would be the bridge in the summer and the tunnel in the winter.

"Customs and Immigration are two separate services," Armond Salturelli, U.S. Immigration Director for Detroit pointed out.

"We (Immigration) deal primarily with people; they (Customs) with merchandise or goods — but we work together. Inspectors for both services take turn on the auto lines. When a problem comes up they refer it to the right office.

"Detroit is the largest port of entry on the northern United States border — 16 million a year pass through here," Salturelli continued. "We are really proud of our women inspectors — they are right on an equal work and time basis with the men."

OVER AT the U.S. Customs Office, Director Louis Mezzano said women inspectors had been working the auto line for about two years.

"We try to schedule the girls on all shifts around the clock and rotate them for duty at the three stations, so we will have one on hand in case we need her for 'strip searches.'

"Occasionally there is an intensive search when all cars are stopped and searched," Mezzano said, "but mostly its just a matter of judgment by the officer in charge. Narcotics are one of biggest problems now.

Inspector Kathy Ottgen, of Woodhaven, was one of the officers on duty at the airport two weeks ago when the Customs services located 3½ kilos of cocaine.

"IT WAS COLD!" Kathy said when interviewed at the airport. "I mean we had no tip or advance notice. My supervisor just thought these people seemed suspicious. I found cocaine under their wigs and taped to the small of the backs underneath girdles."

One of the biggest immigration service problems in Detroit, according to Inspector Kathryn Wahl, of Rochester, are people who live in Canada and work in the United States without a visa.

A GRADUATE of Oakland University, Miss Wahl has been with the the Immigration Service for a year and a half and regards it as a fascinating career — she not only works at all three regular locations but from time to time boards foreign ships docked in Detroit to check immigration papers.

Other women immigration inspectors in Detroit are Audrey Hertlik, Detroit, and Georgia Franz, Harper Woods.

Customs inspectors in addition to Mrs. Latiker and Miss Ottgen are: Gloria A. Boni, Karen L. Mikeshock, Mary L. Sites and Mary Murdock, all of Detroit.

Others are Deena Henry of Inkster; Ann E. Peterson of Westland; Angela Raiti of Dearborn; Mrs. F. J. Lewis of Dearborn, Linda Czajka of Belleville; and Mary Fernandez, of Southgate.

Detroit News

Fig. 9.2 *A story with a variety of quotations and speech tags.*

in some contexts may imply that the speaker was owning up to a misdeed. Confessions and admissions in many readers' minds are related to wrongdoing. Be careful in using these words.

Some verbs are too formal for most uses. Presidents, governors and high public officials make statements. To say that the average speaker *stated* something is usually an exaggeration. Save *stated* and *announced* for formal and important occasions.

Some verbs are misleading. *Revealed*, for example, implies that something that has been hidden or kept secret is finally coming to light. *Said* or *announced* is usually more appropriate. *Added* or *concluded* may be misleading if they give the wrong impression of the order in which the speaker made the statements. Writers usually present their facts in a different order than the speaker used. Writers frequently take something from the end of a speech or interview and put it near the top of their story. Don't use the words *added, concluded* or *went on to say* unless you are presenting the statements in the same order the speaker used.

This is not intended to be an exhaustive discussion of the meanings of all substitutes for the verb *to say*. It is meant only to suggest some of the problems you may encounter if you use the verb in the speech tag to convey information about the manner in which a statement was made or the circumstances surrounding it. There are a number of readable and helpful guides to newspaper usage, and news writers, even experienced news writers, find them useful. Some of the better guides to usage are listed in the back of this book.

Word Order in Speech Tags

Since the speech tag is nothing more than the subject plus verb of a normal English sentence, it might be supposed that normal word order would be preserved. And it should be. But too many beginning news writers and careless older ones feel called upon to twist word order for no apparent reason. Normal word order would be:

Smith said
Gov. Wallace said
the mayor said
she said

Probably 90 per cent of all speech tags preserve this normal word order. And ordinarily there is little reason to reverse it. Readers are helped when word order is expected or usual; they have to slow down if they meet the unexpected, the unusual. You don't often want to slow them down and you don't often have a good reason for drawing their attention to the speech tag. Nothing in the following sentence calls for the shift from normal word order in the tag:

> "It was what we wanted and what we expected," said Mellin.

Sometimes, however, there is a reason for departing from normal word order in a speech tag. In the following example, the verb and the subject—the name of the speaker—would have been separated by a long descriptive phrase if normal word order had been preserved:

> "Frankly, my friends," said S. C. Van Curon, editor of the Frankfort State Journal, "your public image reminds me of a coal-camp youngster who has been playing on the slate dump all day . . .

In this case, the word order of verb plus subject sounds better. Note the contrast:

> S. C. Van Curon, editor of the Frankfort State Journal, said . . .

> said S. C. Van Curon, editor of the Frankfort State Journal . . .

There are no hard and fast rules to tell you when to use other than normal word order in speech tags. You must develop you own ear. If normal word order would separate the verb and the name of the speaker too widely, then try something else. In most cases, however, it is best not to invert verb and subject in speech tags.

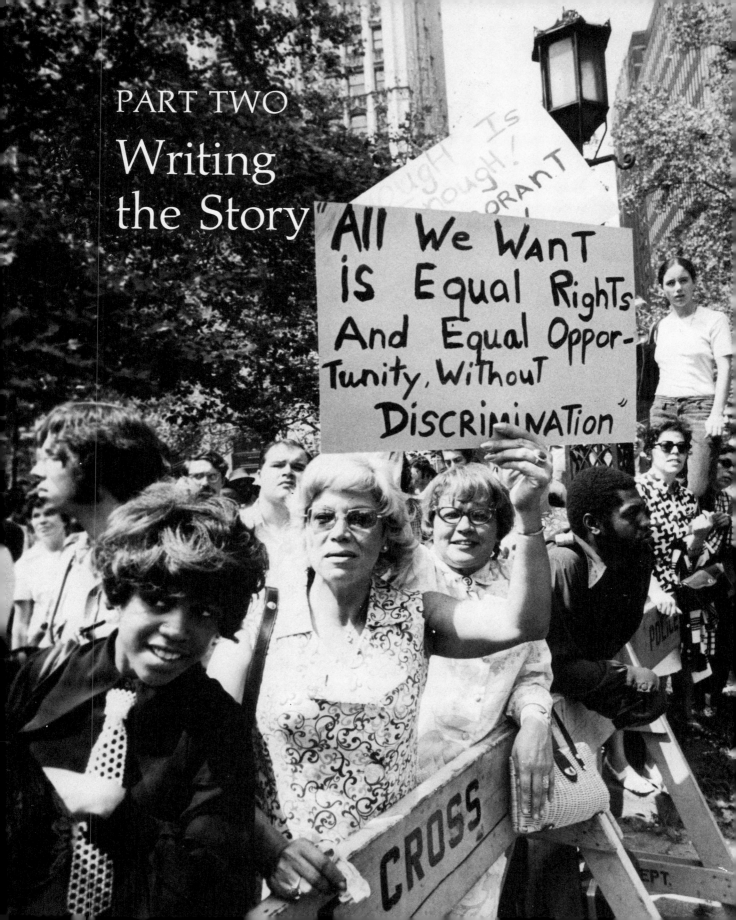

PART TWO

Writing
the Story

CHAPTER TEN

The Speech Story: Leads

SPEECH STORIES are basic to news writing. They require so many of the techniques and skills of news writing that they provide excellent training for beginners. Schools of journalism have traditionally started young news writers off with assignments to cover sermons, speeches and meetings.

In this chapter we will discuss a variety of news stories, all grouped under the general heading of *speech stories* because they all basically depend on what people have said. Speech stories in this sense include stories about sermons, lectures, public meetings, panel discussions, press conferences, trials, public hearings and interviews. They ordinarily involve reporting what one speaker said, but sometimes must incorporate what two, three or even half a dozen speakers said.

Not only must news writers have considerable reportorial skill to get this material together—handouts of the text are not always provided—but they have to have a lot of writing tricks up their sleeves as well.

Turning the spoken word into the written word and using direct and indirect quotation were discussed in Chapter 9. In this chapter and the next we will discuss news stories that are made up almost entirely of direct and indirect quotes and summaries of quotation.

The lead of a speech story is the first unit or section of the story. It may consist of a single paragraph in a very brief speech story or it may be as long as three or four paragraphs. For example:

> It is time for the medical profession to forget the myth that it takes a brilliant and highly educated person to practice medicine, an officer of the Department of Health, Education and Welfare said here Friday.
>
> Dr. Hazel M. Swann, chief of the HEW Family Health Center Branch, was in Milwaukee to address a dinner meeting of the Cream City Neighborhood Health Center on "Health Care in the '70s."
>
> She said during a press conference that change in medical education is needed to deliver necessary health care in the next decade.
> *Milwaukee Sentinel*

The first paragraph of this lead gives us an idea of the speaker's opinion about medical education and identifies the speaker in general terms. The second paragraph adds more information: details of the speaker's identity and of her reason for being in town. The third paragraph tells us the exact circumstances under which she was speaking and adds something to her first statement about medical education.

At this point the reader should have a good idea of who was talking, under what circumstances and what she was talking about. The story can go on from this lead to a fuller explanation of the speaker's views in the body of the story.

STATEMENT AND ATTRIBUTION

The starting point of a speech story is ordinarily a two-part presentation: first, a statement of what the speaker said, and, second, the attribution. The following first paragraph of a speech story shows the statement in italics:

> Chief Justice Warren E. Burger said today that *delays in Federal courts had become so acute that the burden on the courts should be taken into consideration whenever reform legislation was proposed.*
> *New York Times*

The opening words of the paragraph, "Chief Justice Warren E. Burger said today," are the attribution.

The statement of what the speaker said is linked to the attribution by the word *that*. The attribution is limited to the speaker's name, his identification and a time element. A second paragraph adds something to the attribution and a third paragraph rounds out and concludes the lead:

> In a nationally televised speech that was billed as the first "state of the judiciary" address by a Chief Justice, Mr. Burger took the unusual step of singling out potential areas of Federal legislation and warning against their enactment.
> As an example, he noted that there had been a number of proposals for new Federal legislation in the fields of antipollution and consumer class actions. He suggested that these issues might be left to the states to avoid further burdening the Federal courts.

The statement part of the first paragraph is the meat of the lead. It is the news writer's version of what the speaker told his audience. It is brief, but it gives essential information about the subject of the speech, the speaker's point of view and the general tone of his remarks. It is a good starting place.

You will see as you study the leads of speech stories in this chapter and the next that there is some variation in the kind of statement used in the lead. The best statement is the one that gives the reader the fairest and most complete summary of what the speaker said. Such a statement is generally presented in the news writer's words, although occasionally the writer may pick up a word or two, sometimes a whole phrase the speaker used. But, no matter how it is derived from the words of the speaker or speakers, the statement should be brief, informative and interesting. The success of the entire speech story depends on the effectiveness of the first couple of paragraphs. Here are some examples of summary statements from speech story leads:

> A religious revolution, largely unknown to organized church leadership, is taking place in the United States.

> The most effective check on Dutch elm disease—and the cheapest in the long run—is spraying and community cleanup.

> Theology ought to answer some of the bold new questions about the governments of the world.

Summary statements like these, of course, do not tell the whole story. The reader still needs to know: who made the statement; where; when; under what circumstances. Attribution rounds out the opening paragraph of a speech story lead:

> . . . graduates of the Milwaukee Institute of Technology were told Wednesday night in the Milwaukee vocational school auditorium.

> . . . a forest pathologist said Monday.

> Mayor Richard J. Daley has told top Democratic leaders here . . .

> The chairman of General Motors Corp., James M. Roche, said Thursday . . .

These attributions are brief and to the point. They identify the speaker, sometimes by name, sometimes by general description. Sometimes they identify the audience. They usually tell where and when the statement was made, at least in general.

PLACING THE EMPHASIS

In the speech story the basic elements of the lead—the statement and the attribution—can be arranged in a number of ways. The arrangement the writer chooses will depend on which of these two elements should be emphasized. Should the speaker be given prominence? Or is the substance of the speech the important thing? Or, perhaps, the audience the speaker was addressing is important enough to be given preferential treatment.

The beginning news writer will see that there are a number of fairly standardized approaches to writing leads on speech stories. Certain recognizable and re-usable patterns provide a framework and guide for the beginner learning how to write about what people say.

Attribution plus Statement

One of the commonest and easiest-to-use patterns is *attribution plus statement* which puts the speaker's name first in the lead. This arrangement obviously emphasizes the identity of the speaker. This type of lead recognizes the fact that the importance of the speaker frequently accounts for the importance of what was said, that the source of the story has a great deal to do with its credibility and significance. A diagram of an attribution-plus-statement lead looks like this:

————————————VERB—————— ————

  speaker's name   said   where   when

(that)————————————————————

          statement of what was said

The opening paragraph of speech leads that take this approach look like this:

> WASHINGTON—AP—Sen. Edmund S. Muskie said Monday that President Nixon is abusing presidential power through "a notion of one-man rule over the budget, over inflation and over the Watergate case."

> FREDERICKSBURG—AP—Former Gov. Mills E. Godwin said Tuesday night that he is confident Virginians will "make the choice between continuing our responsible and progressive state government and turning it over to the liberal left and the reactionaries."

Note that in both these leads the attribution not only names the speaker, but tells who he is: Muskie is a senator, Godwin a former governor.

Statement plus Attribution

The first major shift in emphasis is accomplished merely by placing the statement first and following it with the attribution. Now the emphasis is on what was said, rather than on who said it. We can diagram a *statement + attribution* lead like this:

————————————————————————

          statement of what was said

————————————VERB—————— ————

  speaker's name   said   where   when

Leads of this type are generally used when the subject matter of the speech, what was said, is interesting or significant and when the speaker's name might not be immediately recognized by newspaper readers. For example:

> The majority of the rural people who left the Tennessee Valley searching for jobs and a better life could not find it, TVA Chairman A. J. Wagner said here last night.
> *Nashville Tennessean*

> Despite the "prophets of doom," the Catholic Church in America is in the business of education for keeps, Terence Cardinal Cooke,

Archbishop of New York, said Monday.

Philadelphia Inquirer

Audience plus Statement

In some stories about speeches, it is important to emphasize another element: the nature of the audience the speaker addressed. This is often interesting, in some cases highly significant, and when it is, we can emphasize who was being addressed rather than who was doing the addressing or what the speaker said. We can diagram the first paragraph of such a lead this way:

_____VERB_____ _____

audience   was told where   when

(that)_____

statement of what was said

This lead, as you can see from the diagram and from the following example, emphasizes the audience by placing it first. The speaker's name is not even mentioned in this first paragraph.

WASHINGTON—UPI—A Senate Subcommittee was told Tuesday that aspirin was one of the best medications for the common cold, but that hot chicken soup might be better than heavily advertised cold and cough remedies.

Audience plus Speaker plus Statement

It is possible to include both an identification of the audience and the name of the speaker in the first paragraph of the speech story lead:

_____VERB_____

audience   were told by   speaker

_____   _____(that)_____

where   when   statement

Baptists in Northern Virginia were told by a denominational official last night that Southern Bap-

tist inactivity in the racial struggle calls for repentance.

This first paragraph does not say where the speech was given, a fact included in the second paragraph of the lead. This is an acceptable variation. Even where there are patterns and conventions, there is room for flexibility. The second paragraph of this two-paragraph lead:

"It behooves us as a denomination to be repentant, in the light of our tragic failure to bring the full weight of our strength to bear in the racial crisis," said the Rev. Ross Coggins, director of communications of the Christian Life Commission of the Southern Baptist Convention. He spoke at the annual meeting of the Mount Vernon Baptist Convention.

Speaker plus Audience plus Statement

A slightly different lead can be written merely by reversing the order of the speaker and audience, thus:

_____VERB_____

speaker   told   audience

_____   _____(that)_____

where   when   statement

Dr. Joseph Stokes Jr. told a Quaker audience in the Arch St. Meeting-house Thursday night that "no child should come unwanted" into the world.

Philadelphia Inquirer

WASHINGTON—AP—Treasury Secretary George P. Shultz told Congress today he would not be surprised if President Nixon would veto a bill requiring a mandatory across-the-board freeze on prices, rents and interests rates if Congress enacted such legislation.

A Further Variation

A slightly more involved construction requires the use of two verbs to introduce the name of the speaker, identify the audience and tell what the speaker said:

_____ VERB 1 _____
audience   heard   speaker

VERB 2 _____ _____ (that)_____
say   where when

_____
statement

> Republican district officers heard Rep. John Byrnes say here Monday that cuts in the foreign aid bill will help balance the federal budget.
> *Milwaukee Journal*

To review briefly, the first sentence of a speech story lead consists of two elements: a statement of what was said by the speaker or speakers and an attribution. The statement represents the contents of the speech. The attribution identifies the speaker and mentions the time and place of the speech; it sometimes identifies the audience.

SPACE PROBLEMS

One of the essentials of clear, communicative news writing is brevity. And in trying to be brief, the writer will sometimes run into difficulties with the speech story lead. While it may be possible, for example, to present a brief and succinct statement of what the speaker said in the first paragraph of the lead, including the speaker's full name and identity is sometimes awkward and results in long sentences. And long sentences too often are hard to read. To keep the first sentence and first paragraph short, the news writer can employ two useful devices: the *blind lead* and the *delayed identification lead*.

Blind Leads

In the blind lead the speaker is described but not named. And, the description need only give the reader a general idea of who is speaking rather than an exact identification. Here are some examples:

> A University of Oregon economist
> a denominational official
> one of the nation's leading experts on race relations
> the chairman of the House Foreign Affairs subcommittee

The blind lead may be long or short—although the shorter the better. It serves two purposes: first it helps give the story immediate credibility by establishing the speaker's qualifications; and second, it saves a few words by omitting the speaker's name. Fuller identification of the speaker appears in the second or third paragraph of the lead. For example:

> HOUSTON—AP—A nutrition expert says malnutrition threatens the unborn of American middle-class women as well as those of poor women.
> "The low-income woman who is pregnant does not eat well," said Dr. Myron Winick. "The obstetrician tells the middle-class women not to eat much."
> Winick, director of the Institute of Human Nutrition at Columbia University College of Physicians and Surgeons, said weight control during pregnancy may be dangerous because the pregnant woman is eating for two persons.

Such identification is useful as a space saver. The right kind of description also gives the story immediate credibility and overcomes the problem of beginning a story with a name that may not be known or easily recalled by the reader. Many speakers are important because of their jobs, their expertise or for some other reason of which the reading public is unaware. So, many blind leads are written solely to avoid using an unfamiliar name and to permit the writer to describe the speaker in a way that will attract the reader's attention.

Delayed Identification

Delayed identification works much the same as the blind lead, but instead of omitting the name, it uses the name but withholds complete identification or description of the speaker. Delayed identification is useful when identification might be long or cumbersome. In taking this approach, the news writer assumes that readers will recognize the name even if they are not entirely clear about who the speaker is. For example:

> OXFORD, ENGLAND—AP—Sen. George McGovern said Sunday that the United States is "closer to one-man rule than at any time in our history," with Congress, the press and the political parties in full retreat and the American people dispirited.

Identification is withheld from this opening paragraph and given at the beginning of the second paragraph. Readers ought to know who the speaker is. If they don't, if the name just sounds vaguely familiar, they will be clued in when they get to the second paragraph. The first paragraph ran to 10 lines of type, long enough that the writer thought it a good idea not to add the extra line and a half that further identification would require. The next paragraph:

> The Democratic presidential candidate said in a lecture at Oxford University that his loss to President Nixon last November had left him with a "sense of sadness and fury."

No Identification

Some speakers are so widely known that it is acceptable to use their names alone, without identification. People prominent locally or nationally may not need much in the way of identification:

President Ford
Sen. Ted Kennedy

Very few readers would have trouble recognizing these names. In Pennsylvania newspapers it might suffice to refer to Senator Hugh Scott without identifying him further. And in Chicago no one needs to be reminded who Mayor Daley is. Illinois newspapers consider it enough to say Governor Walker without further identification:

> Gov. Walker told legislators today in his first State of the State message that Illinois' future is bright if they cooperate with him in a belt tightening program of "prudent fiscal management."
> *Chicago Tribune*

Holding Back Attribution

In all the leads we have discussed so far attribution has been closely linked to the statement of what was said. Sometimes, however, it is possible to separate them, to present the statement first, unsupported, and then present the attribution separately. The link between statement and attribution is not as strong in this type of lead as it is in the statement-plus-attribution lead where the two elements are presented within a single sentence. However, the reader can reasonably be expected to make the connection as the examples that follow should demonstrate. This is not a common approach but where the news writer has trouble summarizing and condensing the statement of what was said, it may be the best way to proceed. For example:

> There's more than a glimmer of hope that by the turn of the century, Michigan's population count will have stopped climbing.
> That was the good news brought to members of Lansing's Zero Population Growth group Sunday night by Dr. Kurt Gorwitz, chief of the center for health statistics of the Michigan Department of Public Health.
> Lansing (Mich.) *State Journal*

The statement here, set off without attribution in the first paragraph, is not long. The attribution, however, is long and detailed. By separating them the news writer was able to keep both the first and second paragraphs of the lead short and readable.

Holding back all attribution is acceptable upon occasion and should not present any problems for the reader. Of course, a lead like the one just cited could be written differently—as a blind lead or delayed identification lead, perhaps—but the approach the writer used will work just as well.

OTHER CONSIDERATIONS

So far we have discussed the organization and structure of speech story leads in terms of two basic components, the statement and the attribution. And we have seen that these two components can be arranged in a number of ways depending upon whether the writer wants to emphasize what was said or one of the various elements in the attribution. There are some other considerations that ought to be mentioned before we go any further.

Who Leads

In writing speech story leads, we can write a *what lead* that emphasizes what the speaker said. Or we can write a *who lead* emphasizing who the speaker is. The who lead was discussed in Chapter 4, although in other terms. In speech stories the who lead is merely an attribution-plus-statement lead in which the name of the speaker is emphasized, that is, placed ahead of the statement. This lead is generally used when the name of the speaker is of some significance, where it isn't so much what was said as who said it that makes the story. We might call this lead by still a third name, the *Washington lead*, to help us remember the limitations on its use. This lead is used a great deal in stories originating in the nation's capital where news sources are often very important:

> President Nixon asked Congress today to permit him to grant trade concessions to the Soviet Union without linking them to the lifting of its restrictions on free emigration of Jews and other Soviet citizens.
> As part of the message accompanying a trade reform bill, Mr.

Nixon directly opposed the plan of Senator Henry M. Jackson, Democrat of Washington, which is backed by 75 other Senators and a majority of the House of Representatives.
> *New York Times*

Names are supposedly the stuff of which news is made and the who lead pays honor to this journalistic cliché. But the news writer must remember that the name must mean something to the reader. It must be more than a space filler; it must be a genuine attention-getter. If the name of the speaker or news source is important, if it is well known, if it will be recognized and need not be explained, then the who lead—the Washington lead—makes a perfectly good beginning. If the name won't command the reader's attention and by itself lend significance to the story, then write the lead another way. To exaggerate a little, unless you are reporting on a speech by the president or, perhaps, the governor or a big-city mayor, take a different approach.

Direct Quote Leads

Some years ago it was fashionable to use direct quotes in the lead of speech stories. Today it is not. Generally, the summary lead with its concise statement of what was said will tell more and tell it better than a direct quote. The summary gives a broader view of the speech. The direct quote can usually only cover one point the speaker made. However, direct quote leads are used, at least occasionally, and when they are properly used, they can be highly effective. One example of a direct quote lead:

> "They've ruined me, I'm going to retire under a cloud. But I don't mind for myself. I just don't like what they did to that boy."
> The speaker was Clarence E. Hyde, a Federal Mine inspector. "That boy" was Gordon Couch, a protégé of Mr. Hyde.
> *New York Times*

Direct quote leads are not always practical. Usually, in fact, any other kind of lead would be better because it would be more informative. The above example suggests the appropriate use of the direct quote lead. Where the writer has a colorful or emotional statement to use, the direct quote lead can be very effective. However, it is wise not to use this approach too often.

Characterizing Leads

Every lead we have discussed so far has included both a statement of what was said and an attribution. The characterizing lead describes or characterizes the speaker's message instead of presenting a summary of what he said. It comments, interprets, analyzes the effect or potential effect of the speaker's message, tells how the audience was affected or suggests the possible results of what was said.

The following leads show how this is done. Basically these leads are telling about the speech rather than quoting from it. They avoid the statement-plus-attribution structure and find other verbs to take the place of the verb *to say*.

> North Carolina Gov. James E. Holshouser Jr. used his inaugural address Friday for another strong denunciation of the North Carolina Highway Department and for a re-iteration of his campaign promises.
> "If there is one place—and one focal point—for this desire for change," said Holshouser with a wave of his arm toward the Highway Department Building which he was facing, "it is right there in the highway department."
> *Charlotte Observer*

> Presidential Communications Director Herbert G. Klein has accused congressional war critics of applying a "double standard" in denouncing administration war policy after "participating in an election where the President had a very clear mandate to proceed the way he has on Vietnam."
> *St. Louis Globe-Democrat*

When the effect or import of a speech is as interesting as the speech itself—or more interesting—this is a practical approach. If what the speaker said needs some clarification, the characterizing lead may be the best way to start your story.

No-News Leads

Every lead we have discussed so far in this chapter was a device for telling the reader something, for providing information about a speech, a press conference, a meeting of some kind. They are factual and newsy. But, beware the lead which doesn't say anything: the *no-news lead*. For example:

> Flying saucers and other un-identified flying objects were the topic Sunday night at Trinity Church parish house.

> A widely known Protestant clergyman discussed the errors of the younger generation Sunday in his sermon at St. Stephen's church.

> The state Republican chairman Monday discussed his party's program for improving the nation's moral and economic climate.

To leads like these, apocryphal but entirely possible, the average reader is sure to say: "Yup, but what did he say?" These leads don't tell what was said; they merely hint. They avoid being specific about the speaker's message. Writers who resort to identifying the topic, the title of a speech or to saying that the audience was delighted to hear the speaker's views aren't saying much.

No-news leads contain little more information than the advance story the newspaper ran a day or so before the speech. If you don't give your readers something more than they could have learned in a story published before the speech was given, then you aren't giving them much. Don't write advance leads on past events.

Another point. If you desert the verb *to say* for *to discuss*, you will not write a very sharp lead. What did the speaker say? What does the speaker want us to do about it? What does it mean to us? The reader wants to know what the speaker said, not to be tantalized by hints.

President Coolidge is said to have returned to the White House one Sunday after church to be quizzed by Mrs. Coolidge about the service. "What did the minister talk about?" she asked. "Sin," replied the President. "What did he say about it?"

Mrs. Coolidge persisted. "He was agin it," Coolidge responded with finality.

A news writer's version of the sermon ought to be more satisfying, and the lead, in particular, ought to be more informative than was Silent Cal. There are lots of ways to write a speech lead, but whatever way you choose, you must weigh your lead against the emptiness of the no-news lead. You have to be sure you are saying *something*.

Other Possibilities

News writing, at least when it deals with routine stories, is pretty much a matter of averages. There are routine ways of doing things, workable and useful ways of saying things, basic ways of organizing various kinds of news stories that will be useful most of the time. But as long as news writers are human beings and not computers, the ingenious individual will always find new ways of writing. This chapter has discussed a number of practical, useful and accepted ways of organizing speech story leads. Most speech stories have leads like those we have discussed, but there are other possibilities. The following lead takes a different approach:

> Is meaninglessness meaningful: Is the absurd serious?
> That the answer is a resounding yes and no was indicated Monday night in a nonconsensus, by a theologian, a psychoanalyst, a critic, an Off-Broadway producer and two poet-playwrights. Their topic was "The Idea of the Absurd from Kierkegaard to 1966."
> *New York Times*

There are infinite possibilities in news writing and, while the tried and trusted may generally be best, there are times when a story cries out for unusual treatment. You should not be afraid to experiment. It may not come off, but if it does—and gets by the editor and the copy desk—then you can take pardonable pride in your creativity and imagination.

LEAD AND DEVELOPMENT

The Lead as a Unit

So far we have looked closely at what goes into a speech lead. Now let's look at the lead as a whole, and examine the writing of the statement-plus-attribution type of speech lead. This type of lead begins with a brief statement about something the speaker said. Since this is considered a summary lead, our statement should be a highly condensed version, in our own words, of the general tenor of the speech as a whole, or of one of the major points made by the speaker. For example, this statement from the lead on a speech story from the *St. Louis Globe-Democrat*:

> Mayor Alfonso J. Cervantes is breaking faith with the people by seeking a third term as mayor.

To which the news writer adds a very limited attribution:

> Sheriff Raymond Percich charges that Mayor Alfonso J. Cervantes is breaking faith with the people by seeking a third term as mayor.

This is the beginning of a lead, but certainly not all of it. The lead identifies the speaker, but does not fully explain who he is, there is no reference to time or place, and the speaker's charge against the mayor is tossed out provocatively, but not fully explained. The writer offers a little more information in a second paragraph:

> Percich, candidate for the Democratic nomination for comptroller, said Sunday Cervantes is breaking his 1965 promise to seek only two terms as mayor.

The reader now is aware that the speaker is a candidate himself, not just a sheriff, that he spoke on Sunday and that the reference in the first paragraph to "breaking faith" refers to a campaign promise the mayor apparently made several years ago. We are beginning to understand what the speaker is talking about. To help us further, the writer now uses the speaker's own words in direct quotation:

> "This doesn't surprise me," Percich said. "It's just another indication that the people can't trust him (Cervantes) or believe him."

Pretty strong words. But this is a city election campaign and the sheriff is a candidate himself. But why is he so vehement about the mayor? The writer fills us in by adding another paragraph:

> Percich, a long-time Cervantes critic, is backing Comptroller John Poelker for the Democratic nomination for mayor.

The picture is now complete. We know who the speaker is, his involvement in the story, his point of view, and what he said. It took four paragraphs and a careful piling up of small bits of information to do it, but the writer has now given a complete summary of what the speaker was getting at—and why. The lead is complete and we can go on to the body of the story for additional details and possibly some other points made in the course of the speaker's talk. A similar building process is used in the following blind lead:

> The executive director of the National Urban League Wednesday angrily accused both President Nixon and Sen. George McGovern of largely ignoring campaign issues that concern blacks.
> "I really think that black people are out of style in this political campaign," Vernon E. Jordan Jr. declared at a press conference at Gary's downtown Holiday Inn.
> Jordan was in Gary to address the 27th annual dinner of the Urban League of Northeast Indiana at the St. Sava Serbian Hall in neighboring Hobart.
> *Chicago Sun-Times*

The substance of what the speaker said at the press conference is presented in summary in the first paragraph and is amplified and supported by direct quotation in the second paragraph. The attribution is built up carefully over the three paragraphs: first, the speaker's title, second, his name. The time element is included in the first paragraph; the place and circumstances of his remarks are given in the second paragraph; and the explanation of his presence in Gary is completed in the third paragraph.

The speech lead, as we can now see, does a number of things all at once:

1) It gives the reader a brief idea of what the speaker said. In the statement-plus-attribution lead, the first paragraph is largely concerned with summarizing what the speaker said, and the second and third paragraphs enlarge on that brief statement.
2) It identifies the speaker. The first paragraph of the lead may contain a complete identification, or a partial one that is completed in a later paragraph.
3) It explains the circumstances of the speaker's appearance: when, where, why. Although time and place are usually mentioned briefly in the first paragraph of the lead, the circumstances may not be explained until the third or fourth paragraph.
4) It also provides a bridge to the body of the story.

As Fig. 10.1 suggests, a direct line of thought takes us from the lead into the body of the speech story. There are several ways to accomplish this. The lead can be organized in such a way that there is a logical progression from one paragraph to the next. In a sense, the writer provides a 1–2–3 sequence and then moves on to 4 so easily that the reader makes an easy transition into the story. For example, in the Percich story, the writer has carefully built up to the speaker's rebuttal to charges by the mayor:

> Percich rejected Cervantes' charge that he is "nitpicking."
> "I've been sticking to the issues," Percich said, "His eight years is an issue. That's about as long as any city can endure."

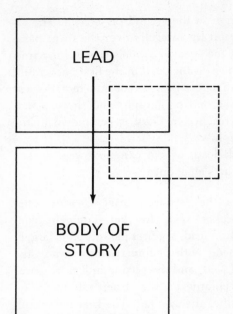

LEAD

BODY OF
STORY

Lead summarizing
sense of speech and
circumstances

Swing paragraph which
overlaps lead
and main part of
story

Body of story: an
expanded version of
lead, containing more
details of what was said

Fig. 10.1 *The speech story can be visualized this way. The arrow indicates the natural progression from the lead to the body of the story. The function of the overlapping bridge paragraph is to make the transition from lead to main part of the story easier.*

The rest of the story will be devoted to a subject now carefully introduced: the issues. The lead in the Percich story consisted of a gradual buildup of detail that moved logically into the main part of the story. There is, of course, a certain amount of linkage between paragraphs, but essentially this lead and the story it introduces presents information step by step in a 1–2–3–4 sequence.

Sometimes there is an overlap between the lead and the body of the story that serves to tie the two together. See, for example, the story in Fig. 10.2.

The story in Fig. 10.2 presents the substance of the speaker's talk in the first two paragraphs and, more specifically, in the speaker's own words in the third and fourth paragraphs. Attribution is limited to identifying the speaker in the first and second paragraphs. Now comes the bridge: a paragraph that belongs both to the lead and to the body of the story, that overlays these two distinctly separate parts.

> Cone told the spring meeting of the American Academy of Pediatricians that he agreed with authorities who called bed rest the greatest nonspecific treatment of our time and one often used needlessly.

The first part of this paragraph, the fifth in the story, is still clearing up points that are usually covered in the lead: identifying the audience Cone addressed:

> Cone told the spring meeting of the American Academy of Pediatricians . . .

The rest of the paragraph elaborates on some of the general references from the previous paragraphs of the lead and begins to get specific:

> . . . (that) he agreed with authorities who called bed rest the greatest nonspecific treatment of our time and one often used needlessly.

At this point the writer has left the lead and is safely into the body of the story. Because this paragraph includes both lead and body elements it helps the reader make a smooth transition from one part of the story to the other; it bridges any gap that might have existed between the two parts.

Whether you depend on the forward impetus of the story or on a carefully contrived bridge, you must give your reader an easy transition from the lead to the body of the story. You don't want to lose your reader before you have said all you have to say.

BOSTON (AP)—Many pediatricians routinely prescribe traditional remedies such as excessive bed rest, vitamin supplements and tonsillectomies even though their effectiveness is in question, a Harvard professor said.

Dr. Thomas E. Cone Jr., clinical professor of pediatrics at Harvard Medical School, says doctors are so used to these techniques that they seldom question whether they are dictated by reason or ritual.

LEAD

"IF WE do, we probably comfort ourselves by reflecting that they must be of some value or they would not be so widely practiced or so long-lived," he said.

"A traditional custom may be very valuable, but it's a good idea to examine ideas critically."

Cone told the spring meeting of the American Academy of Pediatrics that he agreed with authorities who called bed rest the greatest nonspecific treatment of our time and one often used needlessly.

BRIDGE

DOCTORS PRESCRIBE bed rest for colds, sore throats, diarrhea and headaches even though there is no evidence that the time in bed helps, he said.

"A restless child exerts himself more when in bed than he would do if allowed up in his room," Cone said. The confinement bores the child and makes it more difficult for him to sleep at night and less easy for him to play, he added.

BODY OF THE STORY

"A child shouldn't be allowed to exert himself; but say after a fever has peaked, he should be allowed out of bed for activity," Cone said.

A HEALTHY child eating a variety of foods does not need vitamin supplements, but commercial pressures and advertising have created a public demand for vitamins that in turn pressures the physician, he said.

"Vitamins have become symbols of health and are ingested in quantities far beyond possible needs," but doctors take part in the ritual simply because it does no apparent harm and the parents want it, the educator said.

Cone said parental pressure also was a reason for the great number of tonsillectomies performed each year, adding that those committed to the procedure tend to exaggerate its benefits and minimize its risks.

"THERE EXISTS a general feeling among critical observers that the majority of these operations may be unnecessary or actually harmful," Cone said.

Many children get inflamed tonsils at an early age, and this is not a serious problem in most cases, he said, adding that doctors are removing an organ whose function is almost unknown and some studies indicate the tonsil may play a big part in the body's defense system against disease.

Fig. 10.2 *A well-organized speech story with a bridge linking the lead and the body of the story.*

CHAPTER ELEVEN

The Speech Story: Development

ONE WAY to let newspaper readers know what was said at a speech, a meeting, a public hearing or a trial is to print a verbatim text. From this the readers, if they have the time and patience, can pick out the points that interest them and can make their own decision as to what in the text was significant.

This is not done very often in the newspaper world. In the first place, most newspapers do not have the space to print long transcripts. And, in the second place, it is the newspaper's job to weigh, evaluate and select what is interesting and significant in the day's news and to present it to us in a concise and readable form. The success of *Time* magazine ought to convince any skeptic that the reading public appreciates predigested news.

So, reporters who cover speeches or meetings must take notes, tape the speech or verify a prepared text and then prepare a short version for their readers. Some newspapers will, as a matter of record, publish the text of a significant speech—and occasionally verbatim testimony from a trial or public hearing—but they also invariably print a story to fill us in as quickly and effortlessly as possible.

Figures 11.1 and 11.2 show how the *St. Louis Globe-Democrat* reported two inaugural addresses. Reporters covered both speeches and wrote news stories in which they attempted to provide background and explanation that would put the speeches in their proper context. On an inside page the *Globe-Democrat* printed the verbatim texts of the addresses as a matter of record. Some readers no doubt wanted to read the text. Most were probably satisfied with the reporter's considerably abbreviated version.

The *New York Times*, which prides itself on being a newspaper of record, publishes many verbatim texts. For example, the *Times* always publishes the text of the president's annual economic

Fig. 11.1 *The inaugural speeches of the governors of Illinois and Missouri were given full dress treatment by the* St. Louis Globe-Democrat. *The newspaper printed both the full text and news stories.*

Interlude

Shovel under cloudy skies Tuesday, and be ready for a chance of more snow Wednesday. High Tuesday from 20 to 25, low Tuesday night from 10 to 15.
Additional Weather 13A

St. Louis Globe-Democrat

120 Years of Public Service / Founded July 1, 1852

Vol. 121—No. 166

Tuesday, January 9, 1973—3 Sections—36 Pages

c

10¢

Ex-Judge Cady strikes out again

An Editorial, Page 12A

Police Speculate Slain Gunman Was Lone Sniper

By AUSTIN WILSON
Associated Press Writer

NEW ORLEANS — Heavily armed police rushed a rooftop hotel bunker Monday in a search for snipers who killed six persons and wounded 17 others, but found no trace of gunmen.

A room-by-room search of the hotel was begun Monday night, but thfere was no immediate sign of snipers. Police admitted there was a chance one or two snipers had escaped—or even a remote chance there was only one gunman.

One sniper was killed Sunday night by police gunfire from a helicopter which swooped over the roof of the hotel. At that time, police thought there were three snipers.

POLICE SUPERINTENDENT Clarence Giarrusso said Monday night he still believed there were at least two snipers originally, but "if they don't turn up anyone and there was another sniper, then he got away."

"If we don't find anyone, then we're going to admit something went wrong, possibly with us, and return to normalcy,'g' Giarrusso said at a news conference.

"There's a amut of possibilities ranging from police negligence to a superbrain sniper," said Giarrusso.

He said there was a possibility there was only one sniper to start with, "but I don't think so."

THE SUPERINTENDENT said his men, about 200 of them, would search the hotel thoroughly, looking in air-conditioning vents, flase ceilings and anywhere else a man could be hiding.

A gunman was killed by police marksmen firing from a military helicopter Sunday night as he bolted from a concrete block enclosure atop the hotel and ran a zigzag pattern across the roof.

His body lay on the roof all night and all day Monday. Police technicians did not

Continued on Page 5A

Police search the roof of New Orleans hotel for sniper.—A.P. Wirephoto

Christopher Bond takes oath of office with his wife at his side while the outgoing governor, Warren Hearnes, watches, at left. Additional pictures, Page 14A.
—Globe-Democrat photo by Jack Fahland

Bond outlines '4 battles to win'

By JACK FLACH
Globe-Democrat Political Editor

JEFFERSON CITY — Gov. Christopher Bond plans "four battles, all of which must be won," aimed at repairing broken down machinery in state government, he said in his inaugural address here Monday.

Republican Bond's first speech was received warmly but cautiously by Democratic legislature leaders.

"Our challenge, put simply, is to make government work," Bond told a shivering crowd his four points:

— Build a government that merits the trust and earns the confidence of those it serves.

— Every Missourian must share a portion of the responsibility and help, not just those who are employed by state government.

— Government can only work if it has compassion for the problems of the people. "The agenda of human needs is long."

— A government for the people that respects each person's individual dignity. Efficiency is welcome, effectiveness is necessary but the true measure will be responsiveness, he declared.

Complete text . . . 10A

Bond's 15-minute address was void of any specifics, as is customary for inaugual talks. These will come when he presents his program to the legislature in upcoming weeks.

SEN. WILLIAM CASON (Dem.), Clinton, president pro tem of the Senate, said he "appreciates Bond's philosophies about people participating in government.

"I'm looking forward to his specific proposals."

Democratic majority floor leader Lawrence Lee of St. Louis called it a "good speech as far as inaugural talks go."

Democratic House Speaker Richard Rabbitt of St. Louis said "it was a good speech with some good thoughts.

"A lot of the governor's ideas coincide with the Democratic leadership," he delared, "and I think he's given every indication he wants to work with us. Time will tell if this

Continued on Page 5A

Walker to take case to people

By MARION R. LYNES
Chief of The Globe-Democrat
Springfield, Ill. Bureau

SPRINGFIELD, ILL. — Illinois faces a "crisis of lost faith in our own government," Walking Dan Walker, Democrat maverick, declared here after taking the oath of office as the state's 36th governor.

He delivered his inaugural address Monday to a crowd of about 5,000 shivering persons on the east lawn of the State Capitol. A chilling north wind accentuated the 20-degree temperatures.

WALKER MADE NO specific reference to major governmental problems, except loss of public confidence. The tone of his speech was that he was going to take his case to the people rather than to the legislature, where he faces a Republican majority in both houses.

In his address he dwelt on his experiences during his 1,200-mile trek across the state that led to his election. He stressed that he wanted to "let the voice of the people be heard again" rather than "the bureaucrats or those with wealth or power."

Response of the audience was more respectful than enthusiastic. Walker was interrupted by brief applause five times, with the greatest reaction coming when he declared the "free rides" were over for those in government who put themselves ahead of the welfare of the taxpayer.

The ceremony took about 30 minutes. Illinois Supreme Court Justice Walter V. Schaefer administered the oath to Walker, who then delivered the inaugural address.

Complete text . . . 10A

Neil F. Hartigan, Chicago Democrat, was sworn into office as lieutenant governor by Illinois Supreme Court Chief Justice Robert C. Underwood. Hartigan spoke briefly.

Michael J. Howlett, Democrat, who has been state auditor for three terms, was then sworn in as secretary of state by Cook County Circuit Judge Nathan M. Cohen. Howlett also spoke briefly.

BESIDES THE audience of friends and

Continued on Page 5A

Illinois' incoming governor, Daniel Walker, and his wife, Roberta, greet friends before inaugural.
—A.P. Wirephoto

Guard slain during apparent effort to hold up Bell truck

A 23-year-old private security guard was fatally wounded in a gun battle with a man who police said apparently tried to hold up a Southwestern Bell Telephone Co. collection truck.

Edward John Byrne II, a former Ferguson policeman and a security guard for the Sentry Security Agency, Inc., was pronounced dead Monday of a gunshot wound of the side about 1:30 p.m. at Homer G. Phillips Hospital.

A MAN MATCHING the description of Byrne's assailant later was found wounded and lying face down in the snow 50 feet from the hospital's emergency entrance, police said. The man, identified as Dennis Kirksey, 21, of the 1200 block of Walton avenue, was arrested and charged in a warrant with murder in the case.

Kirksey, former convict, had been shot twice in the chest. He was admitted to surgery at the hospital and was listed in critical condition.

Kirksey is a suspect in the robbery of a telephone company collection truck last September. The driver robbed of $2,450 in that incident, Ed Payne, 21, also was the driver involved in Monday's slaying, according to a telephone company spokesman.

PAYNE TOLD POLICE he drove to a pool hall in the 5000 block of Dr. Martin Luther King drive about 1 p.m., to make a collection from a pay telephone there. Byrne, assigned routinely to follow in his private car and guard the collection truck, remained parked outside while Payne went inside to make the collection, police said.

"I was starting to leave when I heard the shots," Payne said. The driver then ran outside and saw Byrne, seated in the front seat of his (Byrne's) car, firing his pistol over his shoulder out a passenger side window.

Payne said he saw a man fleeing down an alley nearby, and later said it was the "same man" who had robbed him last September, according to police.

Homicide Division Detective Sgt. James King and Detective Joseph Priest passed the area moments later and went to Byrne's aid.

"I'M SHOT," Byrne muttered and collapsed.

The security guard's death was the latest in a series of slayings in St. Louis, incuding the robbery-shootings of two city merchants and the killings of two St. Louis police officers.

Police followed a trail of blood from the alley to the 1500 block of Clara avenue, officers said, but the trail ended and police believed the man was picked up in a car.

Kirksey, found later near the hospital, was believed to have been dropped there by whoever picked him up on Clara avenue, police said.

Byrne, who had received his private watchman's license only last month, had worked previously for an insurance firm and as a Ferguson policeman.

"HE WAS VERY eager," a former fellow officer said of Byrne. "He'd go in hell bent for leather. He always did more than was necessary."

A graduate of Northwest High School and a former Marine, Byrne lived with his wife and child at 1222 Marquis ct., Moline Acres.

"He was very conscientious," the Ferguson officer said.

Kirksey, who served less than a year of a two-year sentence for robbery in 1971, was free on $10,000 bond in connection with the robbery of Payne last September, records show.

Payne said he testified against Kirksey during a preliminary hearing on the charge and is scheduled to testify when the case goes to court in February.

HOWEVER, PAYNE SAID he has no reason to believe the two incidents are connected.

Police said they could find no witnesses to the actual shooting and could only presume Byrne's shooting followed a robbery attempt.

"We don't know yet if it was a robbery or what," said Lt. Norman Jacobsmeyer, homicide commander.

However, police were seeking the occupants of, the car believed to have taken Kirksey to the hospital.

Edward John Byrne II

Ed Payne and Dennis Kirksey
Additional photos . . 5A

What's inside

★ ★

Housing still in city's lap
The federal government says it will not take over operation of the city's nine conventional housing projects. Page 3A

Farming the modern way
The modern farmer not only knows farming techniques, but studies the grain market like a stockbroker studies Wall Street. Page 2A

South Vietnam ready'
Secretary of Defense Melvin Laird says South Vietnam is ready to take over the war if peace talks fail. Page 11A

Features . . .

Good morning news

Boys Town can't lose at auction

The annual Kaleidoscope Auction for the benefit of Boys Town of Missouri will be sponsored by Central Hardware Co., beginning at 10 a.m. March 25 at the Three Flags Restaurant in St. Charles.

Central Hardware president Stanley M. Cohen said the goal is to raise funds to continue operating the Boys Town of Missouri Center, a halfway house, in St. Louis. Last year's auction enabled that center to open.

Mrs. F. Joseph Pfeffer, Kaleidoscope Auction chairman, called Central Hardware sponsorship "our greatest source of encouragement to date."

Cohen said several luxury items have already been donated: A 1973 Cadillac given by Boys Town founder Bill James, a 1972 Volkswagen given by Gary Vincel and James Holton, an antique fire engine, vacation trips and antiques.

Persons wishing to make contributions should call the Boys Town state office here, 644-6585, to arrange for pickups. More than 4,000 items are expected to be donated, Cohen said.

New name for program that has not yet begun

WASHINGTON (UPI). — Operation Egress Recap, the Pentagon's code name for the return and rehabilitation of American prisoners of war in Indochina, was formally changed Monday to "Operation Homecoming."

"I have made this change because I feel 'homecoming' is more appropriate," said Secretary of Defense Melvin R. Laird in a message to the military services ordering the change in name.

Snow takes a powder; cold's more lasting

Monday's snow was a pretty, somewhat perilous, almost refreshing phenomenon that began to fade away by midday. Monday's cold is going to stick around a lot longer.

The U.S. Weather Service says the area can expect temperatures no higher than 25 for most of the week, with 30 degree readings finally creeping into the picture Friday.

The snow—an inch covered the ground by the time most St. Louisans arose Monday—basically was a one-day occurrence, although there is a "slight chance" of some snow again Wednesday.

St. Louis apparently was lucky as up to six inches of snow fell in western and southern parts of the state early Monday morning.

The difference here, meteorologists say, occurred in the upper atmosphere over St. Louis where dry air evaporated much of the snow before it hit the ground.

Only minor collisions and a few cases of vehicles sliding off roads were reported to area police Monday. Highway and street crews worked most of the night to have roads clear for early morning traffic.

A warning was issued that heavy floating ice was in the Missouri River from Decatur, Neb., to St. Charles. And all pools in the Mississippi River were covered with floating ice.

The sun did make an appearance several times in St. Louis Monday, pushing the temperature as high as 28 degrees at 1:30 p.m.

Temperatures will be slightly lower Tuesday. Skies will be partly cloudy with winds out of the north 6 to 12 mph.

ST. LOUIS Globe DEMOCRAT **Special**

10A Tues., Jan. 9, 1973

'Come work with us for Missouri'

Text of Christopher Bond's inaugural address as governor of Missouri

It is customary in an inaugural address to talk of a mandate which the voters have extended to those newly entrusted with power.

Today's ceremony is all the more humbling because I know that the people of Missouri in this election did not give an explicit mandate for explicit policies. They said instead: "We trust you." They have put that trust in this administration and in the people who serve it; they have put that trust in all of us here as elected officials.

That trust shall be our conscience as we seek to build the faith of Missouri in its public servants.

THAT TRUST shall be our inspiration as we develop a government to serve people, rather than stifle them.

That trust will be our energy as we seek to meet the long agenda of human needs.

That trust will be our spirit as we seek to instill pride in our state and in ourselves.

The burdens I feel this moment are not a result of the problems of Missouri state government being so unique — but because they are so regrettably similar to those at all levels of government and in all other state capitals throughout the land.

The question is whether this government can meet these problems, whether it can respond to the expectations of our founding fathers, the demands of the present, and the aspirations of future generations.

THE GOVERNMENT'S machinery is in need of repair; the methods of the past are no longer adequate for the complexities of the present; the vision must be of the future.

Our challenge, put simply, is to make government work. To do so, in my view, we must fight four battles; and we must win them all.

First, a government of the people can work only if blessed with their faith. Surely, enough has been said about people's growing cynicism and their lack of confidence in government. We acknowledge it exists.

The first battle, then, must be to build a government that merits the trust and earns the confidence of those it serves.

THE CORNERSTONE of such a government must be integrity. We heed the precept that "nothing is politically right that is morally wrong."

We shall strive to be open and candid with ourselves and with the people of Missouri. The people's confidence depends upon an understanding of the policies and actions of government. It is the duty of those in office to be frank and thorough in their discussion of the objectives and programs they pursue.

"We shall welcome constructive criticism and hope to learn from it.

"We shall seek honest and genuine solutions to the problems we confront, and not just patchwork compromises contrived to avoid offending someone.

"AND I AM confident that my words echo the sentiments of the legislature, when I pledge to them and to you a spirit of bipartisanship from the governor's chair for the next four years. Neither party has a monopoly on virtue or wisdom; and neither party has the right to act as if it does.

"Second, a government by the people can succeed only if its citizens have the pride to support its work and to shoulder its burdens.

"No governor can succeed, no administration can succeed, no government can succeed without your help.

"Come work with us for Missouri.

"THAT IS NOT a political slogan. It is a plea. Government service involves a sacrifice for those who serve, but like any other endeavor, government is only as good as the individuals in it. Whether this administration achieves its goals will depend upon those who serve the administration.

"So we strive to find the most qualified people to serve this government. Advancement in this administration will be based upon proven excellence alone. The rewards for service in this administration must be in inner satisfaction alone.

"Our plea is not, however, just to those who are employed by government; it is to every Missourian to share a portion of the responsibility which is ours collectively.

"From the early days when hearty pioneers first settled this land, Missourians have been willing to help each other. Through civic organizations and individual voluntary action, Missourians have helped their less fortunate neighbors.

THE PROGRESS of our state in the years to come will depend not just upon government programs, but also upon continuing and expanding the role of neighborly service. Leadership to succeed must also promote pride in such service.

"Third, a government for the people can work only if it has compassion for their problems.

"The agenda of individual human needs is long, but it must be the agenda for all of us.

"When some of our children are not able to reach their full potential to work, to earn and to contribute because they have not received the best possible education, then we all share in their loss.

"WHEN AREAS in the inner city and in the rural areas decline and stagnate because of a lack of productive jobs, then all of us suffer.

"When there is waste and destruction of our environment, polluted streams and noxious air, then not only are we the losers, but our future generations are as well.

"When the threat of crime and fear for personal safety inhibit some of us, then the freedom of all suffers.

"When hard drugs claim the bodies and minds of some of us, then all of us are the losers.

"TO MEET these challenges is not merely our goal; it is our obligation.

"Finally, a government of, by and for the people can work only if it respects each person's individual dignity.

"Modern government is too often a failure because it cannot see the trees for the forest. Its economists talk percentage points unemployed instead of human beings. Its tax office computers record digits instead of human beings. Its bureaucrats treat categories instead of human beings. Its politicians see voting blocks instead of human beings.

"EFFICIENCY is welcome; effectiveness is necessary to provide the tools to make government work. But efficiency is not the hallmark of a great democratic government; the true measure is responsiveness.

"Each human being is unique. And each human being's problems are unique. We have to establish broad programs on a statewide basis, but they can never be successful unless we listen first to the voices of the individuals who are to be served. No government can possibly satisfy every citizen within its boundaries, nor would it be desirable for a government to accede to every wish. But at least it should listen.

Gov. and Mrs. Christopher Bond during inaugural festivities.
—Globe-Democrat Photo

"Today, we can begin the long and difficult job of making state government in Missouri the finest and most respected state government in America. From many of you, we need your time; from all of you, we need your ideas. From many of you, we need your energy; from all of you, we need your prayers. With your support, we can have a government that is known by integrity, respect, compassion and pride.

"Those are the qualities of Missouri that will serve us now — as they served Missouri's first citizen, a humble man from Independence, 28 years ago when he assumed the far more awesome burdens of the presidency with words that match my sentiments today: 'I ask only to be a good and faithful servant of my Lord and my people.' "

Walker to attack 'crisis of faith'

Text of Dan Walker's inaugural address as governor of Illinois

Three hundred years ago, Louis Joliet and Father Marquette embarked on their "voyage of discovery" through the land that is now Illinois.

Traveling down the Mississippi River, drifting past what is now Galena, Rock Island and Quincy, they saw a land sparse in people but rich in promise.

IT TOOK vision and courage for the first settlers of Illinois to believe in that promise. James Monroe, writing to Thomas Jefferson a century after that first voyage of discovery, said of our Illinois ancestors that their land will "never contain a sufficient number of inhabitants to entitle them to membership in the confederacy."

Two centuries and 11 million citizens later, we can smile at the fallibility of this forecast. But we can also understand it. It is enormously difficult to envision how different the future can be.

And yet, it is just that sort of vision which has distinguished the people of Illinois. Over the years they have consistently chosen the harder but more rewarding path; they have always looked at a crisis not for the sufferings it threatens but for the opportunity it provides.

—When Chicago was ravaged by fire a century ago, the people of Illinois could have rebuilt the city as it was. Instead, they took a Chicago of wood and cobblestones and built a new city of stone and steel and the soaring architecture of Louis Sullivan and Frank Lloyd Wright.

—WHEN POVERTY stalked our neighborhoods and people seemed helpless, it would have been easy for leaders to hide behind a wall of indifference. Instead, there was Jane Addams, helping others find their voices, to speak for their own needs. And there was John Peter Altgeld, exercising courageous leadership in his fight against the special interest and for the working people of Illinois.

We now have another crisis; the crisis of lost faith in our own government. And as in the past, this crisis provides opportunity.

Two years ago, when I embarked on my own "voyage of discovery" through Illinois, I learned that this state is not just farms, suburbs and Chicago. It is our other great cities such as Rockford, Rock Island, Decatur, Peoria, East St. Louis and Springfield. It is our smaller communities like Blue Mound, Nauvoo, Durand, Du Quoin and Table Grove. I love the names and the places that are rich in history, in heritage, in the qualities of individualism and hard work that honest and good people embody.

And during that voyage I listened and spoke to thousands of you throughout this state. I spoke to those of you in small communities, on farms and in great cities. I spoke to those of you who work — with your hands and with your minds — in overalls, blue collars, hard hats, coats and ties — and to some of you who did not work at all because there was no work.

FOR ALL of your differences, what you had to say about government was disturbingly similar. You simply did not believe government was worth your trust.

This was no partisan view. It was shared by Democrats and Republicans about Democrats and Republicans. It was aimed at no one administration or official. It was instead a pervasive cynicism.

The people of Illinois — like the people across much of America — simply do not believe that our institutions, including government, can do what they say they will do; they do not believe government understands how they live; what they need; what they want for their families.

Government, they said to me over and over, knows how to tax money but not how too spend it wisely. They told me how discontented they were with the grand and elaborate social programs costing millions of dollars but not solving the problems facing people. As one man said to me, "Dan, a dollar's worth of spending can't beat nickel's worth of understanding."

THIS DISCONTENT, this cynicism, reaches from Brookport to Galena, from East St. Louis to Zion, from Warsaw to Wateska, from Cairo to Chicago. It poses, I believe, the most serious dilemma we face. If our citizens continue to lose their sense of faith, it can strike at the heart of democracy; for if we do longer believe hat the people we choose can govern us, we are really saying that we do longer believe that the own capacity for self-government.

I reject this doctrine of doom completely. I believe that here in Illinois and around the nation, the central belief of the founding fathers is sound; the people are the best judge of what they want and need.

And I believe that much of our own loss of faith has happened because too many in government do not believe in this American credo; they believe that only experts, politicians, bureaucrats or those with wealth or power can tell people what to do.

I do not share the belief.

Let government step back, let people step forward.

MY DEEPEST resolve as governor of Illinois will be to sweep the arrogance of bureaucracy from the halls of power, to let the voice of people be heard once again.

And to hear that voice, I will, in the months and years ahead, return to the towns and farms and cities of Illinois. I will hold accountability sessions on a regular basis so that the people whose government this is can tell me what we have done and have not done.

These sessions will not be held behind closed doors or only for those with special power and office. They will be open to every citizen who wishes to attend.

Illinois Supreme Court justice gives oath of office to Daniel Walker.

I want your knowledge and wisdom. I want to know about the mistakes I have made — for we will certainly have our share. I want to know what we have done that's working — so that we can do more of what's right and less of what's wrong. I want to try to be your voice in the councils of decisions.

OTHER administrations before mine have found solutions to difficult problems facing the people of Illinois. I do not pretend that I am the first to try to make government more responsive.

But to do this, government must learn to listen more. It must find better ways to deal with the problems closest to people. These are the ones which too frequently get buried under the business of government: The road that needs repair; the nursing home that is not caring for our parents and grandparents; the neighborhood that needs more policemen; the factory that is unsafe.

And I want to carry with me your fight in the next four years; the fight for a government that exists to serve the people, rather than cater to the special interest; the fight to find ways to save, rather than spend your tax dollars.

To those who have grown rich on the public dollar, to those who have won secret grants and contracts, to those in government who put themselves first and the taxpayers second — to you I bring my first message from the people of Illinois: The free ride is over. And in the weeks ahead I shall be using the government's power of executive order to make this abundantly clear.

TO THOSE who are in mental hospitals; to those who fear the streets of their own neighborhoods; to those with inadequate housing or schools; to you I offer not the certainty of success, but the promise of concern, the hard work of trying to make government work better for people.

To every one of you, I make this pledge: This government is yours. You created it. You pay for it. And it is time you began getting your money's worth.

You have given me the greatest gift possible — your trust and confidence.

I intend to spend the next four years fulfilling that trust.

report to Congress. But, at the same time, it always publishes a detailed story about the president's report: what he said, what the various points meant, the reaction of members of Congress, the impact of the speech on various segments of the economy.

The job of reporters/newswriters, then, is to edit the speech, to select the interesting and important parts, to arrange or structure a story so that it is clear and coherent, and above all, to reduce a great many words to a very few. They must select what ought to be included in the news story and eliminate what need not be included. To do this they must, first of all, understand what was said. They must then be able to summarize lengthy passages and to paraphrase the speaker's words, that is use their own words to convey the speaker's message. And, they must include, where appropriate, some of the speaker's words in direct and indirect quotation.

The job of boiling down a long speech, of condensing a whole day's testimony at a trial or summarizing the often confusing give-and-take of a city council meeting is not an easy one.

Roger Tatarian, former vice president and editor of United Press International, had this to say about reporting in general and the speech story in particular:

> Far more is involved than getting the exact number of dead or quoting the man's exact words. It also involves tone, emphasis, nuance, juxtaposition and similar difficult-to-define factors that very distinctly affect the credibility of the press. If a journalist is not sensitive to these he can produce a story that may be technically correct in specific detail, but a bad story nevertheless.

> The longer the speech and the more controversial the subject, the greater the dangers inherent in trying to condense to a few paragraphs or even to a few hundred words.

Fig. 11.2 *Full texts of inaugural speeches took an entire page in the* St. Louis Globe-Democrat.

Improved justice in Arizona called responsibility of public

NOGALES — An improved quality of justice in Arizona is the responsibility of the people of Arizona, a retired associate justice of the U.S. Supreme Court told Town Hall participants here yesterday.

Speaking at the Rio Rico Inn, the Hon. Tom C. Clark said one of the main problems besetting the justice system is that the public does not take an interest.

"They do not want to get involved," he said. "They want to stay away from the courthouse."

Clark complimented the sponsor of Town Hall — The Arizona Academy — for selecting "The Adequacy of Arizona's Court System" as the discussion topic, but asked why it waited until the 22nd semi-annual meeting to wrestle with the subject.

Clark attacked the traditional election of judges. He called for the establishment of an "Arizona plan, a merit plan" for the selection of judges.

"It costs money for a judge to run for election," he said. "It cost one judge I know $500,000 for a campaign.

"Where does he get the money? From lawyer friends mostly. I tell you it's dangerous to have that subconscious knocking in the back of a judge's head when one of his financial supporters is trying a case before him.

"We must abolish this system of electing judges."

Clark asked the delegates to consider structural changes in the court system that would include bringing justice of the peace courts and municipal courts under the control and supervision of state rules of order and procedure.

"The structure of Arizona's courts is good," he said, "except for this base, this foundation."

He also suggested that Arizona Town Hall panelists look into the possibility of establishing concilliation courts to handle the large amount of domestic relations cases clogging Superior Court calendars.

Another area needing examination, he said, is to consider the use of an omnibus hearing prior to criminal trials. In this hearing, attorneys will make all their pretrial motions.

"I guarantee that by use of this type of hearing you'll get from 90 to 95 per cent guilty pleas without having to plea bargain," he said.

Clark, 74, was born in Dallas, Tex., and received his law degree from the University of Texas in 1921. In 1922, he was admitted to the Texas Bar Association and the Texas Supreme Court.

He served as the civil district attorney for Dallas County from 1922 to 1927. He was appointed assistant attorney general in charge of the anti-trust division of the Department of Justice in 1943 and held that post until he became U.S. Attorney General in 1945.

He served as Associate Justice of the U.S. Supreme Court from 1949 to 1967.

Arizona Republic

Fig. 11.3 *A well-organized speech story with effective use of summary statements and direct and indirect quotations.*

DEVELOPING THE SINGLE-SPEAKER STORY

Figure 11.3 is an example of the end product of such a process of selection, elimination, summarizing and paraphrasing. The speaker's text may have been 10 or 12 typewritten pages long, but the published story runs to just over 400 words, including three paragraphs of biographical background.

The story consists of a lead, the body of the story and a concluding section of background information.

The Body of the Story

The subject of the speech is reported in the body of the story in a series of blocks or units, each

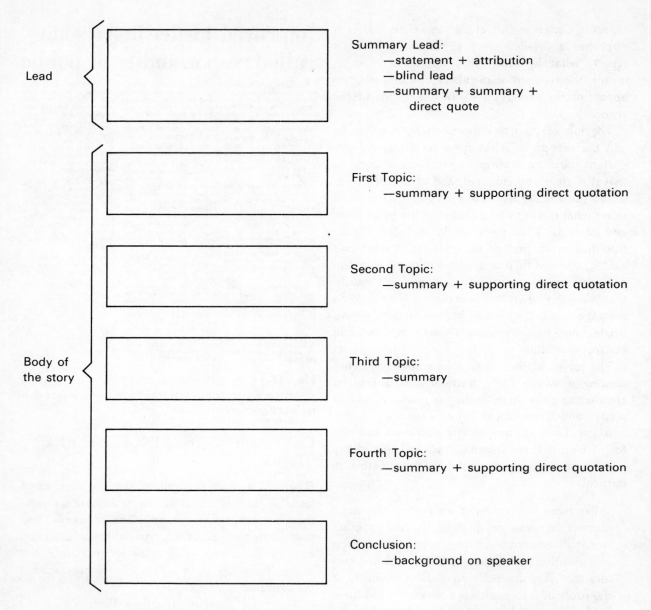

Lead

Summary Lead:
   —statement + attribution
   —blind lead
   —summary + summary +
       direct quote

Body of the story

First Topic:
   —summary + supporting direct quotation

Second Topic:
   —summary + supporting direct quotation

Third Topic:
   —summary

Fourth Topic:
   —summary + supporting direct quotation

Conclusion:
   —background on speaker

Fig. 11.4 *A diagrammatic outline of the Tom Clark speech which shows the organization and structure of the story and calls attention to the use of summary statements and direct and indirect quotation.*

covering a separate topic. In the Clark speech, five topics were covered:

1) The need for an improved quality of justice in the state;

2) The need for a better system for electing judges;

3) The need for structural changes in the court system of the state;

4) A suggestion for a new kind of court, a conciliation court;

5) A suggestion for a new kind of pretrial hearing, an omnibus hearing.

Each block or unit begins with a summary statement and all but one of these summaries are followed by a direct quote which enlarges upon and supports the summary (Fig. 11.4). Here, for example, is the first block:

> Speaking at the Rio Rico Inn, the Hon. Tom C. Clark said one of the main problems besetting the justice system is that the public does not take an interest.
> "They do not want to get involved," he said. "They want to stay away from the courthouse."

This organization is similar to that used to structure the lead of the speech story, as we saw in Chapter 10. And, just like the lead, the topic blocks in the body of the story are built on the solid foundation of a summary statement.

The length of each block will depend on the importance of the topic. As you can see in the Clark story, the blocks vary somewhat in length. The second topic block (the election of judges) takes up four paragraphs: a summary statement followed by three paragraphs of direct quotation. The third block (structural changes in the courts) consists of a summary statement and a single direct quote. The shortest block consists of a single summary statement:

> He also suggested that Arizona Town Hall panelists look into the possibility of establishing conciliation courts to handle the large amount of domestic relations cases clogging Superior Court calendars.

Here is another example, from a story in the *Houston Post* reporting a speech by Former Atty. Gen. Ramsey Clark:

> Touching briefly on foreign policy, Clark suggested that the U.S. aid countries that recognize and extend governmental rights to all their people.

> "The U.S. ambassador to South Africa celebrates independence day in a country where 85 per cent of its people are treated as second class citizens," he said, "and his office is only miles away from a prison camp used to hold political prisoners."

Remember, each topic block starts with a summary statement in the news writer's words and is followed by direct quotation that explains, elaborates on and supports the summary. Of course, the writer may also use indirect quotes to support the summary statement, but direct quotes are generally most effective, since they are in the speaker's own words.

Selecting and Eliminating

As important as knowing how to write a speech story is knowing what to write about. In other words, out of the mass of material at hand, the news writer has to decide which ideas to include in a story and has to eliminate all the rest. There is always much more material available than can be included in a news story. The text of a 30-minute speech is a formidable document. Compare, for example, the fairly brief statement by President Nixon in Fig. 11.5 with the Associated Press story in Fig. 11.6. Only five of the nine paragraphs in the AP story report what the President said. The rest is background and interpretation. The President said, according to the AP, that:

1) He will send his aides to testify publicly as demanded by Senate investigators;

2) He launched a new presidential inquiry into the matter last month;

3) He met Sunday with Atty. Gen. Richard G. Kleindienst and Asst. Atty. Gen. Henry Petersen;

4) "I can report today that there have been major developments in the case . . . real progress has been made in finding the truth."

5) He has told investigators that no officials are exempt from prosecution.

I have two announcements to make. Because of their technical nature, I shall read both of the announcements to the members of the press corps.

The first announcement relates to the appearance of White House people before the Senate Select Committee, better known as the Ervin Committee.

For several weeks, Senator Ervin and Senator Baker and their counsel have been in contact with White House representatives John Ehrlichman and Leonard Garment. They have been talking about ground rules which would preserve the separation of powers without suppressing the fact.

I believe now an agreement has been reached which is satisfactory to both sides. The committee ground rules as adopted totally preserve the doctrine of separation of powers. They provide that the appearance by a witness may, in the first instance, be in executive session, if appropriate.

Expressly Reserved

Second, executive privilege is expressly reserved and may be asserted during the course of the questioning as to any questions.

Now, much has been made of the issue as to whether the proceedings could be televised. To me, this has never been a central issue, especially if the separation of powers problem is otherwise solved, as I now think it is.

All members of the White House staff will appear voluntarily when requested by the committee. They will testify under oath and they will answer fully all proper questions.

I should point out that this arrangement is one that covers this hearing only in which wrongdoing has been charged. This kind of arrangement, of course, would not apply to other hearings. Each of them will be considered on its merits

My second announcement concerns the Watergate case directly.

On March 21, as a result of serious charges which came to my attention, some of which were publicly reported, I began intensive new inquiries into this whole matter.

Last Sunday afternoon, the Attorney General, Assistant Attorney General Petersen and I met at length in the E.O.B. [Executive Office Building] to review the facts which had come to me in my investigation and also to review the progress of the Department of Justice Investigation.

Major Developments

I can report today that there have been major developments in the case concerning which it would be improper to be more specific now, except to say that real progress has been made in finding the truth.

If any person in the executive branch or in the Government is indicted by the grand jury, my policy will be to immediately suspend him. If he is convicted, he will, of course, be automatically discharged.

I have expressed to the appropriate authorities my view that no individual holding, in the past or at present, a position of major importance in the Administration should be given immunity from prosecution.

The judicial process is moving ahead as it should; and I shall aid it in all appropriate ways and have so informed the appropriate authorities.

As I have said before and I have said throughout this entire matter, all Government employes and especially White House staff employes are expected fully to cooperate in this matter. I condemn any attempts to cover up in this case, no matter who is involved.

New York Times

Reporting what the President of the United States says in a formal statement of national import is, of course, a different level of reporting than covering a bush-league speaker at a luncheon club meeting. But in treating the content of the speaker's address, the news writer goes through the same steps: assimilating and understanding the meaning of what was said, selecting the points to include in the news story and deciding how much can be eliminated.

Something is certainly lost in this process: some of the speaker's ideas, many details, nuances and shades of meaning and the color or vigor of the speaker's words in their original sequence. However, something is also gained: a concise news story, covering all the speaker's main points and in a form that may be read by anywhere from hundreds to millions of people who were outside the range of the speaker's voice.

Paraphrasing and Summarizing

Once the news writer has decided what parts of the speech or statement to use the next job is to write as concise a story as possible. Concise does not necessarily mean brief. It does mean direct and precise and without wasting words. The news writer must first reduce the original material to a manageable number of words, and then must *summarize* and *paraphrase* much of it.

Some excerpts from news stories reporting statements made by President Nixon provide examples of this basic news writing technique.

The President's statement:
> All members of the White House staff will appear voluntarily when requested by the committee. They will testify under oath and they will answer fully all proper questions.

Fig. 11.5 *The text of a statement issued by the President. News stories based on this statement selected key passages and summarized much of the text.*

United Press International:

> Nixon ordered all White House aides to testify before a Senate investigating committee . . .

Associated Press:

> Nixon said Tuesday he will send his aides to testify publicly . . .

The President's statement:

> I have expressed to the appropriate authorities my view that no individual holding, in the past or at present, a position of major importance in the administration should be given immunity from prosecution.

The Associated Press:

> But he also said he has told investigators that no officials are exempt from prosecution.

The President's statement:

> If any person in the executive branch or in the Government is indicted by the grand jury, my policy will be to immediately suspend him. If he is convicted, he will, of course, be automatically discharged.

The Associated Press:

> . . . and said he'll suspend any government employee indicted in the case and fire anyone convicted.

As you can see, attribution and explanation are worked into the story with the material actually summarized and paraphrased from the text. And the words of the original can be greatly reduced in bulk.

The following excerpt from a story in the *Chicago Tribune* takes a more radical approach to summarizing. The *Tribune* story ran to several columns and included a running account of testimony at a Senate hearing.

> Testifying with immunity from prosecution before a hushed audience, Magruder, 38, also made these key points during his early testimony.
> —The decision to cover up the Watergate break-in was made because they feared Nixon would lose the election if it was known how deeply the committee and the White House were involved in Watergate.

> WASHINGTON (AP) — The Watergate investigation is gaining momentum after President Nixon abandoned the blanket claim of innocence for White House aides.
> Nixon said Tuesday he will send his aides to testify publicly as demanded by Senate investigators preparing for hearings next month.
> HE SAID he launched a new presidential inquiry into the matter last month, about the time Watergate burglar James McCord began telling his story to a Senate committee and a federal grand jury.
> This time the President's inquiry is being conducted by persons outside the White House staff, some of whose members reportedly have been implicated in McCord's secret testimony.
> In a related development, Nixon's re-election committee was reported to have offered the Democratic party $525,000 in damages to settle a multimillion-dollar package of lawsuits over the Watergate raid. But Democratic National Chairman Robert S. Strauss said he wouldn't accept any offer until it becomes clear that the affair will be aired sufficiently in public inquiries.
> NIXON DISCLOSED his actions in a three-minute statement to newsmen at the White House. No questions were permitted.
> He said he met Sunday with Atty. Gen. Richard G. Kleindienst and Asst. Atty. Gen. Henry Petersen, who gets reports of grand jury testimony.
> "I CAN report today that there have been major developments in the case," Nixon said, ". . . real progress has been made in finding the truth."
> He wouldn't elaborate on the developments or name anyone who might be under suspicion. But he also said he has told investigators that no officials are exempt from prosecution.

Fig. 11.6 *The Associated Press story based on the President's statement shown in Fig. 11.5. A careful comparison of the original statement and the AP story will show how much selection and condensation is possible in reporting speeches or statements.*

> —Also for the first time, the committee heard direct evidence that fired White House Counsel John W. Dean III participated in the planning and the cover up. Dean, Magruder testified, knew of White House desire to gain intelligence information about the Democrats.
> —Former Commerce Secretary Maurice H. Stans was told at least a part of the committee's involvement in the Watergate affair on June 24, 1972, a week after the June 17 break-in. In his testimony yesterday Stans swore he had absolutely no knowledge of the matter.

This summary, representing no doubt a considerable amount of testimony, is a paraphrase. It is concise and it is brief. It presents a lot of information in very little space and makes it possible for the writer to devote the space thus saved to direct quotation where testimony was more interesting or more significant.

Direct and Indirect Quotation

Direct and indirect quotation play an important part in any speech story. Direct quotation of the participants in a news event puts them into your news story in a personal way, enables them to speak directly to the readers. This point and some of the mechanics of handling quotation were discussed in earlier chapters. Now we want to look at some other aspects of using quotation. You will find as you write stories about speeches, public meetings, trials and hearings, that direct quotation is not the same thing as a transcript. A transcript is an exact reproduction of what was said, exactly as it was said: verbatim.

Direct quotes are intended to be the speaker's exact words, but they may not be verbatim; they may vary somewhat from the speaker's original words.

First, unless you have a prepared text in front of you when you write your story, you will have to rely on notes taken during the speech. Your notes may reflect the sense of what the speaker was saying, but will vary slightly from the original since it is almost impossible to take exact notes.

Second, even if you do have a prepared text in front of you, you still may have to deviate a little from the original. Speeches are made for oral delivery and include many rhetorical devices that help speakers in their delivery and enable them to relate more closely to their audiences. Such devices usually have to be edited out or revised in writing a news story about the speech.

Here, for example, is a verbatim quote from a speech:

> All these rights come from the people, and in their Bill of Rights combined with the Fourteenth Amendment, they say they want both— a free press and a fair trial—and it is up to the responsible people in law and in journalism to see that the people have both.
>
> And if we don't see to it—you in your profession and I in mine—then we are both false to our responsibility, and our democracy is in trouble.

Now, look at a news writer's treatment of this passage:

> Kavanaugh, addressing the kick-off luncheon of the 98th annual Michigan Press Assn. meeting at Kellogg Center, said the American people, by virtue of the Bill of Rights, want both a free press and and a fair trial.
>
> "It is up to the responsible people in law and in journalism to see that the people have both," he said.
>
> "And if we don't see to it, then we both are false to our responsibility and democracy is in trouble."

The first sentence of direct quotation is lifted verbatim from the text. The second sentence is altered slightly, that is, some of the words have been rearranged a bit. But there has been no alteration or change in the meaning of the speaker's words. Essentially, all the writer did was revise the sentence to eliminate the parenthetical phrase, *you in your profession and I in mine*, which may have been an effective device in the oral presentation of the speech, but is not as effective or as necessary when the sentence is to be read.

It is not only permissible, it is necessary to do this kind of smoothing out when you use direct quotation in a news story. Unless you overdo it and alter the meaning of the speaker's words, no one will question your revisions. You will find that you have to do much more smoothing out when you work from your own notes or from a transcript of a spontaneous or unrehearsed speech than when you have a prepared text to work from. The average person does not speak in complete sentences nor in direct and concise language.

Indirect quotation, of course, does not purport to be a speaker's exact words and so can be edited or revised somewhat more than direct quotation. The following sentence is exactly what the speaker said; he read from this text:

> That citizen wants his press to be free and he wants his trials to be fair, and I don't think he has much patience with the idea of either one infringing on the other one.

The news writer put this sentence into indirect quotation:

> The citizen wants his press to be free and his trials to be fair, and he has little patience with the idea

of either one infringing on the other, the editors were told.

The changes are minor. The news writer changed the original *I don't think he has much patience* to *he has little patience*. Here is another sentence from the original text:

> If an attorney makes statements that convict a defendant before he is tried, the fault lies with the sense of responsibility of that attorney, and not with the newspaper which prints the remark.

The news writer revised this sentence a little more heavily than the last:

> He said that if an attorney makes a prejudicial statement that convicts a defendant before he is tried, the fault lies with the attorney's lack of responsibility and not with the newspaper which prints the remark.

One of the revisions that usually has to be made in lifting direct or indirect quotes out of context and putting them into a news story is a substitution of nouns and pronouns of reference. In a speech, if the audience is listening, everything is in context. When the speaker says *you*, everyone present understands that the reference is to the audience. In a long discussion of freedom of the press, the speaker may say *they* in referring to the media. Again, the audience can follow the reference without difficulty. The audience knows that *they* refers to the media. But a news story based on only a small portion of what was said will be hard for readers to follow if the news writer picks up every *we, they, you, us* and *it* the speaker used. The news writer must replace the pronouns with the nouns they stand for.

The following excerpt from a verbatim text is a good example:

> Their freedom to rage at us with accusations of censorship, repression and McCarthyism is adequate proof that the alleged "chilling effect" or threat to their freedom is fictional.

The pronoun *their* in the text was perfectly clear to an audience that knew the speaker was talking about the media because of what went before. The newspaper reader might not know this, however, so the news writer was careful to substitute *the media* for the pronoun *their*:

> The Vice President said the media's freedom "to rage at us with accusations of censorship, repression and McCarthyism is adequate proof that the alleged 'chilling effect' or threat to their freedom is fictional."

Transitions

As discussed in Chapter 6, transitions are words, phrases, sentences, sometimes paragraphs that bridge a gap between parts of a story (see Fig. 11.7). When the subject changes, when one speaker stops talking and another begins, the reader needs help in moving from one topic or one speaker to the next. The speech story in Fig. 11.3 uses transitional phrases to introduce the final two topics on which the speaker commented:

> He also suggested that . . .
> Another area needing examination . . .

Words like *also, and, but, however, nevertheless*, all signal to the reader that something different is coming. What follows may be nothing more than an additional fact or it may be an entirely new topic which we have to keep clearly separate from what preceded. It may also be a qualification, an explanation or a disclaimer of something said earlier. The transitional word warns us: "Look out. Think. Something different is coming."

The following excerpt shows a careful transition from one speaker to another in a news story that quotes several speakers:

> Mr. Wattling said that only then could they draft the provision to legalize the present system of classifying real estate property only in Cook County.

Tells Problems Of Teen Mothers

A federal nursing consultant told a group of obstetrical nurses Saturday that teen-age mothers need "more sympathetic, more sensitive" care than older women.

"Society tends to look down on the teen-age mother," said Ione Ripley, regional nursing consultant for the Children's Bureau of the U.S. Department of Health Education and Welfare in Chicago.

"The implication is the teen-age mother is someone who has erred or acted rashly and thus is not entitled to the respect given older individuals."

MISS RIPLEY spoke at the regional Conference on Obstetric, Gynecologic and Neonatal Nursing sponsored by the American College of Obstetricians and Gynecologists in the Pick-Congress Hotel.

She said that in 1961 more than half of first marriages and 38 per cent of all marriages involved teen-age girls.

In 1961, she added, 54 per cent of all married women between 15 and 19 years of age bore children.

"The trend definitely is toward earlier marriages and earlier parenthood each year." Miss Ripley said.

SHE SAID the psychological and financial drawbacks of early parenthood far outweigh the physical advantages. The best child-bearing years are between 16 and 24 and fewer congenitally malformed babies are born to teen-age mothers.

Younger parents often suffer the frustrations of taking on a big family before their income gives them the freedom to enjoy themselves," she said.

YOUNG mothers often "don't know who they are" and are not "ready to take on the responsibility of another person," she said.

Statistics show that teen-age mothers most often give birth prematurely; gain excessive weight during pregnancy; and have either very fast or prolonged deliveries, Miss Ripley said.

The three-day conference, attended by about 400 nurses from the Midwest, ended Saturday.

Chicago Daily News

Fig. 11.7 *This speech story is given coherence and continuity by repetition of references to the speaker and to the speaker's topic. This is the linking technique discussed in Chapter 5.*

Mrs. John B. Mullen, legislative representative of the Illinois League of Women Voters, called the amendment's language so confusing that it clouded the issue of taxes.
"The amendment would do nothing for the people," she said.

The transition is effected easily by naming and identifying the new speaker and giving some brief insight into what she is going to say. The writer is telling us:

1) Here's another viewpoint, that of Mrs. Mullen;
2) She thinks the amendment is confusing;
3) She says it will do nothing for the state or the people.

When you are dealing with only one speaker in a story, this approach can be applied to moving from one topic to another. Then it works most easily if you start with a summary statement or an indirect quote, and follow it with a direct quote. We suggested this structure earlier in the chapter when we discussed topic blocks. For example:

Peabody said he had met yesterday with Gov. George Wallace of Alabama and received support from him.
"He offered us some of the Wallace trailers."

A similar example of summary statement followed by direct quote:

Voris restructured the faculty when he took over two years ago.
"We've added some bright young squirts as a mix with the more experienced teachers," Voris said, "the realists as well as the theoreticians. It did stir up some jealousies and worries. But I like that. It gives our students the advantage of learning from the pragmatist as well as the Ph.D."

Questions are often used as transitional devices, but they must be handled carefully or they are so obvious as to get in the reader's way. The "when asked if" approach should be avoided. It puts the reporter in the story and reporters generally are supposed to be observers and not participants. Furthermore, the reader is more interested in the answer than in the question. If you use a question as a transitional device, make it a rhetorical rather than a reportorial question. Here, for example, is a passage that uses the obtrusive "when asked if" construction:

> When asked how many votes he anticipated, he said "1509," the number needed for nomination.

Here is the same passage, revised, so that the speaker's answer is introduced by a rhetorical question:

> How many votes did Peabody expect?
> "Fifteen-oh-nine," he said.
> A candidate needs 1,509 votes to be nominated.

Another example of this obtrusive kind of questioning and a revision:

> Asked if she thought her pilot training could lead her to the astronaut corps, Lt. Neufer replied: "I haven't given it any thought—I have to take one step at a time."

> Lt. Neufer was asked if her pilot training might lead to the astronaut corps.
> "I haven't given it a thought," she said. "I have to take one step at a time."

Again, a rhetorical question would be preferable:

> Will pilot training lead to the astronaut corps?
> Lt. Neufer hasn't given it a thought, she says.
> "I have to take one step at a time."

OTHER SPEECH STORIES

More Than One Speaker

Most of the speech stories we have analyzed so far in this chapter have quoted only a single speaker. However, you will inevitably have to cope with stories that quote more than one speaker. Then you will find yourself confronting a stage management problem: instead of having one actor to deal with, you will have a whole cast of characters. Stories like this, involving anywhere from two to dozens of people, include panel discussions, public hearings, inquests, trials and conventions. Let's look at some simpler stories of this type: panel discussions and programs where there are two, three or four speakers and they are all dealing with different aspects of a single topic.

Various strategies can be used to handle this kind of a story, but one of the most practical pulls the whole story together in the lead, and then deals with each speaker separately. Here is a good example of this approach:

> Congress must enact a law that will restore the absolute protection of newspapermen guaranteed by the First Amendment to the Constitution, speakers agreed today at the closing session of the annual convention of the American Newspaper Publisher's Association.
> This view was expressed by Clayton Kirkpatrick, editor of the Chicago Tribune; Earl Caldwell, a reporter for the New York Times; and Len H. Small, publisher of the Kankakee (Ill.) Journal.
> *Chicago Tribune*

The first paragraph of this lead summarizes the view of the three speakers, noting that they agreed, and explains where and on what occasion the discussion took place. The second paragraph identifies the speakers. The story then goes on to give some background on the issue and to take up separately the points each speaker made.

The following lead is similar to the one we just discussed, but the story is developed a little differently:

> Representatives of six political action groups met here Wednesday to voice condemnation of the continued air war over North Vietnam and to discuss plans for a Jan. 20 protest in Washington.
> Statements explaining why their organizations oppose continued involvement in the war in Southeast Asia were delivered by:
> Nancy Hendrix Cobb, president of Tennessee Young Democrats.

Sources key issue

U.S. news shield law is vital, publishers assert

By Vincent Butler

Chicago Tribune Press Service

NEW YORK, APRIL 26—Congress must enact a law that will restore the absolute protection of newspaperman guaranteed by the First Amendment to the Constitution, speakers agreed today at the closing session of the annual convention of the American Newspaper Publishers Association.

This view was expressed by Clayton Kirkpatrick, editor of the Chicago Tribune; Earl Caldwell, a reporter for the New York Times; and Len H. Small, publisher of the Kankakee [Ill.] Journal. Caldwell was the reporter whose citation for contempt for refusing to appear before a grand jury in California led to the United States Supreme Court decision that said the First Amendment does not specifically protect newsmen from disclosing confidential sources of information.

SINCE THAT TIME a number of newsmen have gone to jail rather than reveal their sources. Fears have been expressed that unless new legislation is passed to nullify the court's decision, freedom of the press and the public's right to know would be imperilled.

A number of states have passed laws to protect newsmen, but they are not considered adequate. Congress also is considering a number of bills.

Small, who moderated today's discussion, said the A.N.P.A. has not changed its position on what kind of law Congress should pass. He said it was one that would grant "Absolute privilege" as proposed in a bill sponsored by Senators Alan Cranston [D., Cal.] and Edward Kennedy [D., Mass.], which A.N.P.A. helped prepare.

"WE FEEL THAT any legislation to protect the free flow of information ought to be as broad as possible and simple enough for anyone to understand," Small said. "Otherwise it will likely turn off rather than encourage news sources...

"Publishers today are greatly concerned over this issue.

They are deeply committed to the struggle which they recognize as one which may change the course of American journalism and and ultimately affect our form of government."

Kirkpatrick said, "What we want is a charter that gives us the opportunity to fulfill our duty." He called for a bill containing "simple, direct language to prohibit any action by a government that interferes with a newsman in the performance of his duties."

HE SAID THAT since 1968 the Tribune has been forced to answer 107 subpenas. And while officials in Illinois, ranging from a former governor to aldermen were being sent to prison for "moral turpitude," reporters were being threatened with jail for serving a "principle."

Caldwell said that there must be "some kind of relief from the government now." He said that unless there is "we're going to be reduced to dealing with handouts from the government."

He recounted how he had been harassed by government investigators and asked to produce his records and tapes concerning the Black Panther movement in 1968 and 1969, tho he insisted that everything he knew he had told in his stories.

HE WAS CONVICTED of contempt for refusing to appear before a California grand jury, but his conviction was overturned by the court of appeals. Two years later his case was ruled on by the Supreme Court.

Caldwell said that his tapes, notes and files, which he said had great "historical value" and could have had great news value in the future, now have been destroyed.

Chicago Tribune

Fig. 11.8 A more involved speech story reporting *what three speakers said in a joint discussion of a single topic.*

Cindy McCarver of the Student Mobilization Committee.

Kitty Smith of Concerned Citizens for Improved Schools.

Randy Shannon of the People's Coalition for Peace and Justice.

Tom Baker of the National Peace Coalition.

John Hawkins of Medical Aid for Indochina.

Nashville Tennessean

If you examine the First Amendment story (Fig. 11.8), you will see that the writer was quite careful to tell us who was speaking at all times. The material attributed to each speaker is carefully identified with the speaker's name: *Small said, Kirkpatrick said, Caldwell said.* The structure of this story is diagrammed in Fig. 11.9, which appears below.

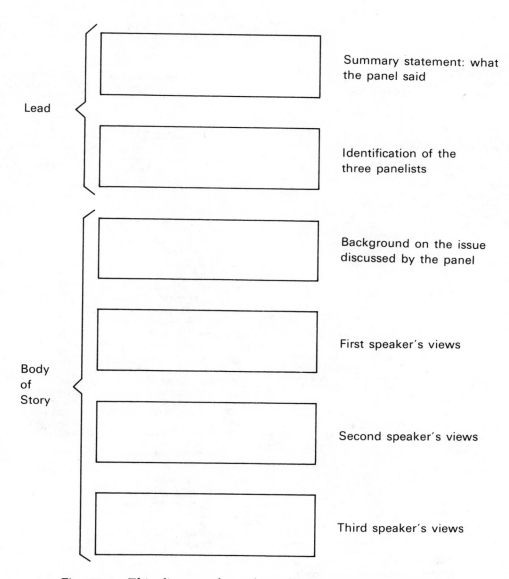

Fig. 11.9 *This diagram shows how the First Amendment story in Fig. 11.8 was organized. This is a highly functional structure, easy for the writer, easy for the reader.*

Heirs Salute 'Oppie,' Genius of Generation

By WILLIAM HINES
Star Staff Writer

American physicists paid homage last night to the memory of the greatest one of their ranks who ever lived.

For two hours at the Sheraton-Park Hotel, members of the American Physical Society heard J. Robert Oppenheimer extolled as the guiding light of a generation of scientists. Two Nobel Prize winners joined in "celebrating—and rejoicing at—a very remarkable life."

These were the words of Charles H. Townes, provost of the Massachusetts Institute of Technology who won the Nobel Prize for his work on lasers. They opened the unusual ceremonial evening, which closed with Oppenheimer's own words played from a tape-recording by Atomic Energy Commission Chairman Glenn T. Seaborg, who won the Nobel laurels for discoveries in connection with atomic energy.

Oppenheimer, s o m e t i m e s called the father of the atomic bomb, died of cancer Feb. 18 at the age of 62. In his scientific lifetime the center of theoretical physics shifted from Western Europe to the United States, partly through his efforts as a teacher and inspirer of younger men.

From the Beginning

Robert Serber, professor of physics at Columbia University, was one of these younger men, who studied under Oppenheimer at the University of California in the 1930s. He spoke last night on "The Early Years"—from the mid-'20s when Oppenheimer was a student in Germany until the outbreak of World War II and start of the atomic bomb project.

"Oppenheimer's fascinating personality played an important role in his impact as a teacher," Serber recalled.

Serber first encountered "Oppie" at the University of Michigan on summer.

"I was on my way to Princeton but after listening to him at Ann Arbor I reversed my direction and went to Berkeley" (where Oppenheimer was regularly teaching).

The seminars Oppenheimer held for his graduate students ranged across what was then the gamut of physics "and after we finished our problems the discussion would turn to wider topics." The action would continue well into the night, Serber recalled, sometimes "at a Mexican restaurant in Oakland or a good restaurant in San Francisco" where Oppenheimer would be host.

In those days there was no bridge across San Francisco Bay, and the students and their teacher would spend the hours waiting for an infrequent late-night ferry boat "in some waterfront bar."

The Presence

Not only Oppenheimer's intellectual brilliance — which all speakers emphasized — "but also his social presence" greatly influenced the lives of his students who emulated his way of speaking and his gestures, Serber said.

"We all of us owe him more than we can say for his greatness and for the greatness of his instruction," he concluded.

Victor Weisskopf, MIT physicist who until recently headed the European Center for Nuclear Research (CERN), discussed "The Los Alamos Years" when Oppenheimer built up the secret center in New Mexico where the atomic bomb was produced.

"The year 1939 changed many things," Weisskopf said. "It was the beginning of the most destructive war of all times, and also the beginning of a different kind of science."

This different kind of science was the discovery by the Germans Hahn and Strassmann of the fission, or splitting, of uranium. "The greatest change of our time came from the discovery of fission," Weisskopf said.

"Many of us," he recalled, "hoped that the number of neutrons produced in fission would be small enough so that no chain reaction would be possible. Oppenheimer was one of these."

Feasibility of the chain reaction was established late in 1942 and "Oppenheimer was chosen as the leader of the most critical part of/(the) venture"—to build an atomic bomb.

Weisskopf drew laughter when he commented that "Oppie did not have what could be called administrative experience," but went on to say that he brought a special kind of leadership to bear at Los Alamos.

Forging the Prima Donnas

"He did not direct the development from the head office. In the laboratory and in the seminar room he was intellectually and physically present." And, Weisskopf added:

"It was a pleasure to see how Oppie handled that strange mixture of international prima donnas and forged them into a working organization."

Oppenheimer's problems with "security"—which were unwittingly the source of great trouble a decade later—were with him in the '40s, Weisskopf said. He continually fought the military's efforts to compartmentalize the difficult business of building a bomb:

"Everybody must know what is going on if he wants to have creativeness," Weisskopf quoted Oppenheimer as saying.

At the height of the atomic bomb effort, Weisskopf added, "Within this fence of Los Alamos the great world of physics was assembled, and we liked to think that the fence was there not to fence that world in, but to fence the rest of the world out."

Speaking of the aftermath of the bomb project, Weisskopf said, "We do not know the balance of the work at Los Alamos—whether it changed the world for the better or the worse. . . .

"One thing is certain, however. . . . We are sadly in need of the wisdom and the insight of Robert Oppenheimer."

Humiliation

Abraham Pais of Rockefeller University, New York, discussed "The Princeton Years" after World War II when Oppenheimer headed the Institute of Advanced Study at Princeton, N.J.

This was the period of what Weisskopf earlier called "the humiliation of this great man"—the time when Oppenheimer was stripped of his security clearances and subjected to an investigation by a board of the Atomic Energy Commission.

Speaking of Oppenheimer's trial, Pais said:

"The man was treated with gross injustice, but this is not the evening to elicit our own anger."

Pais did not speak of Oppenheimer's reaction to the security investigation. It is said to have embittered him, although he strove not to show his feelings.

Pais summarized Oppenheimer's contributions to science as "his own research work in physics, his influence as a teacher, his work at Los Alamos and his work at the Institute for Advanced Study and as its director."

Moved almost to the point of tears at the end of his talk, Pais said, "We remember Oppenheimer as one of the most outstanding personalities of this century."

Seaborg, representing the AEC which 13 years ago publicly degraded Oppenheimer, spoke of the scientist's "Public Service and Human Contributions." The choice of this official to make this talk was interpreted by physicists in the audience as a final government attempt to make amends for "the Oppenheimer case."

"It is not generally appreciated," Seaborg said, "how much of Oppenheimer's efforts at . . . meetings (of the AEC's General Advisory Council) went toward strengthening the commission and our country's national defense."

After listing commission after commission on which Oppenheimer served, Seaborg added, "This enumeration of his services to his country is only a small fraction of his total contributions."

As a result of thses services, Seaborg said, Oppenheimer "was honored by three presidents" — Harry S Truman, who gave him the Medal for Merit; John F. Kennedy, who invited him to the White House Nobel Prize dinner and had planned to award him the Enrico Fermi Prize; and Lyndon Johnson, who actually conferred the $50,000 Fermi award upon him.

Seaborg did not mention former President Eisenhower, who ordered "a blank wall" to be erected between Oppenheimer and all government secrets.

Washington Star

A different approach, and one quite commonly used, is to focus on one speaker in the lead and most of the body of the story, and then to tack on the other speakers in the last third or quarter of the story. Stories like this are written just as if they were single-speaker stories until the last few paragraphs, when other speakers are introduced. This is a typical solution to stories about long meetings, conventions, public hearings and similar affairs.

As you can see, most stories based on more than one speaker are organized along physical lines. The lead and the body are structured so that what was said is constantly related to who said it. The First Amendment story (Fig. 11.8 and 11.9) illustrates this approach to organization quite clearly.

In the story about the tribute paid to J. Robert Oppenheimer (Fig. 11.10), what the speakers said is organized topically. The story reports what was said at a two-hour meeting at which former students, colleagues and friends spoke about what J. Robert Oppenheimer had meant to them and to modern physics. The story is organized around the different aspects of Oppenheimer's life and work, and the emphasis is on what the speakers said rather than who the speakers were. The following excerpt, for example, introduces the discussion of one episode in Oppenheimer's life:

> Victor Weisskopf, MIT physicist who until recently headed the European Center for Nuclear Research (CERNR), discussed "The Los Alamos Years" when Oppenheimer built up the secret center in New Mexico where the atomic bomb was produced.

Trials and Hearings

Stories reporting trials and public hearings present several problems. First, the news writer is faced with a mass of material representing as much as eight or 10 hours of statements, questions, answers and verbal exchanges. Second, several, sometimes many speakers are involved and the problems of identification, background and transition become more difficult. Third, the subject matter tends to become more complicated: there may be conflicting views, long chronological narratives, sometimes even lengthy exchanges of questions and answers before a significant point is made. Finally, the story is sometimes so obscured by wearisome details and roundabout presentation that the news writer needs extreme skill at summarizing.

Public hearings are covered in detail more frequently than trials, so let's look at this type of story first. Hearings may be pretty informal, involving the presentation of statements by interested citizens; or they may be more formal, involving the calling of witnesses, taking of testimony and sometimes questioning and even cross-examination of witnesses. The story in Fig. 11.11 is a report of a formal public hearing before a congressional committee.

Stories about trials frequently require the reporting of long exchanges between witnesses and the attorneys examining or cross-examining them. This kind of exchange can be handled in the form of an unattributed series of questions and answers, usually referred to as Q. and A.:

> Conti said he begged off, pointing out that he had no rifle, but only the grenade launcher.
> He continued, "They got on line and opened up firing."
> Q. Who is they?
> A. Lt. Calley and Meadlo.
> Q. Where were they firing?
> A. Directly into the people.
> Q. How long did they fire?
> A. A minute, two minutes.
> Q. What did the people do?

Fig. 11.10 *This story represents quite a different approach: it is organized around topics rather than around the identity of the speakers.*

WASHINGTON, Jan. 10—AP— A four-star admiral denied today that Gordon Rule, a chief civilian cost cutter, was illegally demoted, transferred or harassed because of his controversial testimony before a congressional committee.

Summary lead and views of one witness.

And Rule, former chief of procurement control for the Navy Material Command, apologized for his remark that an appointment by President Nixon was so bad "old Gen. Eisenhower must be twitching in his grave."

Another witness speaks out on a controversial point.

"I was guilty of a verbal excess and I do apologize," Rule told the Joint Economic Committee.

After first refusing a request to testify, Adm. Isaac C. Kidd, chief of the material command, appeared at the hearing.

Transition to body of the story.

"I attempted to take Mr. Rule up on his previous offer to retire . . . because he apparently found it impossible to stay within the outfield limits of the ballpark which I had laid out for him . . ." Kidd told the committee.

Direct quotation of witness

The admiral described Rule as one of the Navy's finest procurement experts and called his record "superb."

Summary.

But he said Rule refused to stay within his areas of competence and failed, in his testimony Dec. 19, to obey an order not to comment on "delicate" negotiations between the Navy and two separate defense contractors: Grumman Aerospace Corp. and Litton Industries.

Summary.

Sen. William Proxmire (D., Wis.) chairman of the committee's priorities subcommittee, said he could not accept Kidd's explanation

Summary of remarks by a member of the committee.

concerning Rule. Proxmire also said he believes a federal law barring the intimidation of federal witnesses may have been violated.

Kidd complained Rule had not made it sufficiently clear to the committee in his first appearance before the panel he was testifying on his own and in no way represented official Navy positions.

Back to testimony by principal witness.

"He was in an area in which he had no first-hand knowledge and yet he felt constrained to speak for the United States Navy in details, depth, and adjectives . . ." Kidd said, and added:

Direct quotation.

"I just lost confidence in him, sir, and that's what I told him . . . We don't need that kind of help and I told him that."

Proxmire, commenting on Kidd's initial decision not to testify, said the admiral's reasons were "absurd" and "unacceptable."

Another interjection.

In his previous appearance, Rule said Grumman had been all but permitted to "buy into" a huge contract to produce F-14 jet fighters for the Navy and that the $500 million it now seeks in increased costs approximates the amount of the low bid.

Background on reason for present hearing.

He said also Litton has mismanaged large shipbuilding contracts with the Navy and recommended that if the firm fails to meet contract deadlines by February, the contracts be "terminated for default."

Chicago Tribune

Fig. 11.11 *A well organized story on a formal hearing.*

A. They screamed and yelled. I guess they tried to get up. They were pretty messed up. There were lots of heads blown off, parts of them.

Associated Press

The Q. and A., you will notice, was introduced by a summary statement and a direct quote which tells us who is speaking, that is, answering the questions. The identity of the questioner was made clear earlier in the story. In this kind of exchange

the quoted statements are not enclosed in quotation marks. In the following example, however, the exchange is not marked Q. and A., and the questions and answers are attributed and enclosed in quotation marks. Either approach is acceptable.

He said Calley asked the priest several times whether he was a Viet Cong and the priest "would say no."

"Lt. Calley hit him with the rifle butt," Sledge continued.

"Where?" Daniel asked.

"In the mouth."

And what did the priest do?" Daniel asked.

"He sort of fell back ... sort of like pleading.'

United Press International

In all these stories you will note the extensive use of summary to keep the story under control and to provide transitions linking the verbatim testimony or direct quotation.

Occasionally when a trial or a public hearing is of special interest, newspapers run full or partial transcripts of testimony. Transcripts do not, of course, take the place of a news story which summarizes and explains the proceedings. Transcripts, even full ones, are only adjuncts to a well-organized news story, they are not substitutes. The news story will ordinarily make extensive use of summary, but will include direct quotation and frequently extensive passages of questions and answers. It is balanced, brief, interpretative. It predigests, as it were, lengthy proceedings for the reader who doesn't have the time or patience to wade through columns of verbatim testimony.

Interviews

You will find that interviews present more complex reporting problems than other kinds of speech stories. When you interview someone, you have to initiate the discussion, guide the speaker along the lines you want to cover, and generally take charge. You have to ask intelligent questions and prod and pull until you get the material you came after. This is quite a different situation from the lecture or panel discussion where the reporter merely takes notes on what is said. However, once you have your notes, the problems of writing your interview story are not very different from those you encounter in any speech story.

It is usually a good idea when you write an interview story to say explicitly that that is what the story is—a private conversation between a reporter, sometimes several reporters, and an interview subject (see Fig. 11.12). This is only a matter of attribution, but since interviews fre-

NCC Has Future, Says Mrs. Wedel

Green Lake, Wis. – Even though the December assembly of the National Council of Churches may be the last of its kind, the NCC president says the federation is "on its first legs," n o t its last, as some have feared.

Mrs. Cynthia W e d e l of Washington, D.C., gave her views in an interview after she had spoken to the 27th annual Laymen's Conference here.

T h e National Council, a federation of 33 Protestant a n d Eastern Orthodox denominations, will have plenty to do, for church co-operation w i l l be around for a long time, she believes.

Though t h e Consultation on Church Union for a multi-denominational merger seems to be marking time, Mrs. Wedel said she thinks union of all churches w i l l come "in God's own time."

"God is leading us," Mrs. Wedel said, "and He won't let us see the end results. He never does. G o d is saying, 'Come on, take one step at a time.' "

She said her own view of ecumenism includes t h r e e conditions:

● Mutual acceptance of all persons who sincerely believe they are Christians.

● Acceptance by denominations of each others' ministers.

● Admission of all Chris-

Mrs. Cynthia Wedel

tians to all Christian Communion altars.

"If we meet these condit i o n s, our denominational structures w i l l not make much difference," she said.

S h e said she hoped also that other chasms between a n d within denominations would close, such as the differences between "liberals" and "conservatives."

T h e NCC restructuring plan, which puts out of the picture the delegates meetings held every three years, will not detract from the organization, she believes.

"The delegates aren't real-ly in a position to make the decisions," she said. "Even the ones who are chosen to attend many assemblies come together only once in three years. For some of them it is their only c o n t a c t with NCC."

The NCC assembly, which has m e t every three years for more than two decades, will meet in Dallas, Tex. The G e n e r a l Board will meet three times a year, as usual.

Mrs. Wedel said that some leaders are thinking of hav i n g an "ecumenical cong r e s s" periodically — probably every five years — but that would not be a group responsible for decision making.

She said most of the work of the NCC is not engaged in controversial "social action" pronouncements, but in missions abroad and services to churches, denominations and areas in public l i f e in th e United States. T h e s e, she said, will continue.

Milwaukee Sentinel

Fig. 11.12 *This story was based on an interview rather than on a speech, a fact carefully pointed out in the second paragraph.*

quently have quite a different tone from other speech stories, the reader ought to be prepared.

Published Sources

Quite often news stories are based on published reports, an article in a journal or magazine, or on a copyrighted story that appeared in another newspaper. These are speech stories, but they are based on a printed record, rather than an oral source. Stories based on published sources are handled exactly like other speech stories, except that it is essential to specify the nature of the source. Here are two examples of attribution to a published source:

This was disclosed in the AEC's annual report, released yesterday,

along with a reiteration of the agency's program to improve strategic missile warheads.
Washington Post

In a prepared senate speech, Proxmire reported that....
Milwaukee Journal

Speech stories based on published statements frequently alternate the verb *to say* with the verb *to write:*

He wrote that the recent trend of political thinkers to emphasize the enlightened self-interest approach to foreign policy at the expense of a moralistic approach still produced a Vietnam.

Chicago Today

Identifying the Platform

Speech stories, as must be apparent by now, are stories based on what people say in many different situations and in many different circumstances. These include: speeches, panel discussions, conventions, public hearings, public meetings, trials, inquests, press conferences, interviews and formal and informal statements. They also include television and radio programs and a variety of published sources and texts including press releases, official reports, scholarly studies, copyrighted stories in other newspapers, magazine stories and books.

These are legitimate news sources and are all used, most of them frequently, some less frequently. Regardless of the source of the information, all speech stories have some things in common: the need for a considerable amount of summary to reduce the original material to suitable length for a newspaper story, and the use of direct and indirect quotation.

Whatever the source of the material, you should identify it. In a story based on a speech, the attribution ordinarily identifies not only the speaker, but the place and time of the speech.

Frequently the audience is also identified, often in the lead. In stories drawn from other sources it is important that these also be identified. The circumstances under which statements are made frequently have a lot to do with their significance. There may be quite a difference, for example, between what a politician says to a reporter's hurried questions in an airport waiting room and what that same politician says under oath at a public hearing.

The following lead illustrates this. This story differs from routine stories about routine speeches only in the circumstances under which the statements were made. The speaker is giving a press conference which he arranged so as to get public attention for his views. There is an obvious bias in what he has to say and readers had to be warned about it, as they were in this paragraph of the lead:

Fogel, *in a press conference* called to explain his reasons for resigning to become corrections director in Illinois, said either man is qualified to continue the programs he set in motion since his appointment in March 1971.

Minneapolis Tribune

In the following story, the lead and body are based on a question asked by a reporter at a press conference. The nature of the forum again is important to the story and the fact that the speaker's views were not volunteered is an integral part of the story:

Philleo Nash, U.S. commissioner of Indian affairs, said Thursday that all Americans must be allowed to vote "even if it means registering illiterate persons."

Nash was asked *at a press conference* whether he favors an order by the U.S. attorney general's office to register Navajo Indians in Arizona's Apache County who do not speak English.

"The rights of citizenship involve franchise, even if it means registering illiterate persons," Nash said.

The following excerpt makes it clear that the

speaker's remarks were made under carefully controlled circumstances:

> Mr. Anderson made his remarks *during a meeting with reporters* at his Overlea home where he is recuperating from a recent illness that hospitalized him for five days.
> *Under the groud rules*, questions were to be limited because of the county executive's health.
>
> *Baltimore Sun*

Sometimes reporters add to a story, or get an entirely different story, by interviewing a public official or prominent person who has just made a prepared speech. The fact that the resulting story did not come from the scheduled address should be made clear:

> Mrs. Cynthia Wedel of Washington, D.C., gave her views *in an interview after she had spoken* to the 27th annual Laymen's Conference here.
>
> *Milwaukee Sentinel*

Of course, the usual forum is identified, too, as we have seen in examples of leads from stories about public speeches, meetings and programs:

> McGovern *spoke in a lecture* at St. Catherine's College on the campus of Oxford University yesterday.

CHAPTER 12

Feature Technique

WE HAVE SEEN that news stories can be written so as to emphasize any of the conventional elements that go into them: we can write a what lead, a who lead or a why lead. We can also localize a story to emphasize the fact that it is connected with our own community or its vicinity, in order to satisfy our readers' interest in local news. And we can play up the latest events in a story, in order to satisfy their desire for the most up-to-the-minute information.

In the same way we can also emphasize unconventional elements: the unusual, the odd, the humorous, the pathetic or sometimes even the commonplace. When we emphasize these, or similar, elements we say we are *featurizing the* story, and the incidents or situations that we play up or emphasize are called *feature angles*. Feature stories may be long or short, organized in a variety of ways, have different kinds of leads, but they are alike in their emphasis on a feature angle. Here are some typical feature situations culled from newspaper pages:

- Police raided a cockfight in a rural area.
- A city council proposed to outlaw tattooing.
- A youngster made some nitroglycerine with his chemistry set and caused an explosion.

- A man found a boa constrictor in his car.
- A citizen called police to help find the owner of a large sum of money he found in the street.
- A political message turned up in a batch of Chinese fortune cookies.
- University students staged a "study-in" to protest limited library hours.
- A thief was caught fishing money out of a bank's night depository with a line and a set of fishhooks.
- Movers made a mistake and moved the wrong building.
- A large number of small boys and girls turned up to buy bikes at a police auction.
- A young couple fell in love under unusual circumstances.
- A mistake was made in a newspaper ad and customers rushed to a local store for a "bargain."

The list is endless. We must not forget the lost child, the puppy that needs a home, the family reunited after many years, the child orphaned by an automobile accident or an air crash, the ring found after all these years, the two-headed calf, the chicken with four legs, the quintuplets born to a local couple, the surprised parents who expected one child and got twins or triplets, the cat in a tree, the man, woman or child who fights back against some real or fancied wrong perpetrated by the bank, the draft board, the Internal Revenue Service or the telephone company, the fraternity that does good deeds instead of hazing its pledges, the divorced couple that remarries, the naive elderly person bilked in a confidence game, the repentant criminal, the lost child. . .

All kinds of things happen to people and human events run in cycles. The same things happen, generation after generation, year after year, but since people are interested in what happens to other people, these things make news, or more properly, features. It doesn't matter that the events and situations we are talking about here are not really important, except perhaps to the people involved, for they are interesting. They are something to laugh about, sigh or cry over, and newspapers will continue to print such stories and readers will continue to read and enjoy them.

WRITING THE FEATURE

The news writer has two problems with features: first, learning to recognize the situations, the little twists in events, which represent feature angles; and second, learning to write features so as to emphasize the feature angle and to present the facts so that they have the desired impact on the reader. The variety of situations and events that make a feature story have been suggested here and a number of good examples of short features appear in this chapter. The treatment is brief but suggestive, and should be enough to help you on your way toward developing your own instincts about features. In this chapter we shall be concerned primarily with writing the feature, not finding it. Once you have a feature story in your hands, how do you go about writing it?

Summary Leads and Chronology

Feature stories may be written in a number of ways, but one of the simplest is to write a brief summary lead and then to tell the story chronologically. The feature that follows has been handled this way. The summary lead consists of two brief paragraphs that make simple statements about the events of the story. It is a summary because it tells what happened in the story: the puzzled motorist found out what was making the noise in his car—it was a turtle. But the lead does not spoil the story by telling too much—just enough to stimulate our curiosity. It doesn't spoil the story because the feature angle stimulates our curiosity: "That's odd," we say to ourselves. "Now, how did that happen? It never happened to me." Here's the story:

> MEMPHIS, TENN.—UPI—C. B. Roach has discovered what that funny noise was in his car.
> It was a turtle, and it had been living behind a panel for four months.
> "I thought I was going nuts," Roach said. "I'd be driving along and hear this scratching, then kerplunk. I looked a hundred times and couldn't find anything."
> Finally, Roach decided he'd had enough. He took the car to a mechanic and told him "I don't care what you do. Take the car apart. Just find that noise."
> The mechanic found the turtle behind an upholstery panel.
> Roach was so happy to solve the mystery that he fed the turtle, then gave it to the zoo.

The final episode in the turtle story, the conclusion, is an important element in many feature stories. It wraps up the story and answers the readers' obvious questions. In this case, if we hadn't been told, we would certainly have asked: "What did he do with the turtle?" Not all features, however, have a conclusion.

In the next feature, the summary lead tells us all we need to know and the bare chronological account is complete without any conclusion. We have all the facts when we finish the chronology and there is no need for the news writer to add anything. In fact, in cases like this the writer should not do any more:

> A 24-year-old Pontiac man told police he was bilked of $65 yesterday after another man approached

6 Policemen Arrive, Big Shootout Fizzles

By RICHARD S. VONIER
Of The Journal Staff

George Jefferson parked his car at N. 18th st. and W. Wisconsin av. Tuesday and walked off carrying a toy pistol for his 7 year old son in near-by Milwaukee Children's hospital.

"First, I put it in my pocket," he explained, "but then I went to light my cigar. When I slipped my hand in the pocket for my lighter, there was the gun sticking out. So I pulled it out and folded it in the newspaper I was carrying."

In the hospital lobby, Jefferson met his wife, Ruby, who was waiting for their son, Lawrence. The son was having X-rays taken.

"I sat down in a chair, you know, and laid the newspaper down on a table," Jefferson continued. "Then, when I started to read the newspaper, I gave the gun to my wife, and said, 'Here, put this in your purse.'

"I forgot to bring him the gun Monday, and me being so forgetful, I figured I'd better give it to my wife so she'd remember."

While they were waiting, the Jeffersons decided to get coffee in the cafeteria. Jefferson made a stop in the men's room.

"There was a big cop standing there with his hand on his gun when I came out," he reported. "He was looking at me awful hard. Then he went in the rest room.

"Then we went into the coffee shop and he came in there and looked at me again. Then he went out again, but came back with another uniformed policeman and a detective.

"The detective showed me his badge, and wanted to know if I was George Jefferson. He said to come along with them.

"He said, 'You'd better get your cap,' so I guess that meant I was on my way.

"When we got outside the coffee shop, my wife wanted to know what this was all about. The detective said they had had a call that I put a gun in my wife's purse.

—Journal Photo

George Jefferson

"Suddenly, it all began to unfold."

[Actually, Jefferson learned later, there had been two reports. The first one said a man carrying a gun in a newspaper walked into the hospital. A caller had noted Jefferson's license number, and that's how the police—six responded — knew his name.]

"I took it out of the purse by the barrel—very carefully," Jefferson said. "They was looking pretty serious, and I wasn't going to take no chances that they'd think that I was going to come out shooting.

"The detective kinda looked at the gun. Then he looked at the officers. Then he said, 'Well!'

"It was one of those plastic jobs. A six shooter, you know, with a big hammer on it. I guess it looked like an old .45.

"One of the officers asked a doctor if he had a bag. He said, 'Let's keep it in the bag until you get it up to the room, so someone else doesn't make a mistake.' "

Jefferson, 50, of 5734 N. 75th st., an overhead crane operator at the Harnischfeger Corp., said he had to leave for work and couldn't stay to see his son.

"I also had to go get me something for my nerves," he added.

Milwaukee Journal

Fig. 12.1 *An artfully told feature story from the* Milwaukee Journal. *Much of the effect of this story comes from the use of the principal actor's own words.*

him at a downtown bank and asked for "help" in making a deposit.

Elden O. Lloyde Jr., who gave his address as 16 S. Perry, said he was making a deposit at the Community National Bank, 30 N. Saginaw, when a man sought his assistance.

Lloyde said the man then walked outside the bank, showed "a large sum of money," and offered Lloyde $50 to help him deposit the money in the bank if Lloyde would put up $65 "security."

The man then wrapped Lloyde's money and the $50 into a blue handkerchief and left, according to the victim.

Lloyde said he opened the handkerchief only to find some folded newspaper sheets.

Pontiac Press

The feature story's effect depends first of all on the feature angle. The story itself is interesting and all the writer has to do is tell it simply. In the two stories just discussed this means a summary lead followed by a chronological account in which the writer almost lets the story tell itself. Adding unnecessary facts, forced cleverness or explaining things readers can grasp for themselves can easily ruin a good feature. Keep it bare, keep it brief.

Using Simple Structure

Keeping a story simple may, in some instances, mean dispensing with the lead. The feature about George Jefferson and the big shootout (Fig. 12.1) is an interesting example of this technique: there is no lead, just a bare chronological account of what happened. The story starts at a convenient point in the chronology and goes on from there. The first paragraph does identify the principal actor in the story and describes what he was doing, but it contains no other lead elements. And, it certainly is not a summary lead, for there isn't the slightest hint as to how the story came out. This story is a little longer than the two previous features and is told to a large extent in the first person, in the words of the principal actor. Only here and there does the writer insert a few words to keep the story moving along properly. As it reaches the end we can see that it comes out all right, but the news writer adds a concluding statement, still in the words of the man involved in the story.

Involving the Reader

The conclusion in this story (Fig. 12.1) is a direct bid for reader reaction. "Boy, so would I," says the reader. "So would I." Again, note the simplicity of this story: a straightforward account in the first person with only a few additions by the writer. The story is light, entertaining and the first-person account involves the reader. We just listen as George Jefferson tells us what happened to him. And the conclusion is a final, subtle touch. It pulls us right into the story by making us say: "If it happened to me, I'd feel the same way." Fig. 12.2 is another good example.

This is the great appeal of the feature story whether it is funny or sad. Features deal with qualities of human nature and situations which we all understand because they are the kind of things that happen, or could happen, to anyone. The feature exploits our interest in other people and reminds us that we all share a common experience.

Holding Back Facts

When the summary lead is followed by a chronological account, the summary usually tells just enough of the story to stimulate the reader's curiosity without completely satisfying it. The lead has to set the stage, hint at the nature of the story, but hold back enough of the details to force us to read on. The following feature has a summary lead which tells the outcome of the story, but in such a way that we have to read on to satisfy our curiosity about how and why:

CINCINNATI—UPI—Jerry Held, 27, of suburban Delhi Hills, rang up $90 worth of apologies in police court Saturday.

Held was arrested Friday night as he walked across a downtown street against a red light and yelled at a passing police cruiser.

Patrolman Charles Greenert said Held continued to argue loudly when he stopped. He charged Held with disorderly conduct.

Summary lead tells the feature angle, but holds back the details. First episode— how it started and what happened—in chronological order.

Surprise: You're for sale, son

LIVERMORE, Calif. — (AP) — Like many mothers, Muriel Doggett is used to hearing her four children joke that they wished they could be an only child.

So, as a surprise for her son Jim's 14th birthday, Mrs. Doggett decided to run an ad in the local newspaper offering him for sale: "14-year-old boy with paper route & rat. Needs room to roam. Would prefer to be only child. Best offer."

That item greeted startled readers of the Livermore Herald-News classified section Jan. 29.

"The phone began ringing at 8 a.m.," Mrs. Doggett sud. "People called and said, 'about your ad . . .' I am sure many of them were deadly serious about wanting to buy him."

Mrs. Doggett said she received 20 or more calls that day.

"I tried to jump in before anything disastrous happened, but when I told them the phone number was put in by mistake, that only made it worse.

Jim Doggett

"Then I tried to explain it was Jim's birthday, and you should have heard some of them bawl me out for doing a thing like that."

Meanwhile, Jim was at school in this suburban community 40 miles east of San Francisco, unaware of the ad, when his assistant principal told him there was a policeman waiting to talk to him.

Muriel Doggett

The Livermore juvenile squad had spotted the ad and, using a reverse phone directory, identified what it assumed was a family with serious problems.

"Are you Jim Doggett?" Jim recalled the sympathetic detective asking him. "Do you have a paper route and a rat?"

"Who is it you're having trouble with, son, your mother or father?"

"I knew right away what it was," Jim said. "But boy, did you ever try to explain something like that to a cop? It's embarrassing."

Eventually the calls stopped coming, the police were convinced it was all a mistake, and now the Doggett family would just as soon forget the whole thing.

"I'm really sorry that I might have caused some people some unhappiness," Mrs. Doggett said. "We joke a lot in this family, but we wouldn't really sell him. Still, though, there are days . . ."

Detroit News

Fig. 12.2 *A light and entertaining feature which doesn't need any special effects to bring it off. The basic devices here are a chronological structure and extensive use of direct quotation from the principals in the story.*

In police court Saturday Held told Judge Robert V. Wood he had apologized to Greenert Friday night.

"That cuts the fine from $100 to $50," said Wood.

"I also apologized again this morning," Held said.

"That cuts it to $25," Judge Wood said. "Now if you will apologize to me that will cut it to $10."

Held apologized to Judge Wood and paid a fine of $10 and costs.

Second episode—what happened in court. Still a chronological account.

Final episode—the apology and the end of the chronology—and a tie back to the lead.

Another way to tell a feature story is to write a lead that gives a partial summary, but does not give away the outcome of the story. The story is then developed in the suspended-interest format with the punch line carefully withheld until the very end. Not every story lends itself to this treatment, but when the situation is right, the suspended-interest format can be very effective. For example:

BENTON HARBOR—UPI— Two Benton Harbor men have decided that a professional towing service has its advantages.

Robert Ross, 27, had trouble with his car which stalled.

Sampson Sally, 22, started towing Ross' car Sunday night. Sally's car, a convertible, ran out of gas. There were no gas stations nearby.

The two men took a felt hat and drained gasoline from the Ross car for the Sally car. They had no flashlight and Ross struck a match to guide the operation.

Sally's convertible was destroyed by flames.

The lead hints at a problem situation and tells how it started with a stalled car.

The story is revealed chronologically. One fact presented at a time. The punch line in last paragraph.

How dull this story would have been if the news writer had not taken advantage of the reader and held back the punch line. The story would not have been the same with a summary lead that started out:

A convertible belonging to Sampson Sally, 22, of Benton Harbor was destroyed by fire last night.

This story is not unique. It has happened before and will happen again. It is a frequent subject of humor. But, properly told, it has an impact on the reader, and it is this impact that the news writer is after.

Another good example of the suspended-interest format can be seen in the following feature. The story is simply told in chronological order. The punch line is held back until the final sentence. And the writer has added to the impact by deliberately misleading the reader with the words *well prepared* in the first paragraph:

GRANT—UPI—Jimmy Morrison, a local restaurant operator, made sure he was well prepared before setting off on a three-day deer hunting trip to Michigan's northland.

He made a thorough check of his maps, made sure his camping equipment was in good shape and packed plenty of ammunition, food and warm clothing before driving 75 miles to the hunting grounds north of Baldwin.

Morrison returned to Grant Wednesday empty-handed.

He had left his rifle at home.

One more example. The following feature is also a suspended-interest story, although it doesn't have a punch line. We are led into the story with an unobtrusive teaser lead. Then the explanation reveals the point of the story to be one we didn't expect at all. This use of a teaser lead followed by the revelation of the facts is a useful and satisfactory feature format.

SAN FRANCISCO, CALIF.–AP —More than 100 physicians whose specialty is the study of why and how folks get fat dined Wednesday night at the Mark Hopkins Hotel. They had:

Beef stroganoff, shrimp newburg, cold cuts, cheese, chicken salad, green salad, potato salad, bread, butter and pastries.

OTHER APPROACHES

Playing with Words

In the feature stories examined so far, the emphasis has been on simplicity. The leads are all brief and reveal just enough to draw the reader into the story. In each case once the lead was constructed the story practically told itself, usually in simple chronological order. There was no need for any trick writing. Indeed, overwriting or trick writing would have spoiled those stories, for the feature angle was inherent in the event or situation itself. The main problem for the writer was to do as little as possible and to let the story tell itself.

There are times, however, when some aspect of the story, some little twist, enables the writer to add a creative touch. This added touch may be necessary to make the story worthwhile, or it may just be an added bonus. A good example of this is the following lead on a story about high meat prices and a housewives' meat boycott:

> LIVERMORE, CALIF.—AP—
> The meat boycott is a lot of tripe, and housewives deserve the higher prices they are getting, says Margie Thompson, who has been in the butchering business 30 years.

Here the writer is playing with words to add interest to the story. It's a useful device to pep up a routine story as well as to add luster to stories that are inherently interesting. The feature that follows is a perfectly good story in itself, but the writer has taken pains to add a little something in the lead:

> BALTIMORE, MD.—AP—Only by sticking to his guns, standing his ground and keeping a stiff upper lip did George Gorney emerge victorious in his battle with the U.S. Internal Revenue Service.
> It started in September, when Gorney watched a friend in a boatyard fill out a form for a rebate of the excise taxes he had paid on gasoline for a powerboat.
> Gorney, 38, a salesman, claimed a similar rebate for gas used in operating his mechanized lawn mower.
> Back came a letter from IRS, rejecting the claim.
> "I called the fellow who signed the letter," he said.

> "Then I got disconnected or something. I thought he got mad or something so I hung up." Then came another letter, saying his claim had been re-considered.
> And last Thursday, Gorney received a check covering the rebate, which—figured on the basis of the three gallons of gas he used in the mower—totaled six cents.

A familiar saying, proverb, aphorism or cliché can frequently provide a bond of immediate understanding between the news writer and the reader. The tax story used several clichès: *to stick to one's guns, to stand one's ground, to keep a stiff upper lip.* The following feature lead depends on a pun, the contrast between the colloquial meaning of the word *loud* and the conventional meaning. The writer is playing a verbal game with us, but by the time we discover this we are well into the story—too far in to back out.

> George Wilson has the loudest suit on Pleasant Street.
> It's not so much the color that bothers his neighbors, it's the material. And it bothers their ears, not their eyes.
> George Wilson's suit is made of steel. It weighs 90 pounds and it once belonged to a fighting knight of the 16th century. It is a genuine suit of armor from the middle ages —and when Wilson wears it, he sounds like a Sherman tank in low gear.
>
> *Chicago American*

The following lead also takes advantage of a pun:

> SHERWOOD, OR.—AP—A woman opened a box of cake mix Saturday and found a lot of dough— nearly $4,000 in U.S. Savings Bonds.

Sometimes a literary, historical or topical allusion serves as a good starting place in a feature story. In the following example, the writer makes effective use of a poem familiar to all high school graduates:

Daley pedals away, Bilandic jogs along

By Judy Nicol

Michael J. Bilandic, alderman of Mayor Daley's 11th Ward, often walks closely in the footsteps of the mayor.

But on Tuesday Bilandic outdid himself. He ran for several blocks in the bike treads of the mayor.

Bilandic said that when he arrived for the 8 a.m. ribbon-cutting ceremonies at Clark and Walton opening the Clark and Dearborn bicycle lanes he thought the mayor's appointment schedule would permit him to "just cut the ribbon and run off."

So when Bilandic was offered a bicycle and the opportunity to try out the new bikeway with the other dignitaries, he declined.

Just getting started

"I didn't want to leave the bike stranded a block or so south (of Walton) when the mayor got back in his car to go to City Hall," he said.

Bilandic jogged along behind His Honor as the group, which included Police Supt. James B. Conlisk Jr., Illinois Central R.R. president Alan S. Boyd and environmental control commissioner H. Wallace Poston, set off.

"After three blocks the mayor was just getting warmed up," said Bilandic, astonished. "I was a little behind him so he couldn't see me, and I didn't dare tell him to slow down. I never would do that.

"Any block I thought it was going to end," he said, but the mayor pedaled past Chestnut . . . Chicago . . . Superior . . . Huron . . . Ontario . . . Ohio . . . Illinois . . . Kinzie . . .

Pretty good jogger

Bilandic, attired in a green business suit, shirt and tie, was not dressed for the occasion, but luckily he is a pretty good jogger. He said.he can do a mile in about 8½ minutes.

Finally the mayor jumped off his bike at Wacker Drive. Fellow Democrat Bilandic was still with him.

"It was a photo finish," he said. "I'm waiting for the pictures to be developed."

Chicago Sun Times

Fig. 12.3 *Politics can be amusing as well as serious and this light feature makes the most of the humor in the incident. The writer also makes effective use of colloquial speech.*

> "The fog comes on little cat feet. It sits looking over harbor and city on silent haunches and then moves on."

LONDON—When Carl Sandburg wrote the above, he wasn't describing British fog.

A London pea-souper has no endearing feline qualities. It is more like an infuriated tomcat that bites and claws and bludgeons.

Washington Post

Here is another example of this approach in a lead which depends for its effect on the reader's familiarity with a song from "The Music Man."

IOWA CITY—Well, folks, there may be trouble in River City . . . lots and lots of trouble . . . but it was nothing compared to the trouble in Iowa City.

You spell it with "T" and rhyme it with "P" and "P" stands for pass . . . and that's how Iowa beat Michigan Saturday.

Detroit Free Press

Some feature leads depend, not on word play, but on the highly selective choice of just the right word to set the tone of the story. Here is a lead in which the use of one or two choice words in the right place catches the reader's attention:

One of the last of the great non-spenders, Alfred J. Tennyson of Pawtucket, is about to retire after nearly 20 stingy years in the state budget office.

Providence Journal

More creative feature leads:

"Ruly teenagers entering building . . . 9,280."
"Unruly teenagers entering building . . . 17."

New York Times

A seven-foot water snake went out for a writhe yesterday, it being that kind of a day.

Washington Post

Richard Hays was in jail, while his twin brother, Kenneth, was out. But for a while, Kenneth was in and Richard was out when Richard was supposed to be in and Kenneth was supposed to be out.

Associated Press

Richard and Regina Eife went home from Frankford Hospital yesterday with 22 pounds 14½ ounces of babies—in four almost equal parts.

The Eifes are the parents of the quadruplets born at Frankford Hospital June 3.

Philadelphia Bulletin

A school which teaches hope has opened here for children who are victims of cerebral palsy, and staff members say the simple function is to "teach the children to do things for themselves."

Los Angeles Times

Franklin D. Roosevelt Jr.'s Liberal campaign for Governor got off to a dismal start in Harlem yesterday—a fizzle in a drizzle.
New York Times

Anyone can forget where he parked his car for a day. Or maybe even a week. But for one year, six months and 22 days?
for Reuters

Michigan has a problem it seeks to solve through an iffy sale of a Pontiac warehouse on a maybe basis.
Detroit News

Pathos

So far, most of the examples of feature leads we have used in this chapter have been taken from humorous or light stories. Not all features are funny, however. The account of the budget official's retirement, for example, was in no way intended as a funny story. Many of the devices we have discussed and the various ways of organizing the lead and development in a feature lend themselves especially well to writing short, breezy, light and often humorous pieces (see Fig. 12.3). These are page brighteners and editors and readers love them. But they are not the only kind of feature.

Many feature stories wring our hearts, and these, too, are good stories. They evoke reader response—frequently a surprising response which reaches out and offers aid and comfort to the bereaved and injured. The feature in Fig. 12.4 is a sad story, but in its structure and organization you will find it quite similar to the lighter features we have discussed.

More Than One Way

As you can see from the examples in this chapter, there are a number of ways of featurizing a story. Given a single story, different writers, or even the same writer, can find different ways of writing the story. Let's look at two featurized versions of the same story (Figs. 12.5 and 12.6).

The *Detroit Free Press* version (Fig. 12.5) was featurized by using a simple literary device, putting the reader into the story. Just imagine, the writer says, that this was your idea, and then continues to talk out loud at us and to us throughout the entire story.

The writer has, as you can see, involved the reader in the story. "Imagine this, get that, do this," the writer says. "Wouldn't it be a good idea? Why not?" And he makes effective use of conversation. He talks out loud so the reader may follow his thoughts.

> Voilà!
> Cognac. Tomato juice. A drink.
> Call it a "Bloody Napoleon."

And, he talks directly to the reader:

> Quick, Henri, more Cognac. Forget the bloody tomato juice. I'll drink it straight.

CHICAGO—Marie Dujka knew her last child was dying. She had known it for 15 months.

She had had two other children. They too were both dead.

The first son had died at 17 after an auto accident in 1970.

Her first daughter, Jenny, died in 1958, before her first birthday.

It was July of last year when the doctors told her that Mary Sue was dying.

The little girl had bumped her arm. The pain didn't go away when it should.

Mrs. Dujka and her husband, Rudolph, took the girl to a doctor. The diagnosis was bone cancer. They gave the 7-year-old girl two years to live.

As the cancer progressed, Mary Sue grew weaker and became frail. She lost most of her hair. She had to stop going to school, and spent most of the day in bed watching television. Once a week, her parents took her to Children's Memorial Hospital for treatments.

The Dujkas' neighbors and friends held fund-raising drives to help pay the medical expenses.

And Mrs. Dujka watched her little girl die.

On Friday Rudolph Dujka came home from work and found the house empty. His wife was missing. So was Mary Sue.

Then he noticed a light in the garage, opened the door and found the family car inside, the windows rolled up, the door closed, the accelerator wedged down so the engine would run faster.

Inside the car were the bodies of Mrs. Dujka and her daughter.

The family's wait for death was over.
Chicago News Service and *UPI*

Fig. 12.4 *Tragedy is a proper subject for feature treatment.*

NAPOLEON, OHIO—Imagine for a moment that it is your job to promote the sale and consumption of a good French brandy, a Cognac called Courvoisier and known as the "brandy of Napoleon."

Wouldn't it be a good gimmick to somehow tie that brandy into a solid little northwestern Ohio community bearing the French emperor's name? Voilà!

Napoleon, O., population 7,300, is about to celebrate the 150th anniversary—more or less—of its founding by French-Canadian fur trappers and also to mark the opening of the annual Tomato Festival and the Henry County Fair.

Why not somehow combine all these ingredients? Yes, but how? Voilà!

Cognac. Tomato juice. A drink. Call it a "Bloody Napoleon."

Get all the 7,300 residents—or at least all those old enough to drink—and have them toast the festival and fair with "Bloody Napoleons." Zut alors!

Contact the Chamber of Commerce. Call the French consul. Bring in some prominent people from Toledo, 40 miles to the northeast. Contact the newspapers.

Change the name of Main Street to Rue de Courvoisier.

All set. Raise the glasses. Clink. Clunk.

Only 17 people turn out for the toast.

At the crowded fairgrounds, where most of Napoleon's 7,300 residents—at least those old enough to walk—are milling around, looking at the prize tomatoes, a woman says:

"Napoleon Bonaparte? Oh, yes. I remember that name from school. He was some Frenchman, wasn't he?"

Quick, Henri, more Cognac. Forget the bloody tomato juice. I'll drink it straight.

Detroit Free Press

Fig. 12.5 *Putting the reader into the story.*

NAPOLEON, OHIO—UPI—Apparently the 7,300 residents of this community 40 miles southwest of Toledo don't care much for their namesake—Napoleon Bonaparte.

The local Chamber of Commerce had planned to have the entire population turn out en masse for a birthday toast to the little emperor on what would have been his 197th birthday.

The party was to have been the first acknowledgement of the namesake since the community was founded some 150 years ago by French Canadian trappers.

A new drink, the Bloody Napoleon—made by combining the juice of the main production of Henry County, the tomato capital of the world, with Courvoisier cognac, the brandy of Napoleon—was to have been used in a mass toast to the opening of the Tomato Festival and the Henry County Fair.

The toast never came off. Not enough people showed up.

Perhaps the problem was summed up by one woman interviewed on the fair grounds who remarked, "Napoleon Bonaparte. I remember that name from school. He was some Frenchman, wasn't he?"

Fig. 12.6 *A low-key approach.*

BRISTOL, CONN., May 4—Mrs. Bernice Wyszynski got the keys Tuesday for an automobile that she bought for a bunch of bananas.

Mrs. Wyszynski, who lives in nearby Pequabuck, answered an advertisement in the Bristol Press that has asked 1,395 "bananas" for a 1962 Pontiac-Tempest on sale at the Stephen Pontiac-Cadillac Company of Bristol. She showed up with the 25 "bananas" requested as a down payment.

The firm told her the dollar sign before the word "bananas" had been dropped in the advertisement, and refused to sell her the car. Mrs. Wyszynski then complained to the State Consumer Protection Department. Today, after several days of publicity, Stephen Barberino, head of the automobile agency, accepted the bunch of bananas for the car. The bananas were donated by the United Fruit Company.

New York Times

Fig. 12.7 *A feature told simply and briefly.*

Fragments of high school French also help jazz the story up a bit: a *voilà* here, a *zut alors* there.

The United Press International story of the same event (Fig. 12.6) also uses a feature format, but it tells the story in a low key without using any tricks. The UPI story has a simple feature lead, the statement of a situation which raises the question, why? The story is told chronologically and employs a bit of conversation, a direct quote, as a conclusion. Both stories are effective, but the *Free Press* version is a little more flamboyant.

Let's look at another example of how different writers treat the same story. This story, however, had such an obvious feature twist—the play on the word *bananas*—that it was used in the lead of both versions (Figs. 12.7 and 12.8).

The *New York Times* version (Fig. 12.7) has a summary lead and the story is developed chronologically. It omits many details, but nothing the reader really needs to know. The story has inherent feature appeal. Simply and briefly told, it stands on its own merits.

BRISTOL, CONN.—UPI—The housewife and the car dealer have come to terms on the late model sedan and all agree the deal was just the bananas. She gets the car. He gets the 1,395 bananas.

Dealer Joe Degone said he's also been getting a few raspberries for being outmaneuvered so handily by Mrs. Bernice Wyszynski.

And, he said, he still means bucks when he advertises cars "for only 1,395 bananas," even though he will take the fruit for the car this time.

Mrs. Wyszynski snapped up Joe's offer and plopped down a 25-banana down payment on his desk. She told the salesman she wanted the car.

They started eating the down payment.

"Your bananas are very delicious, lady, but you got to be putting us on." she said the salesman told her. Mrs Wyszynski said she wasn't.

She complained to the state Consumer Protection Commissioner Attilio J. Frassinelli.

Degone then called Mrs. Wyszynski and said she could come down and get the car, but "bring the bananas."

"Don't worry," the housewife said. "I called the fruit man and he said he could get them for me on a moment's notice."

"I figure that at 18 cents a pound

and three to a pound, those bananas will cost me $75 to $100."

Degone said he will give the bananas to the Newington Home for Crippled Children and that, after a long talk with Mrs. Wyszynski, "we're the best of friends."

He said he did not think anyone put her up to the deal.

"She just saw a way to get a car and took it. It was a sharp deal on her part."

Degone said business has picked up and that now everybody calls his agency about a car and wants to buy it for peanuts.

Fig. 12.8 *Using quotes and colloquialisms.*

WASHINGTON—AP—"I do believe, Gordon," said Mrs. Gordon B. Desmond, looking up from the chemical dictionary she was reading, "I do believe I would like a mink stole for Christmas."

"Why?" asked Desmond, a retired Army major.

"So I can wear it when I go lobbying for good old-fashioned foodstuffs."

"I do believe that is the funniest excuse a woman ever gave for requesting mink," the major said.

But he bought it.

That was last Christmas and, heartened by mink, Ruth Desmond has been redoubling her efforts ever since—for more peanuts in peanut

butter, baby food minus sodium carboxymethyl, for the banishing of sodium nitrate from junior frankfurters and for the defeat of pending legislation which would permit the use of cotton fiber cellulose in jelly beans.

Mrs. Desmond, a grandmother, is president of the Federation of Homemakers.

This six-year-old organization has its headquarters in nearby Arlington, Va., in a small suite of offices cluttered with mail, government reports on food, and such formidable volumes as "Gleason's Toxicology of Commercial Products."

Mrs. Desmond won't say how many members the federation has.

But she announces proudly that it has enlisted 800 new ones in the last five months.

Currently, her efforts are centering on the Food and Drug Administration's hearings on whether it should go through with its proposed rule that peanut butter must contain at least 90 percent peanuts.

To be called peanut butter, she tells FDA, the product should contain 95 percent peanuts, a standard which would alter the composition of much of the peanut butter now on the market.

Mrs. Desmond, a native Washingtonian and an alumna of American University, was a legal secretary before her marriage.

Fig. 12.9 *A feature touch dresses up an otherwise routine story.*

The United Press International version (Fig. 12.8) is longer and jazzier. It has a few touches, particularly in the direct quotes, which are probably more fiction than fact. And, it is a bit overwritten. The UPI story insists on going beyond the basic pun on the word *bananas*, to include puns on *raspberries* in the second paragraph and *peanuts* in the final paragraph. Note also in the UPI version the effective use of colloquial language: *bucks, plopped down a 25-banana down payment, snapped up Joe's offer, a sharp deal, been getting a few raspberries, buy it for peanuts, I figure that.*

In Chapter 10 you were warned that direct quotes generally do not make effective leads for

speech stories. This is true of the speech story, but not necessarily true of the feature, as the story in Fig. 12.9 shows. Although it is basically a background story that did not require anything more than routine treatment, the news writer took the feature approach and built up the human interest by focusing on the dynamic president as well as on the work of her organization.

The conversation in this feature is no doubt fictionalized, but it is probably based on something Mrs. Desmond told the writer. You have seen similar freedom taken with direct quotes in other features in this chapter, especially in the story about the Bloody Napoleon and perhaps to some extent in the UPI version of the banana story.

Featurizing calls for creativity and imagination. There is no reason not to embellish the facts a little in the interest of entertainment. But there is a line between featurizing and faking. Stick to the story. Dress it up a little. Make the most of the facts you have been given. But do remember that while featurizing is an art, faking is an unforgivable violation of the rules of the game.

CHAPTER 13

Structuring the Larger Story: I

MOST OF THE writing strategies and organizing techniques we have discussed so far have been directed at fairly simple and routine kinds of news stories. Let's turn now to the larger story. Larger stories aren't necessarily longer stories, though many will be. For the purposes of this chapter, larger means more involved, more detailed, more complicated. Disaster stories, for example, get both complicated and detailed. They involve many people, many public agencies and may even involve several events occurring simultaneously at different places. Weekend accident roundups fall into this category. So do major weather stories.

This chapter and the next will suggest ways of handling larger stories: ways to make involved and detailed stories easy to read, ways to control the various angles to a multiple-incident story.

Not all the excerpts and complete stories used as examples in this chapter are complicated. They do go well beyond the simplicity of the single-incident story and they suggest the kinds of complications you will encounter in longer and more involved stories. This chapter will present the tools and techniques for dealing with larger stories so that you will be ready for them when they come along.

THE LEAD

Summary Leads

Whether the story is long or short, whether it is a breaking story or a news feature where timeliness is not so important, a summary lead is a good, workable device for getting started. The summary leads we will discuss here are not much different from the five W leads discussed in Chapter 4, although the stories they introduce are longer and more involved. However, since the stories are longer, the leads themselves tend to be longer and more detailed. The structure remains the same. The following lead is a good example. It introduces a fire story that runs almost two full columns in length:

> A battlefield-like explosion shook an East Side neighborhood today, touching off fires that destroyed homes, businesses, and cars and sent sleepy-eyed occupants scurrying into the pre-dawn streets.
>
> No one was reported killed or seriously injured in the devastation.
>
> Fire Commissioner Robert B. Howard expected damages to reach

between $300,000 and $500,000. No cause was listed.

Three taverns and four homes were destroyed and 15 other buildings and 11 cars were damaged by the fast spreading flames.

One man, trapped in his upper apartment, was rescued by two policemen using a ladder carried to the burning building by a neighborhood youth.

Buffalo Evening News

This lead could stand by itself as a complete story except for its lack of detail. It is a good model for an accident or disaster story. The first paragraph summarizes the story and succeeding paragraphs highlight events common to any fire, accident or disaster story: the dead or injured, property damage and rescue efforts.

The following summary lead is from a different kind of story and is structured somewhat differently:

Amid angry exchanges over state building programs in downtown Lansing and the suburbs, legislative leaders Friday agreed to set aside $100,000 for a new series of site studies.

Of the total, $75,000 would cover potential expansion in downtown Lansing.

Another $25,000 would be designated for the secondary state government complex in Windsor township.

Action came during heated debate in the Joint Capital Outlay Subcommittee over:

—Whether new state office space is actually needed.

—Providing new quarters near downtown Lansing or in outlying areas at less expense.

—Trying to cut down on rental costs by investing state funds in state-owned properties.

Lansing, Mich., *State Journal*

This lead, too, is almost a complete story. It tells what happened, under what circumstances, and adds details: a breakdown on how the money will be used and a breakdown on topics covered at the subcommittee meeting.

Note that the first paragraph is short, although not as short as some leads we have seen: 28 words.

And it is backwards, in the sense that it tells what happened only after it describes the circumstances under which the story developed: the writer added color and interest to the lead by moving the phrase *amid angry exchanges* ahead of the main part of the lead. The experienced writer knows when to try a different approach. This is a better lead, more interesting and attractive, than it would have been if written the other way around:

Legislative leaders Friday agreed to set aside $100,000 for a new series of site studies for state buildings.

The decision followed angry exchanges over state building programs in downtown Lansing and the suburbs.

The *State Journal* lead also introduces a new technique, the careful breakdown of summarized information that:

1) Makes the lead clearer by presenting facts in small and easily understood bits;
2) Helps the reader by serving as an outline for the rest of the story.

The $100,000 figure is broken down into two sums and the use to which each sum will be put is explained. The *angry exchanges* are also broken down and explained as a heated debate over three questions. The reader should have no trouble following the story after this simple explanation of what happened and what the issues are.

Itemizing Leads

The more involved a story is, the more important it is that the writer organize and simplify it for the reader. The following examples will give you some idea of the possibilities offered by a lead which breaks details down into itemized lists:

A determined Warren teen-ager was finally brought into custody by Warren police Sunday after:

—Leading the police on a 100-mile-an-hour chase.

—Smashing into a tree.

—Running down a patrolman.

—Wrecking a police car.

—Being shot at six times.

—Smashing through a roadblock.

—Hurtling a ten-foot ditch.

—Fleeing on foot from his wrecked car.

Charged with resisting arrest and assault with a deadly weapon (his auto) was....

Detroit Free Press

The itemizing lead, as you can see, is a list which presents each item in a separate paragraph. The items can be marked with dashes, as in the *Free Press* lead, with big black dots (called bullets) or by numbers. However marked, the trick is to make each point stand out on its own.

In accident stories the names of the dead and injured are commonly listed in the lead. This makes each name visible and enables readers to scan the list rapidly and identify any names they may know. The following lead is a good example:

A spring vacation trip to the Bahamas ended in the deaths of four Wisconsin young people when their light plane crashed while attempting a landing at the Athens (Ga.) airport.

The victims, three of them University of Wisconsin-Milwaukee students, were identified Sunday as:

Roger Papiham, 28, son of Mr. and Mrs. Jerry A. Papiham of 13333 W. Prospect Dr., New Berlin. Papiham was a sophomore at UWM.

Richard W. Pearson, 22, son of Mr. and Mrs. George Pearson of 621 Elm Ave., South Milwaukee. Pearson was a junior.

Michael Scharenbroch, 20, of 3245 N. Oakland Ave. Scharenbroch, the son of Mr. and Mrs. Alphonse J. Scharenbroch of Kiel, was a sophomore at UWM.

Miss Rosemarie Andes, 26, of 1601 N. Farwell Ave. Miss Andes was the daughter of Mrs. Sophie Andes of 4626 W. Concordia Ave.

Milwaukee Sentinel

Roundup Leads

Roundup leads are summary leads. They may also be itemizing leads. They differ from the leads already discussed only in that they introduce several stories that are to be treated as one. For

Four state residents, including a Dairyland father and one of his 13 children, drowned during the weekend in Wisconsin waters.

The victims:

Eugene W. Sikorski, 53, Dairyland.

Miss Rose Sikorski, 19, his daughter.

Florian L. Schellinger, 40, West Bend.

Earl Koehnke, 38, Menasha.

Washburn County Sheriff Arnold Drost said Sikorski had taken several of his 13 children to Bear Track Lake near Minong Friday to swim.

When his daughter Rose disappeared while swimming, Sikorski tried to rescue her.

One of the other children ran to a nearby public beach and summoned help when he failed to reappear. Six youths recovered the bodies and attempted to revive them.

The young men told authorities that both victims seemed to respond for a brief period. The father, however, was dead

at the scene when the ambulance arrived. His daughter died in an ambulance enroute to a Spooner hospital.

Schellinger drowned Saturday when he fell off the rear of a boat about 100 feet from shore on the Iron River.

Bayfield County authorities said several persons were standing on the shore of the river when Schellinger fell into the water.

His body was recovered within a few minutes by a bystander.

The body of Earl Koehnke, who drowned Friday off the north shore of Lake Winnebago, was recovered Saturday.

The Menasha Police Department said Koehnke was in a boat with four other persons when he stood up near the rear of the craft and tumbled into the lake.

Efforts by his companions to rescue him failed.

Milwaukee Sentinel

Fig. 13.1 *A roundup story of weekend drownings across the state from the Monday morning Milwaukee Sentinel.*

example, the following lead is from a roundup of five different traffic accidents. Instead of writing the stories separately and either grouping them on one page or scattering them throughout the paper, the stories are pulled together under a single lead which stresses their common denominator: death in a traffic accident.

Six more Minnesotans have died in accidents on state highways, bringing the 1972 road toll to 690, compared with 763 at this time last year.

The victims were identified as:

Minneapolis Tribune

A similar story, a roundup of drowning accidents over a weekend, is shown in Fig. 13.1. See also Fig. 13.2.

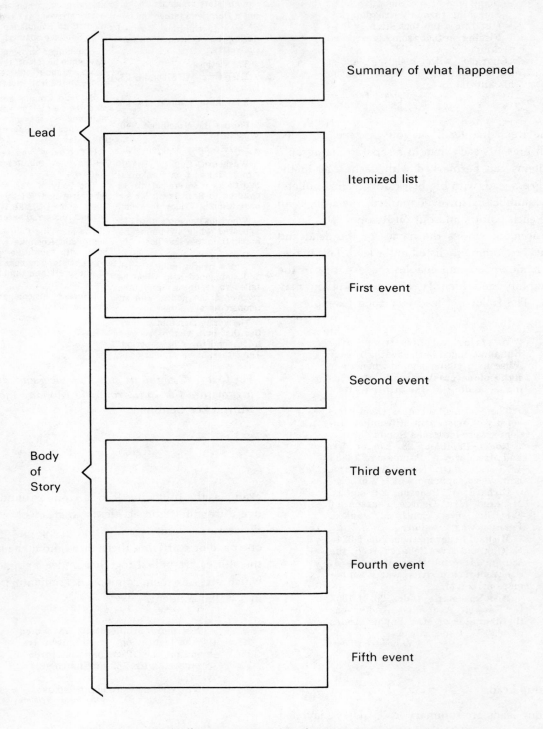

Fig. 13.2 *Overall organization of the roundup story like the weekend roundup of accidents or drownings. Compare this with the story shown in Fig. 13.1.*

The roundup is a practical solution to handling a number of small stories with a common theme: traffic and other accidents; various elements or incidents related to severe weather; crimes; separate speeches at a convention; views of several speakers on a panel.

Some roundup stories pull together completely unrelated events (like the roundup of weekend auto accidents or drownings) that can be tied together because they are similar in nature (accidental deaths from a common cause). Other roundups are a single story—but one that develops over a period of time and that may involve events or incidents which happened in a number of places. Severe weather stories are a good example. In such cases, the roundup pulls the various events together under a common lead that reflects the entire story, rather than just a part of it (see Fig. 13.3).

The following lead is an example of this kind of roundup. The story involves a series of gambling raids in several places and the arrests of a number of people. The raids all resulted from a single investigation. The story has a common thread, but a number of angles and a good many details:

> Fifteen persons were arrested today in raids on several locations on Buffalo's East Side, Eggertsville, and North Boston in connection with an alleged organized gambling ring believed to have done a brisk $500,000-a-year business.
>
> Capt. Kenneth P. Kennedy, commander of the Buffalo Police Bureau of Vice Investigation, said the half-million-dollar figure was "a conservative one" based on results of a day-by-day investigation. He said the investigation included wiretapping.
>
> In custody pending arraignment later on misdemeanor gambling charges are:
>
> *Buffalo Evening News*

Second-Day and Follow-Up Leads

Another common lead is the second-day or follow-up lead. The second-day lead has two functions: first, to tell the reader about new developments in

a story; second, to refresh the reader's memory about the events of the previous day.

The stories about the serious train wreck in Chicago are a good example of this kind of lead. The first-day story, of course, contains all new information. Second-day and follow-up stories include new and old information. The lead on the first-day story as it appeared in the *Boston Globe*:

> CHICAGO—UPI—A crowded commuter train plowed into the rear of a double-decked train yesterday, trapping dead and injured passengers in shredded debris in the nation's worst rail disaster in 14 years. Forty-five persons were killed.
>
> More than 320 others were injured —some critically—in the morning rush-hour collision on the Illinois Central Gulf Railroad commuter line three miles south of the Loop, the shopping and business district.

The crash occurred about 8 a.m. Monday. The *Globe* story first appeared in the Tuesday morning paper printed Monday evening. The *Detroit News* carried a second-day story in its early Tuesday editions printed Tuesday morning. The second-day lead in the *News*:

> CHICAGO—AP—Federal Safety officials investigating the commuter train collision which killed 44 persons raised questions today about the strength of the lightweight steel cars used by commuter lines.
>
> More than 300 were reported injured yesterday when an Illinois Central Gulf Railroad commuter backing into a South Side station was rammed by a second IC electric commuter during the morning rush hour.
>
> Transportation Secretary John Volpe inspected the wreckage in a 40-minute tour. He and Hendy Wakeland, director of the department's Bureau of Transportation Safety, said the strength of the lightweight steel and aluminum cars would be studied.
>
> It took six hours to extricate the last of the dead and injured from the wreckage of two of the cars.

This is a good example of a second-day story lead. As you can see, the lead introduces the

Winter's first major storm brings snow, rain to N.E.

By Al Larkin
Globe Staff

The first major Nor'easter of winter swept into New England late yesterday slowing rush-hour traffic to a crawl while dumping more than a foot of snow in northern regions and lesser amounts to the south.

Heavy snow warnings and watches were in effect until about 9:30 last night for most of Maine, New Hampshire, Vermont and western Massachusetts, and travelers advisories were issued for coastal regions, where the snow was expected to turn to rain.

Major snow accumulations in ski country, expected to reach 18 inches by this morning, were seen as a boon to weekend operations. One Vermont area proprietor described the storm as "a real blockbuster."

State Police said highways were busy last night as optimistic skiers made their way north in anticipation of the heavy snowfall.

Driving conditions were reported as "extremely hazardous" on virtually all highways, and police reported hundreds of minor automobile collisions and breakdowns.

One storm-related death had been reported by 9 p.m. last night, but local hospitals braced themelves for the usual flurry of heart patients as New Englanders begin digging out from beneath the heavy, wet snow·

Mrs. Bernadette T. Sweeney, 51, of 155 Beacon st., Lowell, was killed early yesterday afternoon on snow-swept Rte. 125 in North Andover.

STORM, Page 5

Boston Globe

Fig. 13.3 *A weather roundup story from the* Boston Globe. *The story has a straightforward Five-W lead. Note the number of different events, incidents, problems included in this story, all of them fitting comfortably under the umbrella of the lead.*

second-day angle, the new part of the story, in the first paragraph; it ties back to the original story in the second paragraph; and then quickly summarizes those of the previous day's events that took place after the crash.

The entire story, except for the list of dead and injured at the end, appears in Fig. 13.4.

A follow-up, carried in the Thursday morning editions of the *Chicago Tribune*, is almost an entirely new story that refers to the original event in only a few places. The bulk of the follow-up was devoted to the investigation into the cause of the crash. The first part of the *Tribune* follow-up appears in Fig. 13.5.

Fig. 13.4 *A second-day story on a serious accident. The story contains very little new information, but a complete retelling of the original story.*

CHICAGO — (AP) — Federal safety officials investigating the commuter train collision which killed 44 persons raised questions today about the strength of the lightweight steel cars used by commuter lines.

Second day or follow lead

More than 300 were reported injured yesterday when an Illinois Central Gulf Railroad commuter backing into a South Side station was rammed by a second IC electric commuter during the morning rush hour.

Tieback to yesterday's story

Transportation Secretary John Volpe inspected the wreckage in a 40-minute tour. He and Hendy Wakeland, director of the department's Bureau of Transportation Safety, said the strength of the lightweight steel and aluminum cars would be studied.

It took six hours to extricate the last of the dead and injured from the wreckage of two of the cars.

President Nixon expressed his sorrow and canceled plans for a downtown campaign motorcade scheduled for today in Chicago.

The President said, "The heart of the nation goes out to the victims of this tragedy and to the people of Chicago."

Sen. George McGovern, campaigning in Pittsburgh, called off a torchlight parade scheduled tomorrow in Chicago.

The Democratic presidential candidate said his "heartfelt sympathy goes out to the families of the victims of the terrible tragedy."

Volpe headed a federal investigation team dispatched from Washington to study the collision, the nation's worst rail disaster since 1958, when 48 persons were killed in Elizabethport, N.J.

Gov. Richard B. Ogilvie ordered a state investigation.

Developments after the crash and rescue efforts: second day story expanding on first paragraph

Railroad officials said they could not determine immediately how fast the second train was traveling when it struck the rear of the first commuter.

Transitional paragraph

The first commuter, a shiny, four-car, double-decked HighLiner, overshot the 27th Street station and was backing up when it was rammed by the second train. Whether the backing was a violation of railroad rules could not be learned immediately.

The second train was made up of six 1926-vintage coaches. Each train carried about 500 passengers.

Officials said that when the first train overshot the station it may have tripped a switch which changed a signal from red to yellow, misleading the engineer of the second train.

They said the yellow signal permits a train to travel toward the station at approximately 30 miles an hour, but also indicates to the engineer that the track is clear for 2,000 yards. (a mile and one sixth).

The engineer of the second train, Robert W. Cavanaugh, shouted a warning to passengers before the collision. Cavanaugh, who was injured, was among the last victims freed from the wreckage. He was removed by one of four helicopters which joined a dozen ambulances in speeding victims to hospitals.

Officials said the engineer of the lead train, James A. Watts, told them he overshot the 27th Street station by about 250 feet. When asked why this occurred, H.F. Mullins, the railroad's head of passenger service, said, "Maybe he was going faster than he should have."

Review of crash and rescue efforts: yesterday's events as introduced in second paragraph of the lead

Detroit News

STRUCTURING THE LARGER STORY: I / 137

Poor visibility and changing signal lights are being investigated as probable causes of Monday's crash of two Illinois Central Gulf Railroad trains.

This was disclosed yesterday by a key official in the federal inquiry into the crash, in which 44 persons were killed and 350 injured. The official, who asked not to be identified, said the investigation is proceeding on this "hypothesis."

A study of the scene tends to support this theory as do statements yesterday by John H. Reed, chairman of the National Transportation Safety Board. Reed said at a press conference that the investigation so far indicates nothing was wrong with mechanical or electrical systems of the trains involved or the roadbed.

At 7:27 a.m. Monday, train 720, consisting of six old-style cars, crashed into the rear of train 416, consisting of four modern, steel, double-decker cars, which was backing into the railroad's 27th Street Station at the time.

The basis for this theory, the official said, follows:

Thru error, the first train, No. 416, passed thru a block signal 100 feet north of the 27th Street Station's platform. This caused the block signal there to turn red, and a block signal at 31st Street to turn from red to yellow, calling for a train entering the 27th–31st block to travel at speeds up to 30 miles an hour with caution.

Train 416 then backed up to the station to pick up a passenger. This caused the signal just north of the station to turn green and the signal at 31st Street to become red, calling for approaching trains to halt.

By this time the second train, No. 720, had passed the 31st Street signal. The engineer was concentrating on the overhead signal light at 27th Street, which at this time was green, and indicated to him that he should proceed. He may even have picked up speed.

Chicago Tribune

Fig. 13.5 *A follow-up story, almost entirely new.*

The *Tribune* story is a typical follow-up, with its emphasis on new developments and only brief details about the original event (see Fig. 13.6).

The second-day and follow-up stories shown here are fairly routine. They do an effective job of relating new information and background in such a way that the reader gets a complete and coherent picture of the news event and its aftermath. You can find your own examples in newspapers and perhaps some of them will solve the problem differently. There is no one way to organize and write a news story.

The *Milwaukee Journal* story in Fig. 13.8 shows another approach to shirt-tailing. Again there is a main story and the minor details are shirt-tailed on at the end. But, the *Journal* set the shirt-tailed material in smaller type as an additional space-saving device.

Shirt-tailing is routine on the sports desk where statistical summaries are regularly appended to game stories (Fig. 13.9). In game stories there is a clear and obvious division between the action of the game and statistical summaries that result from the action.

SHIRT-TAILING

Another organizing device in larger stories is *shirt-tailing*. This is a simple procedure which involves writing a story about the major aspects of a news event and then appending a lot of minor details. A story from the *Louisville Courier-Journal* (Fig. 13.7) is a good example of shirt-tailing. The first and longer part of the story deals with one remark the governor made during a televised panel discussion. Other points the governor made were shirt-tailed to the end of the story and introduced by a transitional phrase *On other topics, the governor said*. Note that this transition calls for a colon.

CONCLUSIONS

Another recognizable part of a news story, and one that is often carefully structured, is the conclusion. Bringing some stories to an end is simple. The writer just stops and lets the story trail off at the last paragraph, as in the brief inverted-pyramid format. In longer stories, and especially in more involved ones, it is sometimes essential to write a formal conclusion. The formal conclusion is much like taking your leave at the end of a party. You have to say something to your hostess before going. But you don't stand around chatting all night with the front door standing open. You make it short.

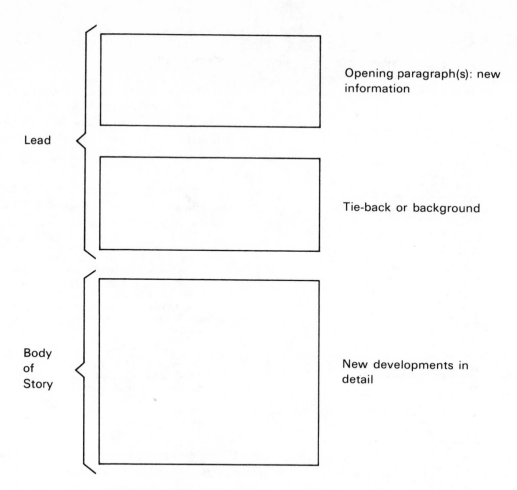

Fig. 13.6 *The follow-up story on the Chicago train crash published in the* Chicago Tribune *(Fig. 13.5) is organized like this.*

Feature stories generally require a formally organized conclusion. A *Detroit News* feature (Fig. 9.2) about women customs and immigration inspectors was concluded with a list of the women inspectors.

An action-packed feature about two escaped convicts who terrorized an Illinois couple ended this way:

> Day by day the fugitives run their race, but the snare tightens.
> And Mrs. Odetta Politte remembers the words of a "houseguest" who bore the name of Kane.
> "We will never go back."

A feature story explaining the step-by-step process by which civil suits are tried ends with the quip:

> Ready, set . . . sue!

A feature story about alcoholism ends this way:

> A few months ago, Luke quit his construction job of four years. He was tired of it. He thinks about going back to school, but he's afraid he won't be able to get back into studying. At loose ends, he's trying to make a living by repairing cars at home. He worries about falling off

Ford suggests
he won't run
for U.S. Senate

By SY RAMSEY
Associated Press

Gov. Wendell H. Ford yesterday indicated strongly that he plans to serve out his term as governor rather than run for the U.S. Senate in 1974.

He all but ruled out any Senate candidacy, despite what he called bantering remarks to newsmen last Thursday during a visit to Washington.

When asked then if he were interested, he hedged saying, "I'm not giving my support to anyone else at this time."

But during a WHAS-TV panel interview broadcast yesterday, the governor told a reporter:

"I want to serve out my term . . . and be a good governor and do the responsible thing for the people of Kentucky. Period. And I think you know what I mean."

Republican incumbent Marlow Cook will be up for re-election in 1974, and among the leading Democratic prospects to oppose him are former Gov. Edward T. Breathitt and fried chicken king John Y. Brown Jr.

Breathitt decided not to enter the Senate primary this year, leaving the field clear for now Sen.-elect Walter (Dee) Huddleston.

Breathitt implied at the time of his decision that Ford and State Democratic Chairman J. R. Miller had committed themselves to support him as a senatorial candidate in 1974.

"Would Breathitt have any reason to expect you and Miller owe him a little more consideration than you do the other prospective candidates for the Senate?" the governor was asked.

"I would say he would probably expect that, yes," Ford said.

"Would he have a right to expect it?" the governor was asked.

". . . Yes," he replied.

But Ford suggested that Breathitt might be content as an official of Southern Railways and not want to become a candidate.

On other topics, the governor said:

✔ Kentucky coal production has increased for the past 14 weeks and the industry is healthy despite "a scare they (the coal people and their advocates) tried to put up" last fall.

He said 25,000 persons are employed in the industry, up from last year, and receipts from the recently-imposed severance tax are coming in as well as anticipated.

✔ He favors a federal law regulating strip-mining that would clean up streams coming into Kentucky.

But he would oppose any provision with the effect of banning strip-mining in Eastern Kentucky by lowering the allowable slope degree for such activity.

Ford said he believes in handling the problem on an individual permit basis—which he said his administration now is doing—hinged to the feasibility of reclaiming the land.

✔ He will put the state's portion of federal revenue-sharing funds, estimated at about $29 million, into a trust fund.

"We'll think through (the way to spend it) for the next two years and I'll present it to the next session of the legislature," the governor said.

✔ He believes the death penalty ought to be reimposed in Kentucky to conform with U.S. Supreme Court requirements.

The high court recently ruled that capital punishment as now practiced in most states is unconstitutional.

Ford said he favors the death penalty "in certain areas, but I have not crystallized in my mind what those areas would be."

Louisville Courier-Journal

Fig. 13.7 *A news story with minor elements of the story shirt-tailed onto the main story.*

the wagon: "I hear stories about guys who are sober 20 years and then had that first drink."

This conclusion not only brings the reader up to date on the young alcoholic who is the main figure in the story, but it has him give his own picture of the future, the long days of worry and apprehension that face the alcoholic who is trying to control his illness.

In the following conclusion from a light feature in the *Milwaukee Journal* Robert W. Wells describes the visit of a high school French class to a French Line freighter calling at Milwaukee:

> By then the students were using their skills as French speakers quite bravely. One officer was drawn aside and asked how la classe de français de Wauwatosa was faring in its battle with the language.
>
> "We can understand them," he said gallantly. "They do well. But the accent—It is like mine when I speak English. You would not mistake me for an American, no?
>
> "If they were in France, one would not suppose Wauwatosa was near Le Havre."

Direct quotation is not the only useful device for putting together a conclusion. David G. Gladfelter of the *Milwaukee Sentinel* ended the first part of a four-part series on poverty with a simple statement about how he reported the story. In the first paragraph of his story he said:

> In four days, one cannot begin to know poverty. One can only sample it.

And a paragraph or so later:

> For four days my assignment was to live on a public assistance budget. I was to spend what a 30-year-old single man on relief rolls would spend. I was to go where he would go; do what he would do.

He ended the first installment of his series, thus:

> And so I went out where Milwaukee's poor men are: listening,

This Time the Pigeon Drop Nets $1,200 and Ring

A 74 year old widow was the victim Thursday of the old pigeon drop scheme.

She was persuaded to give $1,200 and her diamond ring to two women she met while walking home from a grocery store.

Police gave this account:

Mrs. Frances Volk, of 5715 W. Capitol Dr., met the two women in an auto parked in the 5700 block of W. Capitol Dr. They told her they had found an envelope containing $31,000. They showed her a brown envelope containing what appeared to be bills an inch thick. Three or four $100 bills were on the top of the pile.

Joined by Mrs. Volk, they drove to 6114 W. Capitol Dr.,

where one woman said she would consult an attorney. The woman entered the building. When she came out again, she said an attorney had told her that the money was Mafia gambling money and that they could keep it, but they each should put up money to show good faith.

They then drove to 47th and Capitol, where one woman got out, supposedly to get money. The other woman drove Mrs. Volk to the First Wisconsin National Bank in Capitol Court, where she withdrew $1,200 from her savings account and placed it in an envelope.

They picked up the other woman, who said she had cashed a $5,000 check and

drove back to the building at 6114 W. Capitol Dr.

One of the women went into the building and returned, saying the attorney had advised that they exchange envelopes as a good faith gesture. Mrs. Volk also gave the women her $500 diamond ring.

Mrs. Volk was told that she should go to see the attorney. She found no attorney in the building, but when she went back outside, she found that the car with the two women was gone.

Among other crimes reported.

ARMED ROBBERY

Clark Service Station, 905 W. Center St. Two men, both armed with revolvers, demanded money from attendant who gave them $100 before they fled.

ROBBERY

Spic & Span Cleaners, 3285 N. Green Bay Ave. Man entered store, displayed

an atomizer and sprayed the clerk's face with a chemical irritant, fled with $53.18.

ATTEMPTED RAPE

Girl, 12, walking near 14th and Center, accosted by 16 year old youth who dragged her into a parking lot behind 1315 W. Center St., displayed a small revolver and told her to remove her clothes. He fled before raping her.

BURGLARIES

F. W. Woolworth Store, 1243 W. Vliet St. Display window broken by piece of concrete, five radios and electric organ taken.

Moose Lodge No. 49, at 5476 S. 13th St. Window pried open, $44 and liquor, beer and cigars taken.

Residence of Neil Johansen, 5822 W. Custer Ave. Door case knifed, tape recorder and blender taken.

Residence of Elizabeth Giese, 5823 N. 69th St. Entry gained through unlocked hall door, kitchen window glass broken, $50 taken.

Resident of Ira Grimes, 3743 N. 18th St. Rear door unlocked from milk chute, camera, movie projector, man's wrist watch taken.

Residence of Ray Alexander, 2824 N. 10th St. Basement window opened, kitchen door forced, a television, radio and 200 pennies taken.

Uptowner, 1032 E. Center St. Front door pried open, metal box with $844 taken.

Residence of Joan Ashford, 218 E. Hadley St. Rear door forced, television, AM-FM radio, woman's watch, camera, two

women's leather coats and a boy's leather coat taken.

Residence of Joyce Killebrew, 2455 N. Palmer St. Kitchen storm window pried off, unlocked inner window opened, television, clock radio, phonograph, sewing machine, bracelet watch, pendant watch, five quarts of liquor and assorted jewelry taken.

Residence of Judson Hull, 2572 N. Newhall St. Wooden panel covering previously broken window forced and door unlocked, television, two tape recorders and camera taken.

Residence of Lillie M. McGee, 2652-B N. 16th St. Storm window pried open and inner window opened, 12 gauge shotgun, stereo, television and sweaters taken.

Residence of Willa Williamson, 2938 N. 1st St. Front door case knifed, television, radio and checks taken. Three juveniles arrested.

Residence of Louis Scherbarth, 6715 W. Burleigh St. Window broken and unlocked, metal box containing papers, a bank, a man's diamond ring and gold ring with three rubies, and $175 taken.

Milwaukee Journal

Fig. 13.8 *Material shirt-tailed to this news story is in summary form and set in type smaller than the usual text type.*

Redskins' Harraway leads title clincher

Associated Press

PHILADELPHIA — "We've fulfilled our immediate goal . . . win the division title, but now we've got to go on from there," said coach George Allen yesterday after his Washington Redskins defeated the Philadelphia Eagles 23-7.

Washington clinched its first National Football League Division title in 27 years by systematically grinding down the surprisingly tough Eagles, who still smarted from last week's 62-10 humiliation by the New York Giants.

The Washington dressing room was strangely quiet. There was no champagne, no back-slapping, very little jubilation. It appeared in keeping with the low-key philosophy of their coach. The big job, the Redskins indicated, was still ahead, the playoffs and the Super Bowl.

The Eagles' charged-up defensive unit held the league's leading ground-gainer, Larry Brown, to only 70 yards, forcing Washington to turn to super-blocker Charley Harraway for key yardage. The Redskins also got three clutch field goals from Curt Knight.

"After the first half, I had my doubts (about winning)," said Allen, who in two years rebuilt the Redskins from a perennial also-ran to champions of the National Conference Eastern Division. "We were on the ropes, but we turned things around in the second half because the offense controlled the ball 75 per cent of the time."

Knight stakes early lead

Losing coach Ed Khayat said, "you're never pleased when you fail to win, but at least we hit some people out there today . . . there's no tougher team to face than the Redskins."

The last time Washington won a divisional title was in 1945 when it finished with an 8-2 record and then lost to the then-Cleveland Rams 15-14 in the NFL championship game. The 11 victories recorded so far this season are the most ever for a Washington team. The previous high was 10 in 1942 when the Redskins finished 10-1-0 and went on to win the league title over the Chicago Bears.

The Redskins took an early 3-0 first period lead on a nine-yard field goal by Knight but fell behind early in the second quarter as the Eagles scored on a 10-yard touchdown pass from rookie John Reaves to Howard Carmichael. Harraway's one-yard TD run rallied Washington to a shakey 10-7 half time edge.

Washington's tough defense held the Eagles scoreless in the second half, while quarterback Billy Kilmer directed the offense to a pair of field goals and a touchdown. Knight booted three-pointers from the 14 and 46, and Kilmer tossed a three-yard scoring pass to Charley Taylor.

Statistics

	Redskins	Eagles
First downs	19	9
Rushes-yards	50-170	20-66
Passing yards	155	54
Passes	12-15-0	7-21-0
Punts	3-40.3	6-41.5
Fumbles-lost	4-0	2-1
Penalties-yards	6-81	8-48

WASHINGTON REDSKINS . . . . . 3 7 3 10—23
PHILADELPHIA EAGLES . . . . . 7 0 0 0— 7

Wash—FG, Knight, 9. Phi—Carmichael, 10, pass from Reaves (Dempsey kick). Wash—Harraway, 1, run (Knight kick). Wash—FG, Knight 14. Wash—FG, Knight 46. Wash—Taylor, 2, pass from Kilmer (Knight kick).
Attendance—65,770.

Louisville Courier-Journal

Fig. 13.9 *Statistics, box scores and other details are routinely shirt-tailed to game stories.*

absorbing, hoping to meet them as one of them.

An anecdote is frequently an effective way to bring a news feature to a conclusion. It illustrates, explains, and at the same time provides a final note. In a story in the *New York Times* which reported Arlo Guthrie's wedding, Fred Ferretti brought his account to an end this way:

> As he (the justice of the peace) said "man and wife," the hill erupted with "Yea, yea, whoopie," the conch shells sounded and presently the rock band began playing "Wedding love, earthly love, everyday love."
> But before the band did, everybody on the hill sang the Baptist hymn "Amazing Grace, How Sweet the Sound."
> And Alice cried.

Questions frequently provide a good stopping point. In this conclusion to a feature in the *Lapeer County Press*, the writer tries to show two sides to the lives of "sad old men," widowers who live out their remaining years alone. Here is his concluding paragraph:

> Then the final question: Was Bobby Stillman really a worthless old bum? Or was he a victim of a rural social malignancy that we are either too blind or too cowardly to face?

The concluding question hits hard at the premise of the story and suggests that the reader must consider the question, and the problem, a personal one.

Rhetorical questions, of course, are based on information presented in the story. They are intended to end the story on a now-its-up-to-you note. They ask the reader to get involved, to think seriously about the story; they urge him to do something. A conclusion with a question is a goal and a stimulus. It is intended to nick the reader where it hurts, in his conscience.

CHAPTER 14

Structuring the Larger Story: II

IN CHAPTER 13 we examined leads and conclusions and one special organizing device, shirttailing. In this chapter we will look at a number of devices for organizing the body of the story and we will discuss the structure and organization of the story as a whole.

THE BODY OF THE STORY

In shorter news stories, the body can be written as a unit. The development might be chronological or an inverted pyramid using a series of summary statements. But, when the story gets longer and when it incorporates a number of angles or points of view, it may demand the use of several organizing devices. The development of a larger story may take advantage of a whole bagful of writing tricks, each one used to tell part of the story and all of them tied together with transitional devices.

None of the organizing devices we are about to discuss will be new to you. We discussed them all before, in connection with other writing problems. Here we will see them used to construct the larger story.

The Inverted Pyramid

In a larger story each part is organized in response to the nature of the material. Quite often the material is a set of facts that must be presented logically; that is, main fact first, then the supporting facts. This is, of course, nothing more than the inverted pyramid format we have seen used over and over again in shorter news stories. Here, for example, it is used to present one part of a longer story about a plane crash:

> Deputy Coroner Sidney Berman said nine bodies, all burned too badly to be identified, had been brought to a temporary morgue at the airfield and "we have accounted for everyone." The dead were six women and three men, he said. Nearby hospitals treated at least 15 injured persons.
> Names of the victims were not released last night pending notification of relatives. North Central said six of the nine victims were bound for Madison, Wis., and three for Duluth.
> All of the dead were aboard North Central Flight 575 taking off at 6:01 p.m. on a flight to Madison and Duluth with 45 persons aboard. Visibility was one-quarter of a mile.
> *Minneapolis Tribune*

A similar account of an automobile accident which was part of a weekend traffic accident roundup story:

> Mrs. Cacha died Friday when the car she was a passenger in and two others collided on Hwy. 7 east of Hutchinson, Minn.
> Her son Dale, 22, who was driving the car, was taken to a Hutchinson hospital where he was treated and

Among a list of more than two dozen demands for reform being considered by the commissioner and his staff are:

—A change in bylaws which would require election of Blue Shield board members by subscribers, rather than by a doctor-dominated group, much as shareholders elect officers of proprietary concerns.

—The right to participate in Blue Shield should be conditional on the doctor's taking a minimum number of hours of refresher courses a year.

—Salary limits for hospital-based doctors.

—Only board-certified surgeons should be reimbursed by Blue Shield.

—Blue Shield should require all participating physicians to prescribe drugs generically. (A similar provision was inserted in the renegotiated contract between Philadelphia Blue Cross and participating hospitals.)

—Blue Shield should not pay for surgery performed in un-accredited hospitals nor reimburse doctors who perform surgery in specialty areas outside their competence.

Boston Globe

Fig. 14.1   *Itemizing, point by point.*

released. The other drivers were identified as Philip Johnson, 25, Grove City, Minn., and Lyle Braun, 17, Young America, Minn.

Minneapolis Tribune

Itemizing

Presenting information point by point in an itemized list is as useful for organizing part of a story as it is for organizing a lead. The itemized unit consists of an introductory paragraph followed by a series of long or short paragraphs presenting separate but related points on a single topic. The items may be numbered or set off with a bullet or other typographical device. Figure 14.1, an excerpt from a lengthy news story, is a good example of this technique.

The example below shows itemization using short paragraphs:

EPA said its mission will include studies of:
• Effects of noise at various levels.
• Projected growth of noise levels in urban areas through the year 2000.
• The psychological and physiological effects on humans.
• Effects of sporadic and extreme noise such as jet noise near airports as compared with constant noise.
• Effect on wildlife and property including values.
• Effect of sonic booms on property.
• Other noise problems involving the public health and welfare.

St. Petersburg Times

Lists

Occasionally a story has to include many names and one of the easiest devices for organizing names is a list. One simple way to arrange a list is in alphabetical order, although there may be other logical ways of doing it. In the following excerpt, the writer developed categories suitable to the story:

The list of permit officers hired since May 16 includes at least six of Gov. Ford's 1971 county campaign chairmen or co-chairmen—Earl A. Houchins of Edmonson County, Russell O. Young of Monroe County, Kenneth G. Teague of Trimble County, Lewis M. Britton of Woodford County, William B. Mineer of Fleming County, and Jack L. Thompson of Rowan County.

The list also includes three former state legislators—Pearl Strong of Ary in Perry County, James T. Alexander of Versailles and Archie Craft of Lexington, formerly of Whitesburg; two former sheriffs—James C. Harris of Lincoln County, and Young, of Monroe County; the son of Logan County Judge Robert R. Brown, Bobby R. Brown; the son of Logan County Clerk Marion Johnson, Larry E. Johnson, and the wife of State Livestock Sanitation Director Tom Maddox of Owensboro, Mrs. Mary A. Maddox.

Louisville Courier-Journal

Sometimes lists are shirt-tailed onto the main story:

Here is how much Greater Philadelphia area governments would receive:

Delaware County (total)	$6,076,805
Delaware County government	2,350,254
Townships (total)	2,147,504
Chester City (Boroughs)	891,103
Aldan	15,490
Brookhaven	22,282

Philadelphia Bulletin

"That's the one," said Mrs. Hendler. "This is the one in the window? The genuine smoky topaz?"

"Yes."

Mrs. Hendler bought the pendant, paid $17.05 including tax, then, as the jeweler handed her the pendant wrapped in Christmas paper, she asked:

"It's genuine smoky topaz?"

"Of course."

"It's not really, is it?" she asked.

"Of course it's genuine."

"It's really quartz, isn't it?"

"It's smoky topaz quartz."

"It's quartz, isn't it?"

"Yes, it's quartz."

Mrs. Hendler reached into her shopping bag and pulled out her wallet. She flipped it open and showed it to the man. It said "Esther E. Hendler, Supervising Inspector, Bureau of Weights and Measures, Department of Markets." Gently she asked the jeweler:

"Why don't you advertise it as quartz?"

"Everybody knows its quartz."

"Who?"

"Everybody."

"The consumer?"

"Certainly, the consumer knows."

New York Herald-Tribune

Fig. 14.2 *Dialogue as an organizing device.*

It was close to midnight, the lonely time when one nothing day fades into another.

Driver Ed Marks took the call. "Woman slashed her wrist."

Mullen reached for the phone to the police radio room. "An 801–X," he said and gave the address.

He turned back to Marks. "You mean her wrists."

"No, just one of them."

"They never cut one. Always both."

They brought the redhead in and strapped her down. "I want to go home," she moaned. "Leave me alone."

Dr. Ted C. Woy held her arms while Nellie Shepanski, a pert blond nurse, cleansed and bandaged her wrist.

"Come on, Dorothy," Woy said when they let her up. "This way."

"My name's not Dorothy," she snapped.

They led her to a cell with a padded floor and a low bed and the screaming started again. "Oh, please. I don't want to be by myself. I've been that way for three days."

It took four of them to get her inside. They locked the door.

San Francisco Examiner

Fig. 14.3 *Another example of effective dialogue.*

When lists are shirt-tailed onto a story they may be set in the newspaper's regular body type, but frequently (as was the case of the above example, they are set in somewhat smaller type, usually six point.

Chronology

We have to cite chronology again as a basic and useful organizing device, this time for its uses in smaller segments of a story. The following is an excerpt from a column-long story about a plane crash:

Clarke County sheriff's officials said the pilot radioed the Athens control tower at 10:20 p.m. inquiring about food and fuel at the airport. The plane was about 12 miles from the airport at the time.

Witnesses said the pilot approached for a landing but apparently overshot the landing strip. Bobby Smith, an airport communications operator, said the plane touched down then surged back into the air, cleared a hangar and crashed.

The plane broke in half but did not burn.

Sheriff's officials said the three men were thrown from the plane. Miss Andes' body was found inside the badly mangled wreckage.

Officers said they found scuba diving gear and other vacation equipment in the wreckage.

Milwaukee Sentinel

Dialogue

Conversation or dialogue is another useful device for organizing parts of a larger story. In some instances this takes the form of an exchange between two people in the story, participants; sometimes the exchange is between an outsider (the reporter or other observer) and a participant. The excerpt in Fig. 14.2 illustrates this technique. Such exchanges are vivid, real. They take us right into the story so that we can observe the action. You will notice in both Fig. 14.2 and 14.3 that there is minimum attribution. The writer clearly establishes who is talking, but once that is done much of the dialogue is not directly attributed. Look at Fig. 14.3.

Question and Answer

In covering trials or public hearings, newspapers frequently reproduce verbatim testimony, or questions and answers (Q. and A.). This device can be adapted to many different situations and can be a very effective means of presenting information in the words of participants in a story. It is somewhat more formal than dialogue: dialogue usually records spontaneous conversation while Q. and A. is a planned or structured exchange.

In a story about court cases or public hearings, Q. and A. is the exchange between a questioner and a witness, both participants in a legal or quasi-legal proceeding. In a feature story, the Q. and A. may be an exchange between a reporter, an outsider, and someone involved in the story. It would be more formal than conversation between participants in an event, such as that between the jeweler and the weights and measures inspector (Fig. 14.2). The following excerpt from a story explaining the intricacies of a presidential order for a wage and price freeze is even more tightly structured:

> The following questions and answers on the freeze are based on official statements, the replies of agency spokesmen concerned and a White House fact sheet.
> Q. How can a consumer check on whether a merchant is complying with the freeze?
> A. The presidential order requires that all persons in the business of selling or providing goods or services must "maintain for public inspection a record of the highest prices or rents charged for such or similar commodities during the 30-day period ending Aug. 14, 1971."
> Q. Are dividend payments and interest charges also frozen to previous levels?
> A. No. Mr. Nixon has asked the nation's bankers to hold the line on interest. Lacking authority to control dividends, he is asking corporations voluntarily not to raise their dividend payments.
> *Detroit News*

There was considerably more of this, but this brief excerpt will give you an idea of the technique. The writer has constructed a series of carefully-thought-out questions as a means of presenting information gathered from several sources. His Q. and A. is constructed after he has gotten his notes together, not as part of the reporting process. The questions are formulated by the reporter to provide a means of presenting the answers he has in his notes. This is quite different from reporting actual dialogue, although the format is the same. Here is another example of this technique:

> Now the Michigan Legislature is to be redistricted all over again, which must confuse some voters. Here are some questions some citizens may ask, and the answers.
> Q. Why are we going through this all over again?
> A. Because the Supreme Court has ordered it.
> Q. Why did the court do this?
> A. Because five of the eight justices agreed with the Republicans who brought the suit, that the existing plan should be replaced by a new and better one—that the existing plan was only temporary in the first place.
> Q. What's wrong with the existing plan?
> A. Nothing technically; it has districts of equal population except for one where a mistake of a few thousand voters was made. But the Republicans claim "Gerrymandering," that is, a plan that . . . .
> *Muskegon Chronicle*

As you can see from the first paragraph of this excerpt, the writer is using a carefully contrived dialogue, not a spontaneous one. The writer made up some questions about the redistricting plan in order to provide a structure for talking about the plan and explaining how it would work.

Q. and A. can be used to present a small part of a larger story, or to organize an entire story. The principle is the same, however: it is the writer who organizes information that has come from one, sometimes from several, sources.

Direct Quotation

Sometimes the most effective way to organize information is to let the sources speak in their own words. This may mean quoting a few words or lengthy passages, but in a longer story it is just one of several organizational techniques. In a somewhat involved column-long story from the *Buffalo Evening News,* the writer used direct quotation in two instances in a story about a supposed plot to murder two sheriff's deputies:

> Roman was arrested again Sept. 14 on a felony drug charge when deputies reportedly found about 6 pounds of marijuana in his home. That arrest was connected with another arrest the same day in which another 35 pounds of marijuana was seized, deputies reported.
>
> "The problem started Sept. 15, the day after we arrested him the second time," Chief Tuttolomondo said.
>
> "We started receiving threatening telephone calls, but figured they were just cranks. Over that weekend, undercover men received information that made us think maybe there was more to it," he added.

Farther down in the story, the writer again quoted the chief of police:

> Officers reported the plan to kill both officers the same day at their homes—Chief Tuttolomondo was to be first, then Capt. Caffery.
>
> "They were going to wait for us outside our homes until we came home and kill us as we got out of our cars or they were going to get us on the way out of our houses," Chief Tuttolomondo said.
>
> Roman was arrested about 3:15 a.m. today in a tavern on Kenmore Ave. near Englewood Ave.

Summary

Summary involves reducing large amounts of information to a few essential points and rendering them in the writer's own words. We have seen how to use summary in writing speech stories. But, it is also an important device for organizing the longer or more complicated story. In this excerpt, from a story in the Mount Clemens, Mich., *Macomb Daily,* the writer uses two paragraphs to summarize and explain a complicated voter registration suit:

> The residents filed suit the following week in U.S. District Court against Mrs. Jorgenson, Bruff and Austin, charging them with interfering with their right to register and vote by their "dilly-dallying" in determining whether they qualified as Harrison residents.
>
> The suit, which was filed on behalf of the Selfridge residents by Robert J. Lord, attorney for Tri-County Citizen Action, Inc., also challenged a provision in the state election law which has been interpreted as preventing military personnel from registering to vote in a nearby municipality.

In another story about the same case, the writer summarized the history of the lawsuit to provide background for readers who may have missed earlier stories. This longer story is reprinted in Fig. 14.4.

The suit was filed against Mrs. Jorgenson, Secretary of State Richard H. Austin and Harrison Township Attorney John B. Bruff, who, the Selfridge residents claim, had "denied, delayed and limited" the residents' right to register and vote.

Last February, a group from Selfridge asked Mrs. Jorgenson to register its members to vote in Harrison Township elections, but she denied the requests pending an opinion from Austin's office on whether they were actually Harrison residents.

Mrs. Jorgenson's request for clarification was "mislaid" in Austin's office and was not dealt with until last month when Attorney General Frank Kelley issued an opinion on the matter, which still left Mrs. Jorgenson confused.

Asked to interpret Kelley's letter, Bruff said that the Selfridge residents must own property, have a car registered or have some other "permanent" connection in Harrison in order to vote.

But Austin's office said a person had only to "declare" this "intention" to reside in Harrison and instructed Mrs. Jorgenson to register the Selfridge group.

Mrs. Jorgenson and her staff on Oct. 4, 5 and 6 registered the Selfridge personnel, but the suit in federal court claims that not all the residents were given "sufficient opportunity" to register because of the legal "haggling" by Mrs. Jorgenson, Bruff and Austin.

The Selfridge residents claim that they are "naturally" residents of Harrison, since the township surrounds the base. Harrison officials say they are not.

Mount Clemens, Mich., *Macomb Daily*

Fig. 14.4 *Use of summary to provide background.*

To summarize is to present the substance of a story, event or situation in a condensed or concise form. It is to be brief, to give the essential facts stripped of detail and adornment. It is, in short, a device for crowding essential information into very little space. The examples just given are skillful summaries of a complicated situation. The beginning news writer who wants to become a skilled professional must learn the art of summarizing. It is one of the news writer's essential tools.

How can you acquire the skill? Practice telling your friends about things you have seen or heard. If you are not summarizing adequately, you'll be cut short. If you leave out essential details, you'll get questions. Another way to practice is to rewrite news stories, trying to reduce them by half at first, then by two-thirds, then to a few essential paragraphs. It is not easy. Summarizing is a mental process, not a mechanical one. In order to summarize you must first understand the material, then select those ideas or facts that must be retained and discard the rest. Then you must write the summary in your own words in clear, direct and orderly sentences.

OVERALL ORGANIZATION

Up to this point we have discussed ways to organize parts of larger stories: leads, segments of the development, conclusions. Now let's take a look at some strategies for organizing an entire story.

Chronology

In previous chapters we have seen a number of examples using chronology to tell a story. Chronology is a useful device in an action story, even a short one, and in short feature stories. It is equally effective in telling a larger and more involved story. The *Chicago Daily News* story about the two escaped convicts (Fig. 14.5) makes very effective use of chronology to structure a long

story. There is only one break in the strict chronology that starts in the lead—a few paragraphs of background. This interruption, starting with the words *four hours earlier*, is also told in chronological order. A concluding section includes some summary, but it appears in its proper place in the chronology.

Shifting Scenes

Sometimes a story has two sides or two different points of view and the writer can best present the story by shifting from one point of view to the other. This device was effectively used by J. Anthony Lukas in a *New York Times* story under the headline "The Two Worlds of Linda Fitzpatrick." This lengthy feature tells about an 18-year-old girl who was murdered in Greenwich Village. The contrast between her life as she lived it and as her family thought she lived it is expressed both by organization and typography—the family's view in roman and the reality in italic. An extract from this moving story appears in Fig. 14.6.

Somewhat similar is the approach taken in the story in Fig. 14.7. Here the writer alternates paragraphs of a story about a young alcoholic with paragraphs of comment by doctors and other people who work with alcoholics. Again, two views: from the inside and from the outside.

Step-by-Step

Another useful approach for organizing certain kinds of stories is the serial or step-by-step format. This is the cookbook approach: how to bake a cake, how to put together a Christmas toy, how to enroll for winter term classes. The excerpt in Fig. 14.8, from a story which explains how a civil suit is processed, is a good example.

A Little of Everything

Chronology, shifting scenes and step-by-step formatting are somewhat specialized approaches to the overall organization of the larger news story.

It is more common to use a variety of techniques to organize different parts of the story.

The story in Fig. 14.9 shows how one writer used a number of techniques to tell a long and involved story about a crime, the subsequent investigation and the trial of the accused men. The story has been annotated to help you identify the techniques and devices discussed in this chapter and in Chapter 13.

Doug Shuit's story is interesting and well told. It is not a blueprint for every lengthy story. You might tackle the story in some other way. But it is instructive and provides a kind of sampler of techniques useful in structuring larger stories.

By Donald Zochert

It was 6:50 p.m. on Thursday, Nov. 14, when they knocked at the front door.

Bernard Politte got up from his easy chair and swung the door open. Two men stood outside. One of them, the older one, raised his hand.

In it he held a shiny gold badge.

"Would you step outside a moment?" he asked.

Bernie did and the man raised his other hand.

In it he held a snub-nose revolver.

"We need shelter," he said. "Let's go inside."

Bernie Politte backed into his living room.

The older man, square-jawed and soft-spoken, introduced himself. Patrick Kane. Then the younger man, his eyes intense despite their lightness. Dale Wilson. What's your name? Where's your wife? In the bedroom? Call her. Her name is Odetta? Okay, Bernie. Okay, Odetta. No one will get hurt.

It was all according to Emily Post: terror on a first-name basis.

Patrick Donald Kane, white male, age 43, brown eyes, hair graying at the temples. Bank robbery.

Dale Glennon Wilson, white male, age 24, hazel eyes, pockmarked face. On his right forearm, tattooed, "love and hate." Kidnaping. Murder in prison.

They were strangers to each other.

Four hours earlier, near Warrenton, Mo., they had overpowered the deputy U.S. marshal and special-duty St. Louis police officer who were transferring them from Leavenworth Penitentiary to St. Louis.

Kane was to attend an appeal hearing, Wilson to stand trial for murdering a fellow inmate. They couldn't wait.

They handcuffed the guards, drove down toward Pacific, Mo., and put the lawmen in a shack in the woods.

From Officer Robert Gentry, of the St. Louis police department, Kane took $240 and a revolver. "I'll see that you get this back," he said, "but I need it now."

From Vernon Whitlock, deputy U.S. marshal, Kane took a gold badge and a ring.

Then he and young Wilson got in the car and headed for St. Louis. In Bridgeton, a suburb west of the city, Wilson spotted a red and black 1968 Malibu parked in a driveway. Not bad.

It was getting dark and they were hungry.

Patrick Donald Kane and Dale Glennon Wilson decided to pay Mr. and Mrs. Bernard K. Politte a visit.

They stood around in the living room, four people and a gun, and Kane said sit down and nobody will get hurt. Wilson didn't say anything.

At 7:30 p.m., Ronnie Politte, 13, came home, through the garage and family room and into the living room. Now there were five.

Two were still hungry.

Kane took the Malibu and drove down to the shopping center, a few blocks away. Wilson waited. He paced back and forth in the living room, seemed nervous, but said nothing.

In a half hour, Kane came back. He brought two big steaks, a bag of potato chips, a couple of onions, some beer, whisky and a bottle of champagne. He also brought paper plates.

"I don't want to mess your kitchen up," he told Odetta Politte.

Kane tossed one steak in the refrigerator and cooked the other—medium. Then they ate, he and Wilson. He had a beer and two glasses of champagne; Wilson sipped the whisky.

The hostages watched.

After dinner, Kane and the Polittes went into the living room. They sat down and talked.

Kane was a good talker. He put his gun in the holster and stretched his legs and talked. He talked about prison.

Ronnie Politte was only 13 and no one was going to spoil his evening. He went into his bedroom and began to play rock 'n' roll records.

Wilson, tight-mouthed and a little wobbly, went with him. Kane watched him go.

"I don't know this boy too well," he said to the Polittes. "If you don't want him back there with your son, just tell me."

Three times, Kane got up and walked over to the boy's bedroom to see that everything was okay. It was.

At 10 p.m., they were still counting the hours. Wilson wandered out of the bedroom, saying nothing, and they all sat down to watch the news on television.

Two convicts had escaped, the newscaster said, and one of them—Patrick Donald Kane—was a bank robber and murderer.

"That's a lie!" Kane snapped at the television. "There's your murderer right there!"

He pointed at Wilson.

There wasn't much more to talk about.

At 3 a.m., Wilson took Ronnie Politte into the boy's bedroom. He tied Ronnie's hands and feet with hosiery. But first he gave the boy a $5 bill.

"Be nice," he said. "Don't turn out like me."

Kane took Bernard and Mrs. Politte into the master bedroom, tied their hands with hosiery, and lashed them to the bed with drapery cords.

Fig. 14.5 *A good example of chronological order.*

"Is that too tight?" he asked. It wasn't.

"I want you two to stay here for a couple of hours," Kane said. Then he left.

From the bedroom, the Polittes heard the radio go on—loud. They heard the sound of the shower.

Kane and Wilson were cleaning up. It was time to move out. They found about $800 in cash. They took some clothes: a blue suit, five sports shirts, two black windbreakers. They took Bernie Politte's billfold and his credit cards.

And then there was only the sound of the radio.

It was 9:30 a.m. Friday, Nov. 15.

At a table in the North Grand Club, 1024 N. Grand E., Springfield, Ill., two men sat looking at the morning's edition of the Springfield State Journal.

One of the men was getting gray at the temples. The other looked young enough to be his son.

Eight blocks away, near Springfield Junior College, a red and black 1968 Malibu with Missouri license plates was parked. It was empty.

The waitress in the North Grand Club walked over to the men and asked for their orders. For the older gentleman, a fish sandwich and a mug of draft beer. For the younger man, a fish sandwich and a Pepsi.

While they ate, they thumbed through the paper. They were looking for used car ads.

At 10 a.m. the older man got up and went to the pay telephone. Name's Ben Johnson, he said. Want to buy a car for my son. Got anything for around $100?

A few blocks across town, at Jack's Auto Sales, 704 N. Ninth St., Jack Means sat in his office and told the man on the telephone sure, he had some junkers.

The caller said he and his son were at the North Grand Club having breakfast. Could they get picked up in about an hour? It was a deal.

Patrick Donald Kane put down the phone and walked back to the table. The waitress came over and they chatted. They seemed like average Joes.

The boy had an accident with his car, Kane explained, and were going to pick him up another one.

"Don't be too hard on him," the waitress chided. "All kids have accidents."

Dale Glennon Wilson didn't say anything.

Jack Means finally showed up at 11:30 a.m., in a 1957 Pontiac he had just swapped for, and the waitress in the North Grand Club lost her two customers.

They didn't leave her a tip.

Jack showed the two men around the lot. There seemed to be no hurry.

Finally the older man, Ben Johnson he said his name was, decided maybe he liked that '57 Pontiac best, so they went into the office to close the deal. Ben pulled a fresh fifth of whisky from his pocket and offered it around.

No takers.

They sat there for 15 minutes, gabbing—"trying to beat me down on the price," Jack Means said. And then they closed the deal. The men gave Jack two $100 bills, and Jack gave them $50 change.

At 1 p.m., the two men headed downtown in the Pontiac to buy 1968 Illinois license plates. But 15 minutes later they were back.

"You forgot your dealer's plates," friendly Ben said to Means, "so we brought them back."

A nice touch. The world's not full of bums after all.

Patrick Donald Kane and Dale Glennon Wilson drove across the street to a gas station. They fastened the 1968 license plates, SM 7363, to the car, and pulled out into Ninth St.

Up the road was Route 66.

It was 1:30 p.m. and four hours to Chicago.

At 6 p.m. on Friday, Nov. 15, Kane and Wilson checked into the Villa Motel, 5952 N. Lincoln, Chicago. They gave their names as Ben and James Johnson, father and son, Springfield, Mo.

The clerk gave them Room 9.

Now, for about 48 hours, Kane and Wilson dropped from sight. Perhaps they slept.

They had been busy.

After dark on Sunday evening, Nov. 17, a powder-blue Volkswagen drove past the Villa Motel.

In the car were a 23-year-old Air Force veteran from Michigan and his blond bride. They had been married in Michigan Saturday, and had come to Chicago for their honeymoon.

A sign advertising color television caught the bride's eye. They decided to stop.

The clerk gave them Room 11.

The newlyweds had been in their room 20 minutes when there was a knock at the door. They ignored it. Ten minutes later there was a metallic tapping on the picture window.

The bridegroom went to the window and pushed back the drapes. A man peered in the window. He had a key in his hand.

"Hey!" the man shouted. "You left your key in the door!"

The bridegroom went to the door and opened it.

Two men stood there. One was middle-aged, graying at the temples. In one hand he held a shiny gold badge. In the other he held a snub-nose revolver.

Kane and Wilson pushed themselves into the room and shut the door behind them.

This time, they didn't introduce themselves.

It was 9 p.m.

"We're not police officers," Wilson said. "We're here to rob you."

"Where's the girl," Kane said.

This was no pleasant conversation. Nothing was according to Emily Post.

The two men bound the hands and feet of the honeymooners with adhesive tape. They ransacked the couple's personal effects, pocketed $400 in cash and took the bridegroom's identification papers.

Then they unwound the tape from around the ankles of the bride.

Kane raped her first.

The room was quiet.

Wilson left and came back in a few moments with an armful of sheets and pillow cases.

Then he raped the girl.

Kane and Wilson worked quickly. They ripped the sheets and pillow cases into shreds and tightly bound the newlyweds.

Earlier, they had moved the old Pontiac from the motel parking lot and left it parked a block and a half away, in front of 5828 N. Whipple St.

They didn't need it anymore.

Now they had a powder-blue 1967 Volkswagen, with wedding gifts and a sun roof.

But there was no sun.

It was midnight, Sunday, Nov.

Fig. 14.5 (continued)

17. Patrick Donald Kane and Dale Glennon Wilson really had reason to run.

Three days later, Mrs. Odetta Politte of Bridgeton, Mo., had her red and black 1968 Malibu back. The police had found it parked in Springfield, Ill.

The car had been driven 211 miles and something was wrong with the ignition.

Mrs. Politte drove the car to a garage in St. Charles, Mo., to have it worked on. It was almost 1:30 p.m., on Wednesday, Nov. 20.

And she heard sirens.

A few minutes earlier, two men had walked into the First State Bank of St. Charles at 121 N. Main St., a block from the Missouri River and three doors from the St. Charles police station.

One of the men carried a carbine. The other, graying around the temples, carried a snub-nose revolver.

They forced 15 bank employes and customers into a rear room.

"I want everyone to be careful," the man with the revolver said. "I'm Kane."

The young man with the carbine stood guard over the employes while Kane prodded cashier Russell Kanseiner around the bank, ordering him to open cash drawers and the big bank vault.

He stuffed the cash, an estimated $50,000 in a white laundry bag.

Then he and Wilson fled.

Two days after the robbery, a letter arrived at the St. Louis police station. It was addressed to Robert Gentry, the officer who was with Vernon Whitlock when Kane and Wilson escaped.

The letter bore a St. Louis postmark, dated Nov. 21. But Gentry was off.

On Monday, Nov. 25, he returned to work. His sergeant handed him the letter and he opened it.

Inside were 100 $20 bills—$2,000—and a note. The note said: "Take care of Whitlock."

The note wasn't signed. It didn't have to be.

It was only three days before Thanksgiving.

Since then, there have been steady developments in the manhunt for Kane and Wilson.

Area 6 homicide Lt. John Glas, of the Chicago police department, said the newlywed couple from Michigan has positively identified photographs of the two fugitives as their assailants.

The $2,000 in cash sent to Robert Gentry is being checked to deter-

mine whether it came from the bank robbery.

The Volkswagen stolen from the honeymooners in Chicago was found this week abandoned on Eads St. in St. Louis.

And the FBI says it has identified a South St. Louis residence where Kane and Wilson stayed the week of the bank holdup.

They are the hunted. The Chicago police seek them on charges of rape and robbery.

St. Louis-area authorities seek them for holding the Politte family hostage the night of their escape.

The Federal Bureau of Investigation, with positive identifications from bank employes, seeks them on a warrant charging them with the robbery of the First State Bank of St. Charles.

A report that one of the men was involved in a bank robbery in Shreveport, La., the same day of the St. Charles holdup has been discredited by police.

Day by day, the fugitives run their race, but the snare tightens.

And Mrs. Odetta Politte remembers the words of a "houseguest" who bore the name of Kane:

"We will never go back."

Chicago Daily News

Fig. 14.5 (continued)

According to her family, Linda's last summer began normally. In mid-June she returned from Oldfields after an active year during which she was elected art editor of the yearbook. She spent several weeks in Greenwich, then left with the family for a month in Bermuda.

"The family always takes its summer vacations together; we always do things as a family," said Mr. Fitzpatrick, a tall, athletic-looking man in a well-tailored gray suit, blue tie and gold tie-clip. "Sometimes we went to Florida, sometimes to the Antibes, but for the past few summers we've rented a house in Bermuda. This time it was at Paget."

The family included seven children—Linda and 9-year-old Melissa ("Missy) from this marriage; Perry, 32; Robert, 30; Carol, 27, and David, 25, from Melissa ("Missy" from this marriage, which ended in divorce,

and Cindy from Mrs. Fitzpatrick's first marriage, which also ended in divorce. But this time only Linda and Missy accompanied their parents to Bermuda, while Cindy and her husband joined them later for 10 days.

As the Fitzpatricks remember it, Linda spent "a typical Bermuda vacation"—swimming in the crystal ocean; beach parties on the white sands; hours of painting; occasional shopping expeditions to town.

On July 31 the family returned to Greenwich, where Linda spent most of August. Again the family insists she was "the girl we knew and loved."

They say she spent most of her time painting in the studio in the back of the house. But she found plenty of time for swimming with friends in the large robin's-egg-blue pool, playing the piano, and sitting with Missy.

"Linda and Missy were terribly close," their mother said, biting her lip. "Just as close as Cindy and Linda were when they were younger."

If Linda went to New York during August, the family said, it was "just a quick trip in and out—just for the day."

Friends in the Village have a different version of Linda's summer.

"Linda told me she took LSD and smoked grass [marijuana] many times during her stay in Bermuda," recalls Susan Robinson, a small, shy hippie who ran away last May from her home on Cape Cod. "She talked a lot about a fellow who gave her a capsule of acid [LSD] down there and how she was going to send him one."

Susan and her husband, David, who live with two cats and posters of Bob Dylan, Timothy Leary and D. H. Lawrence in a two-room apartment at

Fig. 14.6 *Shifting to give two viewpoints of the same event.*

537 East 13th Street, first met Linda when she showed up there sometime early in August.

The Robinson apartment served this summer as a "crash pad"—a place where homeless hippies could spend the night or part of the night. Scrawled in pencil on the tin door to the apartment is a sign that reads: "No visitors after midnight unless by appointment please." It is signed with a flower.

"Linda just showed up one evening with a guy named Pigeon," Susan recalls. "She'd just bought Pigeon some acid. We were fooling around and everything. She stayed maybe a couple of hours and then took off."

"But we liked each other, and she came back a few nights later with a kid from Boston. She turned him on, too [gave him some LSD]. She was always doing that. She'd come into the city on weekends with $30 or $40 and would buy acid for people who needed some."

David Robinson, a gentle young man with a black D. H. Lawrence beard who works in a brassiere factory, recalls how Linda turned him on on Aug. 22. "We went to this guy who sold us three capsules for $10 apiece," he said. "She put one away to send to the guy in Bermuda, gave me one and took one herself. She was always getting burned [purchasing fake LSD] and that night she kept saying, 'God, I just hope this is good.' We were out in the Square [Tompkins Park] and we dropped it [swallowed it] right there. Forty-five minutes later — around midnight — we were off.

"We walked over to a pad on 11th Street just feeling the surge, then over to Tompkins Park, then to Cooper Union Square, where we had a very good discussion with a drunk. By then we were really flying. She was very, very groovy. At 8 A.M. I came back to the pad to sleep, and Linda took the subway up to Grand Central

and got on the train to Greenwich. She must still have been flying when she got home."

That weekend in Greenwich, Mrs. Fitzpatrick was getting Linda ready for school. "We bought her almost an entire new wardrobe," she recalled, "and Linda even agreed to get her hair cut."

For months Mr. Fitzpatrick had complained about Linda's hair, which flowed down over her shoulders, but Linda didn't want to change it. Then at the end of August she agreed. "We went to Saks Fifth Avenue and the hairdresser gave her a kind of Sassoon blunt cut, short and full. She looked so cute and smart. Hardly a hippie thing to do."

The first day of school was only 11 days off when Linda went to New York on Sept. 1. When she returned to Greenwich the next day, she told her mother she didn't want to go back to Oldfields. She wanted to live and paint in the Village.

"We couldn't have been more surprised," Mrs. Fitzpatrick said, fingering her eyeglasses, which hung from a gold pin at her left shoulder.

"Linda said her favorite teacher, who taught English, and his wife, who taught art, weren't coming back. She just adored them—when they went to Europe she just had to send champagne and fruit to the boat—and she couldn't face going back to school if they weren't there.

"What's more, she said there wasn't anything else she could learn about art at Oldfields. They'd already offered to set up a special course for her there, but she didn't want more courses. She just wanted to paint. She thought she'd be wasting her time at school."

Mother and daughter talked for nearly two hours that Saturday morning of the Labor Day weekend. Then Mrs. Fitzpatrick told her husband, who at first was determined that

Linda should finished school.

"But we talked about it with all the family and with friends all through the weekend," Mr. Fitzpatrick recalls. "Finally, on Sunday night, we gave Linda our reluctant permission, though not our approval." Linda left for New York the next morning and the family never saw her again alive.

"After all," her mother put in, "Linda's whole life was art. She had a burning desire to be something in the art world. I knew how she felt. I wanted to be a dancer or an artist when I was young, too."

The Fitzpatricks' minds were eased when Linda assured them she had already made respectable living arrangements. "She told us that she was going to live at the Village Plaza Hotel, a very nice hotel on Washington Place, near the university, you know," her mother said.

"'I'll be perfectly safe, mother,' she kept saying. 'It's a perfectly nice place with a doorman and television.' She said she'd be rooming with a girl named Paula Bush, a 22-year-old receptionist from a good family. That made us feel a lot better."

The Village Plaza, 79 Washington Place, has no doorman. A flaking sign by the tiny reception desk announces "Television for Rental" amidst a forest of other signs: "No Refunds," "All Rents Must Be Paid in Advance," "No Checks Cashed," "No Outgoing Calls for Transients."

"Sure I remember Linda," said the stooped desk clerk. "But Paula Bush? There wasn't no Paula Bush. It was Paul Bush."

Ruffling through a pile of stained and thumb-marked cards, he came up with one that had Linda Fitzpatrick's name inked at the top in neat Greenwich Country Day School penmanship. Below it in pencil was written: "Paul Bush. Bob Brumberger."

New York Times

Fig. 14.6 (continued)

Most societies have rituals to mark the passing into manhood. In America, drinking liquor and smoking cigarettes represents being old enough to do as you please, says Dr. Faruk Abuzzahab, assistant clinical professor in psychiatry and pharmacology at the University of Minnesota.

Luke was getting to be a nasty drunk. That didn't bother him much, because he couldn't remember things the morning after. Blackouts.

"People started coming up to me and saying, 'God, were you sloppy last night.' And I'd say, 'What, me sloppy? We were just having a little fun—drinking and smoking a little grass.' And they'd say, 'Sure, and crawling around the floor and puking.' They used to watch me hug the commode for half an hour every morning after a party."

He moved out of the house he had shared with other young men and moved home with his folks. That curtailed his drinking somewhat. Occasionally, he'd not drink for a few weeks, in order to show himself that he wasn't hooked on alcohol. After proving it to himself, he'd go out and get bombed.

Sometimes he'd give his father five bucks to buy him a bottle, and the two would drink the evening away at home. His father, Luke says, had the philosophy that young people should be introduced to alcohol at home, so when they'd be grown they'd have an understanding of alcohol.

Luke's father may have gone about it wrong was but fine. Dr. Abuzzahab regrets that young people in our society are not taught how to drink, much less what to drink, how much to drink and what alcohol does to the human body and mind. A taboo against showing children how to drink creates naive teenagers, he says.

To celebrate his 21st birthday, Luke had "a hell of a party" at his folks' house. They were on vacation and not witness to the destruction of their home. "That place was a real mess," Luke says. "It took five guys eight hours to clean it up."

A week later, he realized he was of legal drinking age and had not yet done a real bar scene. So with the law on his side for the first time, he went to a tavern and ordered his usual, Windsor and water. Another. And another. He figures he downed a quart of whiskey. He bought himself a bottle and went to a party.

"I blacked out. I don't remember going home. The next thing I remember was sitting under the clock in jail, getting fingerprinted. They dropped me in the drunk tank. It gets a little crowded at 4 in the morning. There were a lot of people to step on you, and you waited in line for the commode. If you could wait.

Minneapolis Tribune

Fig. 14.7 *An excerpt from a feature story in the* Minneapolis Tribune *in which two sides to the story alternate. Note the use of typography to emphasize the contrasting views.*

Saturday, the nation observes Law Day . . . a day to honor the county's judicial system and the fundamental premise that government in the U.S. is built on laws, not men. One aspect of the law very close to all of us is the process of civil court damage suits. M. P. Fleischer of The Times staff traces such an action through the twists and turns on the road to resolution of a damage suit.

By M. P. FLEISCHER
Of The Times Staff

So there you are walking along minding your own business and WHAM — you're suddenly hit in the head with a board — carelessly, you think — being toted along by some carpenter working on a constructin project.

"Purely an accident," he says.

"Ouch," you say.

You're injured — not only actually but legally. After a trip to the hospital to get your wounds dressed, you go off to see your lawyer to find out how he can ease your aching head.

"Sue," says he.

"Fine," says you, and your lawyer draws up the complaint.

You're on the brink of the courts game, you're now a plaintiff.

THE FIRST THING your lawyer does is go to the clerk of the Circuit Court's office and file the complaint. That starts the game in motion.

The next move is up to a deputy sheriff. He has to find that board-toting carpenter and serve the complaint on him. When he does, board-toting carpenter becomes a defendant.

Suppose your board-toting carpenter decides to take a six month African safari. You have no suit until he returns. You'll have to wait. Then, he'll become a defendant.

The next move is up to the defendant. He goes to see his lawyer — and they do one of three things:

✔ They either file a motion to dismiss or quash or strike or any one of a number of other things. If one of these motions is granted by the judge, go back to step one.

✔ They can turn around and file a counter-claim against you. "After all," they say, "you Mr. Plaintiff were walking on the sidewalk at the same time as Mr. Defendant and stopped to ask one of his co-workers a questions. When Mr. Defendant's board hit your head, he fell and skinned his knees.

"You contributed to the accident. You're responsible for Mr. Defendant's injuries through contributory negligence." Or they can sue Mr. Defendant's empolyer. "If Mr. Defendant hadn't been working for you Mr. Third

(See COURT, 4-D)

St. Petersburg Times

Fig. 14.8 *Steps in a civil suit: an excerpt.*

By Doug Shuit
Times Staff Writer

On a hot August night in 1969, a pretty 15-year-old babysitter was murdered in a field in Palmdale. *(simple statement of fact; summary and outline of story that follows)*

The investigation that followed, which concluded 13 days ago with the sentencing of the second of her two slayers, required the unprecedented combination of:

—Astronomers at the Griffith Observatory re-creating for a jury the sky as it looked the night of the murder, including the phase of the moon, the position of the stars and cloud cover. *(itemizing)*

—Scientists at Caltech using Space Age technology to identify photographs of vague shoeprints which almost defied measurement.

—Detective work that, among other things, took investigators to more than two dozen shoe stores in search of a single pair of shoes.

The unusual combination of police work and science was the result of an attempt to solve a crime that at first appeared to offer a relatively simple answer.

The nude body of Darlene Marie Smelcer, 15, was found Aug. 9, 1969, in a freshly plowed field about two blocks from a Palmdale home at which she had been babysitting the night before. She had been raped and strangled. *(summary)*

Less than two weeks later, Joseph Lee Jenkins, then 22, who at the time was on parole for conspiracy to commit murder, surrendered to police.

He claimed innocence but witnesses told police they had seen Jenkins lead Miss Smelcer in the direction of the field the night before her body was found, and repeated their stories in court.

And when Jenkins' alibi was disproved, a jury found him guilty of first-degree murder. The recommended penalty of death was later reduced to life in prison.

But the case was not that simple. Despite the conviction, there were several questions that remained unanswered, according to the prosecutor, Dep. Dist. Atty. Herman Herzbun. *(transition)*

Those questions and their resolution, constitute the anatomy of a successful criminal prosecution.

First, though all the evidence *(itemizing)* pointed to Jenkins, a pathologist said that more than one man had raped the girl.

Second, photographs of the earth around the girl's body showed the vague outlines of what appeared to be two different shoe prints. Miss Smelcer was not wearing shoes the night she was murdered.

Third, the chief prosecution witness at Jenkins' preliminary hearing, Clemmie Earl Henderson, then 21, was discredited by a change in stories and a failed lie-detector test.

Because Henderson failed the lie-detector test, Herzbrun decided not to use his testimony at Jenkins' trial, though it could be highly damaging, both to Jenkins and to Henson. Because of the test, the latter had also become a suspect. *(transition)*

Among other things, Henderson testified that he had seen, from about 12 feet away, Jenkins struggling with the girl in the field, but that he "ran" when he heard the girl cry, "No. No. No."

But aside from suspicion, Herzbrun and three Sheriff's Department detectives, Sgt. Robert Wood and Dets. Charles Sharp and Willia Wilson, had little physical evidence.

"Then one night I went out to the field, to the spot where the girl's body was found. It was pitch black. There were no lights of any kind," said Herzbrun, a career prosecutor in his mid-30's. *(direct quotation)*

"I got to thinking about the 12-foot distance," he continued. "I said, 'Hell, you can't see 12 feet ... you can't even see 4 feet.'"

Herzbrun said he went back to the field with a deputy sheriff and, clad in a white tee shirt, knelt down approximately in the same place the girl's body was found.

He told the deputy to walk toward him, following the same path Henderson said he took. *(indirect quotation)*

"I wore the white tee shirt on purpose," Herzbrun related. "We knew what Joe Jenkins was wearing; he had on dark clothes the night of the murder. The deputy came within 20 paces of me before he could even see a form, and even then he almost tripped over me. We knew Henderson was lying ..." *(direct quotation)*

Herzbrun said he next examined photographs taken of the murder *(transition)*

Fig. 14.9 *A story using a variety of techniques.*

scene by the Sheriff's Department and had enlargements made of the sections that showed the outline of shoeprints made in the soft earth of the field.

direct quotation

"We compared the photos and thought one imprint looked an inch or so smaller than the other. The prints were of a left and a right shoe. One appeared to have been made by a fairly conventional shoe. The other showed the outline of a toe and a heel that looked like it had been made by a European shoe, Italian, maybe," Herzbrun said.

The prosecutor said the photographs confirmed his suspicions of Henderson. The latter had testified that he was wearing Italian shoes the night of the slaying.

In the transcripts of Jenkins' preliminary hearing, there is the following exchange between Henderson and Antelope Valley Municipal Judge William J. Wright:

question and answer from the transcript

"What kind of shoes are those, Mr. Henderson?" asked Wright.

"Italian."

"They have a hand stitch around the shoe, lining the entire top of the shoe?" continued the judge.

"Yes."

"And the size?" asked Wright.

"The size? Nine and one half."

Herzbrun said he pondered the transcript and the photographs and concluded that what looked like the imprint of the Italian shoe was closer to size 11 than 9½.

direct quotation

"So now I knew he was lying about the distance and probably about the shoe size. A lot of people saw what kind of shoes he was wearing the night of the murder, so he couldn't lie about that, but he could lie about the size of the shoes," said Herzbrun.

transition

Shortly after, a charge of murder was filed against Henderson.

To win a conviction, Herzburn said he had to prove two things: that Henderson couldn't possibly have seen what he said he saw, and that the footprint made by the Italian shoe was Henderson's.

The most immediate problem, the prosecutor said, was to prove the footprint was Henderson's.

summary

Herzbrun took the photographs to a San Fernando Valley orthopedic foot specialist, who backed up the prosecutor's earlier thought: that the probable size of the Italian shoe was in the range of 10–11, and that the conventional shoe imprint was smaller, possibly size 9½.

Measurements were then taken of both Jenkins' and Henderson's feet, and the measurements were highly damaging to Henderson. A shoe specialist, who later testified at Henderson's trial, said the suspect had a natural shoe size of 12, though calluses on the ridges of his toes indicated he wore a smaller size shoe, possibly size 11. Jenkins' shoe size was 9½.

But there was still no solid evidence that the vague outline of the shoe imprint in the photograph was a size 11 shoe.

transition

Then Herzbrun read an article in The Times describing crime detection work being done at Caltech's Jet Propulsion Laboratory.

The prosecutor went to JPL, the agency responsible for the U.S. unmanned planetary space program, and talked to Dwain Spencer, manager of JPL's Space Technology Applications Office, who had a federal grant to apply space technology to urban problems, including crime.

Herzbrun described his problem to Spencer, who assigned Dr. Belliot Paul Framan and a mathematician-systems analyst, Ramuald Ireneus Scibor-Marchocki, to work with the prosecutor.

An immediate problem became apparent: the photographs were one-dimensional, viewed from the top, and therefore would not lend themselves to conclusive analysis. A three-dimensional model was needed.

Thus began a long search to find a shoe that matched the description of Henderson's shoe, a task made more difficult because there was no model of the shoe, only Judge Wright's verbal description.

The search for the Italian shoe led Herzbrun, Wood and other investigators to more than two dozen shoe stores from downtown Los Angeles to Palmdale.

summary

The legwork paid off one day when a district attorney's investigator, Roger Reid, found a pair of shoes matching Wright's description in the display window of the Hardy Shoe Store in North Hollywood. The shoes were taken to the judge, who said they were identical to the ones

Fig. 14.9 (continued)

Henderson wore to the preliminary hearing.

Herzbrun and the others then got eight pairs of the store's shoes sizes 8 through 12, plus 16 pairs of two similar-style shoes, and took them to Framen and Scibor-Marchocki.

The shoes were measured to a 1000th of an inch, using a Univac 1108 computer, and the measurements were compared to the photograph of the Italian shoe imprint.

The findings, read to a jury at Henderson's trial, were: "Thus, the overall conclusion is that the evidence photograph is of a print of a Hardy shoe, probably of size 11."

transition

The prosecutor then set out to prove that Henderson would have had to be inches, not feet, away from Jenkins and the girl to see what he said he saw the night of the murder.

list

Among the persons he talked to during this part of the investigation, all of whom later testified at Henderson's trial, were:

—Rolf Thorvaldson, a civil engineer for the Los Angeles County Road Department who went out to the field on a night similar to the night of the slaying and took a light meter reading.

—Reanard R. Lawrence, a Southern California Edison Co. official, who said the street light closest to the part of the field where the girl was murdered illuminated only 420 feet, which would leave much of the field blanketed in darkness.

—George Rader, a Federal Aviation Administration air traffic controller in Palmdale, who described atmospheric conditions the night of the slaying, such as the type of clouds, their altitude, visibilities, temperatures and wind velocities.

—Three persons who had businesses near the field who said there were no lights in their shops that would have shined on the field that night.

But even this was not enough.

transition summary

To prove his case, Herzbrun went to Dr. William J. Kaufmann, director of the Griffith Observatory, and Kaufmann's associate, astronomer Paul Roques, and asked them to re-create the atmospheric conditions the night of the crime.

They agreed and one day during Henderson's trial, everyone involved in the proceeding went to the Griffith Planetarium, including the jury, attorneys, the defendant and Superior Judge Harry V. Peetris.

The jurist consented to the virtually unprecedented display—for a murder trial—only after testimony established that all conditions were exactly the way they were the night Miss Smelcer was slain.

Herzbrun placed a mannequin, a likeness of the girl's body, across the backs of auditorium chairs at one end of the planetarium.

"The lights were turned down to where they coincided with Mr. Thorvaldsen's light meter," Herzbrun said, "Then the moon was cranked to the right location, height and brightness and they even put in a cirrus cloud."

Beginning about 60 feet away, the jury and others in the plantarium began moving toward the manikin, peering into the darkness from atop a step ladder.

Finally they were 12 feet away. Each person in the room climbed atop the ladder to see what was there.

All they could make out was a vague form, and that was all . . . until the lights were turned up.

The jury had their backs to the mannequin. Unknown to them, a sheriff's deputy was standing behind the mannequin playing the role of Jenkins as Henderson had described it. He posed so as to make it appear that he was kneeling over the body.

As the jury turned around, still in semidarkness, they saw the image of killer and victim, thoughts of which were already imbedded in their imaginations, and were startled.

"Several of them let out loud gasps," said Herzbrun, remembering the reaction in his Van Nuys office.

transition and summary

The jury's verdict? Guilty, of voluntary manslaughter, a lesser penalty than first-degree murder because the jury apparently felt Henderson had no "malice aforethought." He was sentenced to up to 15 years in state prison.

direct quotation as clincher

"We just didn't want to have one guy facing a death penalty in San Quentin and another guy outside laughing," said Herzbrun when asked what motivated him.

Los Angeles Times

Fig. 14.9 (continued)

CHAPTER 15
Clarity

THE MAJOR PURPOSE of the newspaper is to inform the reading public, to present news of events, of trends, of ideas and many other things in such a way that readers know more when they put their paper down than when they picked it up. To inform, the news story must be written clearly, understandablly and accurately. It must be organized so that its meaning is readily apparent.

Clarity is not easily attained but it is an ideal for which news writers should strive. Facts, even when verifiable, can often be interpreted in different ways. Whatever we write is bound to be biased; after all we are human and can only write from our own experience and knowledge. So with these built-in limitations on our writing, it is essential that we write as clearly, as unambiguously and as accurately as we can.

HOW MUCH DO READERS KNOW?

In addition to our human limitations and the varying interpretations that can be drawn from any set of facts, the newspaper and news writer must consider the limitations of the readers, the people we are trying to inform, educate, entertain or persuade.

Newspaper readers are not dumb. The average American has more education today than ever before. In many communities, newspaper readers are extremely well educated: in college and university communities, for example, or communities with highly sophisticated industry. Some newspapers, like the highly specialized *Wall Street Journal* and the *New York Times*, have well-educated, well-informed and very critical readers.

But whatever their audience, news writers must consider two factors: our readers are intelligent enough to understand what we write, but probably not as well informed on any given subject as we might expect. There's a well-known rule-of-thumb in newsrooms: "Never understimate your reader's intelligence, but don't overestimate his facts."

Older readers have forgotten things that happened in their youth and younger readers have never heard of some things that older readers take for granted. Newcomers to a community won't know the names of pioneer settlers or be able to identify the local hero for whom the high school was named. College freshmen will be ignorant of important events that took place on campus just the year before. We must remember in news writing that some of our readers are knowledgeable and some are not. We must write for our entire readership—informed and uninformed.

Newspapers seek to appeal to the largest possible audience. News stories must be written so clearly, explain facts so precisely, define terms so carefully that no readers, no matter how uninformed on the subject, will wrinkle their brows and mutter, "How's that again?"

This does not mean that we write down to our readers. It is not always necessary to use second-grade language. Often the context will make even a very learned word clear and understandable.

DEFINE AND EXPLAIN

Context and Background

A basic tenet of clear, understandable writing is that the background or context of a story should be made clear to readers. In Chapter 13 we saw, for example, how second-day and follow-up stories include a brief résumé of earlier events so that readers can place the new developments in their proper context. The *New York Times* regularly publishes biographical sketches of people connected with the major news stories to help readers better understand the stories.

When an engineering firm billed the Town of Falmouth some $2,600 more than the amount they had originally estimated for doing a study for the town, the *Falmouth* (Mass.) *Enterprise* published a lengthy story about it (Fig. 15.1). The story explains how engineers, supposedly pretty accurate people, could make such an error. The newspaper was not satisfied merely to report that the cost would be higher than anticipated. Readers might ask why. The *Enterprise* apparently felt that an explanation was in order.

A *New York Times* story reporting that three railroad officers were jailed and fined for taking kickbacks explained in detail just how the scheme worked. And a *Milwaukee Journal* story about a renewed investigation of the Weathermen included a background insert on two Wisconsin people associated with the Weathermen (Fig. 15.2). An Associated Press story about the excavation of the ancient Italian city of Sybaris included a detailed explanation of the importance of Sybaris and an account of its destruction. Not all newspaper readers know ancient history, but if such a story is given enough background many readers will read it with interest.

When Charles H. Kuhl died in Mishawaka, Indiana, several years ago, the Associated Press identified him as the soldier slapped by the late Gen. George S. Patton Jr. The slapping incident was a sensation in 1943, but even readers who followed the story at the time might have forgotten the details after three decades. The AP story gave the background so that even the most uninformed reader would understand the story.

The experienced news writer is careful to provide the background for a story, to place people and events in context, to explain how things came about, how things work. The experienced news writer does not ask readers to remember, to guess or to look it up in the almanac or encyclopedia.

Obscure Details

Harold Ross, the founder and longtime editor of *The New Yorker* was a stickler for clarity in articles that appeared in his magazine. He went over every line and every word with extreme care. James Thurber, in his biography of Ross, said that whenever Ross did not recognize a name, he would pencil in the margin, "Who he?" Don't give your readers the opportunity to ask, "Who he?" Tell them. The following excerpt shows how one writer handled it:

> He told a Senate subcommittee investigating snooping and wire-tapping activities:
>
> "I can sit here and point to George Wilson and I can say that he is the Dr. Strangelove of the Boston office."
>
> Mr. Wilson is group supervisor of intelligence in the Boston revenue office.
>
> Dr. Strangelove was a fictional evil nuclear mastermind in a motion picture.
>
> *United Press International*

Several years ago James J. Kilpatrick, then editor of the *Richmond* (Va.) *News Leader*, created the Beadle Bumble Fund, a modest trust to give a helping hand to the victims of official stupidities, as news stories explained. The stories also explained the odd title of Kilpatrick's fund. Most newspaper readers today are not familiar with

Town Will Likely Come Up With Extra Money For Dump Engineers

Falmouth will probably end up paying $2,600 more to have its dump study completed. Finance committee Tuesday night heard representatives of the consulting engineers, Metcalf & Eddy, explain their mistaken estimate of $16,000.

Metcalf & Eddy said early last year they could study the town dump as required by 1971 state law and that it probably would cost the town $16,000.

Public Works commissioners asked the town for $16,000 at the annual town meeting last March.

Town meeting voted the $16,000.

The DPW commissioners signed a contract with Metcalf & Eddy as they often had before.

The contract was elastic in that it allowed the engineers to go over the $16,000 estimate with the approval of the town if the time required for the job exceeded their own estimate.

The billing is not unlike the hiring of a plumber or a mechanic. It is unlike the hiring of a dentist who fixes a tooth for a fixed price whether it takes him five minutes or 25 minutes.

The $16,000 in "professional engineering services" would not be exceeded, said the engineers, without the prior approval of the town.

DPW Director Ellis could not remember ever having the cost of an engineering project exceed the professional estimate of the engineer doing the job.

Billing to the DPW was, as usual, in increments. One day last summer, however, a bill came which the DPW could not pay. The amount of the bill would have pushed the total paid out to more than the $16,000 appropriated by the town meeting. No approval had been given for further work.

A telephone call from project engineer, Paul R. Calloe, provided the explanation. The job required another $2,600 in work, said Mr. Calloe.

Preparation of the sample contract to be used for hiring a dump operator was more complicated than Metcalf and Eddy had expected it would be.

Additional time would be required to complete the job, and the additional time would cost more.

The commissioners argued with Metcalf & Eddy by letter.

Finally, DPW Director Ellis asked for an "upset price", a term which Webster defines as "the price fixed on as the minimum for property offered in a public sale."

Engineers don't use it that way. Fixing an upset price for engineering costs means shifting the computation from "time-charges" toward a lump sum, a

little more like the dentist and the tooth.

It wouldn't cost more than $4,000 to finish the work, said the engineers. This meant that the engineers were saying that their original professional estimate could not have been wrong by more than 25 per cent. It also gave them a little bargaining room. The project engineer had told the commissioners that it would cost $2,600 to finish the job but, when pressed, wanted an additional $1,400 of leeway.

Special town meeting, on the recommendation of the finance committee, rejected the DPW request for $4,000.

Falmouth still did not have its dump study, and the notices of violations from the state kept piling up.

Manuel Couto's contract to operate the dump expired and Albert W. Lawrence was given an interim contract until the study could be completed and the town could decide whether to run the dump itself or have a contractor do it.

Mr. Ellis tried to arrange a meeting between the finance committee and the engineers and at the same time submitted two dump budgets to the finance committee, one assuming management of the dump by the town and the second assuming a contract operation.

There was money left in the reserve fund and the fund was

Continued on Page 3

Fig. 15.1 *The* Falmouth *(Mass.)* Enterprise *explained a minor detail in the town's budget in great detail. Readers are entitled to enough background to enable them to understand the facts in a news story.*

How Consulting Engineers Charge For Job

Continued from Page 1

open until Jan. 10, but Selectman Richard R. Paine got there first and got $7,000 for the redistricting of the town.

John Podger, senior vice-president of Metcalf & Eddy, who signed the contract with the town but had not met the men who had signed for Falmouth, couldn't get to town before Jan. 10.

Finally, Tuesday night, they all got together.

The finance committee met for a brief period before the engineers and the commissioners arrived.

Chairman Richard J. Fish was there as were Manuel F. Rapoza and Mr. Ellis. Mr. Fonseca was absent.

Mr. Calloe, a tall, modishly dressed engineer in his thirties, took a seat next to John Podger, the senior vice-president of the old Boston firm.

Mr. Podger after the meeting presented his embossed "M & E" business card to reporters. So did Mr. Calloe, whose card is printed. Mr. Podger is a slightly built man. He dresses in conservative tweeds and speaks softly but directly with a slight accent that might be British.

Mr. Podger held the Falmouth folder while Mr. Calloe turned its pages to find the correct reference, and Mr. Podger did the talking. He wanted the matter resolved, but he also wanted the $4,000.

He said that the firm usually prefers the "time charges" method of bill computation because, he said, it protects the firm and it protects the town from paying more than it might have to pay.

He held up a manual of a professional engineering association and said that the "time-charges" method was the one that the engineers had decided was the best way to charge customers.

Unusual Difficulties

"Rather unusual difficulties" had caused the overrun, he said, but asserted that the $16,000 was not an "upset" limit.

"We're used to not signing contracts that are open ended" said Finance Chairman Joseph C. Martyna.

George Pinto asked if the firm had billed in excess of the $16,000.

"A billing did get through which was in excess of the $16,000," admitted Mr. Podger. It was an accounting error, he said, an accounting error which the company admitted.

"It was just an accounting error; you hadn't done the work?" asked Mr. Pinto.

"Yes, we had done the work," replied Mr. Podger,

Mr. Pinto wanted to know if the $4,000 is an "upset" limit.

Project Engineer Calloe started to speak.

"Why don't I answer this," said Senior Vice-President Podger, smiling expansively.

"Yes," was his answer.

"We may well come in for less," he said. "We don't anticipate any problems with the state," he added, in response to a question.

Mr. Martyna didn't think the engineers had fullfilled their "moral obligation" to the commissioners by emphasizing the possibility of overrun.

"Twenty-five per cent is quite an overrun," said the finance committee chairman.

"I think they have a moral obligation to work this out," said Mr. Pinto. "Principle is more important than money."

Bargaining Begins

Both he and Mr. Martyna were broadly hinting toward a deal — something less than $4,000.

"We will bend in order to get this thing resolved and finished," said Mr. Podger. "We'll take the $2,600 as the upset limit," he said.

Bargaining had begun, but George Pinto didn't think the finance committee should be involved.

He suggested to the commissioners and engineers that they "go back upstairs" and conclude the negotiations.

Mr. Rapoza and Mr. Fish indicated they would be amenable to the new figure.

Mr. Martyna told Mr. Ellis that the final figure could either be included in a revision of the DPW capital outlay budget or as a separate article.

Mr. Ellis said that he wanted the figure buried in his budget.

"I don't want to have a big fight on town meeting floor," he said.

The commissioners and the engineers moved upstairs to negotiate.

After the meeting with the finance committee, according to Mr. Ellis, the commissioners agreed that $2,600 was all right. They now await a letter from Metcalf & Eddy confirming that agreement.

What now?

Mr. Ellis told The Enterprise that he believes it was "a misunderstanding that should not reflect on future work."

"I think their intent was honest," he said, noting that he thought the misunderstanding was "as much our fault as it was theirs."

It was, he said, "a nothing job to them."

"They're not going to make any money on this job," he asserted.

He said he has no intention of not recommending the firm for a future town job. That, he said, would be "a slanderous thing."

Falmouth (Mass.) *Enterprise*

Fig. 15.1 (continued)

'Weatherman' Probe Revived

By Sanford J. Ungar

Washington Post Service

Washington, D. C. – The Justice Department has launched a new investigation into activities of the radical leftist Weatherman organization and hopes to indict some of its members — including federal fugitives now living underground — in connection with bombing incidents nationwide.

One grand jury probe by the department's Internal Security Division has been underway in San Francisco for more than two months, and another reportedly will open soon in an undisclosed city.

Nixon administration officials, including Asst. Atty. Gen. A. William Olson, chief of the Internal Security Division, are confident that their new drive against the Weathermen will bring more cases into court. It is said to be based on recently obtained intelligence information.

One Fugitive Located

Officials admit to frustration, however, in their attempts to track down some the best known members of of the group. Several have been fugitives for more than two years.

[Among the fugitive Weathermen is Bernardine Dohrn, a leader and founder of the organiziation, who went underground in the spring of 1970 after she and 12 others were indicted by a grand jury in Detroit on charges of conspiring to bomb public buildings.

[Miss Dohrn, 30, a native of Chicago, graduated from Whitefish Bay (Wis.) High School in 1959. Her younger sister said last year that Miss Dohrn was "alive and working for the revolution."

[Another fugitive is Ronald Kaufman, 34, son of Mrs. Sonia Kaufman, 817 E. Fairy Chasm Rd., Bayside. He graduated from Riverside High School in 1955 and from the University of Wisconsin in 1961. He was charged early this year with planting time bombs in three bank vaults. None exploded.]

One fugitive, Joseph Edwin Schock, under indictment in Idaho for the destruction of 29 military vehicles, has been located on the French Caribbean island of Martinique, but the French government has declined to extradite him to the US on the ground that Schock is sought for a "political crime."

Milwaukee Journal

Fig. 15.2 *The* Milwaukee Journal *provided some background for its readers with this insert in a Washington story.*

minor characters in Charles Dickens's works and the stories about the fund had to identify Mr. Bumble:

> The fund is named after a fictional character in the Charles Dickens novel "Oliver Twist" who

called the law "a ass . . . a idiot" if the law supposed a wife acted under the direction of her husband.

Detroit Free Press

Explanations did not go so far as to define a beadle.

New Terms

New words and terms, technical terms, unfamiliar words and references ought to be explained in news stories. Don't let your readers stumble over a word or a term. They may get discouraged and stop reading. Do you know what *Antabuse* is? What does *nunc pro tunc* mean? What exactly is *salmonella*? How loud is a *four-decibel sound*? What are *pork barrel* funds? What is a *yarmulke*? What is a *captain's mast*? You cannot expect your readers to know everything and when new words or technical matters crop up in news stories they must be explained. Sometimes it is possible to substitute a more understandable or commonly used word for the unfamiliar one. Short, everyday words are often better than longer, more learned words. But you can't always write in words of one syllable—nor should you.

The newspaper is a great educational force because it makes new facts, new ideas, new words familiar and understandable. Twenty-five years ago *astronaut, orbit, perigee, apogee* and many similar technical terms were not part of the vocabulary of the average newspaper reader. Today the space program, reported in detail in newspapers, magazines and over the air, has made many previously unfamiliar technical words part of everyone's vocabulary. Use an unfamiliar word or a technical term if that is the exact and proper word, but explain it.

The excerpts in Fig. 15.3 contain technical terms that are important to the story and that had to be used. But each story includes a brief and clear explanation of what the term means. And, you will notice, no matter how technical the term, the explanation is in familiar, everyday language.

Jargon and Gobbledygook

Jargon and gobbledygook are pretty much the same thing—nonsensical, incoherent or meaningless language. Jargon is an old word, gobbledygook a fairly new one. Both describe a very real problem for the news writer. If we are to communicate with our readers, we must write clearly, precisely and intelligibly. Jargon and gobbledygook are roadblocks.

Nonsensical, incoherent or meaningless language originates with people in specialized trades, professions, groups or classes: with doctors, lawyers, teachers, public officials and politicians, the military, scientists and many others. It originates in the need for technical terms to describe things, processes, concepts or situations. It is "in" language, understandable to members of the profession, trade or group, but unintelligible to the rest of us.

And, since newspapers are written for the rest of us, the news writer must learn to avoid jargon

A Navy Spokesman said John Randolph Warren, 21, of Worthington, Ohio, will be brought before Captain John H. Carmichael, commanding officer of the Naval station here, for a captain's mast.

The procedure is similar to a preliminary hearing in which the commanding officer determines the future of the case. This could include dismissal of the charge, recommendation for a special court-martial or non-judicial punishment.

Associated Press

The report made public today estimated overland supersonic flights by regular commercial flights might subject 20 million Americans to five to 50 severe sonic booms a day.

The boom is produced by the shock wave caused by compression of air at speeds faster than the speed of sound (660 miles an hour at high altitudes).

The noise intensity was likened to that produced by a large trailer truck passing at 60 miles an hour at a distance of about 30 feet. More millions would be exposed to lesser noises.

New York Times

To clear up the confusion, Miss Hash has proposed to Superior Court Judge Laurens Henderson that he file all 200 decrees nunc pro tunc—in other words, doing now what should have been done in the first place.

Associated Press

A candy company official said Wednesday a day's production of two of its products was being withdrawn from the market because some of it was contaminated with salmonella.

Salmonella is a micro-organism that can cause violent stomach upsets. An FDA spokesman said the agency viewed the contamination as a "potential health hazard."

United Press International

Fig. 15.3 *Making jargon understandable.*

Reading a report about a family on relief, County Judge Christ T. Seraphim was stopped Wednesday by this sentence:

"In the area of functional failure, our prognosis is 'modification.' This modification we expect to take place at a very slow rate."

"Explain this gobbledygook to me," Judge Seraphim demanded of the report's author, George Gochinas, a welfare department case worker.

Somewhat flustered, the case worker began: "There should be some kind of modification here...."

"Don't use that word 'modification.' Nobody here knows what it means," said the judge.

What the report was trying to say, Gochinas explained, was that the parents lacked education and the welfare department was trying to help them improve.

The case involved a 30-year-old mother charged with neglect of her 14 children. Judge Seraphim adjourned the case until the father could be found.

Milwaukee Journal

Fig. 15.4   *A case of gobbledygook.*

and gobbledygook and use language that the average reader can understand. But in many cases the reporter and news writer gets his stories from people who use jargon. So, he must learn to translate. The story in Fig. 15.4 will give you an idea of the problem.

Examples of jargon are easy to come by. The Bureau of Public Roads referred to an "impact attenuation device" which turned out to be oil drums placed around an obstruction to warn motorists away or soften the bump if a car did run into the obstruction. When questioned, a brigadier general explained that when a program is *definitized* the army means that it makes "a definite list of equipment and training that you feel is popular with that country. So many this, that, the other thing, and it becomes definite." In this case, the explanation is as much jargon as the original.

Checking into a neighboring school district's application for federal funds, a newspaper questioned an item about "self-contained learning packages." A self-contained learning package, it was explained, is a book. Another newspaper, reporting on affairs in Washington, found that in government circles, reading a government notice to reporters is referred to as a "verbal posting." And a press briefing is known as a "verbal information opportunity."

A famous example of bureaucratic gobbledygook came to light at one of President Roosevelt's press conferences during World War II. The President read to reporters a blackout order which he said had been prepared by the director of civilian defense:*

> Such preparations shall be made as will completely obscure all federal buildings and nonfederal buildings occupied by the federal government during an air raid for any period of time from visibility by reason of internal or external illumination. Such obscuration may be obtained either by blackout construction or by terminating the illumination. This will of course require that in building areas in which production must continue during a blackout, construction must be provided that internal illumination may continue. Other areas, whether occupied or not occupied by personnel, may be obscured by terminating the illumination.

Roosevelt directed that the order be rewritten as follows:

> Tell them that in buildings that will have to keep their work going, put something across the windows. In buildings that can afford it, so that work can be stopped for a while, turn out the lights.

President Johnson had his difficulties with bureaucratic jargon, too. Bill Moyers, at one time Johnson's press secretary, recalled this incident:†

*Quoted from "Editorial Workshop" by Roy H. Copperud in *Editor and Publisher*, November 28, 1959.

†Quoted from "Across the Pedernales," by Bill Moyers in the *New York Times*, January 26, 1973.

Another time he ripped into a group of Government lawyers who had drafted an Appalachian assistance bill. "Who the hell can read this gobbledygook?" he thundered. "But that's a technical document, Sir," one of the men replied. The President gave him a long, merciless stare, then with his own black felt pen he rewrote the establishing clause. "There!" he said, holding the document out before him with a flourish. "Now they'll know down in Morgantown what we're talking about."

Presidents Roosevelt and Johnson were articulate speakers who used plain language to get their ideas across to the American public. Like them, experienced news writers are against jargon and are expert at translating obscure language into easily understood words. Editors and copyreaders are generally quick to catch offending language and return it to the writer for translation. But jargon occasionally does slip through. A newspaper recently referred to a grade school child who "underachieved in school and socialized poorly." Apparently the child wasn't learning anything and couldn't get along with other kids. Another newspaper said that in Pennsylvania one of the presidential candidates was "stepping into as many media markets as he could." Presumably, the candidate was appearing in cities where there were newspapers and broadcasting stations and skipping the little places where there wouldn't be any reporters to cover his appearance.

Be wary of words, phrases, sentences and paragraphs that you don't understand. If you don't understand them, neither will your readers. Ask the source to translate. If you understand the idea yourself, you can find plain language, simple terms, in which to explain it to your readers. This doesn't always make the experts happy; they like jargon. A *Detroit News* reporter recalled this encounter with an expert:

At a press conference I attended some time back an expert on water pollution scolded the press for saying that Lake Erie was dying and that it was dying because it was dirty.

"It's not dying," he said. "It is slowly deteriorating in terms of natural plant and animal growth because of an increase in the amounts of effluent being poured into it."

"That's what we've been saying in the papers," one reporter replied: "It's dying because of all the crap that's being tossed into it."

Translation is not to hard once you get the knack of it. To *finalize* means to finish, to *annualize* means to put on a yearly basis, *civilianization* means that jobs once done by soldiers will now be done by civilians, *a dichotomy* just means that there are two sides to the question.

ACCURACY AND COMPLETENESS

Considering the staggering number of facts and bits of information that even one issue of a newspaper contains, it is surprising that more errors do not creep into the pages of the newspaper. There are many mechanical errors—typographical errors, lines out of place and awkward word divisions perpetrated by the computer—but not too many errors in fact. Those errors in fact that do get by the network of news writers, copyreaders, editors and proofreaders are usually the result of human error. Some errors, even obvious ones that everyone should have noticed, slip by occasionally because of carelessness or momentary lack of attention. No human work is ever going to be entirely free of that kind of error. Other errors are caused by the failure of the reporter, news writer, copyreader or editor to check a fact with a reliable source.

Careful reporters check facts with their sources. You can usually count on your sources to know how to spell their own names, what age they are and what their address is. Some of the other information they give you may need to be double checked against other sources. If you are working on the rewrite desk and take a story over the telephone from a reporter, you must check the facts carefully with the reporter. Then recheck the names, addresses, highway numbers, references to localities and similar facts with a city directory, almanac or map, for example.

The experienced editor always tells beginners in the newsroom: "Never take anything for granted." That means check and check again. Check spellings of names. Check addresses. Check the locations of streets. Check titles of public officials. Check dates. Check figures in a city or county budget. Check the accuracy of direct quotes. Verify the wording of a state law. Add up the column of figures. Refigure the percentages. Be ready to stand behind all the facts in a story when you turn it over to your editor.

Where and how do you verify facts? Some can be checked quite easily by asking the source. Other facts can be verified in readily available published sources. Your newspaper library will have some of these, others will be available in the newsroom. You should have in your own desk such obvious sources of information as a city street map and a state highway map. Your newspaper library may also have a detailed county map and many newsrooms have large-scale maps on their walls. You should also have ready access to a telephone book, a city directory and, if one is available, a directory of local public officials.

Your newspaper library should have a copy of the most recent state government manual. There is sometimes, too, a special state government telephone directory. For verifying facts about the federal government there are the *U.S. Government Organization Manual* and the *Congressional Directory.* Statistical data abstracted from the census can be found in the *Statistical Abstract of the United States* and in the *Historical Abstract of the United States.* Much demographic data is broken down usefully in the *County and City Data Book* published by the Bureau of the Census.

Your newspaper library should have a large atlas with enough detailed maps to enable you to check most geographical facts. Atlases usually contain a gazetteer, a list of place names by states and countries, and much other useful data. The *Associated Press Almanac* is authoritative and very useful.

Another useful source of information is the newspaper itself. A number of major newspapers are indexed, chief among them the *New York Times.* If your newspaper library does not have the *New York Times Index,* a large public library or university library near you will. The index won't tell you much more than the date a story was published, but once you know the date you can go to a microfilm file and read the original story to find what you're after.

A word of warning, however. Errors do get published in newspapers and are sometimes repeated and republished later, not only by the newspaper that published the original error but also by other newspapers that have copied the data without verifying them. Treat all sources with healthy skepticism. Do your own verifying.

Words, Quotations, Allusions and References

In addition to checking and verifying facts, we must frequently verify the accuracy of literary quotations, the names of literary figures, the meanings of words or phrases, or the titles of plays or songs. We cannot depend on memory or on the helpfulness of the reporter at the next desk. Newspaper reference libraries have some of the basic tools we need for verifying information, and, beyond that, there is the reference desk at the public or university library.

If you need to check the spelling of a word or are seeking a more precise definition, you go to the dictionary. One widely-used dictionary is the Merriam-Webster *Third New International Dictionary of the English Language.* This is an unabridged dictionary and a complete, reliable and useful reference. Another equally useful dictionary is the *American Heritage Dictionary of the English Language,* not as large as Webster, but published more recently. In addition to these standard works, there are several dictionaries of slang and popular usage which can be quite helpful at times. H. L. Mencken's *American Language* is a useful source of information about words either in the original study with its two supplements or in the one-volume revised and abridged edition.

In addition to slang, there are dictionaries of technical words such as acronyms, space terminology, military words and terms, foreign words and phrases, scientific terms, political words and even words used by journalists and printers. If a word is in use, it is likely to be defined for you in some dictionary.

Quotations from literature, from the speeches of statesmen and politicians, generals and other quotable people are frequently garbled in transmission. You should not rely on your memory when it comes to using a quote, nor on anyone else's memory either. Look it up in the appropriate reference work. The standard reference for quotations is Barlett's *Familiar Quotations*.

If you want to check the spelling of a name in literature, that is, the name of a fictional character, or the title of a work of fiction, you have to take a different tack. If you are verifying a reference in a literary classic—the King James Bible, for example—you may find what you need in a concordance. A concordance is an index of all the principal words in a work with a reference to their locations. It's handy if you want to check on the chapter and verse of a biblical reference or the act and scene of a Shakespearean reference. There are also dictionaries of fictional characters which may help if there is no concordance for the work or the author you are checking. Another useful work is the *New Century Handbook of English Literature* which contains some 14,000 articles on British authors, literary works, fictional characters and common literary allusions.

If you are checking on a real person of more than local importance or interest, you start with *Who's Who in America*. There is also *Who Was Who in America*, useful if the person is no longer living, and the *Dictionary of American Biography*. Another useful biographical reference is the *New York Times Obituaries Index* and various more specialized sources such as the *Directory of American Scholars*.

Some other useful reference works include:

For speeches, the *New York Times Index*, since the *Times* frequently prints the full text of important addresses by the president and other major figures, and *Vital Speeches of the Day* for lesser mortals.

For presidential press conferences, the *New York Times Index*.

For book reviews, *Book Review Digest* and the *New York Times Index*.

For sports, *The Baseball Encyclopedia* and similar volumes for other sports.

You can verify many facts yourself, quickly and easily, once you get the knack of it. However, you will occasionally be stumped. At that point, go to a professional librarian in your newspaper reference library, public library, university or state library. You may not even have to go in person. Usually a phone call will do. Librarians are remarkably adept at finding information. There is nearly always a handy source and the librarian knows what the source is and how to use it.

Plugging Holes

Not only must you make your story clear and accurate, but you must make it complete. If your story raises questions that it doesn't answer, it has holes in it. Plug the hole before your readers write or telephone your editor for more information.

The following story is a good example of a story with an obvious hole in it:

> ENCINO, CALIF.—AP—Ten days ago Mary Wilson told her parents she was going to stop by a friend's home after school. Instead, she went to Bangkok, Thailand, and vanished.
>
> Today, as the State Department and United States embassies in the Far East pressed a search, her mother landed in Bangkok not at all sure her 16-year-old daughter was there.
>
> Sitting by two telephones at the family home in the Los Angeles suburb of Encino, Dr. George Wilson is baffled by his daughter's disappearance.
>
> "This came completely out of the blue," the physician said.
>
> In a letter from Tokyo, the girl apologized for buying airline tickets on her mother's credit card and promised to pay back the money

after working a year in an orphanage.

Then a cable arrived telling the parents not to worry and that their daughter was coming home. The cable was signed "Mary." But the girl still has not been found.

It makes us wonder, but does not tell us, how a 16-year-old girl from Encino, Calif. can get all the way to Bangkok without money and a passport. The gaps in the story were probably the result of the haste with which the story was reported and written—a frequent failing of both wire services and newspapers. An afternoon paper carried the story with the same lead, but it was now updated to fill in the gaps (Fig. 15.5).

The later story does explain a great deal that the earlier story did not. Which is better?

Some other examples of stories with holes in them:

—A story in a college daily about a man arrested on campus and charged with sexual assaults on women students. The story said the man lived in a graduate residence hall and that he was a parolee from a state prison. But it did not say whether he was a student (it later turned out that he was) or why or how an ex-convict on parole gets admitted to a university.

—A story about tax loopholes which identifies in the headline and in the story a new dodge

---

BANGKOK, THAILAND—AP—Ten days ago, Mary Wilson, 16, told her parents in Encino, Calif., that she was going to stop by a girl friend's home after school.

Instead, she flew to Bangkok on her mother's American Express credit card and went to work for an orphanage.

Monday, thanks to a news dispatch from the United States and a newsman's memory, she and her worried mother were reunited in Bangkok.

Mrs. Wilson arrived in the Thai capital early Monday to try to pick up her daughter's trail.

Meanwhile, Alan Darby, a newsman at the English language Bangkok Post, read an Associated Press dispatch about the girl's disappearance and recalled a recent article about the Peirra Foundation, a Bangkok orphanage.

Darby called the orphanage and learned that Mary had been working there for a week. He called the United States embassy, by chance found Mrs. Wilson there, and told the embassy where Mary was.

"I'm so thankful that she's safe and sound," said Mrs. Wilson after the reunion with her daughter. "She's a do-gooder and a rather religious girl."

Two friends, Mr. and Mrs. William Shope, took the two to their home and refused to allow newsmen to see them.

A spokesman at the orphanage said Mary came to the institute last Tuesday inquiring about adoption of a child.

She was asked to wait until an official of the foundation could be located, but left before the official arrived.

She returned the next day with her luggage and after a conference with Dr. Peirra Vejabuo, head of the orphanage, moved into the establishment.

"She's a very quiet girl and spent most of her time singing with the orphans," said a spokesman. "She obviously loves children very much."

The foundation cares for about 80 orphans.

"Thank God she's safe," said the girl's father, Dr. George Wilson, in Encino.

It was shortly after midnight on Nov. 19 that the Wilsons discovered that Mary was missing when they called the girl friend's home only to be told that Mary had not visited there. Nor had she attended school that day.

After questioning her friends, the Wilsons learned from a travel agency that she had inquired in May about flying to Cambodia.

Other clues included a duplicate from the credit card purchase of tickets to Bangkok and a passport application showing that Mary had used her older sister's birth certificate to get a passport.

Then a letter and a cable arrived from Tokyo, adding to the mystery.

In the letter, Wilson said Mary apologized for using her mother's credit card and promised to repay her mother from her earnings as an orphanage worker.

The cable, however, told the Wilsons that she was returning and not to worry.

Wilson said a physician who was treating Mary for a hyper-thyroid condition theorized that "her disease had altered her basic rationale and logic" and perhaps led her to seek adventure.

From papers found in her room, Wilson said he believed that Mary had gone to Bangkok to work in the orphanage founded by Genevieve Caulfield, 77, a humanitarian in the far east and aunt of actress Joan Caulfield.

Fig. 15.5 *The gaps filled in.*

called "the Mexican vegetable rollover." But the story does not explain how the dodge works nor how reluctant taxpayers have benefited from it.

—A story about a new strain of rice developed in Japan which, according to the story, enables a single grain of seed to produce 57,100 grains of rice. Talk of the miracle of the loaves and fishes! If the story is correct, how does this botanical marvel take place?

—A story about the signing of a labor contract for hospital workers. The story reported that the contract called for a wage increase of 15 cents an hour for the first year and 10 cents an hour annually for the next four years. The story, however, did not indicate what kind of an hourly wage the employes had been earning, how much it might mean in weekly or monthly terms nor what the wage increase would cost the hospital. Figures in isolation have little meaning.

—A story about a Catholic priest who was arrested for burning rubbish in front of a newspaper office. The rubbish was a trashcan filled with copies of the newspaper. The story failed to explain why the priest was demonstrating so pointedly in front of the newspaper office.

Confessing Error

There was a time when newspapers only reluctantly acknowledged mistakes, for publishers did not want readers to doubt for a moment their paper's infallibility. The *New York Sun's* motto was: "If you see it in the *Sun*, it's so." There is a probably apocryphal story of the nineteenth-century editor to whom a reader brought a complaint. The paper had printed a news item reporting that the reader was dead. Not so, the reader emphasized. This put the editor on the spot. His newspaper never made mistakes. If the paper said

the man was dead, obviously he must be. The editor thought for a while. Finally he brightened. "I'll tell you what I'll do," he said. "I'll put you in the birth announcement column."

Today's newspaper more readily concedes that it makes mistakes. Some newspapers have ombudsmen to whom readers can take complaints about errors. Others simply make corrections routine, even to the point of having a daily paragraph or two in a regular corrections column. For example:

> Because of a typographical error, a story in Monday's Eagle about the possible purchase of land in Sheffield for a recycling shed incorrectly stated that $50,000 per square foot would be paid for the land. The sentence should have read that the tract is about 50,000 square feet in size. Also, the property shown in a picture which accompanied the story is owned by the Old Parish Church and is not under consideration for the recycling project. The tract which the town may buy is to the west of that shown in the picture.

The need to print corrections is annoying to editors. They generally make corrections as unobtrusively as possible and they seldom explain how the error happened. Not so Russell Baker, *New York Times* columnist, who admitted error handsomely and publicly at the end of one of his columns. Baker wrote:

> This column's recent suggestion that President Nixon might take unique satisfaction from the opportunity to receive the Nobel Peace Prize in Sweden was dumb, since the Nobel Peace Prize is presented in Oslo, Norway, and not in Sweden. The error resulted from the writer's ignorance.

Obviously, it is best to avoid errors, but it is good policy to correct mistakes promptly and clearly. At least the readers will know their newspaper is trying.

PART THREE
Technical
Matter

CHAPTER 16

Spelling

NOTHING IRRITATES an editor more than a news writer who can't spell. There was once, it is said, an editor who believed that if someone was a good reporter it didn't matter whether the person could spell. For every editor like that there are hundreds who will throw a temper tantrum at the first misspelled word in a new staff member's copy.

The late Stanley Walker, the famous city editor of the *New York Herald-Tribune*, used to keep a list of words misspelled by his staff. Periodically he would issue a list of misspellers and their errors, much to the embarrassment of his staff.* Some years ago the Arizona Newspapers Association approved a resolution urging schools of journalism not to give degrees to students who couldn't pass an examination in the fundamentals of spelling, punctuation, vocabulary and grammar. Newspaper recruiters who visit schools of journalism consistently ask about the ability of graduating seniors to write well and spell correctly.

Journalistic tradition demands that the news writer spell words as they appear in the dictionary or stylebook.

*I am indebted for this story to "Oh, For a Good Aardvark Stampede" by John O'Reilly in the *Saturday Review*, May 13, 1967.

DEVELOPMENT OF A SPELLING SYSTEM

History

There are irregularities, anomalies and inconsistencies in the spelling of English words. And there are good historical reasons for this.

English was written first in the runic alphabet and our earliest records of written English are spells, charms and epitaphs carved in runes on stone. When the Christian missionaries came to England they adapted the Latin alphabet to English, that is, they used Latin letters to represent the Germanic sounds of Old English. Where there were no Latin letters for certain sounds—as in the case of the *th-* in words like our Modern English *there* and *then*—letters were borrowed from the runic alphabet. Pronunciation and spelling matched fairly well at this period and irregularities in spelling were largely due to the various dialects of English then in use.

The Norman Conquest smothered written English for a time and when the English once again used their own language for literary purposes several generations after the Battle of Hastings, there had been significant changes in both the sound and syntax of the language. Since that time there has been a struggle to devise a system of spelling that would most closely reflect the pronunciation of the time.

Various ingenious systems were developed, adapted and modified before the arrival of the printing press in England brought order out of chaos. The printing press came into use at the beginning of the Renaissance. As printing became widespread, and as usage became standardized, printers began to regularize spelling for the sake of efficiency and consistency.

What the printers did in practice during the productive years of the sixteenth and seventeenth centuries was eventually enshrined in the dictionaries of the eighteenth century. Although there had been earlier dictionaries, the first great, standard dictionary of Modern English was Samuel Johnson's *A Dictionary of the English Language* published in 1755. Johnson was authoritative and dogmatic. He set out to make English spelling consistent and uniform, and for the most part he built on established usage. Johnson's dictionary was immensely popular and was published in successive editions for many years. It was widely used even in this country and was only supplanted by the new dictionary which Noah Webster first published in 1828.

Since Johnson, the dictionary has been regarded by nearly everyone as the authority on usage and spelling. Even when dictionary editors introduce changes in spelling—Webster Americanized many spellings, for example—the dictionary has been a conservative and standardizing influence.

Unfortunately, Johnson's dictionary enshrined a great many irregularities, inconsistencies and errors which have been maintained to some extent down to this day. For instance, he inconsistently entered *receipt*, from Middle English *receit*. And he retained such unetymological spellings as *debt* and *doubt* from the Middle English words *dette* and *douten*.

Johnson's dictionary standardized a spelling system which was better suited to the English language of the fifteenth and early sixteenth centuries than to the middle of the eighteenth. It also fixed forever the etymological nature of English spelling; that is, it made historical forms permanent and made it nearly impossible to alter spelling as pronunciation changed. English spelling retains, for example, the *gh* which represents a sound that disappeared from standard English in the late Middle English or early Modern English period— well before Johnson's lifetime. For example, the words *eight, night, fight, bought, thought, wrought.*

Not only is spelling today made difficult by the influence of outmoded pronunciation, but it is also complicated by the hybrid nature of the vocabulary of the modern language. Modern English grew out of the merger of two great languages: English and French. Neither side of the family is pure. English as it was when William the Conqueror came to England was a mixture of West Germanic dialects strongly influenced by Scandinavian dialects. French came to England in the form of Norman French and the more prestigious Central French.

As English evolved after the Middle Ages, it was a mixture of these two streams. The Renaissance brought a great influx of Latin words, taken both from the classics and from contemporary French and Italian. From the Elizabethan period on, English has borrowed avidly from other languages. English has naturalized many borrowed words and has preserved something of the spelling system of both the Germanic and Romance languages. English also makes widespread use of borrowed words in their original forms: words like *sputnik, blitzkrieg, chauffeur* and *hors d'oeuvre.*

The wonder is, not that English spelling is as irregular and chaotic as it is, but that we have been able to systematize it at all.

Competing Spellings

Our spelling system is further complicated by the presence of two acceptable spellings for some words. *Adviser*, for example, can be spelled perfectly correctly with an *-er* or an *-or; employe* is as acceptable as *employee;* and you may use either *controller* or *comptroller.*

Many technical words have two spellings, one reflecting the original form of the word, the other representing an attempt to adapt it to English. You may choose either *subpoena* or *subpena*, *apothegm* or *apophthegm*.

You may choose to write *color, center, realize* or *traveled,* or you may use the British spellings *colour, centre, realise* and *travelled.*

You might choose to write *donut, tho, thru* or *holsum,* simplified forms in popular usage especially in advertising, but that do not have enough sanction to appear in the dictionary. You might be better advised, in these cases, to choose the standard forms: *doughnut, though, through* and *wholesome.*

You might choose to describe a woman as a *blonde,* a *brunette,* an *authoress* or an *aviatrix.* Or, you might use the words *blond, brunet, author* and *aviator.*

How do we know?

Spelling Preferences

No one working for a publishing house, magazine, journal or newspaper will be long in doubt as to what standard of spelling to follow. There is always a preferred dictionary, a stylebook and a fixed preference for spelling wherever reasonable alternatives exist.

Some form of stylebook is in use wherever the English language is written and edited for publication. These guides to usage generally solve the problem of alternative spellings by requiring the use of the first version or of the shorter form. The wire services joint stylebook requires the use of the short form as given in Webster's *Third.*

Stylebooks also contain lists of exceptions and preferred spellings. The wire services joint stylebook contains a list of words "often used and frequently misspelled." This stylebook expresses a preference for *adviser, cigarette, employe, goodby* and *subpoena,* all words with two acceptable spellings. The *Chicago Tribune* stylebook reflects the paper's long interest in simplified spelling. The *Tribune* insists on the following spellings: *altho,*

breakthru, burocracy, catalog, etiquet, demagog, tho, thru, and *thoro.* The *Tribune* also prefers *clew,* a variant spelling of *clue.*

MASTERING SPELLING

Some Problem Words

There are many problem words in the language, words that appear often in print and which, despite frequent use, are often misspelled. The list that follows is certainly not exhaustive. It is derived from newspaper stylebooks, from lists of frequently misspelled words compiled by editors and from a list of words commonly misspelled by students and collected by the author of this book over the years.

1. Among words that cause difficulties are those ending in *-ent* or *-ant* and in *-ence* or *-ance.* Some of the difficulty lies in the fact that vowel sounds in unstressed syllables are undifferentiated. In some cases the difficulty lies in regional pronunciation:

acquiescent	acquiescence
competent	competence
consistent	consistence
different	difference
independent	independence
insistent	insistence
precedent	precedence
exorbitant	exorbitance
	grievance
relevant	relevance
resistant	resistance

2. Words ending in *-ible* and *-able* also cause some difficulty, especially in the following words:

accessible	accessibility
admissible	admissibility
compatible	compatibility
discernible	
permissible	
resistible	irresistible

indispensable
inseparable

3. Words ending in *-er* and *-or* are also confusing, again because the vowels are not ordinarily distinguished in speaking:

adviser*   debtor
conquer   councilor*
coroner   counselor
observer   impostor
propeller
worshiper

4. The following words are often troublesome because of doubled consonants. These words are commonly used and commonly misspelled:

accommodate   innuendo
affidavit   miscellaneous
bailiff   occurred
ballistic   parallel
bookkeeper   questionnaire
colossal   sheriff
dissertation   surveillance
drunkenness   tariff
embarrass   uncontrollable
harass
inflammation

5. Words of Latin or Greek origin are troublesome and they do turn up regularly in news stories:

deity   naphtha
fluoridation   hygiene
nonagenarian   hemorrhage
subpoena*   diphtheria
rhetoric

6. There is a rule in English spelling that says: keep the silent *e* before a suffix beginning with a consonant and drop it before a suffix beginning with a vowel. Of course there are exceptions:

*The *American Heritage Dictionary* shows alternate spellings for words marked with an asterisk.

judgment   changeable
wisdom   knowledgeable
            mileage*

Despite the fact that they are regular in terms of this rule, there seems to be a tendency to misspell *likable, salable, sizable* and *usable*. No *e*, please.

7. Four words that cause trouble are *eye, dye, die* and *tie* when they are given the *-ing* ending:

eye   eyeing*
dye   dyeing
die   dying
tie   tying

8. A few words prove troublesome because of prefixes that double consonants:

innocuous   misspelled
irreligious   offense

9. Foreign plurals can be a cause of difficulty. For example:

Negro   Negroes
tornado   tornadoes
tomato   tomatoes
attorney   attorneys
phenomenon   phenomena
alumna   alumnae
alumnus   alumni
medium   media
datum   data

10. When it is used as one element in a compound word, *full* is spelled with a double *l: full-blooded, full-fledged.* When it is a prefix or a suffix, a single *l*, as in:

fulfill   armful
fulsome   awful
           playful
           masterful
           skillful

11. One rule of spelling that everyone knows, even erratic spellers, is that *i* comes before *e* except after *c* and in words like *neighbor* and *weigh*.

Despite the rule, words with *ie* or *ei* still cause difficulties:

ei after *c*	rec*ei*ve, rec*ei*pt	
	per*cei*ve	
	de*cei*ve	
ei	w*ei*gh	s*ei*ze
	sl*ei*gh	l*ei*sure
	n*ei*ghbor	for*ei*gn
	sl*ei*ght	
ie	f*ie*nd	
	bel*ie*ve	
	l*ie*n	

12. Words with the suffixes *-ege* and *-edge* are frequent offenders:

> privilege   knowledge
> sacrilege
> sacrilegious

13. Words from names are often misspelled. Three quite common offenders are:

> philistine
> nemesis
> quixotic

14. The following words frequently give trouble, probably because their pronunciation does not indicate the presence of certain vowels or consonant letters. In other cases related words may confuse the user.

aerial	
liaison	
missile	
parishioner	(parish)
provocateur	(provoke)
repetitious	(repeat)
skiing	(ski, skied, skier)
stability	(stable)
subtlety, subtleties	(subtle)
temperament	
vacuum	
veterinarian	

15. The following list consists of words susceptible to misspelling, but which don't fit any of the previous categories:

a lot	kidnap, kidnaped*
all right	minuscule
all-right (adj.)	mold
anecdote	oriented*
asinine	paraphernalia
athlete, athletic	pari-mutuel
aura	peninsular
caricature	picnicking, (picnic)
categorically	plaque
chauffeur	predator
coconut	prejudice
complexion	preventive*
consensus	rarefy
defunct	rehearsal
dietitian	relict
disease	restaurateur (restaurant)
dormitory	satellite
drought	sergeant
dumbbell	soluble (dissolve)
dumfound*	strait jacket
edifice	strait-laced
gauge	strict, strictly
good-by*	supersede
hypocrisy	supposed, supposedly
immerse, immersion	temblor
inaugurate	tentacle
incalculable (calculate)	verbatim
indict, indictment	vernacular
inoculate	
intramural	

Homophones

Homophones are words that sound alike, but that have different written forms. More and more beginning news writers have trouble with these sound-alikes because they know and use a word, recognize it when they hear it, but fail to distinguish in writing between the word they want to use and its homophone. The author has found that among journalism students who read newspapers, magazines and books this is not a serious problem. But students who rely more on television and radio often have trouble with spelling and are more likely to use the wrong form. Some commonly confused forms:

to/two/too	do/due
site/sight/cite	rite/right
wet/whet	compliment/complement
shear/sheer	cue/queue
council/counsel	aural/oral
capital/capitol	hale/hail
principle/principal	bus*/buss
their/there/they're	canvas/canvass
straight/strait	

The Almost Right Word

This is probably the appropriate place to take up another problem of usage: the confusion of similar words. Words that are similar in their written forms and frequently in their pronunciation can be even more confusing than homophones. *Affect* and *effect* are examples of words commonly confused because they are pronounced alike. *Nauseous* and *nauseated* are similar words which are frequently confused despite their quite different meanings:

> The offensive odor *nauseated* him.
> His political views were *nauseous* to many people.

Many English words are pronounced or spelled enough like other words to confuse the careless. Careful readers and careful writers know the difference. They write precisely. As Mark Twain observed, they use the right word, not the next one to it. A partial list of similar words that can cause trouble follows:

affect	effect
allude	elude
allusion	illusion
anecdote	antidote
apposite	opposite
appraise	apprise
censor	censure

consul	council, counsel
continual	continuous
eminent	imminent
empathy	apathy
expatiate	expiate
flout	flaunt
healthful	healthy
historical	historic
illusive	elusive
imply	infer
ingenious	ingenuous
nauseous	nauseated
odious	odorous
ordinance	ordnance
perspective	prospective
populous	populace
prostrate	prostitute
ravage	ravish
relic	relict
rend	render
restive	restless
tenet	tenant
tortuous	torturous
uninterested	disinterested
venal	venial

A little investigation in your dictionary will make it abundantly clear that these words are not interchangeable. In any given context, one is correct, precise, meaningful, and the other is meaningless and misleading. For example, this sentence from a news story:

> A senator often is just a conduit between some ghost rider and the Congressional Record.

Guidelines for Good Spelling

Becoming a good speller is not so much a matter of genius as it is a matter of discipline. In the author's experience, there are few really bad spellers. Most newcomers to journalism are undisciplined and careless. When they become convinced that correct spelling is important, most of their problems disappear.

There are no rules for becoming a good

speller—or a better speller—but there are some general guidelines.

First it is necessary to see words on the printed page. If you read a lot, if you understand what you read, you will find that recognition of the written forms comes naturally. Second, it is important to build up your working vocabulary, words you know and can use.

The beginning news writer should not only use the office dictionary, but should own a dictionary, preferably a substantial desk dictionary which gives adequate definitions as well as etymologies. Knowing how a word developed from its earliest recorded use to its present form often makes it easier to spell.

We all have words we find difficult. Some of us are unsure of *principle* and *principal*, others of *hail* and *hale*. You can make a list of words you find troublesome and either memorize them or keep the list available for ready reference.

And it is a very good idea to master the list of preferred spellings or trick words that appear in the stylebook used in your newsroom.

Read your copy carefully before you turn it in to your editor. Read it line by line and word by word, carefully. You can catch typing errors and careless mistakes in spelling. And you can remind yourself that this word or that is on your "not sure" list. Look these words up before your editor gets his hands on your copy.

You cannot rely on the city editor and the copy desk to back you up and catch errors that slip through. Careful writing and careful editing is expected of you before you turn your copy in.

Discipline yourself, work systematically, check your copy carefully. The copy desk will back you up, but it won't carry you.

Human beings inevitably make mistakes and no one can turn in error-free copy every time. But you must try.

CHAPTER 17

Grammatical Problems

ASK A CARPENTER how to build a house or a shipwright how to build a boat and they can tell you. Ask a writer how to put a sentence together and 9 times out of 10 the writer will freeze, inarticulate and terrified. Yet the writer has written many sentences and spoken an even larger number. Most writers, however, are unable to describe what they do when they put a sentence together. They can do it, but they can't tell you how they do it.

Grammar should not be mysterious, for if we speak a language we are using its grammar. We are familiar with the way words are put together and sentences arranged, and we know how sentences can be combined so that meaningful communication is possible. We make daily use of all the grammatical elements and arrangements of our language.

Grammar as a technical term is nothing more than a handy word to describe a body of knowledge, knowledge about language. The grammar of English, for instance, is a systematically arranged series of observations about the way native speakers of English talk and write. For example, let's look at the following sentences:

The boy _____ running a good race.
The boys _____ running a good race.

If we ask a native speaker of English, you for example, to insert the verb to be in the above sentences, you will put is in the first sentence and are in the second. You would probably explain this choice by saying: "That's the correct way to do it." What you mean, of course, is that your choice is usual or normal for you and for the people you know.

That's grammar: observations about the usual or normal use of our language as well as about usage that is not usual, that most people do not use or that they consciously avoid using.

None of the grammatical problems we will discuss in this chapter are mysterious or difficult. They represent some usages and habits that are common to news writing but that may differ somewhat from the way other people in other circumstances write or say things. Some of the points we will cover will be *descriptive*: observations of the way things are generally done in news writing. Other points will be *prescriptive*: suggested, preferred or recommended usage where choices exist.

Word Order

The words in English sentences are arranged in a consistent manner. In the most common sentence structure, we find nouns first, verbs second and another noun after the verb: subject plus verb plus direct object. Like this:

The boy hit the ball.
The ball struck the fence.

This word order has a distinct advantage in communicating because it is normal and listeners or readers are able to anticipate what is coming. And anticipation greatly facilitates understanding. Normal journalistic usage, then, calls for us to identify the subject first, to follow that with an appropriate verb, and to follow the verb with information about the subject:

Governor Smith was reelected Tuesday.
The car struck and injured two passersby.
The speaker will be the Rev. Henry L. Hadley.
The judge fined the prisoner $100.

Occasionally, for effect, we change things around and arrange words in a way that is a little out of the ordinary. We change emphasis and with it some elements of meaning. For example, this sentence, from a story by Fox Butterfield in the *New York Times:*

Rare is the Vietnamese in Saigon who buys Tin Song, the small pro-government afternoon newspaper.

Putting the adjective at the beginning, instead of at the end, of the sentence has the effect of emphasizing this key word: *rare*. Notice the difference:

The Vietnamese in Saigon who buys Tin Song, the small pro-government afternoon newspaper, is rare.

Use normal word order most of the time, because it is predictable. Use unexpected word order for effect because it has a certain shock value that enhances meaning. Here is another example, a lead from a *United Press International* feature:

Backwards ran machines in this northern port city when an engineer a wrong switch pulled.

On movie screens, actors in reverse maneuvered; from oil tanks in the harbor flowed oil back into tankers.

Obviously, the chance to write this kind of a sentence, and make sense, doesn't come along every day. But there are plenty of occasions when a shift such as that in the *Times* example above is an effective device. Here, for example, is a sentence from the *Milwaukee Journal:*

To the standard fare of candy, apples and popcorn handed out to Halloween beggars, a biology teacher has added three new items: Live white rats, mice and rabbits.

Lists of Names

Newspapers frequently have to print lists of names in news stories: names of dead and injured in accidents, names of people elected to office, names of people competing in various events. A useful journalistic device in lists is to use sentences that start with the verb. For example:

Charged with murder and armed robbery were Michael Clark, 21, of 7624 S. Normal Av.; Nathaniel Burse, 23, of 50 W. 71st St.; Reuben Taylor, 22, of 9719 S. Prairie Av.; and his brother Donald Taylor, 21, of 7000 S. Parnell Av.
Chicago Tribune

Few readers would wade through that list of names if it preceded the verb as it would in normal word order. And until they get to the verb, the readers aren't going to know what is going on. Here is the *Chicago Tribune* paragraph rewritten in normal order, subject first, with the subject enclosed in brackets:

(Michael Clark, 21, of 7624 S. Normal Av.; Nathaniel Burse, 23, of 50 W. 71st St.; Reuben Taylor, 22, of 9719 S. Prairie Av.; and his brother Donald Taylor, 21, of 7000 S. Parnell Av.) were charged with murder and armed robbery.

Lacks punch, doesn't it? Some other examples, with the list of names omitted:

> Treated at St. Joseph Intercommunity Hospital were:
> Dead are . . .
> Found innocent of the same charges yesterday were:

Many newspapers, including some of the most carefully edited ones, accept such inverted constructions. Other newspapers prefer normal word order and introduce lists of names like this:

> *Those* charged with murder today are:
> *The* dead are:
> *Four men were* found innocent of the same charges yesterday. *They* were:

Sequence of Tenses

Ordinarily the principal verb in a sentence determines the tense of verbs that follow it. For example:

> He *tried* to do a good job whenever he *was asked.*
> He *asked* for and *received* his fee.
> He *does* whatever he *likes.*

This is normal or expected usage and no one has trouble with it. But sometimes adhering too rigidly to normal usage causes confusion, as in this sentence:

> He *said* he *would* go tomorrow.

As we know, the past tense of the verb *to say* requires a past tense so that *will* becomes *would.* However, since the implication is simply one of futurity, the word *would* doesn't really make sense. Be flexible, break the rules of ordinary usage and write the sentence:

> He *said* he *will* go tomorrow.

In the following examples the past tense, *said,* is followed by another verb in the past tense, to the detriment of good sense and understanding:

Gov. Albertis S. Harrison Jr. declared today that Virginia was rapidly becoming an urban state.

The question now, Waters said, was whether to expect the current year to produce another $40 billion increase.

If what these people said was true when the reporter heard it, it would probably be true the following day when the paper reached the hands of the reader. In these cases it would have been better to have said: "Virginia is rapidly becoming an urban state" and "is whether to expect."

Even worse is the mixing of verb forms that follow the main verb in a sentence. The following example, gleaned from the *UPI Reporter,* shows what can happen:

> The union *said* it *had* reliable information that trainees in the program *will* be assigned to state hospitals . . .

Since the sentence would make perfectly good sense if the two verbs following *said* were in either the past or the present tense, the problem is one of consistency. The writer should have used either *had/would* or *has/will,* but should not have used both tenses.

The Passive Voice

Every construction, usage, or tense has its uses. And so with voice. The active voice has its place. And when you need it, the passive voice is also highly useful. In the examples below, the first sentence is in the passive voice, the second is in the active. Which would you accept as more usual?

> Smith was struck by a pitched ball.
> A pitched ball struck Smith.

Since the elements closest to the front of the sentence get the most attention, the writer has to decide which element to emphasize, and what grammatical construction will do the trick.

For example, the following sentence is in the active voice and the emphasis is on the university board of regents. The coach's name is subordinated.

> MOUNT PLEASANT—AP—The Central Michigan University Board of Regents *approved* Wednesday the appointment of Jerry Green, former Dowagiac High School coach and University of Michigan freshman defensive co-ordinator, as assistant football coach.

If the writer had wished to give more prominence to the new assistant coach, he would have used the passive voice:

> A University of Michigan freshman defensive co-ordinator *was appointed* assistant football coach at Central Michigan, University Wednesday.

Here are some more examples of the passive voice to demonstrate its usefulness:

> DAKAR, SENEGAL—AP— Amilcar Cabral, one of the most prominent leaders of the African struggle against white supremacy, *was assassinated* Saturday night in front of his home in Conakry, capital of Guinea, a broadcast heard here said.

> Rivers Hills Village trustees *were asked* Wednesday by President Reuben Lueloff to tour the village of substantial homes and bring in a list of things that need cleaning up in the community.
> *Milwaukee Sentinel*

> An East Side man *was shot* to death by a nervous young gunman during a robbery attempt Sunday evening at Deco Restaurant, 901 Broadway.
> *Buffalo Evening News*

> Many banks, which have been grumbling for weeks that a six per cent prime is too low, *are expected* to follow suit next week.
> *Detroit Free Press*

Empty Subjects

When *there is, there are* or *there were* are used as sentence openers the results are often very awk-

ward, although we can also find many good sentences that begin in this way:

> There were giants in the earth in those days . . . mighty men which were of old, men of renown.

> There are more things in heaven and earth, Horatio,
> Than are dreamt of in your philosophy.

> There were in the the same country shepherds abiding in the field, keeping watch over their flocks by night.

It would be difficult to improve upon these well-known passages from the King James Bible and *Hamlet*. However, these awkwardly constructed sentences which also begin with *there* are not in the same class:

> There is a good portion of the advertising which is done in color.

> There are more than 20 federal agencies that have data about individuals in the United States.

> There were only a handful of people living in the endangered area, he said.

> There are 3,150 new students expected on campus next year.

These sentences can be quickly and easily revised for the sake of readability by getting rid of the *there are* or *there were* openers:

> A good portion of the advertising is done in color.

> More than 20 federal agencies have data about individuals in the United States.

> Only a handful of people are living in the endangered area, he said.

> Some 3,000 new students are expected on campus next year.

Fronting of Modifiers

In normal usage, writers have a stylistic choice: they may place modifiers before or after the word they modify. For example, these two perfectly grammatical sentences:

He demanded a jury trial.
He demanded a trial by jury.

In the first sentence the noun *jury* appears in front of the noun that it is intended to modify *(trial)*. In the second example, a prepositional sequence (preposition plus noun) is placed after the noun it modifies. Both of these arrangements are perfectly acceptable and both are perfectly clear. However, news writers increasingly tend to use a noun in front of the word it modifies rather than a prepositional sequence after it. Where the meaning is clear, this is perfectly acceptable. Where the meaning is not clear, or where too many nouns start accumulating in front of another noun, then for the sake of clarity it is better to use the prepositional sequence after the word to be modified. Look at these examples:

cousin marriage or *marriage between cousins*
claim payment or *payment for a claim*
student status or *status as a student*

If long and short forms are interchangeable and both are usual, you might use the shorter form in order to save space: *jury trial* rather than *trial by jury*. If the short form is more usual, use the short form: *income tax* rather than *tax on income*. If there is the slightest possibility that a reader might hesitate over your meaning, use the longer and usually more precise form: *vote by the committee* rather than *committee vote*. Where placing modifiers in front of a noun results in the accumulation of more words or terms than a reader can easily assimilate, then place the modifiers after the noun. We are, after all, interested in making it easy for readers to assimilate our stories:

a two-car rural intersection accident
a two-car accident *at a rural intersection*

an attempted July 16 gas station robbery
an attempted robbery *of a gas station on July 16*

Western District of Michigan federal grand jury
federal grand jury *for the Western district of Michigan*

Don't let too many modifiers pile up in front of the noun. Strike a balance between modifiers that belong in front of the noun and those that can be placed after the noun. For example:

a 15-cents-an-hour wage increase
a *wage* increase *of 15 cents an hour*

Sometimes you will also find that choosing between locating the modifier in front of the noun or putting it after the noun, is choosing between two entirely different meanings. For example:

Miss Favor is a French teacher
Smith is a handicapped teacher

Do you mean that Miss Favor teaches French or that she is a French national, a citizen of France? And does Smith teach handicapped students or is he himself handicapped? Placing the modifiers *French* and *handicapped* after the noun *teacher* and using a preposition might make your meaning clearer:

Miss Favor is a teacher *of French.*
Smith is a teacher *of the handicapped.*

Misplaced Modifiers

Modifiers can be placed either before or after the word they modify, but their placement is guided by meaning, not by whim. A modifier in the right place means one thing, in another it may mean something quite different. Take the following example:

. . . reported that someone stole a $15,000 diamond ring and five $100 bills from his motel room, which he had left in a dresser drawer.

The sequence *which he had left in a dresser drawer* is out of place and the result is comic: it seems to indicate that the hotel room had been left in the dresser drawer. This should be revised to read:

. . . a $15,000 diamond ring and five $100 bills left in a dresser drawer in his motel room.

Another example of a misplaced modifying phrase:

Ten years ago, a coin worth $4 would sell today for as high as $500.

The writer should have written:

A coin worth $4 some 10 years ago would sell for as much as $500 today.

In the following example the writer has inserted a long modifying sequence in the middle of a sentence when it should have come at the end:

Elaborate security arrangements, to protect Pope Paul VI from the moment he leaves the Vatican for India until his return, were set in motion Saturday.

This would make more sense if written this way:

Elaborate security arrangements were set in motion Saturday to protect Pope Paul from the moment he leaves the Vatican for India until his return.

If we assumed that the following sentence was grammatically correct, it might make us wonder about the county nurse:

After a discussion of making diapers for the county nurse, the meeting was adjourned.

This is probably what the writer meant to say:

The meeting was adjourned after a discussion of making diapers to be distributed by the county nurse.

Split Infinitives

The split infinitive is not a very important problem, but since so many beginning writers seem to

worry about it, it will be treated here briefly. An infinitive, of course, is any combination of the preposition *to* and a verb: to go, to run, to hide, to speak, to say and so on. Splitting the infinitive, means placing an adverb between the preposition and the verb and, by the way, it is not a crime:

to immediately run
to quickly go
to subsequently hide
to later speak
to immediately ask

It is not wrong, ungrammatical or illegal to split an infinitive. You should put your adverbs where they sound best. You have to develop a sense of what will be clearest to the reader. If a construction seems awkward or unclear, recast it.

Omission of Definite Articles

A lot of time is wasted on this subject since it is really a matter of preference. What does your ear tell you? Some newspapers prefer to drop what they regard as superfluous articles. Others think that dropping articles makes sentences sound choppy and telegraphic. Bob Casey, in his entertaining account of Chicago newspapers and newspapermen, *Such Interesting People,** relates the following anecdote:

One of the pundits decided that no story in the [Chicago] *Examiner* should begin with *A, An,* or *The*. And shortly after the promulgation of the rule Mr. Avery [a rewrite man] was called upon to write a piece about the finding of the body of an unidentified woman in the river. That did not bother Mr. Avery.
"Hello everybody," he wrote. "Take a look at this. The body of an unidentified woman . . . etc." That got into type and the rule was changed the next day.

That was a long time ago and many newspapers in later years would have permitted: "Body

*From *Such Interesting People* by Robert J. Casey: The Bobbs-Merrill Co., Indianapolis, 1943, p. 127.

of an unidentified. . ." Many newspapers today do permit or encourage the omission of articles where clarity or meaning is not affected. The following paragraph is typical:

> Democratic Town committee meeting scheduled for Thursday has been canceled, so that members may attend a talk on education being presented by Rep. Richard E. Kendall at the public library.
> *Falmouth* (Mass.) *Enterprise*

Articles are useful when they help make meaning clear. There is certainly some difference in the following sentences. The first is the original version:

The visiting nurse went to Mashpee two half-days a week.

Visiting nurse went to Mashpee two half-days a week.

A visiting nurse went to Mashpee two half-days a week.

The wisest course would be to omit definite or indefinite articles only after some thought. You may be writing less clearly without them.

The Wrong Suffix

We ought to be able to assume that beginning news writers—and certainly seasoned news writers—know the difference between a noun and an adjective. Experience, however, shows that this is not so.

Confusion often arises because both nouns and adjectives can be used properly in a modifying position before a noun:

We had a *nice* time.   (adjective)
We had a *fun* time.   (noun)

However, where there are two related forms which differ only in the suffix, it would be best to use the adjective in what is more properly an adjective position:

He expected to get the *Democrat* vote.
(noun)

He expected to get the *Democratic* vote.
(adjective)

The adjective *Democratic* with its characteristic *-ic* suffix sounds better than the noun. In the following example the adjective is again a better choice:

She was studying *journalism* ethics.
(noun)
She was studying *journalistic* ethics.
(adjective)

In each of the sentence pairs below, the second sentence would be accepted as the most usual, most grammatical. These examples have all been gleaned from newspapers. They are common mistakes that are frequently the result of pure ignorance of meaning or usage:

an old-fashion picnic	(unacceptable)
an old-fashioned picnic	(acceptable)
an alumni of the state college	(unacceptable)
an alumnus of the state college	(acceptable)
the county prosecutions office	(unacceptable)
the county prosecutor's office	(acceptable)
an indigent defender who . . .	(unacceptable)
an indigent defendant who . . .	(acceptable)
arrested for drunk driving	(unacceptable)
arrested for drunken driving	(acceptable)

Confusion of Form

Strangely enough, some of the most commonplace words in the language are often used incorrectly in writing, but not in speech. The words that cause trouble occasionally for the beginning news writer are those that sound alike, but that have different written forms. These words are, technically, *homophones*, that is, sound alikes. Be on guard against these:

He went to the classroom.	*to,* preposition
John went too.	*too,* adverb
Two boys went.	*two,* article
The two boys went.	*two,* modifier
The two are together.	*two,* noun

It's a nice day.   *it's* contraction
                                    (it is)

I like its looks.   *its*, pronoun
It's been a nice day.   *it's*, contraction
                                    (it has)

The meeting was held there.   *there*, adverb
They held their meeting.   *their*, pronoun
They're all here now.   *they're*, contraction
                                    (they are)

Your book is here.   *your*, pronoun
You're the new reporter.   *you're*, contraction
                                    (you are)

Empty Words

In Chapter 10, the verb *to say* was described as useful because it lacks color. Using the verb *to say* to link the name of a speaker with what was said does not add meaning to our story, it is merely a useful device for giving people credit for the words they speak. *Says* and *said* are empty words and useful because of it.

Other empty words may be less useful. For example, the word *etcetera*, usually abbreviated *etc.*, which means *and so on* or *and so forth*. Writers often use *etc.* when they don't know what to say next or how to cut off a sentence. For example:

> The mayor said that taxes are too high, expenditures are too great, the budget is out of balance, etc.

The *etc.* in this sentence adds nothing. If the mayor cited other examples of the city's fiscal problems, the writer should have included them. If no further examples were cited, the writer should not have implied they were with the *etc.* Avoid such empty words. If there is something to say, say it. If there is nothing to add, end your sentence.

Empty Verbs

There are fads in words and one of the current fads among news writers is the verb *to receive.* Used in its proper sense, it is a useful word: "He received your letter this morning." As it is being more and more misused, however, it produces awkward and wordy sentences and blurred meanings: "The store did not receive an inspection by the state." What the writer means is: "The store was not inspected by the state." The writer has ignored the direct approach and gone the long way around. The sentence using *receive* is vague and wordy; the sentence using *inspected* is short and direct. Some other examples:

> He was the second man *to receive* a sentence of capital punishment.
> He was the second man *to be sentenced* to death.

> He pleaded guilty and *received* a $100 fine.
> He pleaded guilty and *was fined* $100.

> He *received* the degree of doctor of philosophy.
> He *was awarded* the degree of doctor of philosophy.

Watch out for *receive.* It may be substituting for a stronger, more meaningful verb. Here are some other verbs that get misused in much the same way:

> The boy got ready *to take* a swim.
> The boys got ready *to swim.*

> *There was* a heavy snow.
> It *snowed* heavily.

> The Smiths *were* in attendance at the wedding.
> The Smiths *attended* the wedding.

> The board *reached* a decision on the matter yesterday.
> The board *decided* the matter yesterday.

Possessives

Beginners often overuse the -'s which ordinarily indicates possession. We find usages such as:

> Detroit's chief executive
> Florida's governor

the board's vote
the university's fencing team
the association's membership

The use of these so-called false possessives is widespread and growing. It is probably too late to restrict the use of this possessive ending to cases of genuine possession by an animate being: *the boy's book, the mother's two youngsters.* We certainly cannot argue with the *nation's capital, Long Day's Journey into Night, at day's end* or *states' rights.* But, where there is a more direct way of saying something the possessive *-'s* should not be used. Here are two examples of the unnecessary use of *-'s* and their revised versions.

Over one-half the people at the meeting left quickly after the board's vote.
Over one-half the people at the meeting left quickly after the board voted.

He cited the reason for the planning commission's denial of the special use permit.
He cited the reasons the planning commission gave for denying the special use permit.

In many instances, the *-'s* is substituting for a more usual and readable construction employing the preposition *of.* The Book of Revelations, for example, is unrecognizable as Revelation's Book. Nor would Roosevelt's ringing phrase *day of infamy* have sounded the same if he had said *infamy's* day. Avoid *-'s* constructions. For example:

the mayor of Houston, not   *Houston's mayor*
the governor of Florida, not   *Florida's governor*
the president of Harvard, not   *Harvard's president*

In other instances, the *-'s* is superfluous and can be deleted without any change in sentence structure:

University of Oregon's School of Journalism
University of Oregon School of Journalism

Would you accept a headline that said "10 Die in Traffic's Accident?" Watch those possessives.

Participial Constructions

Many, probably most, sentences which use subordinate elements introduced by a present participle—a verb ending in *-ing*—can be improved by rewriting. For example:

Having held the lieutenant governor's post in 1954–56, Hart has been a U.S. senator for the past years.

This is an extremely awkward sentence, partly because it implies a cause-and-effect relationship between being a lieutenant governor and being a United States senator. What the writer no doubt meant was:

Hart was lieutenant governor for two years and has been a U.S. senator for six.

Here are some other examples of unsatisfactory participial afterthoughts and their revisions:

The State Department refused to send speakers, contending the conference was set up to be one-sided.
The State Department refused to send speakers to what it claimed was a one-sided conference.

The fire broke out in a basement, filling the structure with smoke.
The fire broke out in the basement and filled the building with smoke.

In both of the preceding examples, the past tense makes a more emphatic sentence than the present participle.

Parallel Construction

This grammatical device is used a great deal in news writing and is neither mysterious nor difficult to execute. The itemized leads listing dead and injured in accident roundups are examples of parallel construction. So is an itemization like this one, which comes from the body of a story:

Effective with the fall semester, the promotions include:
James R. Sweeny, instructor of history, to assistant professor.

Benjamin F. Clymer Jr., assistant professor and head of the library reference department, to associate professor.

Elizabeth S. DeBedts, assistant professor and head of the library circulation department, to associate professor.

Norfolk (Va.) *Virginian-Pilot*

The list goes on, but you get the idea. Each item in the list is presented in exactly the same order: name, present rank and position, (promoted to) new rank. This presentation of items in the same order is called *parallel construction*.

Here is another example, this time one without names. The parallel construction consists of a series of sentences each starting with a figure:

Other major suburban projects in the program include:

$5.1 million for a new bridge over the Sanitary and Ship Canal at Wil-

low Springs Road and German Church Road in Willow Springs.

$4 million for widening Route 83 from Devon Avenue to Woodland Road in DuPage County.

The Trib

There were 15 more items in the list, but this excerpt is enough to show the parallelism. The trick, of course, is to maintain the parallelism throughout an itemized list.

Another example, this time not an itemized list:

Springfield—Members of the Illinois Education Association tried the personal touch in the General Assembly this week regarding bills of interest to the association.

They came up with two reactions:

They were criticized for being overly aggressive to the point of being hostile.

They were praised for demonstrating their right to express their desires to their legislative representatives.

The Trib

CHAPTER 18
Punctuation

PUNCTUATION IS NOT a serious problem for most beginning journalists. There are a few specialized uses of punctuation marks in news writing, and these will be reviewed here.* For the most part, however, common sense provides adequate guidance for beginners. And, when that fails, there is always the stylebook to fall back on.

LINKING

The colon, the dash, the hyphen and the semicolon are punctuation marks that link elements together.

The Colon

The colon is widely used in news writing and causes little difficulty, although some beginners have a tendency to use a semicolon in its place.

*The author is indebted to the *Milwaukee Journal-Milwaukee Sentinel Stylebook* and the *Chicago Tribune Stylebook* for suggesting some of the punctuation problems discussed in this chapter. The organization of punctuation into linking, separating and enclosing marks follows the views set forth in Harold Whitehall's *Structural Essentials in English.*

The colon is most frequently used in clock time where it links the hour and the minutes:

1:12 a.m.   4:15 p.m.   12:01 a.m.

The colon is also used to link an introductory statement and a list:

The class winners were:
Those elected to the board are:
Those killed in the crash were:
Police identified the arrested men as:

Here is an example of this usage, where the itemized list follows the lead in a weekend accident roundup:

The dead are:
Miss Elizabeth Brownsher, 48, of 7000 Plymouth Ave., University City.
Mrs. Lubertha Hogan, 77, of 1423 North Taylor Ave.
Robert Mriscin, 25, of Alhambra, Ill.
Johnny Almo, 26, of Lonedell, Mo.
Mrs. Dorothy Bauer, 38, of 2609 Logan St., Granite City.
St. Louis Globe-Democrat

The colon also links an introductory statement and a list of points which may be numbered or marked by bullets or some other typographical device:

> The proposals include:
> –Land use and transportation programs to be contained in a comprehensive planning report from the State Planning Commission.
> –General interior renovation of the county courthouse here.
> –Construction of a county-wide park.
> –Development of a county-wide solid waste disposal system.
> –Construction of a multi-purpose office building and civic center.
> –Provision of a county park and outdoor recreation facility.
> *Nashville Tennessean*

The colon is also used to link an attribution or speech tag with quoted material:

> A spokeman said:
> "The main objection is that no one knows the freshman candidates."

The quoted material may be a single sentence, several sentences or even the complete text of a speech, but the device is the same. In the example above, as in earlier examples of itemized lists, the writer indented for a new paragraph after the colon. In the following examples, the speech tag and direct quote are not separated. This is acceptable form and saves a little space:

> He concluded his speech by declaring: "The only thing I have against the Democrats is that there are too many of them."

> Rep. Walter Fuller, D-Mass.: "This appears to be just another extension of the federal power over interstate commerce."

The Dash

A single dash is used to connect the main part of a sentence with a subordinate part. For example:

> He will quit Common Council next month to become a higher-paid

Council employee—city deputy auditor general.

> Jack Church is a successful student—he has a 3.5 grade point average, is president of his class and tutors other students in math in his spare time.

> Worse than that—the firm's out of business.

The Hyphen

The hyphen is used to link two or more words together, to link numbers and words, to link letters and words and to link prefixes to words.

Hyphens are used in word combinations such as the following, whether they are established by usage or are created for the occasion:

editor-in-chief	do-it-yourself
bread-and-butter	come-as-you-are

Hyphens are used in numerical combinations such as:

23-year-old soldier	6-inch pipeline
6-foot-3-inch athlete	10-pound hammer
20-20 vision	half-mile highway extension
12-6 final score	three-quarters completed million-dollar price tag

Hyphens are used in double names where both elements are of equal importance:

German-American
Landrum-Griffin Act
Columbia-Presbyterian Medical Center
City-County Building
city-county reporter

Hyphens are also used in noun-plus-noun combinations which describe dual jobs or dual qualities:

actor-manager	writer-director
soldier-statesman	secretary-treasurer

Hyphens are used in some political titles and designations:

congressman-at-large
secretary-general
ambassador-designate

Hyphens are used in compound units of measurement:

foot-pound light-year
kilowatt-hour year-round

Hyphens are used in compound words where the two parts of the compound conflict:

serio-comic
socio-economic

Hyphens are used in compounds of family relationship:

great-grandfather bride-to-be
great-great-grandfather mother-in-law
son-in-law   father-in-law

Hyphens are commonly used in word combinations that include a present or past participle:

man-killing job half-baked idea
hard-working man twice-told tale
man-eating tiger new-driven snow

Hyphens link combinations of letters and words, and numbers and letters:

H-bomb X-ray
A-bomb A-1

Most prefixed words are set solid, that is, without a space and without a hyphen, as in *unrecorded, supermarket, transoceanic*. In newspaper usage, however, the following prefixes require the hyphen:

all- all-university
ex- ex-champion
out- out-take
self- self-insured
no- no-fault

Hyphens are used in prefixed words to avoid doubling vowels or tripling consonants:

pre-empt shell-like
re-elect quick-kick
co-op (but cooperative and cooperation)

Hyphens are used to distinguish a prefixed word from a homonym:

re-cover, as opposed to *recover*
re-sent, as opposed to *resent*
re-view, as opposed to *review*

Hyphens are used where a prefix precedes a noun beginning with a capital letter:

pre-Raphaelite Pan-American
un-American trans-Atlantic

In combinations such as the following the hyphen is required:

sit-in hoped-for
once-over put-on
head-on put-down
lean-to

Combinations with *-like* are hyphenated if the usage, is colloquial or if there is a need for clarity:

crazy-like
flu-like

Hyphens are not used with adverbs formed with the derivational suffix *-ly:*

fully informed
newly elected
recently named

Avoid suspensive hyphenation where you can. The following example is hyphenated correctly, but it is awkward:

He was sentenced to a three- to five-year term in prison.

This sentence will read better if it is revised to avoid the hyphenation:

He was sentenced to three to five years in prison.

The Semicolon

The semicolon is used to link closely related ideas into a single sentence. For example:

> The maximum sentence for perjury is seven years; the sentence for subverting justice is left to the judge.

Because this leads to longer sentences, news writers seldom use the semicolon this way. If you are tempted to, don't. Use a period and start a new sentence.

In news writing the semicolon is used most often in lists where too many commas would lead to confusion. Since this is a separating and not a linking function, it will be treated later.

SEPARATING

The use of the period and question mark are so common and so widely understood that it is pointless to recapitulate here. Some journalistic uses of the period, for example its use in initials like U.N., are adequately explained in the *Basic Guide to News Style* at the back of this book.

The use of the exclamation point is also simple. However, it is rarely found in news writing because the breathless kind of writing that uses it is generally poor writing.

The comma and semicolon, however, are extensively used in journalism in situations which, for some reason, cause problems to beginners.

The Comma

As a separating punctuation mark the comma can be disposed of quickly. It is used primarily to separate figures:

> Aug. 1, 1974
> $1,150
> 10,000

The comma is also used to separate words in a series, but in journalistic usage the final comma before *and*, *or* and *nor* is omitted:

> The student was tall, handsome, intelligent and neatly dressed.

> Red, white and blue are our colors.

> Johnson, Smith and Burke were re-elected.

The Semicolon

The semicolon is used in lists where the comma would not provide enough clarity, as in lists that include names, ages, addresses, titles or other descriptive items. For example:

> Those to be honored are Sen. Edward M. Kennedy, D-Mass., the main speaker; the Rev. Theodore M. Hesburgh, president of the University of Notre Dame; author Mary McCarthy; M. Stanton Evans, editor of the Indianapolis, Ind., News; Patrick Healey, a government consultant; Preston E. James, professor emeritus of geography at Syracuse; and Charlotte M. Young, professor of medical nutrition at Cornell.
>
> *Associated Press*

Another list, much on the same order, but this time with addresses, again shows how the semicolon separates and improves clarity:

> Others on the television panel included Kenneth A. Gibson, Newark, N.J.; Neil Goldschmidt, Portland, Ore.; Ben Boo, Duluth, Minn.; and Pete Wilson, San Diego, Calif.
> *United Press International*

Lists of names, ages and addresses also require the semicolon for clarity:

> John Smith, 17, of 103 E. Grand River; Myron Brown, 44, of 234 MAC Ave.; Harris O'Connor, 26, of 723 Michigan Ave.; and Max Cohen, 22, of 442 Western Ave.

ENCLOSING

Paired Commas

Commas come in pairs when they enclose and set off parenthetical material inserted into a sentence. For example, this sentence is grammatical and complete:

John Smith was arrested Monday.

Additional information about Smith can be inserted in this sentence after his name:

John Smith (age 37) was arrested Monday.

Replace the brackets with a pair of commas and you have the usual sentence:

John Smith, 37, was arrested Monday.

Beginning news writers tend to forget that when a name is followed by age, address and sometimes an occupational label, these additional bits of information are optional, the sentence is complete without them. They are, in a sense, parenthetical insertions. No one would dream of setting this material off with a single parenthesis. But when commas are used, the second comma is frequently overlooked.

When more than one item of information is included after a name, each item is a separate parenthetical insert and must be set off by paired commas. For example:

John C. Smith, 37, (of 2134 Madison St.) was arrested Monday.

Replace the brackets with commas and this becomes:

John C. Smith, 37, of 2134 Madison St., was arrested Monday.

Note that the comma after 37 and before *of* now serves to enclose and set off both the 37 to its left and the *of 2134 Madison St.* to its right. Both items have commas before and after, that is, are still set off by paired commas. We can go one step farther:

John C. Smith, 37, of 2134 Madison St., (a laborer) was arrested Monday.

We again replace the brackets with commas, and use the comma after *St.* to replace the left parenthesis. We don't use two commas together.

John C. Smith, 37, of 2134 Madison St., a laborer, was arrested Monday.

Paired commas are also used to set off a year inserted after month and date:

The eclipse occurred on June 30, 1973, over a wide area of the continent of Africa.

Paired commas are used to set off the name of a state or political district inserted after the name of a city:

The student lived in Madison, Wis., before coming to the university here.

Washington, D.C., is a beautiful city.

Paired commas, of course, are used to set off other parenthetically inserted matter:

Robert McCormick, NBC News correspondent in Washington, joined the discussion.

The students, despite the fact they felt unprepared, did well on the examination.

Her son by a previous marriage, Eldon McKee, is the manager of the boat line.

Senate Republicans want to see Governor Walker, a Democrat, keep his promises on flood control.

Paired Dashes

Paired dashes can be used instead of paired commas or parentheses to set off material inserted in a sentence. They represent a somewhat more emphatic break and are generally used to set off material that is explanatory or interpolative:

Four nations—The United States, Russia, Great Britain and China—are the powers to be watched.

The President—it was generally conceded—owed the Congress an explanation.

Smith—at bat for the first time this season—faced the pitcher warily.

Paired dashes are a nice compromise between commas, which are all right for routine use, and parentheses which are usually too emphatic an interruption in a smoothly flowing sentence. Paired dashes are informal, easy to accommodate while reading, well suited to the general tone of news writing.

Parentheses

Parentheses are not much used in news writing because they interrupt the reader in the midst of a sentence. Paired commas and paired dashes are better for setting off parenthetically inserted material, while parentheses are useful for enclosing and setting off single words, initials or brief interpolation:

The program began shortly after noon (EST) on the Capitol steps.

Smith was a reporter for the Marion (Ind.) Chronicle-Tribune at the time.

He was arrested by Cuyahoga County (Cleveland) officers on a fugitive warrant.

The bill was sponsored by State Senator Frank Perkins (R-8th) and Rep. James Meek (R-31st).

The land-use bill (House Bill 1122) was approved by the committee Monday.

The Environmental Protection Agency (EPA) was asked to investigate.

Not all these examples follow the *Basic Style Guide* included with this book, nor do they all conform to the wire services joint stylebook. They are all, however, structurally correct and suggest the kinds of uses to which parentheses can be put.

CHAPTER 19
Style and the Stylebook

BEGINNERS in the newsroom are confronted almost immediately with the need to spell, punctuate, capitalize and abbreviate—among other things—in a certain way. If they ask why, as they ought to, they will be told: "That's our *style*."

Style is the way things are done around the newsroom. Style is the way you are supposed to do things. And style, as you will quickly find out, is often arbitrary, unreasonable and confusing. But it is terribly important and the first thing beginners should do is get a copy of the stylebook that governs writing practices and usage in the newsroom where they are working and learn its rules.

Most newspapers use a stylebook. Many use the stylebook prepared jointly by the Associated Press and United Press International. Many large newspapers have their own stylebook, some agreeing in most cases with the press associations joint stylebook and some differing considerably. Book publishers, public relations agencies, the Government Printing Office and the armed forces also have stylebooks. Most books on news writing, including this one, contain a basic style guide for beginners.

WHY HAVE A STYLE?

A Need for Consistency

Stylebooks are devices for enforcing a consistency in writing throughout the newspaper. This does not mean that the newspaper wants every one of its reporters, writers and editors to write in exactly the same way. Far from it. No newspaper wants its pages to sound like the homogenized columns of *Time* magazine or the *Reader's Digest*. But it does want consistency in punctuation, capitalization, abbreviation, spelling, the use of numbers and related matters. The press associations joint stylebook, for example, says:

> 2.4. ABBREVIATE St., Ave., Blvd,, Ter., in addresses, but not Point, Port, Circle, Plaza, Place, Drive, Oval, Road, Lane.

This rule is intended to assure that every news story originating with either press association will abbreviate or spell out these words in exactly the same way every time. In this and other matters of style, consistency is considered both a virtue and a necessity. Editors want capitalization, punctuation, abbreviations and numbers to appear in the same form on every page of the newspaper all the way from the front page to the market news on the inside of the back page. They want sports writers and police reporters and columnists to follow the same rules in the use of titles and nicknames. They want locally written news stories to follow the same spelling rules that press association stories follow.

Preference and Tradition

Style is basically a preference for one way of doing things over another way when there are two or more acceptable ways of doing it. You could, for example, capitalize the word *Street* in addresses; or you might not. You could abbreviate it or spell it out. In any case, whatever choice you make would be perfectly clear to your readers. The choice you make is a matter of preference, not a matter of one way being right and the other wrong.

Style, in the sense of providing rules for spelling, punctuation, capitalization, abbreviation and the use of numbers, is a product of the printing press. It is a visual matter. In the case of punctuation, it provides visual clues to meaning that we would get orally if we were listening to someone talk. In the case of spelling, the various rules reflect what was originally an attempt to indicate how the words sounded.

Style is to a large extent traditional. It grew up with the development of printing and with the growth of the printing and publishing industries. The earliest printers and editors sought consistency as they created a new written form of the English language. There is a long tradition that language ought to be consistent, that there must be true and correct forms and that the right way to use the language must be preserved and enforced. These views do not take into account such well-established phenomena as changes in sound, in meaning and in usage. But attempts at establishing the "correct" forms have persisted. Style falls

within this tradition as it attempts to establish certain forms and usages.

MECHANICAL ASPECTS

The most mechanical and least interesting aspects of style have to do with punctuation, capitalization, abbreviations and the use of numbers. In all these matters the written language permits considerable variation so that stylebooks are attempting only to provide some consistency in such matters. They needn't bother to remind us that the first letter of the first word in a sentence is capitalized; nor that a sentence ends with a period. But the press associations joint stylebook does tell us, for example:

> 3.16 The comma separates words or figures:
> What the solution is, is a question.
> Aug. 1, 1960
> 1,235,567

> 3.17 The colon is used in clock time:
> 8:15 p.m.

> 3.38 The prefix "ex" is hyphened:
> ex-champion.

Capitalization is an area in which there are a few well-understood rules and a lot of leeway for personal choice. For example, we all agree that the initial letters of personal names should be capitalized: John, William, Henry Fonda. But the AP-UPI joint stylebook instructs us in some other matters which are not so generally agreed upon:

> 1.5 Capitalize titles of authority before a name, but lower case them when standing alone or following a name: Ambassador John Jones; Jones, ambassador; the ambassador.

> 1.25 Capitalize common nouns as part of a formal name: Hoover Dam, Missouri River, Barr County Courthouse. Lower case dam, river, courthouse, etc., standing alone.

Abbreviations are anybody's game and stylebooks have much to say on this subject. For example, the AP-UPI joint stylebook, warns:

> 2.12 Spell United States and United Nations when used as a noun. U.S.A. and U.N. as nouns may be used in texts or direct quotations.

Stylebooks generally set rules for abbreviations of state names and for religious and military titles. Look these up when the need arises.

Numbers are a problem, but news style has one generally accepted rule: write out numbers one through nine and use arabic figures for 10 and above. That sounds easy, but when you turn to the section on numbers in the press associations joint stylebook, you find that there are some exceptions. For example:

> 4.3 Casual numbers are spelled: A thousand times no! Gay Nineties.

> 4.12 Write it No. 1 boy. No. 2 candidate, etc.

These examples turn the old one-through-nine rule upside down. You will find that the rules for the use of numbers are fairly simple and, because we use so many numbers in news stories, not too difficult to master with a little practice. Again, when in doubt, refer to the stylebook.

An Aid to Readability

Many rules found in stylebooks are there to make news stories easier to read and understand. And easier to write, too, once some of the more common rules are learned. For example, the AP-UPI joint stylebook cautions:

> 1.6 Long titles should follow a name: John Jones, executive director of the commercial department of Blank & Co. Richard Roe, secretary-treasurer, Blank & Co.

News style is gradually eliminating unnecessary punctuation as a means of keeping sentences uncluttered and flowing smoothly. You will find that most stylebooks ask you to eliminate the comma before *and* and *or* in a series, thus:

He saluted the red, white and blue.
He asked for apples, pears or oranges.

The apostrophe is also done away with, where meaning is perfectly clear. The *Milwaukee Journal-Milwaukee Sentinel* stylebook, for example, requires:

> Do not use the apostrophe to form irregular plurals: ABCs, the three Rs, 2x4s, 1920s. Exception A's (baseball team), and any other ambiguities.

News style calls for the use of *a.m.* or *p.m.* with all references to clock time. Readers should not be confused about when things happened—or will happen.

News style is also very particular about the use of names, and while there are some exceptions, the basic rule is to identify people by their first name, middle initial and last name. Where street addresses are used after a person's name and age, news style requires the insertion of the word *of* between the age and the address, thus:

John C. Smith, 37, of 241 S. Cedar St.

The word *of* in this case is a safety precaution against getting the numbers in the age and the address mixed up. Who lives at 37241 S. Cedar? It might *not* be Mr. Smith and he might *not* like his name associated with the other address.

The *Chicago Tribune* stylebook requires writers to use extreme caution in handling street addresses:

> Include N., S., E. or W. in every street address: 2900 S. State St., even though many readers know that no 2900 N. State St., exists.

In the interest of readability and clarity, stylebooks frequently urge news writers to use short sentences and to avoid the kind of punctuation that encourages long sentences. The *Detroit News* stylebook warns:

> Semicolons should be used sparingly in news writing. When semicolons might be used in more formal writing, periods usually are better in a news story.

As you become familiar with the contents of the stylebook, you will find many rules and suggestions that will not only make it easier for you to put your story together, but which will also make your story easier to read and understand. Rules about style help structure and organize news writing and, although this takes away some of your freedom of choice, it does speed up production. You don't have to stop whenever a decision is called for; the decisions have already been made for you. Once the rules are learned and become second nature, the copy rolls out much faster.

Style and Usage

In addition to the more mechanical matters like punctuation, stylebooks tend to get into the meanings and uses of words and phrases. There are some good reasons for this, although reason and logic do not account for all the rules of usage enforced by stylebooks. In the first place, the newspaper is concerned with the clear, accurate and truthful presentation of information so that precise meanings of words are important. Do you mean *allude* or *infer*? Are you sure it is *convince* or should it be *persuade*? Second, the newspaper is seeking to present the news in readable, informal and understandable prose. There has to be a balance between the informal, slangy, irreverent popular speech and the stiff, formal and traditional written language of literature and scholarship. Finally, editors have quite a conservative streak and many resist manfully any changes in the language and hold onto old words and old usages whether they make sense or not.

Precision in the use of words is important if our readers are to understand us. News writing must be so accurate that readers get the same meaning out of a story that we put into it. Hence, suggestions such as the following from the AP-UPI joint stylebook:

> 6.6 An automatic is not a revolver and vice verse, but "pistol" describes either. A bullet is the metal projectile of a cartridge which includes the propellant powder, casing and primer.

And the *Milwaukee Journal-Milwaukee Sentinel* stylebook cautions:

> oral, verbal. Not synonymous. Oral means spoken as opposed to written. Verbal means expressed in words, either spoken or written.

And the *Chicago Tribune* stylebook has this to say:

> *less, few.* Less applies only to things that are measured by amount and not by number or size or quality: Less manpower; fewer men.

Popular speech, of course, is the real source of the written language and journalism has always drawn on the everyday language of the street, the police station, the theater, sports, politics—and everything else—to enrich its language. Yet some words and phrases are banned by stylebooks on the grounds that they are too slangy, too common. The *Chicago Tribune-Chicago Today* stylebook bans the use of *O.K.* except in headlines; rules out *cop*; and says of *lawman*: "Forget those TV westerns. Make him a policeman, a sheriff or whatever he is." The *Milwaukee Journal-Milwaukee Sentinel Stylebook* also bans *cop*: "Derogatory as synonym for policeman."

Many of the prohibitions in stylebooks, however, are due to tradition and conservatism, even of prejudice, in language, and some are due to a refusal to accept the fact that ours is an ever-changing language. Many stylebooks object to coining new verbs from existing nouns: for example, *shotgunned to death, suicided, hosted a party, authored a book.* But this objection is grammatical nonsense, since speakers of English have been creating useful verbs in this way since the days of King Alfred. It is true that some newly coined verbs are awkward, some are not as familiar as older words or phrases and some won't last. However, others will survive because they meet the needs of our times. Newspapers are full of such words. Nevertheless, stylebooks continue to ban some of them from newspaper columns and we have to follow the stylebook.

Many stylebooks ban the use of *contact* and *finalize* and various verb coinages such as *guested*, *premiered*, *debuted* and *readied*. Other prohibitions which are traditional, but hard to explain logically:

The use of *feel* for *believe*; *following* as a preposition in the sense of after; the use of *sustained* in the phrase *he sustained injuries*; *lady* for *woman* the phrase *given a sentence*; *over* for *more than*; *Xmas* as an abbreviation for *Christmas*.

Such prohibitions are arbitrary and confusing. Many of the words banned from newspaper columns are in common use in everyday speech; many are part of the standard language as proven by their inclusion in the dictionary; many will be found in carefully edited books and periodicals. But, if your newsroom stylebook bans a word, you have to go along. The preference of your editor and your office stylebook govern usage.

Spelling presents another problem since some words have several acceptable spellings and consistency demands that one spelling be selected as the preferred usage. Most stylebooks contain a list of preferred spellings which staff members must use. Generally, they favor shorter spellings: *employe* with one *e*, for example. Sometimes the most commonly used spelling is preferred, even if it is longer: *taboo*, not *tabu*. In other cases spellings that most accurately reflect the history, or etymology, of the word are specified: *bandolier*, rather than *bandoleer*, for example.

Newspapers in the United States generally prefer American to British spellings: *tire* not *tyre*; *theater* not *theatre*; and *glamor* not *glamour*. Noah Webster shortened or changed a lot of British spellings and newspaper style follows his lead.

Some newspapers prefer to maintain the distinctions between masculine and feminine forms. The *Chicago Tribune* stylebook insists on *brunet* and *brunette*, *employe* and *employee*. Most stylebooks require writers to observe distinction between *fiancé* and *fiancée*.

Stylebooks may also contain lists of preferred or correct geographical names, including local or regional names. They sometimes also gives lists of frequently misspelled words.

Style and Policy

Stylebooks generally contain some rules or guidelines to the newspaper's policy on such matters as courtesy titles, racial designations, the use of epithets, vulgarities and obscenities, and the use of legal, technical or scientific terminology: for example terminology concerned with sexual matters, that might be offensive to some people.

The *Milwaukee Journal-Milwaukee Sentinel* stylebook, for example, contains a detailed explanation of the newspapers' policy governing the use of *Mr.*, *Mrs.*, *Miss* and *Ms*. Most stylebooks insist that *Mr.* always be used with the name of the president of the United States if the title *President* is not used: President Ford or Mr. Ford, never just Ford. Most stylebooks ban the use of racial designations unless they are relevant to the news story.

The use of words or phrases that may be offensive to some readers are a problem. Very few words or phrases are banned outright today, although some newspapers are still a little squeamish. *Rape*, for example, long felt to be too strong a word to appear in a family newspaper is now acceptable and stylebooks may prefer *rape* to such circumlocutions as *statutory offense* or *sexual assault*.

Not all newspapers published the exact words Senator McGovern used when, in the closing days of the 1972 presidential campaign, he whispered a blunt vulgarity to a heckler. The more conservative newspapers substituted dashes. What a newspaper does when vulgarities and obscenities are part of a news story is a matter of policy and is or ought to be stated clearly in their stylebook.

Many stylebooks are not as explicit about policy matters as they might be. There have been some enormous changes in the past few years in our use of previously unmentionable or tabooed words and phrases in everyday conversation and in print. Newspapers tend to take a conservative view of language and are just beginning to catch up to their readers in these matters. And, since stylebooks are revised only every few years, many of them do not yet spell out policy on matters—like the use of four-letter words—which are now more or less settled in practice. The *Basic Guide to News Style* which appears at the end of this book attempts to offer some guidance in this area, guidance based on careful observation of what newspapers, press associations and supplementary news services are actually doing.

Long tradition and accepted practices in the newsroom provide some of the authority for the rules given in stylebooks. The authority of tradition and custom may be pretty shaky, especially when you consider that stylebooks are often nothing more than the codification of usage editors learned years ago when they were beginners, or reflect an individual editor's likes and dislikes. The *Chicago Tribune* stylebook inveighs against words ending in the suffix *-wise,* and says that words like *weatherwise, businesswise* "belong strictly to the wastelands of television."

Generally, however, there is some authority behind stylebook rules. Most stylebooks base their spelling preferences on the Merriam-Webster *Third New International Dictionary.* Webster's *Third* is the authority on other matters, too. The *Chicago Tribune Stylebook,* for example, refers staff writers to Webster's *Third* to settle matters of hyphenation not settled in the stylebook. Military titles and designations are based on official use of the armed forces and religious titles and designations are based on careful consultation with the various churches and religious sects. The use of geographic names may be based, in some style-

books, on the authority of the *National Geographic* magazine or on the authorized spellings of the United States Geographic Board. The abbreviations of state names are determined by the authority of the *United States Official Postal Guide.*

The *Chicago Tribune* stylebook refers news writers to H. L. Mencken's *American Language,* Theodore M. Bernstein's *Watch Your Language* and to *Elements of Style* by William Strunk Jr. and E. B. White for matters not covered or fully explained in the stylebook. Presumably, the editors of the stylebook consulted these volumes in making their own decisions. Many newspapers continue to refer to H. W. Fowler's *Modern English Usage* and some of Wilson Follett's *Modern American Usage,* although neither can really be considered an authority on contemporary American English. Fowler is too British and too out-of-date in most matters of usage and Follett is too conservative and old-fashioned to be of much help to news writers who want to write for this generation of newspaper readers.

THE JOINT STYLEBOOK

One of the major influences on news style today is the joint stylebook published by the Associated Press and United Press International. The first joint stylebook was published in 1960 and a revised edition was issued in 1968. Today most newspapers follow the lead of this stylebook, either using it as their own stylebook and making all locally written and edited copy conform, or basing their own stylebook on preferences stated in the joint stylebook.

The introduction of improved technology in the printing of newspapers has also favored the use of the joint stylebook. More and more news copy comes into the newspaper office on punched tape and is fed directly into typesetting machines. Under this system it is too costly to edit wire copy to fit the local style. News stories come into the newsroom, are set in type and printed pretty much as they come from the bureaus of the Associated Press or United Press International.

For the beginner, there is some advantage in the dominance of the joint stylebook. Once you learn style, you will find you can follow it in most of the places you will work.

Only a handful of newspapers compile their own stylebooks and these are generally the largest ones such as the *New York Times, Detroit News, Chicago Tribune* and the *Milwaukee Journal*. These newspapers produce so much of their own copy that it is just as easy to edit wire service stories to conform to their own style as to do it the other way around. Smaller papers generally find it easier to follow the joint stylebook and edit local copy to conform.

THE BASIC GUIDE TO NEWS STYLE

This text includes what might be called a basic stylebook. It contains many statements on style and newsroom practice that are too basic and well understood to be included in the joint stylebook or in most newspaper stylebooks. It omits quite a lot that you will find in other stylebooks, especially typographical matters that are not of immediate interest to the beginning news writer. Since most beginning news writers are working in college classrooms, the basic stylebook covers a number of points that are of greater interest on college campuses than elsewhere—for example, the treatment of academic titles, degrees and rank. As far as possible, this stylebook conforms to the preferences of the press associations stylebook either specifically or by analogy.

NEWS STYLE AND PERSONAL STYLE

News style as we have just described it deals with mechanical matters, with consistency; it smacks of history and tradition; it presents some guidelines for clear and accurate writing and it establishes some matters of official policy. News style offers some useful and workable guidelines for organizing and writing news stories, but it should not inhibit you from developing your own style of writing. You can obey your office stylebook and still develop your own style, your own way of saying things, for personal style is quite another thing. Personal style, the writer's own choice of words, resulted in this lead from the *Detroit Free Press:*

> A 23-year-old Detroit man, clad only in raindrops, tried to climb Scott Fountain on Belle Isle Sunday.

Nude or *naked* might have been the obvious way to describe this Detroit man. Some writers might have said *unclothed*. But the writer of this lead out of an innate genius found a different way of saying something quite ordinary.

Your personal style will have to develop over a period of time and it will probably not start to grow until you have mastered the arbitrary and structured aspects of news style and the basic story structures. Once you feel comfortable with the basic matters of news writing, you will begin to reach out, to be more creative, to develop a style and approach to writing that is your own.

This personal style will not be a matter of punctuation, capitalization and abbreviation. It will be matter of your choice of words, of the range of your vocabulary, of your ability to coin figures of speech, your ear for dialect, colorful words and apt expressions. It will be a matter of sentence length and the rhythm of your prose, of the clarity of your thinking and the logical presentation of your ideas. This style will not come out of an office stylebook, it will come out of you. It will not be a matter of rules, but a matter of feeling. Accept the stylebook for what it is, master it, and go on to learn to write in your own style.

A BASIC GUIDE TO NEWS STYLE

THESE BASIC RULES and guidelines conform in general to practices of the Associated Press and of United Press International. They reflect as much as possible the current practices in the newspaper world.

Abbreviations

1.1 Spell out, do *not* abbreviate, the names of organizations, firms, agencies, universities and colleges, groups, clubs or governmental bodies the first time the name is used in a news story.

There are a few obvious exceptions, like U.N. or FBI, where there is no need to spell out for sure identification.

1.2 The names of organizations, firms, agencies, universities and colleges, groups, clubs or governmental bodies may be abbreviated in second and subsequent references if the abbreviation is standard and will be easily understood by readers. For example, the first reference might be:

European Economic Community
National Organization for Women

Second or later references would be:

the Common Market
NOW

1.3 When an organization, firm, agency, university or college, group, club or governmental body is usually and publicly known by initials or an acronym that might not be familiar to some newspaper readers, you may bracket the abbreviation or acronym after the spelled-out name used in the first reference:

Americans for Democratic Action (ADA)

American Newspaper Publishers Association (ANPA)

The only reason for bracketing the short form after the name is to enable your readers to make the connection when the short form is used in second and subsequent references.

1.4 Do *not* bracket initials, abbreviations or acronyms after the names of organizations, firms, agencies or associations, as suggested in 1.3, *unless* you will use the bracketed identification later in the story.

Do *not* make up initials for organizations where none exist in common usage. Do not use involved, hard-to-decipher or uncommon abbreviations in second and subsequent references. Instead, use an understandable term such as *the group, the association, the committee.*

For example, if the first reference is:

. . . the Italian-American Civil Rights League . . .

The second and subsequent reference would be:

. . . the League . . .

1.5 In street addresses abbreviate these:

street	as	St.
avenue		Ave.
boulevard		Blvd.
terrace		Ter.

However, in general references where a street number is not used, spell out and capitalize street, avenue, boulevard and terrace. See also 1.6 and 2.1.

on West Grand Boulevard
near the corner of Holmes Street

1.6 Do *not* abbreviate these:

Point	Plaza	Road
Port	Drive	Place
Circle	Lane	

1.7 Abbreviate points of the compass in street addresses:

> 1813 S. 59th St.
> 1300 Oakland Road NE

However, in general references where no street number is used, spell out the compass designation which comes *before* the name of the street:

> on South 59th Street
> near West Grand Boulevard

See also 1.5 and 2.1.

1.8 Do *not* abbreviate points of the compass in other use:

> Snow fell south of town.
> He lived north of the tracks.

1.9 Preferred abbreviations for names of states are:

Ala.	Ill.	Miss.	N.M.	Tenn.
Ariz.	Ind.	Mo.	N.Y.	Tex.
Ark.	Kan.	Mont.	Okla.	Va.
Calif.	Ky.	Neb.	Ore.	Vt.
Colo.	La.	Nev.	Pa.	Wash.
Conn.	Mass.	N.C.	R.I.	Wis.
Del.	Md.	N.D.	S.C.	W. Va.
Fla.	Mich.	N.H.	S.D.	Wyo.
Ga.	Minn.	N.J.		

1.10 Do *not* abbreviate the names of the states of Alaska, Hawaii, Idaho, Iowa, Ohio, Maine and Utah. Other state names are abbreviated only when they appear with city names:

He lived in Athens, Miss.

He lived in Mississippi most of his life.

Do *not* use the abbreviations for state names now commonly seen on computerized mailing lists.

He lived in Detroit, Mich., *not* Detroit, MI.

1.11 Do *not* abbreviate the months of March, April, May, June and July. Other months are abbreviated *only* when they are used with a date:

Oct. 21, 1974	October 1973
Sept. 25	September weather
June 8, 1974	April showers

1.12 Names of countries are not abbreviated although there are some exceptions: *U.S.* and *U.S.A.* are acceptable when used to modify a noun:

Mrs. White came to the United States once.
She served on the U.S. Maritime Commission.

1.13 Do not abbreviate days of the week, given names, points of the compass in city names or parts of city names:

Monday and Tuesday, *never* Mon. or Tues.
William and Charles, *never* Wm. or Chas.
East St. Louis, *never* E. St. Louis
Los Angeles and Grand Rapids, *never* L.A. or Gd. Rapids

Do not abbreviate *association, associate, department; professor,* except as a title before a name; *Christmas* as *Xmas; father* as a title, as in Father Smith.

1.14 Degrees—academic, honorary and religious—are abbreviated and capitalized when they follow a name. They are spelled out and lower cased when standing alone.

John C. Smith, B.A.
He earned a bachelor's degree
He studied for a master of arts degree in art.

Standard abbreviations for academic degrees are:

bachelor of arts	B.A.
bachelor of science	B.S.
master of arts	M.A.
doctor of philosophy	Ph.D.
doctor of education	Ed.D.

Note: These abbreviations take periods. See 4.6.

1.15 Abbreviate and capitalize titles before names:

Mr.	Sen.	Gen.
Mrs.	Rep.	Atty. Gen.
Ms.	Asst.	Dist. Atty.
Dr.	Lt. Gov.	
Prof.	Gov.	

Gov. George Wallace	Gov. Wallace
Atty. Gen. Frank J. Kelley	Atty. Gen. Kelley

President is never abbreviated:

> President Gerald R. Ford
> President Ford

1.16 Abbreviate *mount* and *fort* in the names of mountains and army posts, but spell out in city names:

> Mt. Everest
> Ft. Benning (military
> installation in Georgia)
> Fort Meyers (city in Florida)
> Mount Vernon

Capitalization

2.1 A general rule is that with names of places and things, both the distinguishing part of the name and the nondistinguishing part are capitalized:

> Hotel Taft
> Missouri River
> New Trier High School
> Fifth Avenue
> West Central Conference

2.2 Capitalize names of holidays, historic events, church feast days, special events and so on, but *not* seasons:

> Mothers Day
> Labor Day
> National Safety Week
> Welcome Week
> an early fall storm

2.3 Capitalize the names of specific regions, but not points of the compass:

Midwest	an east wind
Middle West	a southern exposure
West Coast	Border States
the South	

2.4 Capitalize trade names and trademarks, that is, names in which the manufacturer, distributor or inventor has a property right:

Coke is the registered trademark of Coca-Cola.
Thermos is a registered trademark.
Scotch tape is a registered trademark.

Use generic or descriptive terms unless you are specifically referring to the trademark item:

> soft drink
> vacuum bottle
> celophane tape

2.5 Capitalize the names of races:

> Indian
> Caucasian
> Negro

Note: White, red and black are not the names of races.

2.6 Capitalize the names of books, plays, poems, songs, lectures or speech titles, hymns, movies, television programs and so on, when the full title is used.

"All in the Family"	(television show)
"Eleanor and Franklin"	(book)
"America the Beautiful"	(song)
"Howl"	(poem)
"Godspell"	(play)

See also 4.7.

2.7 Names of newspapers and magazines are capitalized, but *not* enclosed in quotation marks:

> Houston Post
> Wall Street Journal
> Ms. magazine
> Saturday Evening Post

2.8 Do *not* capitalize occupational descriptions or false titles before a name:

> actor John Wayne
> author James Baldwin
> tennis champion Billie Jean King

Do capitalize titles before a name:

> Gov. George Wallace
> Federal Judge Shirley M. Hufstedler
> Dr. Helen Brooke Taussig

See also 1.15 and 5.12

2.9 Capitalize the names of universities and colleges and the various academic and administrative units within universities and colleges:

> Wellesley College

Howard University
Stanford University
Department of Romance Languages
School of Journalism
Science and Math Teaching Center
Office of Institutional Research
Computer Sciences Program

2.10 Do *not* capitalize general references to subject matter, areas of interest, political philosophies:

> air navigation
> civil engineering
> French history
> democratic system
> communist philosophy

2.11 Names of buildings on campus and other public buildings are capitalized. See also 2.1.

> the Administration Building
> the Book Tower
> Widener Library
> the Pentagon
> the National Archives Building

Numbers

3.1 As a general rule spell out both cardinal and ordinal numbers from one through nine; use arabic figures for 10 and above. For example:

first day	10 days
one man	21st year
nine years	50 more

3.2 Use commas in numbers with four or more digits except in years and street addresses:

> 1,500   23,879

3.3 Exact numbers of more than a million are expressed in arabic figures:

The population of New York City is 7,867,760.

3.4 Round numbers may be expressed in the words *millions* or *billions,* thus:

one million	five billion
23 million	234 billion

Numbers over a million may be rounded off and expressed thus:

2.75 million, rather than 2,750,000

3.5 Arabic figures are used for street addresses:

> 1492 Columbus Ave.
> 1145 E. Grand River Ave.

3.6 Arabic figures are used in ages:

> Mary Brown, 4, who . . .
> Smith, 60, was . . .

3.7 Arabic figures are used to express dimensions, distances, heights, speeds, temperatures, weight, percentages, latitude and longitude, time and scores of sporting events:

dimensions	5 by 9 feet, 11 feet by 23 inches
distances	18 miles, 2 feet
height	5 feet 7 inches
speed	55 miles an hour
temperatures	93 degrees
weight	88 pounds, 15 ounces, 3 tons
percentages	5 per cent, 90 per cent
latitude and longitude	5 degrees west, 10 degrees north
time	8 a.m., 9:15 p.m.
scores	Army 6, Navy 6

Note: In stories with more than one reference to a percentage, follow this rule, but if there is a single, isolated reference to a percentage in a story, spell it out if it is under 10: as *five per cent.*

3.8 Arabic figures are used to express sums of money:

5 cents	$250,000
$1	$100

Sums of money over one million may be rounded off and expressed thus:

> $2.5 billion $1.7 million

Do not round off or express in words sums under one million.

3.9 Fractions alone are written in words, but when part of a modifying unit arabic figures are used:

> three-quarters of a mile
> a ¾-inch pipe

3.10 When three or more numbers appear in a series, either use all arabic figures or spell out all numbers, following the rule for the largest number in the series:

204 pages, 57 dresses and 3 boxes
nine dogs, seven squirrels and four cats

3.11 When a number is used at the beginning of a sentence, spell it out. Do not use an arabic figure to start a sentence:

Seventy-six trombones led the big parade.
Ten thousand people jammed the stadium.

If it is awkward to use a spelled-out number in this way, rephrase the sentence.

The parade was led by 76 trombones.

Sometimes you can round off the number and use a word like *nearly, almost* or *more than* to start the sentence:

Nearly 100,000 people lined the parade route.

3.12 In news writing avoid the use of symbols for cents, degrees, inches, feet, number, per cent and so on. Always spell these out. The only exception is the dollar sign:

5 feet 2 inches   1.6 inches
11 percent $1.50

3.13 Casual numbers, obviously inexact, are spelled out:

A thousand times no!
He can work a hundred million miracles.

3.14 Dates are expressed in arabic figures:

July 4, 1776
November 11, 1918

3.15 Plural dates are indicated by figures and a lower case *s*.

Note the use of the apostrophe:

the 1970s   the early '20s
the 1850s   the late '60s

3.16 References to decades which have acquired names are spelled out:

the Gay Nineties
the depression-ridden Thirties

3.17 Centuries follow the general rule for numbers

(3.1) and are expressed in original numbers.

ninth century   20th century

Punctuation

4.1 The apostrophe is used to indicate omissions in contractions and certain other forms:

it's (it is)
can't (can not)
'60s (the 1960s)

4.2 The apostrophe is *not* used to form plurals:

the 1960s
two MIGs
two Bs and one C

Exception: Write *A's* with the apostrophe.

4.3 A colon is used in clock time:

8:15 a.m.   9:15 p.m.

4.4 The use of the hyphen is complicated and when in doubt it is best to refer to the dictionary. Here are some basic rules, however:

The hyphen is used in phrasal adjectives:

a 7-year-old boy
an off-the-cuff remark

The hyphen is *not* used in sequences like the following where the adverb has an *-ly* suffix:

a gravely ill patient
a relatively easy solution

In combinations of number-plus-a-noun-of-measurement use a hyphen:

a 3-inch bug   a two-man satellite
a 6-foot man

Where prefixes which are usually set solid precede a word normally capitalized, use a hyphen:

unbecoming   un-American
unknown   un-British
unlovable   pre-Raphaelite

A hyphen is always used with the prefix *ex-* as in:

ex-president
ex-chairman

A hyphen is used to separate vowels as in prefixed words like:

pre-empt   co-op
re-elect

Note exceptions like *cooperate, coed, coordinate*.

The hyphen is used in numbers spelled out:

    seventy-six

    twenty-three

4.5 The comma is omitted before Roman numerals, *Jr.* and *Sr.* in names:

    Adlai Stevenson III

    Mrs. John Elliott Jr.

4.6 Periods are used in certain abbreviations, viz:

    U.S. and U.S.A.

    U.S.S.R.

    U.N.

After points of the compass in street addresses, as *16 E. 72nd St.*

In lower case abbreviations, as *a.m., p.m., m.p.h., c.o.d.*

In *B.C.* and *A.D.*, as in *100 B.C.* or *510 A.D.*

In academic degrees, as *B.A., M.S., Ph.D.*

Note that in most other instances abbreviations that are initials do not take periods:

Military abbreviations, as *USAF, USN, RAF, MIG 70, MP, USS Iowa, PO3c, GI*

Points of the compass after street addresses, as *16 Gregory Ave. NW*

Most organizations, as *AFL-CIO, OAS, GOP, MSU, ADA*

Some lower case abbreviations, as *35mm, ips* (tape)

Some company names as *AT&T*

Time zones, as *EDT, CST*

Acronyms, as *CORE, CARE, WAVES, NOW.*

4.7 Quotation marks are used to enclose direct quotations and the titles of books, plays, poems, songs, lecture or speeches:

"The Tonight Show"   (television program)

"Future Shock"   (book)

"What Now My Love?"   (song)

"What's the Matter with   (editorial)
    Kansas?"

"I'm in trouble," he said.

"What," he asked, "is the meaning of that?"

Note that in direct quotation periods and commas are always arbitrarily placed before the closing quotation marks. Other punctuation marks are placed before or after as logic demands.

4.8 Avoid the use of quotation marks with slang expressions or single words where meaning is perfectly clear:

He called the youth a "hippy."   (Wrong)

He called the youth a hippy.   (Right)

He called the word "slang."   (Wrong)

He called the word slang.   (Right)

4.9 Use parentheses to set off names of states in newspaper titles:

    The Boston (Mass.) *Globe*

4.10 In a series omit the final comma before *and, or* or *nor*:

    red, white and blue

    neither money, influence nor votes

4.11 Use quotation marks to set off nicknames:

    Ruggiero "Richie the Boot" Boiardo

    W. C. "Pug" Pearson

    The other players called him "Slim."

Where a nickname has become better known than the person's given name, omit the quotation marks:

He vividly remembers Babe Ruth's 700th home run.

Democrats honor Old Hickory at Jefferson-Jackson dinners.

Name and Titles

5.1 Newspaper usage calls for identifying people in the news by their first name, middle initial and last name:

    Gerald M. O'Neill

    Peter R. Kann

    James A. Bailey

However, where the person prefers and follows some other usage, follow his preference:

Richard Cooper
Barbara Walters
T. John Lesinski
N. Lorraine Beebe
James MacGregor Burns
Sam Ervin
S. Hurok

5.2 Use full identification in the first reference and the last name only in second and later references:

Richard Cooper   (first reference)
Cooper   (second reference)

Most newspapers prefer to use *Mrs.* or *Miss* in second and later references to women:

Miss Walters
Mrs. Beebe

Some women today prefer to use the indeterminate title *Ms.* This is not a fully accepted designation, but where women express a preference for and customarily use it, it is acceptable:

Germaine Greer
Ms. Greer

5.3 In some instances where people have official titles, it is acceptable to use the title and name in second and later references:

Mayor Gerald Graves said today that . . .
Mayor Graves said . . .

5.4 Use the title *Mr.* only in combination with *Mrs.*, as in *Mr. and Mrs. John C. Smith.*
It is customary to use *Mr.* with the name of the President of the United States and with names of living former presidents:

Mr. Ford

It is customary to use *Mr.* in obituaries and in news stories where it is important to convey a tone of respect.

5.5 Identify students in a college or university by class and hometown:

John P. Wintergreen, Little Rock, Ark., senior, was . . .
Mary Williams, Boston, Mass., sophomore, said . . .

Abdul Jamal, Lansing, Mich., senior, said . . .

On some campuses students are identified by class and major:

Janice Keith, journalism junior, was . . .
Eli Whitney, history graduate student, was . . .

5.6 Identify faculty members by rank and department, thus:

Russel B. Nye, professor of English, said . . .
Nancy Perkins, professor of psychology, said . . .
John Bullfinch, instructor in economics, said . . .
Elton Henry, food science technician, said . . .

Note that it is professor *of*, but instructor **and** graduate assistant *in*.

Do *not* use the title *Dr.* for faculty holding the degree of doctor of philosophy.

5.7 Use *Dr.* with the names of faculty and administrators who are doctors of medicine, doctors of osteopathic medicine and doctors of veterinary medicine:

Dr. Ellsworth West, dean of the college of human medicine, said Monday that . . .
Dr. West also said that . . .

Doctors of dentistry and doctors of divinity are treated the same way.

5.8 In referring to Protestant or Catholic clergy, first reference is *the Rev.* followed by full name:

the Rev. John C. Smith (Episcopal, Baptist, etc.)
the Rev. Patrick McGuire (Catholic)

Later references to Protestant clergy may be *the Rev. Mr. Smith* or *Mr. Smith.*

Later references to Catholic clergy may be *Father McGuire.*

Jewish usage follows the same pattern. In first reference it is *Rabbi James Wise.* In later reference it is *Rabbi Wise.*

5.9 *Reverend*, or its usual abbreviation *Rev.*, is not a title and must be preceded by the word *the:*

the Rev. John C. Smith
the Rev. Mr. Smith

It is considered poor usage to say *Rev. Smith* or *Rev. Mr. Smith* or *Rev. John C. Smith*. Always precede *reverend* with the word *the*. The uninitiated tend to forget this and many people don't know about or understand the usage.

5.10 It is customary to identify members of state legislatures and members of the United States Senate and House of Representatives by their political party as well as to give some idea as to where they are from: state, hometown or election district. For members of the legislature from your own state:

Rep. Homer B. Wilson, Alpena Republican, is . . .

Sen. L. Harvey House, Detroit Democrat, said . . .

The United States Senators from your state need not be identified by hometown:

Sen. Edward Brooke
Sen. Philip A. Hart

Members of Congress from your own state are usually identified by party and hometown:

Rep. Charles E. Chamberlain, East Lansing Republican, declined today to . . .

Rep. Charles C. Diggs Jr., Detroit Democrat, announced that . . .

U.S. Senators and Members of Congress from other states are identified thus:

Sen. Edward Brooke, R-Mass., said today . . .

Rep. Shirley Chisholm, D-N.Y., was . . .

5.11 In a list of names and titles, place the name first and the title second:

Harry C. West, president; John Elmer, vice president; Walter Meyers, secretary-treasurer.

5.12 Do not pile up long unwieldy titles before a name. Short titles precede a name, as *Mayor Gerald Graves*, but long titles follow the name and are lower case:

Dr. W. T. Door, Washtenaw county coroner, said that . . .

Dixy Lee Ray, chairman of the Atomic Energy Commission, announced that . . .

Time

6.1 Time in newspaper usage is always *a.m.* or *p.m.*

8 a.m.	8:15 a.m.
9 p.m.	9:20 p.m.

Note that it is *8 a.m.* and not *8:00 a.m.* Keep it short and simple.

Note that *a.m.* and *p.m.* are lower cased and take periods.

6.2 *Midnight* and *noon* are neither *a.m.* nor *p.m.* Write:

noon
midnight

The arabic figure *12* is ommitted:

The ship sailed at noon.

6.3 Use the day of the week and not the words *tomorrow* or *yesterday*.

Today and *tonight* are acceptable where this is clear.

6.4 Using *tonight* with *p.m.* or this *morning* with *a.m.* is redundant.

6.5 In references to events within seven days of the date of publication—before or after—use the day of week only.

In references to events more than a week ahead or previous to the date of publication, use the date only and omit the day of the week.

Use either day or date, according to this rule, *not* both, although there may be occasions when both day and date will be germane to the story.

6.6 In dates do not use a hyphen to indicate *to* or *through*:

They will meet June 11 to June 15.
They will meet June 11 through 18.

Note that *to* and *through* mean different things and that a hyphen is ambiguous.

6.7 Dates are written as cardinal numbers:

Jan. 1   May 3   Aug. 14

Policy

7.1 Be prudent in the use of slang, expletives, profanity and obscenity in news stories. Many readers are offended by their use and newspapers are generally conservative in this matter. Be especially cautious in using expletives or profanity which include references to the deity, and in using so-called four-letter words.

Where such words or phrases are essential to a news story include them. It is preferable, in this case, to spell the words out rather than using dashes or some other coy cover up.

In all matters covered by this section, consult your editor.

7.2 Newspapers today generally avoid euphemisms in referring to diseases and acts once held to be unmentionable. It is preferable to say *rape* rather than to gloss it over by referring to a *statutory offense.* Use of standard and scientific terms is generally acceptable in news copy. Regular reading of daily newspapers will give you an idea of the range of permissibility and the range seems to be growing all the time.

7.3 Do *not* use racial designations unless they are essential to the story. For example, it is pointless to publish a description of a person being sought by police unless you *do* include race or color along with height, weight, sex, degree of baldness, shape of beard and so on.

7.4 Don't make fun of people or use pejorative names, nicknames or phrases that might embarrass or hold people up to ridicule. The following list is suggestive of the kinds of names to avoid, but *not* a complete list:

Dago	Redneck
Bog Trotter	little people
Hillbilly	sky pilot

Avoid using words or terms that tend to indict large groups of people with the offenses of a single individual or a few individuals:

teen-age drug addict   Sicilian gangster
student rioters

7.5 In writing obituaries, avoid euphemisms like *passed away.* Just say that the person died. Don't say that the remains were shipped, but that *the body was sent.*

Generally, use the term *funeral home.*

7.6 Do not describe the method by which a person committed suicide; someone may try to imitate it. It is usually enough to say that the person was found dead and that officials say he took his own life.

7.7 Use the word *innocent* in place of *not guilty.* There is always the possibility the word *not* will be lost:

Smith pleaded innocent to the charge.
(Right)

Smith pleaded not guilty to the charge.
(Dangerous)

7.8 Don't use the word *allege* or *allegedly* as a qualifier with criminal charges or accusations of wrongdoing.

Mr. Smith the missing banker is not an alleged embezzler. He is being sought by police who want to ask him about funds missing at the bank. He may, later, be charged with embezzlement. No matter how serious the charge, every one is innocent until the accusation against him is proved in court.

Smith, the alleged rapist,
  was jailed.   (Questionable)
Smith was jailed. Police said he would
  be charged with rape.   (Safer)
Police are hunting the accused killer.
(Questionable)

Police are hunting Smith for
  questioning about the
  death of his brother.   (Safer)

7.9 Laws in many states prohibit the publication of names of juveniles in criminal cases.

Newspapers generally try to protect the anonymity of innocent victims in criminal cases, especially in cases of violent crimes.

Do not use the names of women who have been raped, even in stories about trials where the woman has testified in open court.

Add Any matter added to a news story at the end. See *insert*.

Advance In press association parlance, a story moved on the wire some time prior to its intended use. For instance, a story intended for use on Sunday which moves on the wire Monday or Tuesday of the previous week. Also, frequently, any story written ahead for later use. Sometimes merely a story written ahead of an event.

Alive or live. Copy intended for use; copy or assignments in the production channels. A live story is one on which a newsman is working and which will be used. See also *kill*.

Assignment Any duty given a newsman, usually a story to cover or write.

Attribution The source of a news story or a fact within a news story. To attribute is to indicate the source of a story or fact and thus give the information authenticity. Also another term for a *speech tag*.

Blind lead A lead in which a person is identified at the beginning, but not named until the second or third paragraph.

Body The main part of a news story; also called the *development*.

Boil Boiling is more drastic than trimming. It implies a close paring of all sentences and the sacrifice of minor facts. Length is substantially reduced.

Box To put a rule around anything; also any story or other matter enclosed in rules.

Bridge A device for carrying the reader from the lead into the body of the story. The bridge could be a word, a sentence or several sentences.

Brief A short news story, usually two or three paragraphs long. Newspapers often collect related short items under a single head; for instance, business briefs.

By-line The line, usually in boldface caps, which indicates who wrote a story; for example, By John H. Smith. By-lines are usually used only on above-average stories, not on routine copy.

Cold type Opposite of *hot type*. Newspapers produced by the cold-type process use electronic devices to create printed images of news and advertising copy and headlines. The copy is produced photographically on paper and is then pasted up into newspaper pages to be photographed, so that either an offset plate or a letterpress plate can be made.

Copy Anything written for publication.

Copy book Sets of copy paper interleaved with carbon paper. They are prepared in advance to save time.

Copy editor Also called copy readers. They read all copy going into the paper to check for errors, improve the copy, add instructions for the composing room. Copy editors, of course, write headlines on news copy and insert subheads. Their job is critical, not creative, as Robert E. Garst and Theodore Bernstein remind in "Headlines and Deadlines."

Copy editing marks Symbols used to indicate corrections or changes in news copy. Copy editing marks always are made at the place a change is desired in the copy as distinct from proofreading marks, which are always made in the margin of a proof. Do not use proofreading marks to correct copy.

Copy paper The white or yellow newsprint on which newswriters type their copy.

Copy pencil A soft lead pencil used by newsmen for taking notes or editing typewritten copy. Only a copy pencil is satisfactory for writing on soft-surface copy paper.

Cut To eliminate all but the most important facts, those without which there would be no story or an incomplete one at best.

Dateline The words preceding news stories which indicate place and date of origin. Datelines need not contain the date, often only the place, of origin. Datelines are not used on local stories.

Dead Copy or type that has been killed. See *alive* and *kill*.

Deadline Time at which news copy is due, that the press is to start or that some particular event must take place. Always meet deadlines. No one stops the presses; they just go without you if you miss a deadline.

Development Another name for the body of a news story.

Direct quote The speaker's exact words, a verbatim report. Sometimes slightly edited to improve syntax or eliminate wordiness. Direct quotes are enclosed in quotation marks. See also *indirect quote, partial quote, paraphrase*.

Down style Newspaper style that tends to avoid capitalization wherever possible. Nondistinguishing nouns in names, for example, are not capitalized, as in *Roosevelt hotel*. Opposite of *up style*.

Dupe A duplicate or carbon copy. Many newspapers

require reporters to make one, two, or three carbons of each story written. Dupes are usually provided by the newspaper to the AP.

Ed and Pub Abbreviated form for *Editor and Publisher,* weekly newsmagazine of the newspaper industry. Required reading for those seriously interested in the press.

Edit In newspaper terminology, either to give the paper editorial direction or to actually carry out the various steps of reporting, writing and preparing news for the paper's pages. To edit copy is to revise, correct, improve news stories. All good newsmen carefully edit their own copy before turning it in.

Editor An editor has been described facetiously as someone who separates the wheat from the chaff and then prints the chaff. Seriously, the editor is an executive who supervises the reporting, writing and editing of the news. He is a skilled craftsman whose job requires a good education, experience and both intelligence and imagination. There are various kinds of editors, titled according to the nature of the job: managing editor, city editor, sports editor and so on.

Editorialize To inject one's own opinions into news copy. Traditionally, newspapers avoid editorializing in news stories and restrict the paper's opinions to the editorial page or signed columns.

Embargo See *hold.*

End mark A symbol, usually # #, sometimes 30, typed at the end of a story to indicate that the story is complete.

Feature The main news angle or news peg of a story; the special point or twist which makes the story worth writing.

Feature A type of news story. A feature, sometimes called a news feature, is hard to define. It is usually not breaking news, but may be a story closely related to the news of the day. Features are often interpretive, give background, playing up human interest, giving the color of an event.

Feature Non-news matter, such as syndicated columns, comics, cartoons and other such which appear regularly in the newspaper.

Feature To give a point prominence in a story; to emphasize it.

Featurize To play up an unusual angle or interesting point of a story rather than to rely on a bare recitation of the Five Ws, the usual straight news approach, which often fails to make best use of the odd, unusual or interesting elements in a story.

First Amendment The first amendment to the U.S. Constitution, which guarantees freedom of speech and of the press; the first item in the Bill of Rights; the cornerstone of the American citizen's civil liberties. The First Amendment also guarantees the freedom of religion, assembly and petition.

Five Ws The six basic questions that news stories must answer: who, what, when, where, why and how.

Flimsy A carbon copy, so-called when the copy is on lightweight paper.

Follow To keep up with a story; to report it as it develops over a period of time.

Follow Sometimes also called *folo.* A story that follows another, giving new facts or bringing the story up to date. Also a *second-day story.*

Fourth Estate The press, a term attributed to Edmund Burke, who is reported to have called the reporters' gallery in Parliament "a Fourth Estate." The three estates of early English society were the Clergy, the Peerage and the Commons.

FYI *For Your Information.* Frequently used to indicate that the material thus marked is for background rather than for inclusion in a news story.

Guild Newspaper Guild, the newsman's union.

Handout News story or other materials prepared for distribution to newspapers and press associations. Usual source is publicity, or public relations, man employed by the person, firm or group that wants a news story to appear in print. Handouts may be one-sided or incomplete and should always be carefully checked and rewritten. See also *press release.*

Hold To delay use of copy. Stories are often given to newspapers for later use and marked "hold for release at such and such a time." Hold orders should not be lightly ignored. AP indicates hold orders by marking stories "embargoed until such and such a time," meaning not to be used before that time.

Hole Something missing in a story. When your editor tells you that there is a hole in your story, he means that you have omitted something essential to the clarity or completeness of the story.

Hot type Process of producing newspapers by mechanical means. Type is cast using molten lead, type metal. Heart of the hot-type production method is the linecasting machine: Linotype, Intertype, Ludlow. Hot type generally also implies letterpress printing.

Human interest An essential element of the news, a recognition of the fact that people have a genuine interest in what other people do. Human interest elements that are especially strong are love, children, success and misfortune. Stories about pets and animals have strong human interest, too.

Indirect quote Not verbatim, but rather a slightly edited version of what the speaker or author said. Indirect quotes are not enclosed in quotation marks. They represent what a reporter, an intermediary, tells us a speaker said. Note change of verb in this example:

"I *will* go," he said.
He said he *would* go.

See also *direct quote, partial quote* and *paraphrase.*

Insert To add matter within the body of a story already written. Also, copy written to be inserted is called an *insert.*

Inverted pyramid The basic news story form with the summary of the story at the beginning and the minor facts at the end.

Itemizing lead A lead which lists or itemizes the several points which the story will cover. Sometimes called a 1-2-3-4 lead. A lead that lists dead and injured in a disaster is an itemizing lead.

Journalism The trade, technique or profession of reporting news for the public by various means. Hence, broadcast journalism, magazine journalism and so on.

Journalism reviews Critical publications whose major interest is study and analysis of the press. Among them are [MORE], published in New York, and the *Chicago Journalism Review.*

Journalist A rather academic or formal name for a newsman. In the United States, newsmen seldom refer to themselves as journalists, indeed are somewhat contemptuous of the term.

Journeyman A competent workman; a craftsman who has completed his apprenticeship.

Kill To destroy matter so that it is not used. A paragraph may be killed or a whole story. Type killed is type melted down or distributed after use or so it will not be used. "Kill" is a final order to prevent matter being used. Kill orders must be strictly observed.

Lead The first paragraph or first several paragraphs of a news story. Pronounced as if it were spelled "leed."

Legman A reporter who covers news, but does not write it. His time is saved for the job of reporting by handing over the writing chore to someone else. Legmen phone their stories in to a rewrite man, who serves as a stand-in for the reporter and writes his story.

Localize To emphasize the local angle of a news story, usually by placing it in the lead or high in the story. To bring a story nearer to the paper's readers by emphasizing their interests.

Lower case Small letters, not capitals. Frequently indicated by the initials *lc* or *LC.*

Media A term used by advertising men, academicians and the public to refer to the press. Media or mass media takes in newspapers, magazines, television and radio. If you are a part of it, do not forget that media is plural and that the singular form is medium.

Memo A memorandum. Newspapers are fussy about instructions and prefer that assignments, reports from reporters, and so on, be written. Always write memos on a piece of paper at least 5½ x 8½, that is, half a sheet of copy paper. Always type memos.

"More" An instruction typed at the bottom of a page of copy to indicate story is not complete and that another page, or pages, follows.

Morgue Traditional term for the newspaper library. Bound volumes of the newspaper, reference books, clipping files of lasting value about people and events, files of photographs which may be useful in the future are kept in the morgue.

"Must" An instruction pencilled on a story that means "this must run."

New journalism Name given to a school of writers, some who are journalists, some novelists, who are attempting to report more accurately and more colorfully the nuances of contemporary life. Most are good reporters, exciting writers, and their example is encouraging new experiments in writing in many segments of the press.

Newshen A coinage intended to serve as the feminine of newsman. The term never became popular, women preferring to be called simply reporters, editors, even journalists, like their male counterparts.

Newsman An employe of the news, or editorial, staff of a newspaper; a press association or news service employe. A man or woman who writes, reports or edits the news.

News Peg The significant or interesting point on which a reporter hangs a story. The angle, feature or twist to a story that makes it interesting or important.

Newsprint A soft, rough-finish paper made from wood pulp and used for printing newspapers. Waste ends of newsprint rolls are cut up into 8½ x 11 sheets and used for copy paper.

No-news lead A lead empty of information. For example, the lead that begins "City Council met last night." They met, but what did they *do?*

Obituary A news story about a death, which reports biographical details about the person as well as information about funeral services and burial. Generally *obit* for short.

Optical character reader An electronic device that

works much like a *Xerox* machine. A scanning light reads down the copy, but instead of producing a duplicate on paper, it creates either an electronic version of the copy that is transmitted to a computer or, alternately, a paper tape that can be fed into the computer. Also called an OCR or simply, a scanner.

Overset Type set but not used because of space limitations.

Pad To add superfluous matter to a story. A padded story has more words, details than necessary. A frequent order on the copy desk is "take the padding out of this;" sometimes "take the fat out of this." Another term for padding is *guff*.

Paragraph An arbitrary division of written matter. Newspaper paragraphs are usually very short, six to eight lines being average. In some newsrooms the term is *graph*.

Paraphrase A revision, summary or editing of a verbatim text; phrasing in the writer's own words rather than in the words of the speaker or author. Paraphrasing is usually done for the sake of brevity. See also *direct quote, indirect quote* and *partial quote.*

Partial quote Verbatim but less than a complete sentence. For best effect partial quotes should be greater than one or two words. See also *direct quote, indirect quote* and *paraphrase.*

Pica A printer's measurement. One pica is one-sixth of an inch. Newspaper columns are today a little less than two inches in width, 10½ or 11 picas.

Play up To emphasize, as to play up a certain angle or fact in a news story. To give an element prominence.

Point A printer's measurement. Type size, that is, the height of the face of the letter, is measured in points. There are 72 points to an inch, hence 8-point type runs nine lines to an inch set solid, that is, without space between the lines. Eight-point type set on a 9-point body will run eight lines to an inch.

Press Originally, printed publications, chiefly newspapers and magazines, but now a broadened term which includes broadcasting insofar as broadcasting deals with news and opinion.

Press release A news story prepared by a publicity, or public relations, man for use by newspapers or press associations. See also *handout.*

Proofreading marks Symbols used by a proofreader to make corrections in proofs of type. These symbols differ from copy editing symbols in a number of cases; also, they always appear in the margin of the proof, rather than directly on the copy.

Public relations The business of presenting information, usually favorable, to the public about a person, firm or group. Public relations is often referred to as information services, as it is in universities, or as public information offices, as it is in government.

Reporter An employe of a newspaper, press association, news service, broadcast station or magazine whose principal job is to gather news and, generally, also to write it for publication.

Rewrite The rewrite desk. Also, copy revised or rewritten.

Rewrite man An employe of a newspaper who not only rewrites stories to improve them, bring them up to date or change the angle from which they were written, but also writes stories telephoned in to the office by reporters. See *legman.*

Roundup A story that pulls together various aspects of a newsworthy event. For example, the weekend roundup of auto accidents provided for Monday papers by the wire services. Such a roundup puts a number of separate stories from a large area under a single roundup lead. Another typical roundup story is the weather roundup.

Q. and A. The device of reporting dialogue in the form of questions and answers. Frequently done in reporting trials and public hearings.

Scanner An optical character reader, OCR for short.

Second-day story A news story written and published on the day after the first stories on a news event have appeared. Second-day stories do not announce news events, they follow them up. They must take into account the fact that readers have already heard about the story and want more facts, later facts or more interpretation or explanation.

Set To arrange type into words and sentences preparatory to printing; to compose. Type can be set by hand or by linecasting machines. Today in the cold-type process, type is set or composed photographically.

Shirt-tail To add secondary matter to a story at the end; also anything so added.

Sidebar A related story; a story that runs alongside another story and carries secondary details, background, color or human interest aspects of the other story.

Slant The tone or direction deliberately given to a story; sometimes, the emphasis of a story. A story directed at a certain segment of a newspaper's audience could be said to be slanted for that audience. Another meaning is, of course, bias, but in this latter sense slanting is to be avoided.

Slug A two- or three-word identification for a news story, typed on news copy at the top of the first page and succeeding pages of a story.

Speech tag Device for attributing a quote or a fact to its source. For example, *police said.* Normal word order in a speech tag is NOUN plus VERB; that is, name or pronoun first, verb second.

Stick or stickful The amount of type that a printer's stick will hold; a few lines of type. Editors frequently ask for a "stickful" on a story, meaning a few lines.

Story From a newsman's point of view, news written for publication. A report of an event in newsman's language.

Stringer Freelance newsman who reports and writes for a newspaper on a production basis, that is, he is paid for what is printed—his "string."

Style Conventions, or accepted usage, regarding punctuation, capitalization, use of numbers and other similar features of written language.

Stylebook A written guide to newspaper or wire service preferences in matters of style.

Summary A brief, inclusive statement of what a story is all about. Newsmen speak of a *summary lead,* which concisely tells what happened, or sometimes of *summary paragraphs,* which briefly wrap up various elements of a story.

Suspended-interest A variety of news story in which the main point of the story is withheld until the end.

Swing Paragraph Another term for a *bridge,* a device for moving the reader from lead to body of the story or from one major division of a story to another.

Take In the hot-metal composing room, a 200- to 300-word section of a news story that has been cut up as part of the composing procedure. Each take is given to a different operator to set into type. Takes vary from a paragraph to a page of copy. If you are asked to write a short take, write 100 words or so.

Thirty The traditional symbol for the end of a story.

Used as an end mark to indicate that there is no more to follow. Origin obscure. Also written -30-.

Transition A word, phrase, sentence or paragraph which carries a story over a break, usually between shifts in topics, sometimes at a point where the story shifts from one speaker to another.

Trim To tighten up a story, chiefly by eliminating superfluous words and by replacing loose phrases with single words that express the thought adequately.

Update To bring a story up to date or to make it more timely. Frequently news stories have to be updated from edition to edition during the day. Sometimes new material is added, but sometimes updating is merely a matter of shifting emphasis to more timely angles in a story.

Up style Newspaper style that tends to capitalize when there is a choice.

Upper case Capital letters. Frequently abbreviated to *UC.* Sometimes also indicated as *CAPS.*

Video display terminal An electronic typewriter. Instead of paper there is a cathode-ray tube, like a small television screen, above the keyboard. A newswriter writes his story just as he would on a typewriter, but his words appear on the screen. He can change what he has written just by typing over it. He can move copy up or down on the screen to review or change what he has written. When he is satisfied with his copy, he pushes a code button and the copy is transmitted electronically to a computer. Also referred to as a VDT or a CRT, cathode-ray tube.

Wire Newspaper terminology for press associations, Associated Press and United Press International. Wire copy is copy supplied by the press associations; wire services refers to the press associations; wire editors handle press association copy.

Working press Those who report, write and edit newspapers and periodicals; newsmen or journalists.

NEWS WRITER'S
REFERENCE SHELF

A selected and selective bibliography of books and periodicals that have proved of interest and use to journalism students and to men and women who write for newspapers and the wire services.

Adler, Ruth. *A Day in the Life of the New York Times.* Philadelphia: J. B. Lippincott, 1971.

An hour-by-hour account of how the *New York Times* is put together on a typical day. Miss Adler is editor of the *Times'* own publication, *Times Talk.*

Associated Press. *Broadcast News Style Book.* New York: The Associated Press, 1972.

Associated Press. *AP Log.* New York: The Associated Press.

A weekly newsletter reporting on the activities of AP bureaus and staffers and the performance of AP.

Associated Press. *Stylebook.* New York: The Associated Press, 1968.

The joint stylebook. Order from the Associated Press, 50 Rockefeller Plaza, New York, N.Y. 10020.

Associated Press. *The APME Red Book.* New York: The Associated Press, annually.

A yearly volume reporting on the convention of the Associated Press Managing Editors Association and APME Continuing Study Committees.

American Newspaper Publishers Association. *Facts About Newspapers—1973.* Washington, D.C.: American Newspaper Publishers Association, 1973.

This and other useful publications are available from the ANPA Newspaper Information Service, Dulles International Airport, P.O. Box 17407, Washington, D.C. 20041.

Bernstein, Theodore M. *The Careful Writer.* New York: Atheneum, 1965.

A sound and practical guide to usage by a former assistant managing editor of the *New York Times.* Bernstein and Copperud should be in every news writer's library.

Chicago Journalism Review

A monthly review primarily concerned with issues and problems of the press in Chicago. Published at 192 N. Clark Street, Chicago, Ill. 60601.

Columbia Journalism Review

A bimonthly journal of comment, criticism and analysis which deals with current issues and problems of the press. Published by the Columbia School of Journalism, 700 Journalism Building, Columbia University, New York, N.Y. 10027.

Copperud, Roy H. *A Dictionary of Usage and Style.* New York: Hawthorn Books, Inc., 1964.

Basic and invaluable to the news writer for its sound and helpful guidance on problems of usage and news style.

Copperud, Roy H. *Words on Paper.* New York: Hawthorne Books, Inc., 1960.

An extremely helpful and informative book which deals with basic problems of newswriting and news style.

Editor and Publisher

A weekly trade publication. Reports broadly on both the business and news side of the newspaper industry.

Emery, Edwin, Philip H. Ault and Warren K. Agee. *Introduction to Mass Communications,* 4th ed. New York: Dodd, Mead, & Co., 1973 (paperback edition).

A primer for journalism students. Broad, informative discussion of the whole field of mass communications. Very useful bibliography.

Garst, Robert E. and Theodore M. Bernstein. *Headlines and Deadlines,* 3rd ed. New York: Columbia University Press, 1963 (paperback edition).

A manual for copy editors, but most instructive for the news writer.

[More]

A monthly journalism review. Informative and stimulating. More critical than the CJR. Largely focused on New York journalism. P.O. Box 2971, Grand Central Station, New York, N.Y. 10017.

Morris, William, ed. *The American Heritage Dictionary of the English Language.* Boston: American Heritage Publishing Co., Inc. and Houghton Mifflin Company, 1969.

A modern, authoritiative and useful dictionary, one of several that have found acceptance in the newsroom.

News

Publication of the Associated Press Managing Editors Association. Informative and current discussion of newsroom problems from the editor's point of view.

New York Times

News writers should also be newspaper readers.

News writers and editors who want to be informed read this important newspaper daily, every Sunday at the least.

Quill

A magazine for newsmen published by Sigma Delta Chi, the professional journalism society. Informed discussion by professionals about the problems of the press.

United Press International Broadcast Services. *Broadcast Stylebook*. New York: United Press International, 1969.

United Press International. *Stylebook*. New York: United Press International, 1968.

The joint stylebook. Order from United Press International, 220 East 42nd St., New York, N.Y. 10017.

United Press International. *UPI Reporter*. New York: United Press International.

A weekly newsletter of considerable interest for its insights into current problems of writing and reporting.

INDEX

DEFGHIJ-H-79876